Lecture Notes in Computer Science 13784

More information about this series at https://link.springer.com/bookseries/558

Venkata Ramana Badarla ·
Surya Nepal · Rudrapatna K. Shyamasundar (Eds.)

Information Systems Security

18th International Conference, ICISS 2022
Tirupati, India, December 16–20, 2022
Proceedings

Editors
Venkata Ramana Badarla
Indian Institute of Technology Tirupati
Tirupati, India

Surya Nepal
CSIRO Data61
Sydney, NSW, Australia

Rudrapatna K. Shyamasundar ⓘ
Indian Institute of Technology Bombay
Mumbai, Maharashtra, India

ISSN 0302-9743　　　　　　ISSN 1611-3349　(electronic)
Lecture Notes in Computer Science
ISBN 978-3-031-23689-1　　　ISBN 978-3-031-23690-7　(eBook)
https://doi.org/10.1007/978-3-031-23690-7

This Springer imprint is published by the registered company Springer Nature Switzerland AG
The registered company address is: Gewerbestrasse 11, 6330 Cham, Switzerland

Preface

This book comprises the proceedings of the 18th International Conference on Information Systems Security (ICISS 2022), held at the Indian Institute of Technology (IIT) Tirupati from December 16 to 20, 2022, in a hybrid mode. The conference received a total of 55 papers from authors in several countries. All the submissions were subjected to two to five single blind reviews by the Program Committee (PC). The PC chairs evaluated and discussed the reviews, and after careful consideration of the merits of the papers, the conference accepted eight full papers, five short papers, and three work-in-progress papers. The net acceptance rate of the full research papers was approximately 14%. A wide range of topics in systems security and privacy are covered, both in theory and in practice, such as attack activity detection, access control attacks on machine learning models, IoT security, and cryptology. In addition to the accepted papers, the conference program featured the following keynote talks by distinguished researchers in the area of system security:

- Ling Liu, College of Computing, Georgia Institute of Technology, USA.
- N. Asokan, David R. Cheriton Chair, University of Waterloo, Canada.
- Chandrakant Patel, HP Senior Fellow, and Chief Engineer, Hewlett Packard Laboratories USA.
- Thomas Hardjono, CTO, MIT Connection Science, USA.
- Ashish Kundu, Head of Cybersecurity Research, CISCO Research, USA.

The conference also had the privilege of having the following expert invited talks:

- Sajal Das, Missouri University of Science and Technology, USA.
- Himanshu Dubey, Quick Heal Security Labs, India.

Further, ICISS 2022 included a panel on Cybersecurity Challenges for National Security moderated by Anil Kapoor and several tutorial workshops. We would like to thank these experts who took their precious time to address the audience live during somewhat odd hours. ICISS 2022 would not have been possible without the contributions of the numerous volunteers who gave their time and energy to ensure the success of the conference and its associated events. We would like to express our gratitude to the Program Committee for their hard work and prompt submission of their evaluations of papers; we would like to thank the publicity and sponsorship chairs for attracting good submissions and sponsorships. Our special thanks go to the local organizing committee, as well as the faculty, staff, and students at the Department of Computer Science and Engineering, Indian Institute of Technology Tirupati, for all the efforts and support for the smooth running of the conference in the hybrid mode. It is our pleasure to express our gratitude to Springer for assisting us in disseminating the proceedings of the conference in the LNCS series. Last but certainly not least, we would like to thank all the authors who submitted papers and the conference participants. We hope you find the proceedings of ICISS 2022 interesting, stimulating, and inspiring for future research.

December 2022

Venkata Ramana Badarla
Surya Nepal
Rudrapatna K. Shyamasundar

Organization

Patron

K. N. Satyanarayana — IIT Tirupati, India

General Chair

Rudrapatna K. Shyamasundar — IIT Bombay, India

Program Committee Chairs

Surya Nepal — CSIRO's Data61, Australia
Venkata Ramana Badarla — IIT Tirupati, India

Steering Committee

Aditya Bagchi — ISI Kolkata, India
Arun Kumar Majumdar — IIT Kharagpur, India
Atul Prakash — University of Michigan, USA
Chandan Mazumdar — Jadavpur University, India
D. Janakiram — IDRBT, India
Pierangela Samarati — University of Milan, Italy
Rudrapatna K. Shyamasundar — IIT Bombay, India
Somesh Jha — University of Wisconsin, USA
Sushil Jajodia — George Mason University, USA
Venu Govindaraju — SUNY, USA

Tutorial and PhD Forum Chairs

Jayanarayan T. Tudu — IIT Tirupati, India
Shachee Mishra — IBM Research Lab, India
Vishwas Patil — IIT Bombay, India

Publicity and Sponsorship Chairs

Kalidas Yeturu — IIT Tirupati, India
Manjul Verma — [24]7.ai, India

Local Organizing Committee

Venkata Ramana Badarla	IIT Tirupati, India
Ajin J. George	IIT Tirupati, India
Anil Kapoor	IIT Tirupati, India
V. Mahendran	IIT Tirupati, India
S. Raja	IIT Tirupati, India
G. Ramakrishna	IIT Tirupati, India
Sridhar Chimalakonda	IIT Tirupati, India
Vamshi Seshasayan	IIT Tirupati, India

Website Design Committee

V. Jayaprakash	IIT Tirupati, India
R. Nagarajan	IIT Tirupati, India

Program Committee

Adwait Nadkarni	College of William and Mary, USA
Anoop Singhal	NIST, USA
Atul Prakash	University of Michigan, USA
Bimal Roy	ISI Kolkata, India
Michele Carminati	Politecnico di Milano, Italy
Chaitanya Kumar	IBM Research, Singapore
M. A. Chamikara	CSIRO's Data61, Australia
Chittaranjan Hota	BITS Hyderabad, India
Claudio Ardagna	University of Milan, Italy
Debdeep Mukhopadhyay	IIT Kharagpur, India
Devki Nandan Jha	University of Oxford, UK
Donghoon Chang	IIIT Delhi, India
Frederic Cuppens	Montreal Technological University, Canada
Gopinath Kanchi	IISc, India
Gowri Ramachandran	Queensland University of Technology, Australia
Guangdong Bai	University of Queensland, Australia
Indrakshi Ray	Colorado State University, USA
K. R. Jayaram	IBM Watson Research Lab, USA
Julian James Stephen	IBM Watson Research Lab, USA
Kapil Singh	IBM Watson Research Lab, USA
Laszlo Szekeres	Google, USA
Lorenzo DeCarli	Worcester Polytechnic Institute, USA
Luigi Logrippo	University of Ottawa, Canada
Mahesh Tripunitara	University of Waterloo, Canada
Mercy Shalinie	TCE Madurai, India
Mohit Kapur	IBM Watson Research Lab, USA
Pierangela Samarati	University of Milan, Italy
Rajat Subhra Chakraborty	IIT Kharagpur, India

Ramesh Babu Battula	MNIT Jaipur, India
Rinku Dewri	University of Denver, USA
Sabrina De Capitani	University of Milan, Italy
Sachin Lodha	TCS Research, India
Sanjit Chatterjee	IISc, India
Sheng Wen	Swinbourne University of Technology, Australia
Somanath Tripathy	IIT Patna, India
Somitra Sanadhya	IIT Jodhpur, India
Udaya Parampalli	University of Melbourne, Australia
Urbi Chatterjee	IIT Kanpur, India
Vijay Atluri	Rutgers University, USA
Xingliang Yuan	Monash University, Australia
Zhi Zhang	CSIRO's Data61, Australia

Abstracts of Keynote Addresses

The Rise of Cyber Physical Security

Chandrakant D. Patel

HP Chief Engineer and Senior Fellow
chandrakant.patel@hp.com

1 Motivation

Engineering in the 19th and early 20th century was about the industrialization of physical and electro-mechanical systems like the steam engine and the utility grid. The latter half of the 20th century was about information management, cyber systems and the Internet. The 21st century is about the integration of the two and the proliferation of cyber-physical systems (CPS) that matter to society. The rise of these cyber physical systems stems from social, economic and ecological trends such as resource constraints, needs of the aging demography, human capital constraints, externalities such as pandemics and environmental pollution. The lack of domain specialized human capital on the supply side - from sub-specialized surgeons to personnel with deep understanding of city scale infrastructures such as power plants – has underscored the need for cyber-physical-human systems such as robotic surgery systems and virtual reality based training systems. Securing these mission critical cyber-physical systems elevates cyber security to cyber physical security.

Cyber physical security applies to physical systems that make up city scale infrastructure verticals such as power, water, waste, transport, healthcare, digital manufacturing. These city scale verticals are built by the integration of operational technologies and information technologies. The operational technologies in the city scales verticals are physical systems with a myriad of actuators e.g. a water treatment and distribution system with pumps and valves. Layered above the scalable and configurable physical systems, are pervasive sensing systems which act together with information technology stack associated with data aggregation, knowledge discovery, and inference. Given the inference derived from the aggregated data, a policy based closed loop control system drives the actuators and provisions the critical resources – water as an example in the water delivery system – to the residents of a city. Security from bottom to top, as shown in Fig. 1, is cyber physical security as it transcends conventional view of cyber security to encompass operational technologies. Operational technologies are built on physical sciences – mechanics of solids, materials, chemicals, fluids and heat.

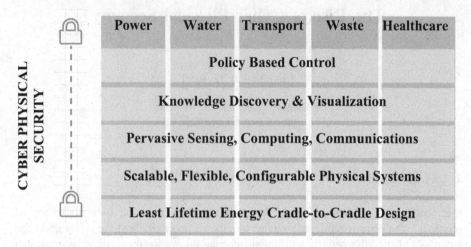

Fig. 1. is a framework that describes future "smart" cities and cyber physical security in that context.

2 Cyber Physical Security Necessitates Transdisciplinary Contributors

Success in cyber-physical security necessitates a deep understanding of the principles of operation of the entire system – from physical (machine age fundamentals) to cyber. Attacks on cyber physical systems that alter the physical functional performance cannot be prevented without a deep understanding of the intricacies of the physical systems that make up a power plant or a digital factory. A contributor in cyber physical security needs to be T-shaped with depth in information sciences and breadth in several subjects in physical sciences.

Consider a modern vehicle. It is a systemic instantiation of operational technologies (OT) and information technologies (IT). The OT are physical propulsion and actuation systems, and sensors, that are integrated with communications, data management and analysis systems. The vehicle, on command of the driver, navigates automatically using a policy based feedback control system. The cyber physical security of the vehicle is integrated across physical and cyber fundamentals and technologies as shown in Fig. 2.

The oft held belief that data and AI (artificial intelligence) with information science will result in a "smart" city, a digital factory or a "smart" automobile belittles domain fundamentals in physical sciences. Deep domain understanding of mechanical engineering, material science, chemical engineering, chemistry and electrical engineering is fundamental to a successful security model. And, cyber physical security of these critical physical infrastructures and systems.

The 21st century cyber physical contributors must have depth in engineering fundamentals of the machine age and breadth in information sciences of the cyber age.

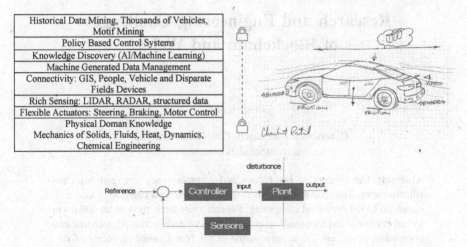

Historical Data Mining, Thousands of Vehicles, Motif Mining
Policy Based Control Systems
Knowledge Discovery (AI/Machine Learning)
Machine Generated Data Management
Connectivity: GIS, People, Vehicle and Disparate Fields Devices
Rich Sensing: LIDAR, RADAR, structured data
Flexible Actuators: Steering, Braking, Motor Control
Physical Doman Knowledge Mechanics of Solids, Fluids, Heat, Dynamics, Chemical Engineering

Fig. 2. Cyber physical security across the transdisciplinary stack

Legions of these T-shaped contributors must be developed through a multi-disciplinary curriculum, learning paths such as dual degrees, continuing education and "learn by doing" projects focused on building cyber physical OT-IT integrated systems.

Indeed, given the socio-economic and ecological challenges, and the urgency to act, the world cannot wait.

Research and Engineering Challenges of Blockchain and Web3

Ashish Kundu

Cybersecurity Research, Cisco Research, USA
ashkundu@cisco.com

Abstract: The concept of blockchain and cryptocurrency emerged from the Bitcoin paper. They have transformed modern distributed computing to a new paradigm of decentralized computing. Several years later, trillions of dollars in virtual economy and thousands of papers, have we truly achieved decentralized computing, or we are yet to solve some of the foundational problems of distributed computing that are key to achieving true and fair decentralized computing. We go over the research and engineering problems that have been solved, yet to be solved. We will also go over what is necessary to make Web3 a framework for enterprises to rely upon.

Security and Privacy in Federated Learning

Ling Liu

College of Computing, Georgia Institute of Technology, USA
ling.liu@cc.gatech.edu

Abstract: Federated learning (FL) is an emerging distributed collaborative learning paradigm by decoupling the learning task from the centralized server to a decentralized population of edge clients. One of the attractive features of federated learning is its default client privacy, allowing clients to keep their sensitive training data locally and only share local model updates with the federated server. However, recent studies have revealed that such default client privacy is insufficient for protecting the privacy of client training data from both gradient leakage attacks and data poisoning attacks. This keynote will describe gradient leakage attacks and data poisoning attacks and provide insights for designing effective privacy and security strategies for combating privacy leakage attacks and data poisoning attacks.

Web3 and the Interoperability of Asset Networks

Thomas Hardjono

Chief Technology Officer (CTO), MIT-Connection Science, USA
hardjono@mit.edu

Abstract: There is today a growing number of digital asset networks that are based on emerging technologies such as blockchains and decentralized ledger technologies. One vision for the Web3 is that it should be an "Internet of value" that builds upon the TCP/IP Internet and extends some Web2 functions. The underlying desire is to permit the various digital representations of assets as value-bearing data-objects to be exchanged and traded seamlessly at a global scale. However, if this vision of Web3 as the Internet of value is to be achieved then one fundamental design goal for Web3 should be the interoperability of asset networks, which in turn permits the ease of the moveability of the digital assets from one user to another across these asset networks. In this presentation we discuss a number of design principles underlying the interoperability of digital asset networks.

Abstracts of Invited Addresses

Securing Cyber-Physical and IoT Systems in Smart Living Environments

Sajal K. Das

Department of Computer Science, Missouri University of Science and Technology, Rolla, USA
sdas@mst.edu

Abstract: Our daily lives are becoming increasingly dependent on smart cyber-physical infrastructures (e.g., smart home/city, smart grid, smart transportation, smart health, smart agriculture). The wide availability of smart internet of things (IoT) devices including sensors and smartphones, are also empowering us with fine-grained data collection and opinion gathering via mobile crowdsensing about events of interest, resulting in actionable inferences and decisions. This synergy has led to what is called cyber-physical-human (CPH) convergence in smart living environments, the goal of which is to improve the quality of life. However, CPH and IoT systems are extremely vulnerable to security threats owing to their interdependence, scale, heterogeneity, human behavior, and trust issues. This extended abstract aims to highlight unique research challenges in smart living environments, build a unified data falsification threat landscape for CPS and IoT systems, and propose novel anomaly detection frameworks and models for securing such systems. Our novel solutions are based on a rich set of theoretical and practical design principles, such as machine learning, data analytics, information theory, prospect theory, and reputation and belief models. Case studies with real-world datasets will be presented to secure smart grid and smart vehicular CPS.

1 Introduction

Nowadays, massive volume of (usually time-series) data are collected via smart devices, such as sensors, smartphones, and Internet of Things (IoT) that form the building blocks of cyber-physical systems (CPS). The collected data are mostly used for intelligent decision making and reliable operations in smart living CPS/IoT applications (e.g., smart home, smart city, smart energy grid, smart mobility or transportation, smart health, smart agriculture, disaster response, etc.) to improve the quality of life. Often such systems are coupled with 'human in the loop' in not only decision making but also information/opinion gathering via mobile crowdsensing through smartphones. This synergy has led to the convergence of cyber-physical-human (CPH) systems at the intersection of three disparate worlds – physical, cyber, and human.

While the governing laws, principles, computation and behavioral models of these three worlds are completely different, our daily life is at stake with interdependent CPH systems that are extremely vulnerable to failures as well as security threats attributed to physical, cyber and human exploits. In particular, the dependence on data analytics, civilian impact of wrong decisions, economic motivations, and vast attack surfaces due to community scale CPS and IoT domains, make the data integrity attacks a common place. For example, it has been observed that unprecedented advanced persistent threats (e.g., Stuxnet, Ukraine power grid attack) can change various telemetry data and alter monitoring processes, when an adversary gains access privileges through a creative zero-day cyber, physical, or social engineering exploit.

Traditional cyber security is designed on the premise that everything within an enterprise or utility network is trustworthy until the perimeter is compromised. Therefore, the main focus of the existing literature has been to protect from external attacks using cryptography, network traffic analysis, network segmentation and fine-grained user-access control. However, many agencies such as Palo Alto Networks, US Department of Defense, and National Institute of Standards and Technology (NIST) have formalized the need for Zero Trust Architecture, which recognizes that (static) trust on users and end point devices are vulnerable. Once inside the network, the adversaries and malicious insiders are free to move laterally and access and modify any data after gaining appropriate privileges. This creates data falsification attacks apart from cyber-physical couplings creating such attacks.

2 Our Contributions

This extended abstract aims to highlight unique research challenges in smart living CPS/IoT environments, build a unified data falsification threat landscape for such systems, and propose novel anomaly detection frameworks and models for securing them. Our novel solutions are based on a rich set of theoretical and practical design principles, such as machine learning, data analytics, information theory, prospect theory, and reputation and belief models. Case studies with real world datasets will be presented to secure smart grid and smart vehicular CPS.

Toward developing a unified a threat landscape abstraction for data integrity attacks that target operational accuracy across smart living CPS/IoT applications (viz., smart grid, smart transportation), we first reveal that traditional cyber-security practices are not enough, and indeed cyber-physical factors make data integrity attacks a credible threat. Next, we propose four facets (namely, attack types, attack strength, attack scale, and attack strategies) that characterize the data integrity threat landscape of IoT/CPS data.

Based on the time series data analytic and machine learning techniques, we develop the exposition of different threat models, attack emulation techniques, and a way to mathematically parameterize the four facets to account for various kinds of adversarial capabilities. This allows an unbiased evaluation of a defense framework where the limits of the defense model can be tested. Our threat model identifies some existing pitfall assumptions that create asymmetry between reality and perception, leading to incomplete threat assessment and biased security performance evaluation. The novelty of our unified approach is that it generates a parameterized threat state space universe, and efficiently detects anomaly based on mathematical invariants and trust models.

References

1. Bhattacharjee, S., Das, S.K.: Building a unified data falsification threat landscape for IoT/CPS applications. IEEE Comput. (2022, to appear)
2. Ranjan, P., Gupta, A., Coro, F., Das, S.K.: Securing federated learning against overwhelming collusive attackers. In: IEEE Global Communications Conference (Globecom), Rio de Janeiro, Brazil, December 2022
3. Gupta, A., Luo, T., Ngo, M.V., Das, S.K.: Long-short history of gradients is all you need: detecting malicious and unreliable clients in federated learning. In: Atluri, V., Di Pietro, R., Jensen, C.D., Meng, W. (eds.) ESORICS 2022. LNCS, vol 13556, pp. 445–465. Springer, Cham (2022). https://doi.org/10.1007/978-3-031-17143-7_22
4. Roy, P., Bhattacharjee, S., Alsheakh, H., Das, S.K.: Resilience against bad mouthing attacks in mobile crowdsensing systems via cyber deception. In: IEEE Symposium on a World of Wireless Mobile Multimedia Networks (WoWMoM), pp. 169–178, June 2021
5. Madhavarapu, V.P.K., Roy, P., Bhattacharjee, S., Das, S.K.: Active learning augmented folded gaussian model for anomaly detection in smart transportation. In: IEEE International Conference on Communications (ICC) – Symposium on IoT and Sensor Networks (IoT-SN), May 2022
6. Madhavarapu, V.P.K., Bhattacharjee, S., Das, S.K.: Generative model for evasion attacks in smart grid. In: IEEE International Workshop on Security and Privacy in Big Data (with IEEE INFOCOM), May 2022
7. Bhattacharje, S., Madhavarapu, V.K.P., Silvestri, S., Das, S.K.: Attack context embedded data driven trust diagnostics in smart metering Infrastructure. ACM Trans. Priv. Secur. **24**(2), 9:1–9:36 (2021)
8. Bhattacharjee, S., Das, S.K.: Detection and forensics against stealthy data falsification in smart metering infrastructure. IEEE Trans. Dependable Secure Comput. **18**(1), 356–371 (2021)
9. Bhattacharjee, S., Madhavarapu, V.P., Das, S.K.: A diversity index based scoring framework for identifying smart meters launching stealthy data falsification attacks. In: ACM Asia Conference on Computer and Communications Security (ASIACCS), pp. 26–39, June 2021
10. Ishimaki, Y., Bhattacharjee, S., Yamana, H., Das, S.K.: Towards privacy preserving anomaly-based attack detection against data falsification in smart grid. In: IEEE International Conference on Communications, Control, and Computing Technologies for Smart Grids (SmartGridComm) November 2020
11. Barnwal, R.P., Ghosh, N., Ghosh, S.K., Das, S.K.: Publish or drop traffic event alerts? Quality-aware decision making in participatory sensing-based vehicular CPS. ACM Trans. Cyber-Phys. Syst. **4**(1), 9:1–9:28 (2020). Special Issue on Transportation Cyber-Physical Systems
12. Bhattacharjee, S., Ghosh, N., Shah, V.K., Das, S.K.: QnQ: a quality and quantity unified approach for secure and trustworthy crowdsensing. IEEE Trans. Mob. Comput. **19**(1), 200–216 (2020)
13. Sturaro, A., Silvestri, S., Conti, M., Das, S.K.: A realistic model for failure propagation in interdependent cyber-physical systems. IEEE Trans. Netw. Sci. Eng. **19**(1), 200–216 (2020)
14. Tan, S., De, D., Song, W.-Z., Yang, J., Das, S.K.: Survey of security advances in smart grid: a data driven approach. IEEE Commun. Surv. Tutor. **18**(1), 397–422 (2017)
15. Das, S.K., Kant, K., Zhang, N.: Handbook on securing cyber-physical critical infrastructure: foundations and challenges. Morgan Kaufmann (2012)

Advanced Persistent Threats: A Study in Indian Context

Himanshu Dubey

Quick Heal Security Labs, India
himanshu.dubey@quickheal.com

Abstract: Cyber Threats have changed drastically over the last three decades. From being a nuisance, they have evolved into

- A financial instrument for Cyber Attackers, with ransomware being the primary tool in attackers' arsenal
- A tool to sabotage operations or exfiltrate sensitive information, using sophisticated attack techniques known as Advanced Persistent Threats (aka APTs)

Attack groups behind APTs are highly sophisticated and well-funded. This enables them to invest heavily in reconnaissance & design attacks before launching them against their intended target. Because of this elaborate planning & inherent complexity, such attacks are extremely hard to detect & protect against. As more & more critical infrastructure systems have started utilizing digital technologies, risk posed by APTs has gone up substantially. In this presentation the following points will be covered:

- How Cyber Threats have evolved?
- What are Advanced Persistent Threats?
- Deep dive into Operation SideCopy. An APT attack that was targeted against Indian defense sector organizations.

Technology Transfer from Security Research Projects: A Personal Perspective

N. Asokan and David R. Cheriton

University of Waterloo, Canada
n.asokan@uwaterloo.ca

Abstract: Taking research results from the lab to the real world is a challenge in any field. Security research is no exception. In this talk, I will describe several security research projects that my colleagues and I have participated in during my stint in industrial research laboratories. For each project, I will describe the motivations that led to the project, briefly outline the technical solutions we came up with and discuss our experience in trying, and sometimes succeeding, to transfer research results from these projects for productization and deployment. From these experiences, I will attempt to draw some lessons for technology transfer of security research results.

Contents

OSTINATO: Cross-host Attack Correlation Through Attack Activity Similarity Detection

Sutanu Kumar Ghosh[✉], Kiavash Satvat, Rigel Gjomemo,
and V. N. Venkatakrishnan

University of Illinois Chicago, Chicago, IL, USA
{sghosh34,ksatva2,rgjome1,venkat}@uic.edu

Abstract. Modern attacks against enterprises often have multiple targets inside the enterprise network. Due to the large size of these networks and increasingly stealthy attacks, attacker activities spanning multiple hosts are extremely difficult to correlate during a threat-hunting effort. In this paper, we present a method for an efficient cross-host attack correlation across multiple hosts. Unlike previous works, our approach does not require lateral movement detection techniques or host-level modifications. Instead, our approach relies on an observation that attackers have a few strategic mission objectives on every host that they infiltrate, and there exist only a handful of techniques for achieving those objectives. The central idea behind our approach involves comparing (OS agnostic) activities on different hosts and correlating the hosts that display the use of similar tactics, techniques, and procedures. We implement our approach in a tool called OSTINATO and successfully evaluate it in threat hunting scenarios involving DARPA-led red team engagements spanning 500 hosts and in another multi-host attack scenario. OSTINATO successfully detected 21 additional compromised hosts, which the underlying host-based detection system overlooked in activities spanning multiple days of the attack campaign. Additionally, OSTINATO successfully reduced alarms generated from the underlying detection system by more than 90%, thus helping to mitigate the threat alert fatigue problem.

1 Introduction

Modern advanced persistent threats (APT) often spread stealthily across multiple hosts in their target enterprises. Detecting APT activities across multiple hosts inside such networks is very challenging. Approaches that deal with this challenge are often *network-based* [22,38,50]. They focus on finding a strong presence of attack artifacts in network data (e.g., DDOS, botnets). However, modern APTs are increasingly stealthy and usually have a minimal footprint on network logs, and are often characterized as "slow and low". Often, most of their actions occur *inside* hosts, while activities like scanning internal hosts or gaining access to new hosts happen over a long period of time.

To be able to detect suspicious in-host activities, *host-based* solutions are needed. Current *host-based* approaches and Intrusion Detection Systems (IDSes)

V. R. Badarla et al. (Eds.): ICISS 2022, LNCS 13784, pp. 1–22, 2022.
https://doi.org/10.1007/978-3-031-23690-7_1

[27,28,45] rely on audit logs to detect attack activities represented as Indicators of Compromise (IOCs) or Tactics Techniques and Procedures (TTPs). However, they are focused on single-host detection and the alerts they raise are mostly about activities inside single hosts. To be able to deal with multi-host attacks, alerts raised on single hosts must be *correlated* with one another.

One way to correlate alerts from multiple hosts involves understanding and detecting *lateral movement* tactics, techniques, and procedures (TTPs) employed by attackers [4,20,34]. In particular, if a *lateral movement* TTP is detected, the two hosts involved in that TTP can be assumed to be victims of the same campaign. However, because such TTPs may be based on zero-day exploits or because of *threat alert fatigue* in human operators of Security Operation Centers [14,16], they may not be detected and the alerts from multiple hosts may not be connected with one another.

In this paper, we present OSTINATO, a tool for efficient cross-host attack correlation across multiple hosts. OSTINATO's design relies on the key observation that a specific APT group uses a finite (possibly large) set of tools during a campaign. In fact, according to MITRE's ATT&CK page listing the cyber threat groups observed in the wild, a vast majority of those groups employ only a handful of techniques and procedures [1,13].

Based on this observation, we design an approach that compares (OS-agnostic) activities on different hosts and correlates those hosts that display similar suspicious techniques used to achieve similar objectives across those hosts. In particular, if similar tactics appear on two different hosts, then it is likely that the two hosts are victims of the same attack and they are, therefore, correlated.

The main challenge in realizing this approach lies in defining an *activity similarity computation* method that can be applied independently of attack peculiarities and thus be used in a general setting in networks with a large number of hosts. To address this challenge, OSTINATO first models the attacker's techniques and the underlying operational procedures as *tagged provenance graphs*, which represent audit logs as graphs that are tagged with attacker-related procedures. Next, OSTINATO defines a novel approximate graph similarity computation method that can be applied to the set of tagged provenance graphs in a pairwise fashion. The main contributions of the paper are as follows.

Graph- and Similarity-Based Correlation. We propose a novel approximate graph similarity-based alert correlation technique by addressing the (often overlooked) problem of determining when entities (e.g., processes, files, sockets, and its respective information flow) associated with alerts from different hosts are similar during an attack campaign. This is particularly useful for cross-host attack correlation involving hundreds of hosts in an enterprise network.

Threat Hunting Application. The second contribution of this paper is the detection of compromised hosts through the correlation between detected attacker activities and other activities across multiple hosts using graph similarity. In this kind of application, OSTINATO can enhance the threat hunting capabilities of existing Security Information and Event Management (SIEM) systems.

Threat Alert Fatigue Mitigation Application. Threat alert fatigue is a common problem in Security Operation Centers (SOC), where human operators pour over hundreds of thousands of alerts generated by the network- and host-based systems. OSTINATO can boost alert scores related to attack activities that are similar across multiple hosts and thus help reduce alert fatigue.

Along with these contributions, we perform the experimental evaluation (Sect. 4) where we use two different datasets collected from several red team engagements organized by DARPA. In the first dataset, the red teams performed various attacker activities across a network of 500 Windows hosts, resembling modern APTs. In this evaluation, the single host-based detection system either missed attacker activities having small footprints that evade its detection threshold or produced many false positives at lower thresholds. In turn, because of similarities among these activities OSTINATO was able to detect 21 additional hosts compromised by the attacker. We also created and evaluated an extensive dataset of more than 1000 graphs (of different sizes) generated by varying the detection threshold of the underlying IDS in each of the hosts from the same data. In the second dataset, we further evaluated OSTINATO on a different attack scenario involving multiple hosts of different OSes and successfully correlated cross-host attacker activities.

This paper is structured as follows: Sect. 2 provides a high level description of the problem. Section 3 describes the approach and architecture, Sect. 4 contains the evaluation, Sect. 5 describes the related work and Sect. 6 the conclusion.

2 Problem Description

In a multi-host system, one of the primary methods for expanding threat-hunting activities to new hosts relies on detection of *lateral movement* activities. In particular, if lateral movement events are seen on one host – e.g., suspicious traffic to a remote Windows SMB host – SOC operators may decide to escalate the alerts on both those hosts to more scrutiny. However, this strategy relies on *known* lateral movement indicators, and it may not always work if those indicators are missing, incorrectly modeled, if attackers modify their tactics so that they do not match known indicators, or if they move laterally via existing benign network communications (living off the land).

Alert fatigue is another cause for failing to process lateral movement indicators. In modern SOC centers, with thousands of hosts and hundreds of thousands of alerts (the majority of which are false positives), without a (relatively) strong signal about lateral movement or initial compromise on a host, it is counterproductive to escalate alerts to a higher level of scrutiny. Operations in such centers are finely tuned to deal with *alert fatigue*, and almost every system incorporates techniques, filtering mechanisms, and knobs that adjust the signals to forward to human operators [10]. Setting such filters to low values ensures reducing false negatives at the cost of having more false positives. Setting them at higher values reduces false positives but can potentially miss true positives. As a result, legitimate lateral movement indicators may be ignored by analysts.

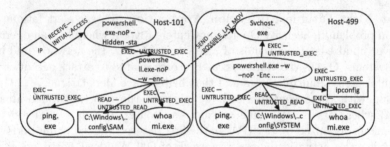

Fig. 1. Example of alarms raised by underlying IDS in multiple hosts in the form of tagged provenance graph

To illustrate the problem, consider the following running example (Fig. 1). An attacker obtains an initial foothold in a host (Host-101) inside a network of several hundred hosts. There (s)he performs several actions on the compromised host using powershell commands. These include pinging other hosts, monitoring running processes, reading sensitive system files, password hashes, and so on. The host-based intrusion detection system (IDS) raises alerts for some of these activities. These alerts are related to events in the audit logs that have some suspicious connotations. However, because they are similar to benign activities, they do not pass the threshold needed to be forwarded to a human operator or, if they do, they may appear together with many other false positive alerts, and thus be missed by human operators. Next, the attacker uses compromised passwords from Host-101 to gain access to another host (Host-499), which is usually accessed remotely by a benign user from Host-101. Because the attacker is mimicking a benign activity, this lateral movement remains undetected. The attacker performs similar actions in the new host including pinging other hosts, monitoring daily activities, sensitive file systems, and password hashes. The IDS running on Host-499 is identical to that on Host-101 and raises similar alerts. However, because the connection between Host-101 and Host 499 is considered benign, alerts are again missed. As a result, the attack is not detected or ignored.

Problem Statement. Our problem statement is as follows: *How can we correlate alerts across hosts without relying on lateral movement detection in a network with hundreds of hosts? How can we obtain an additional suspicious signal related to correlation for SOC operators?* Our key observation to solve this problem is that those attacker activities that are observable in audit logs are a manifestation of the attackers' overall goals (i.e., kill-chain steps) and related techniques [5]. Often, these goals overlap across hosts. For instance, for every host that is compromised, there **must** exist an *initial access* step. Often, initial access is followed by a *discovery* step, where the attacker explores the newly compromised host. To spread to a new host, the attacker **must** perform *lateral movement*. To be able to maintain their presence in the hosts for a long time, the attackers **must** execute some form of *persistence*.

Another *key insight* at the basis of our solution is that the tactics and procedures available to carry out these common goals in multiple hosts during an APT campaign are not infinite but are limited in number. The attackers must, there-fore, execute similar procedures in several hosts. In particular, by the pigeonhole principle, the larger the number of compromised hosts in a network, the more likely it is that similar activities are carried on those hosts. While it is certainly possible that attackers use different procedures for the same goals on different hosts, this would significantly raise the bar of difficulty for the attackers as this would require exploiting several vulnerabilities and increasing the chances of being detected by the underlying IDSes. Several research and survey papers, in fact, confirm the validity of our insight in the wild [3,9,15]. As evidenced by some observations [25], creating novel TTPs often requires significant resources and motivation from attackers.

The main challenge, in correlating cross-host alerts resides in producing a similarity definition for alerts that is general enough to be used across multiple hosts in a network. In particular, because each host can execute processes in many different ways, we must be able to capture the similarity between processes' behaviors inside different hosts. We solve this challenge with OSTINATO, a system that can detect similar behaviors present in the alerts generated by IDS-es, and create additional alerts. OSTINATO's goal is to be used as companion to existing IDS-es and provide an additional signal for attack detection.

3   Approach and Architecture

Threat Model. We assume that the attacker is able to initially compromise a host and, starting from that host, spread to other hosts inside the network, either via relying on vulnerable processes or by using existing tools from the compromised host (e.g., remote desktop services, SSH, etc.). We assume that there is an intrusion detection system in each host that is generating alerts, which may detect part of the attacker's activities. However, these alerts are also buried inside a large number of false positive alerts. Similar to prior research in this area, we also assume that the audit logs data are trustworthy and not modified by the attackers. We also assume that the alerts are derived from existing audit logs systems (ETW, Auditd) and that they contain the system calls generated by the running processes and the process invocations with their command line arguments. We represent the information in these logs and alerts as tagged provenance graphs.

3.1   Tagged Provenance Graphs

Provenance graphs [27,28,35,37,39,44,45,52] are well-known, widely-popular representation of audit logs, where nodes represent system entities (processes, files, registry entries, sockets) labeled by the entity names or paths together with command line arguments (in the case of processes) and directed edges represent system events and system calls (and are labeled by the system call name, e.g., read, write, fork, mmap) that connect those entities.

To represent both the high-level attacker goals and their low-level opera-tional details at the same plane, OSTINATO enhances *provenance graphs* with tags (additional labels) on the edges of the graph representing semantic level details (attacker goals, tactics names, and others). This enhancement is done by OSTINATO based on the graph and its respective alarms generated by the underlying IDS where the edge names are augmented with additional information before storing them in a common database. Examples of such graphs are shown in Fig. 1. The nodes represent different system entities, while edges are labeled by both *system call labels* (`exec`, `remove`) and *suspiciousness labels*, which capture the attacker's goal (`Untrusted Exec`, `Untrusted_Remove`), as a TTP [2] name. This novel enhanced representation, which we call *tagged provenance graphs*, allows us to represent alerts including both system behavior and attacker goals and include these high level details in the search for similar alerts.

Using *tagged provenance graphs*, OSTINATO models the process of alert correlation across different hosts as a search for similar tagged provenance graphs representing those alerts. In particular, OSTINATO first determines *node similarity* between nodes in different graphs. Next, it uses the edge labels and tags to determine edge similarity, and finally combines the nodes and edge similarity values into an overall similarity score for a pair of tagged provenance graphs.

OSTINATO's architecture is shown at the top half of Fig. 2. At the bottom of the figure, we show the hosts of an enterprise network. The IDSes inside each of these hosts produce alerts that are next transformed into tagged provenance graphs and stored in a central database by OSTINATO. It serves as a companion to these IDSes and utilizes the respective tagged provenance graphs. Each of these tagged provenance graphs in the central database are processed by the first phase of our approach, *Node Similarity Detection* (Sect. 3.2), which is responsible for grouping different nodes from different graphs into *buckets* containing similar nodes. Next, the *Graph Similarity Detection* step uses these buckets and a set of edge label similarity rules to compute the final similarity value among the tagged provenance graphs (Sects. 3.3, 3.4). Finally, if the similarity value crosses a specific threshold, OSTINATO raises an alert. The details of each of these stages along with their challenges are explained in the remainder of this section.

3.2   Identifying Similar Nodes

There is a large body of work dedicated to computing graph similarity and related problems, including graph isomorphism [42], iterative (or structural) methods [29], graph pattern matching [24]. At the foundation of these algorithms, often there is an *assumption that an initial mapping between nodes on different graphs already exists*. Such mapping informs these algorithms on which nodes in one graph are similar or match which nodes in another graph. They often assume that nodes have simple labels (e.g., single letters of the alphabet), which can be trivially used to provide an initial similarity measure between nodes. In our setting, however, nodes in the provenance graphs represent different entities, including processes, files, sockets, etc. An initial mapping that can inform about similar nodes across hosts does not exist. Therefore, one question at the core of our problem is: how can we produce such mapping? When can we claim that, for instance, two processes from two different hosts are the same or similar? Is, for instance, a *PowerShell* process from one host similar to a *PowerShell* process from another host? To answer this question, we focus on two aspects of nodes in the graphs: *node label content* and *approximate node behavior*.

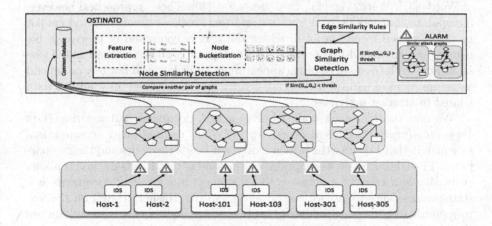

Fig. 2. OSTINATO architecture.

Node Label Content. Node labels consist of text extracted from audit logs information. They typically contain identifiers, e.g., the names and paths of the entities, command line invocation (for processes), flags, and other entity definitions. Because these entities are in different hosts, such labels may not be the same, even for processes often presumed to be similar. For instance, exact string comparison would be unable to identify the two nodes from two different graphs `C:\Windows\System32\WindowsPowerShell\v1.0\PowerShell -noP -w 1` and `C:\Windows\System32\WindowsPowerShell\v1.0\PowerShell.exe -NoP -NonI -w` as similar when actually they behave similarly in the host level. Furthermore, attackers may also invoke processes differently by using different order of similar command-line arguments and other means. An effective node similarity computation method must take into consideration all these factors.

Approximate Node Behavior. Different variations of string comparison would also not result in accurate node similarity. For instance, one can extract only the file name from the path of an image before performing the string comparison so that different directory structures do not interfere with the matching. In this case, labels like `C:\Windows\System32\WindowsPowerShell\v1.0\PowerShell.exe` would match. While such a solution might perform better than string comparison in certain cases, it would perform poorly for complex processes such as Power-Shell, python that act as interpreters. These processes can exhibit multiple different behaviors depending on their input and command-line arguments and cannot be assumed to be similar only because they have the same name.

Solution. In our solution, we consider the node labels as textual representations of the nodes' behavior and use a notion of text similarity to determine node similarity. Beyond the two naive string-based approaches that we mentioned, there are several other approaches used for dealing with text similarity like Bag of Words [31], Word2Vec [43], or ConceptNet [40]. These approaches, however, incorporate concepts derived from natural text, such as synonyms, and cannot be directly used in our problem where the text is composed of processes, file names, and command-line options. In practice, a good solution should: 1) be applicable to the domain of terms appearing in audit logs and not rely or depend on assumptions of natural text, 2) use general intuitions about anomalies in data related to attacker activities.

We first consider each node label as a text document and use the *Term Frequency-Inverse Document Frequency (TF-IDF)* method [32] to create a feature matrix that captures the presence of words inside the nodes and their importance. TF-IDF makes no assumptions on the kind of text it acts on, and it allows evaluating how relevant a phrase is to a document in a group of documents as a statistical measure. Next, we use Locality-Sensitive Hashing (LSH) on the feature matrix [53] to create *similarity buckets*, where nodes in the same bucket are similar to each other. We describe these two steps next.

3.2.1   Feature Extraction

The first step in our approach creates a matrix representation of the node labels in the tagged provenance graphs, which can be used in the next step of the approach. This matrix, which we call *feature matrix* is built by considering the node labels as text documents and applying the TF-IDF measure over them. TF-IDF is a measure for determining how relevant a word is inside a set of documents [32]. The TF part represents the number of times a term appears in a single document (node). The IDF part, on the other hand, represents the informativeness of a term. In particular, a term that appears more frequently in all the nodes is expected to be less informative compared to one that rarely appears in those nodes. In our approach, we define as 'terms' the words inside the node labels separated by white spaces, and we consider each node as a separate document. In particular, each node (i.e., subject or object) is a document d_i: $d_i = \{t_1, t_2, t_3, ..., t_n\}$. We create two sets of such documents D_{sub}, representing all subject nodes (processes), and D_{obj} representing all object nodes (registry, files, IP). In the following details, we describe only the steps related to D_{sub} for space reasons. Steps for D_{obj} are identical. In the first step, we calculate the TF-IDF score for each term appearing in the documents in D_{sub}. This score is the product of the two features: The term frequency of term t in document d_i is shown in Equation 1 where the numerator is the number of times t appears in d_i, and the denominator represents the total number of terms (t') in d_i. The inverse document frequency of the term is shown in Equation 2 where the numerator is the total number of documents (subject nodes), and the denominator represents the number of documents (subject nodes) that contain term t.

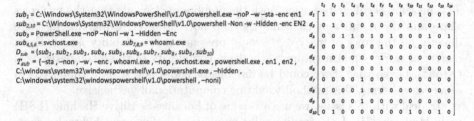

Fig. 3. Example feature matrix. The rows represent node labels. The columns represent words and the cells represent words with TF-IDF higher than median TF-IDF of the corresponding document.

$$(1) \qquad \mathrm{tf}(t, d_i) = \frac{f_{t,d_i}}{\sum_{t' \in d_i} f_{t',d_i}} \qquad\qquad \mathrm{idf}(t, D_{sub}) = \log \frac{|D_{sub}|}{|\{d_i \in D_{sub} : t \in d_i\}|} \qquad (2)$$

After calculating the TF-IDF score for all terms in the documents in D_{sub}, for each $d_i \in D_{sub}$, we calculate the median score $\hat{\mu}$ of the TF-IDF values of its terms. Next, we build a matrix M_{sub} with dimensions $m \times n$ where m equals the number of documents $|D_{sub}|$ and n equals the total number of terms appearing in the documents in D_{sub}. A row in the matrix represents a document, while a column represents a term. If term t exists in d_i:

$$M_{d_i t_i} = \begin{cases} 1, \text{ if } TF\text{-}IDF_t \geq \hat{\mu} \\ 0, \text{ } otherwise \end{cases}$$

The M_{sub} matrix represents the relevance of each term inside each document. The intuition behind this matrix is that we want to keep track of the terms which have appeared in the nodes and, at the same time, are important ($\geq\hat{\mu}$). This means two 1 in two different nodes (i.e., rows) in the same column indicate the presence of an important (relatively rare) term which is $\geq\hat{\mu}$ in both nodes. On the other hand, the terms that are non-relevant and therefore less informative and important ($<\hat{\mu}$) will be represented as zeros. Figure 3 depicts an example of a M_{sub} matrix. The 10 subject nodes in the tagged provenance graphs are shown at the top of the figure. These correspond to 10 rows in the matrix. Each column in the matrix represents one of the words presented in the node labels. The matrix cells represent the presence (1) or absence (0) of a TF-IDF value that is larger than the median TF-IDF in each row.

3.2.2 Node Bucketization

The next step in our approach is to determine the (approximate) similarity between nodes, represented by the rows of the feature matrix M_{sub} (and M_{obj} for the object nodes). In particular, we want to cluster similar nodes into similar 'buckets'. To do this, we compute the similarity between each pair of rows in the TF-IDF matrix M by using the Jaccard similarity measure among them [46].

This measure is calculated using both the number of elements that the two rows share and the number of elements they do not. However, using this measure directly on the rows of matrix M would present some scalability issues. For a matrix of m rows and n columns, the time complexity of these comparisons is $O(nm^2)$. Given that there could be millions of nodes and several (hundreds in some cases) terms, this method would be computationally expensive.

To deal with this issue, we use a version of Locality-Sensitive Hashing (LSH) with Minhash [21]. LSH traditionally employs shingling, which breaks down large documents into sequences of length k of characters called k-shingles. Used traditionally for detecting near-duplicate documents (e.g., plagiarism detection), LSH methods hash data records into buckets such that records similar to each other are placed in the same bucket with a high probability. In contrast, records distant from each other are likely to be placed in separate buckets.

In OSTINATO, we adapt LSH to solve our problem by using the TF-IDF feature matrix M rows instead of k-shingles as input. Because the TF-IDF feature matrix encodes a semantic representation of documents (i.e., nodes) that k-shingles do not have, we believe this is a better approach than using only the LSH method over the documents. In particular, its *Minhash* function, can project high-dimensional binary vectors like M_{sub} to a low-dimensional vector of integers H by reducing the sparseness of the former. This transformation has the property that if the Jaccard index, $J(d_i, d_j)$ between two rows of M_{sub} is high, then the probability value $Pr(H(d_i) == H(d_j))$ is also high. After creating the signature matrix H_M, we calculate pairwise row similarities using the formula:

$$Sim(H(d_i), H(d_j)) = \frac{|H(d_i) \cap H(d_j)|}{D}$$

where the numerator is the size of the row intersection operator (over integers) and the denominator is the size of the rows. The value of this similarity is between 0 and 1. We finally place two nodes in the same bucket if their corresponding similarity is above a threshold J_T. This threshold is specific to the kind of data a system produces and can be tweaked by a domain expert based on their knowledge of the hosts and audit logs they produce.

An evasion technique that attackers may try to use is to change the number of command line arguments in order to have two subject nodes in different buckets. This technique, however, is not likely to be successful for several reasons. To carry this out, the attacker has to include the command line arguments that carry out the objectives in the two subject nodes. To be able to place the nodes in different buckets, the attacker must change the values of the corresponding terms so that the terms' TF-IDF values are below the median in one node (so as to be represented as a 0 in the feature matrix) and above the median in the other node (so as to be represented as a 1 in the feature matrix). We point out that, due to the presence of the IDF, these median values cannot be controlled by the attacker but are a parameter of the system as a whole. Thus, if for instance, an attacker tries to modify the TF term by adding more values in the command line, they would also inherently change the IDF term. This effectively raises the bar of difficulty for the attacker.

Table 1. Edge label similarity rules. *S(name)* denotes the suspiciousness label, *Label.sub* is the subject and *Label.obj* is the object. ≈ denotes string containment.

Information flow similarity	Prerequisites
$E_i \equiv E_j$	System call labels E_i and E_j are the same
Load ≡ Exec	For all cases
Fork ≡ Exec	For all cases
Write ≡ Create	For all cases
Read ≡ Exec	$(Read.sub \approx$ PowerShell$) \wedge (Exec.sub \approx$ PowerShell$)$ $\wedge\ Read.obj \approx \{.ps1, .psd1, .psm1\}$ $\wedge\ Exec.obj \approx \{.ps1, .psd1, .psm1\}$
TaskStart ≡ ProcessCreate	$(S(TaskStart) \in \{$Untrusted_Exec$\}$ $\wedge S(OpenProcess) \in \{$Untrusted_Exec$\})$
Read ≡ Load	if $(Read.obj \in \{$shared_objects$\} \wedge Load.obj \in \{$shared_objects$\})$

3.3   Edge Label Similarity

The edge labels can be very valuable in determining the similarity among tagged provenance graphs. In particular, *system call* labels can inform us about activity similarity at OS level, while *suspiciousness* labels carry much more meaningful information about attackers' goals. To capture edge label similarity, we incorporate several matching rules in OSTINATO. Given the finite number of suspiciousness and system call labels, this task does not need to be automated and can take advantage of domain knowledge. The edge label similarity rules that are used in OSTINATO are shown in Table 1. The first column shows the similarity between edges using system call label names, while the second column shows the prerequisites that must be met for two edges to be considered similar. We also require that the suspiciousness labels are the same for all edge pairs (we do not show this in the table for space reasons). For instance, two edges with *exec* system calls labels are considered similar only if their suspiciousness labels are also the same (e.g., *Untrusted_Exec*). In Table 1 the first row represents the trivial cases where both types of labels are the same (e.g., *read* and *read*). The following rows represent cases where edges with different labels can be considered similar. For instance, the fifths row represents a rule that states that a **read** in host i is equivalent to an *exec* in host j if either subject contains (≈) 'PowerShell' and if the suspiciousness label of either edge is different from *Initial_Compromise*. This rule captures the duality of PowerShell scripts, which can be both read and execute. We point out that this table only deals with similarity among edge labels without considering the nodes. In other words, the table only captures information flow similarity. To fully evaluate if an event is similar to another, we also need to make sure that the nodes connected by that edge are similar to one another. We provide the details about this procedure in the next section.

Algorithm 1: Graph Similarity Algorithm.

1: **function** SIMILARITY
2:     **Input:** G_l, G_s, Buckets map $B : nodes \rightarrow buckets$, Edge label similarity rules
       E_L, MPS = $\{(N_s, N_l) | N_s \in G_s \wedge N_l \in G_l \wedge B(N_s) = B(N_l)\}$, $Len_{MPS} = |MPS|$
3:     **Output:** Final_Sim(G_l, G_s)
4:     **for** $(N_s, N_l) \in MPS$ **do**
5:         MPS = MPS $\setminus (N_s, N_l)$
6:         Total_Acc += Parallel_BFS(N_s, N_l)
7:     Final_Sim$(G_l, G_s) = \frac{Total\_Acc}{Len_{MPS}}$
8: **function** PARALLEL_BFS(N_s, N_l)
9:     Sim = 0
10:    Enqueue(N_s, Q_s); Enqueue(N_l, Q_l)
11:    **while** $(Q_s \neq \varnothing \wedge Q_l \neq \varnothing)$ **do**
12:        N_s = Dequeue(Q_s); N_l = Dequeue(Q_l)
13:        MPS = MPS $\setminus (N_s, N_l)$
14:        $NN_s = \{V | (N_s, V) \in E(Gs) \vee (V, N_s) \in E(G_s)\}$
15:        $NN_l = \{V | (N_l, V) \in E(G_l) \vee (V, N_l) \in E(G_l)\}$
16:        **for** $v_1 \in NN_s$ **do**
17:            **for** $v_2 \in NN_l$ **do**
18:                **if** $(v_1, v_2) \in MPS$ **then**
19:                    Enqueue(v_1, Q_s); Enqueue(v_2, Q_l)
20:                    **if** $E_L(N_s, v_1) == E_L(N_l, v_2)$ **then**
21:                        Sim+= W_1
22:                    **else**
23:                        Sim+= W_2
24:                **else**
25:                    **if** $E_L(N_s, v_1) == E_L(N_l, v_2)$ **then**
26:                        Sim+= W_3
           return Sim

3.4   Graph Similarity Detection

The final step of OSTINATO, is to determine whether two tagged provenance graphs belonging to two different hosts are similar or not. These graphs, however, can: 1) have widely different sizes, depending on the number of suspicious activities detected in each host, 2) be composed of different activities that may or may not be similar. To determine the final similarity score between two tagged provenance graphs, we use Algorithm 1, which performs in parallel two modified breadth first searches over the two tagged provenance graphs while updating a similarity score value during the traversal. This algorithm uses both the bucket information representing the node mappings and the edge label similarity rules to determine whether an initial attack graph is similar to another graph (or a set of graphs) in comparison to the attack behavior and the structure of the graph.

Algorithm 1 takes in input the two tagged provenance graphs, the edge label similarity rules E_L (Table 1), and Matched Pairs Set (MPS), which is the set of pairs of nodes from the two graphs that are in the same bucket. The algorithm chooses one such pair of nodes and performs a breadth first search traversal on each graph using those nodes as roots. Before the traversal, it removes that pair of nodes from the set, so that it does not traverse them a second time later. During the traversal, it only follows the nodes of the two neighborhoods that are in the same bucket (lines 11–16). At any iteration of the loop in line 16, considers three cases of similarity, to which it assigns three different weights: 1) W_1 corresponding to complete edge matching (nodes and edge labels), 2) W_2 corresponding to the two nodes matching but the edge labels being different (E.g., firefox writes to a file in one host and firefox reads from the same file in another host), 3) W_3 corresponding to the case where the subject node and edge labels match but the object names do not match. This approach works across hosts with different OS because even though the names of processes are varied across different OSes, the malicious behaviour and its usage would place the nodes into the respective similar bucket. We use different weights in order to take into account the differences in the number of buckets of subjects and of objects discussed earlier (see end of Sect. 3.2.2). The weights we used in our evaluation for W_1, W_2 and W_3 are 1, 0.2 and 0.8 respectively. From our evaluation, we conclude that these values can be generalized for different OSes or platforms. Additionally, the value of these weights can be customized further by analysts to look for specific nodes during forensic analysis or threat hunting.

After the final similarity score between two graphs is determined in line 7, we raise an alert if it is higher than a predefined similarity threshold. The value of this threshold depends on several factors, including the systems and the filtering actions of the local IDS detectors. We include a discussion about this threshold and others in the Evaluation.

4   Evaluation

This section evaluates OSTINATO by two different experiments using different datasets generated by DARPA red team exercises. The first experiment is part of large-scale 3-day long red team exercise [12] in an environment containing 500 Windows hosts in which the major attacker activities were concentrated in the first two days. The details of this experiment are discussed in Sect. 4.1. We further evaluate OSTINATO on a second experiment which contains two separate multi-host attack campaigns involving hosts with different OSes [11].

We deployed OSTINATO on a desktop with Intel Xeon W CPU @ 3.2 GHz and 32 GB memory running macOS Big Sur. As a local IDS, we used HOLMES, which we obtained from its developers [45]. HOLMES uses rules of *connected* TTPs to detect attacks unfolding inside a single host. Its final output consists of provenance graphs representing the activities detected as TTPs. These graphs are next sent to OSTINATO, which determines similarities among them.

Results Summary. We performed our experiments in a *threat hunting* scenario where, given some attacker activities in one host, we use OSTINATO to find similar activities in other hosts. Thanks to this kind of search, OSTINATO was able to uncover attacks in 14 more hosts than HOLMES on the first day (detailed description in Sect. 4.1) and 7 more (21 in total) on the second day. This is due to the lighter footprint of the attacks on the additional hosts, which fall under HOLMES' detection threshold. In fact, to make HOLMES detect the same attacks as OSTINATO on those additional hosts, we had to lower HOLMES' detection threshold significantly, producing several hundreds of alerts and false positives.

4.1 Ostinato Efficacy

Dataset Overview. We evaluate OSTINATO over two datasets: first, OpTC-NCR2 a large dataset [12] of audit logs produced as part of DARPA's CHASE program. The dataset was collected over a period of two days on 500 hosts. During these days, a red team performed several APT-like attacks on 24 of those hosts. Benign activities were generated both manually and by running scripts. The second dataset was collected as part of DARPA's Transparent Computing (TC) program [11]. During this engagement, the attackers replicated APT-type scenarios across multiple hosts on different platforms.

Ground Truth. The data are accompanied by PDF documents written by the red team describing the attackers' activities performed on each host. The ground truth was built from these descriptions and the process ids contained in those descriptions. In particular, if a tagged provenance graph contains one or more of those process id-s it is considered as an *attack graph*. In addition, we build a ground truth of pairs of similar attack graphs manually.

Detailed Results. Table 2 shows OSTINATO's results for the first two days of the OpTC-NCR2 dataset. The left table (a) contains the results of the first day, while the right table the results of the second day. The tables contain pair-wise similarity scores among tagged provenance graphs that were a part of the attackers' activities and the maximum similarity score (Column B_{max}), and mean similarity score (Column BM_1) between each graph that represents attacker activities and the other provenance graphs that represent benign activities. In Table 2(b), G_a, G_b, and G_c represent 3 tagged provenance graphs generated by HOLMES (and enhanced by OSTINATO) in its default optimal detection threshold setting, which produces true positives and a low number of false positives. These were present on only one host, hence comparisons among them are not calculated. The rest of the tagged provenance graphs from 7 distinct hosts $(G_d - G_j)$ represent activities with a smaller footprint, which were not detected as attacks by HOLMES in its default detection threshold. In our experiments, we reduced HOLMES's detection threshold obtaining a total of 689 more graphs from 500 hosts. Using OSTINATO, we identified 7 (from 7 distinct hosts) out of 689 graphs that were similar to the initial 3 tagged provenance graphs as part of the attacker's activities, while the rest were false positives. In these hosts, the attack's footprint was smaller because the attackers performed only a small number of malicious activities like running some PowerShell scripts in some hosts or communicating to an untrusted C2 server in other hosts. There were several benign graphs generated in those 7 affected hosts, for which OSTINATO generated low similarity scores as per expectations. OSTINATO was able to successfully correlate attacker activities found in the initial attack graphs (G_a, G_b, G_c) among hundreds of other graphs.

Table 2. (a) Day-1 evaluation results, (b) Day-2 evaluation results. Similarity matrices representing the similarity score between attack graph G_x (represented in diagonal) and other attack graphs. The columns B_{mean} represent the average similarity score between the attack graph (G_x) and other benign graphs, and B_{max} represent the maximum similarity score between the attack graph (G_x) and other benign graphs.

(b)

Graph id	G_a	G_b	G_c	G_d	G_e	G_f	G_g	G_h	G_i	G_j	B_{mean}	B_{max}
G_a	x	x	x	0.85	0.81	0.9	0.8	0.8	0.88	0.8	0.15	0.26
G_b		x	x	0.97	0.88	0.9	0.8	0.8	0.88	0.68	0.23	0.54
G_c			x	0.82	0.86	0.9	0.9	0.93	0.88	0.91	0.23	0.28
G_d				x	0.87	0.9	0.8	0.8	0.88	0.6	0.18	0.62
G_e					x	0.9	0.8	0.8	0.88	0.68	0.13	0.37
G_f						x	0.8	0.8	0.9	0.8	0.18	0.52
G_g							x	0.9	0.9	0.8	0.32	0.55
G_h								x	0.93	0.86	0.08	0.14
G_i									x	0.82	0.35	0.57
G_j										x	0.31	0.51

(a)

0.29	0.14	x	G_{18}																		
0.53	0.27	0.66	x	G_{17}																	
0.57	0.23	0.66	0.66	x	G_{16}																
0.44	0.18	0.66	0.66	0.66	x	G_{15}															
0.19	0.06	0.66	0.95	0.66	0.66	x	G_{14}														
0.62	0.37	0.66	0.66	0.66	0.66	0.66	x	G_{13}													
0.22	0.18	0.66	0.66	0.66	0.66	0.66	0.66	x	G_{12}												
0.27	0.16	0.66	0.66	0.66	0.66	0.66	0.66	0.66	x	G_{11}											
0.59	0.24	0.66	0.66	0.66	0.66	0.66	0.66	0.66	0.66	x	G_{10}										
0.58	0.36	0.66	0.66	0.66	0.66	0.66	0.66	0.66	0.66	0.66	x	G_9									
0.31	0.11	0.66	0.66	0.66	0.66	0.66	0.66	0.66	0.66	0.66	0.66	x	G_8								
0.24	0.09	0.66	0.66	0.66	0.66	0.66	0.66	0.66	0.66	0.66	0.66	0.66	x	G_7							
0.52	0.29	0.66	0.66	0.66	0.66	0.66	0.66	0.66	0.66	0.66	0.66	0.66	0.66	x	G_6						
0.39	0.17	0.66	0.66	0.66	0.66	0.66	0.66	0.66	0.66	0.66	0.66	0.66	0.66	0.66	x	G_5					
0.56	0.29	0.93	0.66	0.66	0.93	0.66	0.66	0.66	0.66	0.66	0.66	0.66	0.66	0.66	0.66	x	G_4				
0.41	0.15	0.66	0.86	0.66	0.66	0.95	0.66	0.66	0.66	0.66	0.66	0.66	0.66	0.66	0.66	0.95	x	G_3			
0.64	0.31	0.66	0.91	0.66	0.66	0.85	0.66	0.66	0.66	0.66	0.66	0.66	0.66	0.66	0.66	0.88	0.84	x	G_2		
0.68	0.25	0.66	0.78	0.66	0.66	0.88	0.66	0.66	0.66	0.66	0.66	0.66	0.66	0.00	0.66	0.85	0.90	x	x	G_1	
B_{max}	B_{mean}	G_{18}	G_{17}	G_{16}	G_{15}	G_{14}	G_{13}	G_{12}	G_{11}	G_{10}	G_9	G_8	G_7	G_6	G_5	G_4	G_3	G_2	G_1	Graph id	(a)

Table 2(a) represents the results of the first day of activities. During this day, at its "optimal" threshold, HOLMES detected only four initial attack graphs from three distinct hosts in its default detection threshold with no false positives. However, the attackers conducted activities in several other hosts. These activities do not cross HOLMES' detection threshold. We subsequently reduce HOLMES' detection threshold to capture all possible attacker activities. As a result, we generated 424 more graphs from those 500 hosts. OSTINATO correlated 14 graphs $(G_5–G_{18})$ out of those 424 graphs from 14 distinct hosts to be similar to the initial starting points $(G_1–G_4)$. As can be seen from the table, the average pair-wise similarity values obtained among the attack graphs are significantly higher than those obtained when an attack graph is compared with benign graphs (even with other benign graphs produced from those 14 compromised hosts).

Evaluation on TC Dataset. We evaluated OSTINATO on one additional dataset generated as part of Engagement-5 organized by DARPA [11]. The results are shown in Table 3. The red team used secure ssh sessions to move from one host to another, starting from a pivot host. In each host, the red team performed some suspicious operations (like `nmap, ls, ifconfig`) and exfiltrated a file (`passwd`) back to the pivot machine before moving to a new host. Cadets-1 was a FreeBSD machine in this setup, Theia-1 and Trace-2 were Linux machines, and FiveD-3 was a windows machine. Although the attacks on these different hosts were not identical, due to similar attacker-created processes and invocations across the 4 hosts of different platforms, OSTINATO was able to detect the similarity across hosts successfully.

Table 3. Engagement-5 evaluation results. Multi-host ssh campaign.

Host Name	Cadets-1	Theia-1	Trace-2	FiveD-3	Benigns Mean
Cadets-1	x	0.93	0.86	0.85	0.0
	Theia-1	x	0.87	0.86	0.0
		Trace-2	x	0.93	0.0
			FiveD-3	x	0.0

Similarity Threshold, Precision and Recall. We define a false positive as a comparison between a benign graph and an attack graph that results in a value above a specific similarity threshold. In turn, a false negative is a comparison between two attack graphs that results in a value below the similarity threshold. To determine the optimal threshold in our dataset, we varied the threshold over a specific range and collected the false positives, false negatives, true positives, and true negatives using the ground truth. The results of this experiment are shown in Fig. 4(a), which depicts the values of the precision, recall, F1-score, and accuracy as a function of the similarity threshold. The accuracy metric measures the ratio of correct outcomes over the total number of outcomes ($Accuracy = (TP + TN)/(TP + TN + FP + FN)$). As can be seen in Fig. 4(a) OSTINATO achieves a high accuracy ($\sim$0.97), Evidently, the optimal value for the F1-score is for values of the similarity threshold around 0.5, which produces a total of 15 false positives over both days.

4.2 Node Similarity Accuracy

In this subsection, we describe an independent evaluation of the approach described in Sects. 3.2.1 comparing it with other possible similarity detection methods, in particular, string matching (SM) and k-means clustering technique with a different number of clusters.

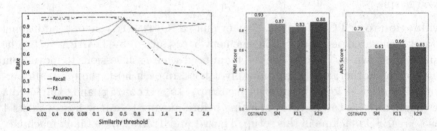

Fig. 4. (a) Precision, Recall, F-Score, Accuracy as a function of the similarity detection threshold. (b) Clustering performance comparison between OSTINATO and other methods using NMI and ARS.

Ground-Truth Dataset. To measure our approach's performance, we created a ground truth dataset of expected buckets for a subset of nodes in the dataset of 3700 subject nodes. We asked multiple security experts to assign each node to a bucket of similar nodes that represents a specific behavior. After this step, the experts met to discuss their assignments, and if there were disagreements, a new step of assignments were executed. This cycle of assignment-discussions was repeated until consensus was reached.

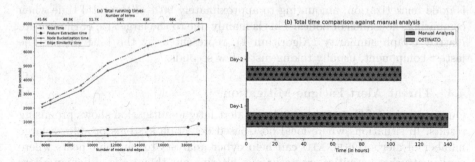

Fig. 5. (a) OSTINATO performance representing the running times of different steps. (b) Total time comparison against manual analysis.

Comparison Against Other Approaches. We compare our approach against several common approaches, including SM and the common clustering approach of k-means clustering with TF-IDF with different k values. To evaluate our approach against the k-means clustering, the most fundamental step is to define the optimum number of clusters (i.e., k). For this step, we chose two approaches. First, we used the number of clusters based on the number of clusters in the ground truth (i.e., $k = 29$). Second, to choose the number of clusters, we used the elbow method [33], a common heuristic approach to determine the optimum number of k which picks the elbow of the curve as $k = 11$ as the optimum k. Choosing two values for k enables us to evaluate our approach against the two probable number of clusters, 1) expected number of clusters based on the ground truth 2) suggested number of (optimum) clusters by elbow method.

To measure the performance of our bucketizing approach against other approaches, we use two standard quality metrics for clustering algorithms: the Adjusted Rand Score (ARS) and the Normalized Mutual Information (NMI) metrics [23] which use different methods to compare the quality of clustering algorithms when the number of clusters in ground truth clustering and that in the prediction are different. The overall results are shown in Fig. 4(b). As can be seen from this figure, our approach outperforms both SM and k-means for different values of k. The main reason for the better performance of our approach is the LSH step, which is able to better capture approximate similarity.

4.3 Run-Time Performance

We measure the run-time performance of OSTINATO by creating sets of tagged provenance graphs of different sizes by varying the underlying IDS detection threshold on the *Day 1* campaign data. The run time performance of the different steps of OSTINATO is shown in Fig. 5(a). To obtain different datapoints, we group the graphs into 7 sets of increasing sizes. The number of nodes and edges in each of these sets is shown in the primary x-axis. The secondary x-axis at the top reflects the total number of words (or terms) present in the nodes of each set. As can be seen from the figure, the most expensive part of the approach is node bucketization, amounting to approximately 90% of the total time when comparing thousands of nodes. This is mainly due to the large size of the feature matrix. Graph similarity (Algorithm 1), represented by the blue line, is the fastest component, usually taking just a few seconds.

4.4   Threat Alert Fatigue Mitigation

Our evaluation of OSTINATO for threat alert fatigue mitigation shows promising results. In situations where local host-based detection systems produce a large number of alerts, OSTINATO can help cyber analysts to pinpoint hosts where similar attacker activities are occurring, filtering out thousands of benign alerts (or false positives from IDS). Across the attack campaign [12] for two days, the underlying IDS produced more than 1000 alerts, which is really unfeasible for manual analysis. Comparatively, when those graphs are fed into OSTINATO along with the 7 initial attack graphs, it successfully correlated to 21 alerts from distinct hosts where it found similar attack behavior. According to several studies [6–8], it usually takes about 10–30 min to investigate an alert manually by cyber analysts. Assuming 15 min on average for each alarm, a cyber analyst would require 140 h to investigate the average alarms of each day produced by the IDS in our experiment. Alternatively, as shown in Fig. 5(b), OSTINATO takes around 167 min to complete the analysis of all the alarms generated, reducing false positives of the underlying IDS by more than 90%.

4.5   Comparison with Other Tools

We compare some of OSTINATO's aspects with some popular graph matching approaches. OSTINATO is much better suited for cross-host attack correlation than compared to other popular graph matching techniques. The features that stand out in comparison with other graph pattern matching approaches is that OSTINATO can perform accurate node label approximations even when similar nodes exhibit different behaviors, does not require training to implement, and performs context relative edge comparison, which is essential for cross-host attack correlation purposes. We outline the qualitative comparison against the existing tools in Table 4. Since majority of such tools are not open source or easily available, an experimental comparison of OSTINATO with those approaches is unfeasible. Out of these only SimGNN [18] is publicly available, however the nodes and edges are much more simpler in it's evaluated datasets and only contains of integers instead of actual names of processes, objects or edges.

5   Related Work

Several approaches have been proposed to deal with cross-host attack detection via cross-host information tracking. These approaches rely on the presence of

Table 4. OSTINATO vs. other approaches

Approach	Node label approximation	Node embeddings	Context-relative edge comparison	Training required
SimGNN [18]	✗	✓	✗	✓
Poirot [44]	✗	✗	✗	✗
Deltacon [36]	✗	✓	✗	✗
OSTINATO	✓	✓	✓	✗

information flow data between entities (e.g., processes) across hosts [30,51]. This approach, however, requires fine-grained taint tracking, which relies on system instrumentation it requires some modifications to existing systems.

Log-Based Threat Hunting: A wide variety of systems leverages different types of logs for threat-hunting purposes. Hercule [48] is a log-based detection system modeled on the community discovery problem. It correlates logs from multiple sources and detects attack communities. Oprea et al. [47], Romero-Gomez et al. [49] leveraged DNS, web-proxy logs in order to detect and visualize threats in a network. Bilge et al. [19] leveraged NetFlow logs to detect Botnet C&C servers and distinguish them from the benign traffic. The DNS logs are also leveraged extensively [17] for the detection of malicious domains. Several systems [27,41,45] make use of different logs just as OSTINATO for efficient threat hunting, forensic analysis, or real-time detection of cyberattacks. Most of the mentioned approaches that deal with cross-host activities rely on network logs, however, while OSTINATO is used over audit host logs.

Provenance Graph Analysis: BackTracker [35] first introduced the concept of generating a provenance graph from the kernel audit logs. In recent years, significant progress has been made for log reduction, compression techniques and tracking OS-level dependencies [26,28,37] in order to facilitate detection of benign events from the suspicious ones as well as to reduce storage overheads. Moreover, recent studies have used provenance graphs effectively for a wide variety of security problems such as identification of zero-day attack paths in ZePro [54], automated provenance triage in NoDoze [27], real-time attack detection and attack scenario reconstruction [45]. While sharing use of provenance graphs, OSTINATO's approach is different from these works. In fact, OSTINATO looks for similar subgraphs across multiple provenance graphs as a signal for multi-host attack correlation.

6   Conclusion

We present OSTINATO, which is based on the intuition that attackers have similar goals on multiple hosts during a campaign. OSTINATO implements an approach for correlating similar attacker activities across different hosts and implements a novel approximate node matching technique. It further uses the attack semantics to detect similarities among tagged provenance graphs. We successfully evaluate OSTINATO on two datasets created by DARPA red team engagements.

References

1. 2021: Year in review. https://thedfirreport.com/2022/03/07/2021-year-in-review/
2. Adversarial tactics, techniques and common knowledge. https://attack.mitre.org/
3. Apt cybercriminal campagin collections. https://bit.ly/364iN8U
4. Detecting lateral movement with windows event logs. https://bit.ly/3hQyF1D
5. Mandiant (2013). https://bit.ly/3MA0N7b
6. Alert fatigue: 31.9% anaysts ignore alerts. https://bit.ly/3MyE9fA (2017)
7. Automated incident response (2017). https://bit.ly/3hPm3Ia
8. New research from advanced threat analytics finds MSSP incident responders overwhelmed by false-positive security alerts (2018). https://prn.to/37hqsS9
9. Destructive attack "dustman" (2019). https://bit.ly/3tHX7YC
10. Dramatic reductions in alert fatigue with crowdscore (2019). https://bit.ly/3IZD9is
11. Tc engagement-5 (2019). https://github.com/darpa-i2o/Transparent-Computing
12. Optc dataset (2020). https://github.com/FiveDirections/OpTC-data
13. Groups (2021). https://attack.mitre.org/groups/
14. Lateral movement (2021). https://bit.ly/3t63ru1
15. Lateral tool transfer (2021). https://attack.mitre.org/techniques/T1570/
16. What makes lateral movement so hard to detect? (2021). https://bit.ly/3hUl0qg
17. Antonakakis, M., et al.: From throw-away traffic to bots: detecting the rise of DGA-based malware. In: 21st {USENIX} Security Symposium ({USENIX}) (2012)
18. Bai, Y., Ding, H., Bian, S., Chen, T., Sun, Y., Wang, W.: SimGNN: a neural network approach to fast graph similarity computation. In: Proceedings of the Twelfth ACM International Conference on Web Search and Data Mining, pp. 384–392 (2019)
19. Bilge, L., Balzarotti, D., Robertson, W., Kirda, E., Kruegel, C.: Disclosure: detecting botnet command and control servers through large-scale netflow analysis. In: Proceedings of the 28th Annual Computer Security Applications Conference (2012)
20. Bowman, B., Laprade, C., Ji, Y., Huang, H.H.: Detecting lateral movement in enterprise computer networks with unsupervised graph {AI}. In: 23rd International Symposium on Research in Attacks, Intrusions and Defenses. RAID (2020)
21. Broder, A.Z., Charikar, M., Frieze, A.M., Mitzenmacher, M.: Min-wise independent permutations. J. Comput. Syst. Sci. **60**(3), 630–659 (2000)
22. Cuppens, F., Miege, A.: Alert correlation in a cooperative intrusion detection framework. In: Proceedings 2002 IEEE Symposium on Security and Privacy (2002)
23. Emmons, S., Kobourov, S., Gallant, M., Börner, K.: Analysis of network clustering algorithms and cluster quality metrics at scale. PLoS One **11**(7), e0159161 (2016)
24. Gallagher, B.: Matching structure and semantics: a survey on graph-based pattern matching. In: AAAI Fall Symposium: Capturing and Using Patterns for Evidence Detection, pp. 45–53 (2006)
25. Hajizadeh, M., Phan, T.V., Bauschert, T.: Probability analysis of successful cyber attacks in SDN-based networks. In: 2018 IEEE Conference on Network Function Virtualization and Software Defined Networks (NFV-SDN), pp. 1–6. IEEE (2018)
26. Hassan, W.U., Bates, A., Marino, D.: Tactical provenance analysis for endpoint detection and response systems. In: 2020 IEEE Symposium on Security and Privacy (2020)

27. Hassan, W.U., et al.: NoDoze: combatting threat alert fatigue with automated provenance triage. In: Network and Distributed Systems Security Symposium (2019)

28. Hossain, M.N., Sheikhi, S., Sekar, R.: Combating dependence explosion in forensic analysis using alternative tag propagation semantics. In: 2020 IEEE Symposium on Security and Privacy (SP), pp. 1139–1155. IEEE (2020)

29. Jeh, G., Widom, J.: Simrank: A measure of structural-context similarity. In: Proceedings of the Eighth ACM SIGKDD International Conference on Knowledge Discovery and Data Mining, pp. 538–543 (2002). https://bit.ly/3HXbqgQ

30. Ji, Y., et al.: Enabling refinable cross-host attack investigation with efficient data flow tagging and tracking. In: 27th {USENIX} Security Symposium ({USENIX} Security 18) (2018)

31. Joachims, T.: Text categorization with support vector machines: learning with many relevant features. In: Nédellec, C., Rouveirol, C. (eds.) ECML 1998. LNCS, vol. 1398, pp. 137–142. Springer, Heidelberg (1998). https://doi.org/10.1007/BFb0026683

32. Joachims, T.: A probabilistic analysis of the Rocchio algorithm with TFIDF for text categorization. Technical report, Carnegie-Mellon Univ., Pittsburgh, PA, Dept. of CS (1996)

33. Ketchen, D.J., Shook, C.L.: The application of cluster analysis in strategic management research: an analysis and critique. Strateg. Manag. J. **17**, 441–458 (1996)

34. King, D.: Spotting the signs of lateral movement (2018). https://splk.it/3vTiQ2C

35. King, S.T., Chen, P.M.: Backtracking intrusions. In: SOSP. ACM (2003)

36. Koutra, D., Vogelstein, J.T., Faloutsos, C.: DeltaCon: a principled massive-graph similarity function. In: Proceedings of the 2013 SIAM International Conference on Data Mining. SIAM (2013)

37. Krishnan, S., Snow, K.Z., Monrose, F.: Trail of bytes: efficient support for forensic analysis. In: Proceedings of the 17th ACM CCS, pp. 50–60 (2010)

38. Kruegel, C., Valeur, F., Vigna, G.: Intrusion Detection and Correlation: Challenges and Solutions, vol. 14. Springer, New York (2004). https://doi.org/10.1007/b101493

39. Lee, K.H., Zhang, X., Xu, D.: LogGC: garbage collecting audit log. In: Proceedings of the 2013 ACM SIGSAC Conference on Computer & Communications Security (2013)

40. Liu, H., Singh, P.: ConceptNet-a practical commonsense reasoning tool-kit. BT Technol. J. **22**(4), 211–226 (2004)

41. Liu, Y., et al.: Towards a timely causality analysis for enterprise security. In: NDSS (2018)

42. McKay, B.D., Piperno, A.: Practical graph isomorphism, II. J. Symb. Comput. **60**, 94–112 (2014)

43. Mikolov, T., Chen, K., Corrado, G., Dean, J.: Efficient estimation of word representations in vector space. arXiv preprint arXiv:1301.3781 (2013)

44. Milajerdi, S.M., Eshete, B., Gjomemo, R., Venkatakrishnan, V.: Poirot: aligning attack behavior with kernel audit records for cyber threat hunting. In: Proceedings of the 2019 ACM SIGSAC Conference on Computer and Communications Security (2019)

45. Milajerdi, S.M., Gjomemo, R., Eshete, B., Sekar, R., Venkatakrishnan, V.: Holmes: real-time apt detection through correlation of suspicious information flows. In: 2019 IEEE Symposium on Security and Privacy (SP), pp. 1137–1152. IEEE (2019)

46. Niwattanakul, S., Singthongchai, J., Naenudorn, E., Wanapu, S.: Using of Jaccard coefficient for keywords similarity. In: Proceedings of the International Multiconference of Engineers and Computer Scientists, vol. 1, pp. 380–384 (2013)

47. Oprea, A., Li, Z., Yen, T.F., Chin, S.H., Alrwais, S.: Detection of early-stage enterprise infection by mining large-scale log data. In: 2015 45th Annual IEEE/IFIP International Conference on Dependable Systems and Networks, pp. 45–56. IEEE

48. Pei, K., et al.: Hercule: attack story reconstruction via community discovery on correlated log graph. In: Proceedings of the 32nd ACSAC, pp. 583–595 (2016)

49. Romero-Gomez, R., Nadji, Y., Antonakakis, M.: Towards designing effective visualizations for DNS-based network threat analysis. In: 2017 IEEE Symposium on Visualization for Cyber Security (VizSec), pp. 1–8. IEEE (2017)

50. Sadoddin, R., Ghorbani, A.: Alert correlation survey: framework and techniques. In: Proceedings of the 2006 International Conference on Privacy, Security and Trust: Bridge the Gap Between PST Technologies and Business Services, pp. 1–10 (2006)

51. Sahabandu, D., Xiao, B., Clark, A., Lee, S., Lee, W., Poovendran, R.: Dift games: dynamic information flow tracking games for advanced persistent threats. In: 2018 IEEE Conference on Decision and Control (CDC), pp. 1136–1143. IEEE (2018)

52. Satvat, K., Gjomemo, R., Venkatakrishnan, V.: Extractor: extracting attack behavior from threat reports. In: 2021 IEEE European Symposium on Security and Privacy (EuroS P), pp. 598–615 (2021)

53. Shrivastava, A., Li, P.: In defense of MinHash over SimHash. In: Artificial Intelligence and Statistics, pp. 886–894. PMLR (2014)

54. Sun, X., Dai, J., Liu, P., Singhal, A., Yen, J.: Using Bayesian networks for probabilistic identification of zero-day attack paths. IEEE Tran. Inf. Forensics Secur. **13**, 2506–2521 (2018)

DKS-PKI: A Distributed Key Server Architecture for Public Key Infrastructure

Abu Faisal[✉] and Mohammad Zulkernine

School of Computing, Queen's University, Kingston, ON, Canada
{m.faisal,mz}@queensu.ca

Abstract. Public key infrastructure (PKI) is the core of authentications performed in secure internet communications. The most popular PKI arrangement is the certificate authority (CA)-based PKI. The traditional security protocols use this CA-based PKI to provide server-side authentications. In this approach, the server-side uses its public key certificate that is the server's public key signed by a *trusted* CA. This CA-based PKI is not able to properly address the challenges associated with the growing demand of secure internet communications. We identified two major problems with this CA-based PKI to be used in secure communications. First, the mis-issuance of certificates or the disclosure of any such CAs' private keys can cause serious problems to the security of these internet communications. Second, revoking an issued public key certificate or any trusted CA's certificate is not a trivial task. In this paper, we proposed a distributed key server architecture (DKS-PKI) that provides a PKI arrangement that can solve the above mentioned problems. The proposed architecture offers registration/issuance, storage, distribution, and revocation of certificates in an efficient manner. It ensures transparency and accountability of the certificate issuers. All the registered/issued certificates and their sensitive identity information are verified and stored into a permissioned distributed storage system. The key-server nodes are responsible to make these issued certificates publicly accessible by means of their associated 256-bit unique identifiers (UIDs). We presented a thorough security analysis of the proposed architecture.

Keywords: DKS · PKI · Authentication · Certificate · Distributed · Issuance · Revocation · Verification

1 Introduction

In public key infrastructure (PKI), digital certificates are used to authenticate entities/participants (e.g., people or organizations) in secure internet communications. The most common format for these certificates is the X.509 standard. Each certificate contains the public key of the entity and some key information, such as domain name, organization name, validity period, and issuer's signature. The issuer's signature proves the trustworthiness of the presented information

© The Author(s), under exclusive license to Springer Nature Switzerland AG 2022
V. R. Badarla et al. (Eds.): ICISS 2022, LNCS 13784, pp. 23–43, 2022.
https://doi.org/10.1007/978-3-031-23690-7_2

in the certificate. The most popular and widely accepted PKI for authentication is the certificate authority (CA)-based PKI. In CA-based PKI, the certificates are issued by the *trusted* certificate authorities (CAs). All the trusted CAs' certificates are already installed in all modern internet browsers and operating systems. Therefore, the entity certificates issued by these trusted CAs can be validated at any time.

The traditional security protocols (SSL/TLS/DTLS) use this CA-based PKI authentication approach to authenticate the server's identity. In these protocols, the client's identity authentication is optional and skipped most of the times. A basic example of the existing CA-based PKI is that a business owner wants to get a public key certificate for his/her online business. After validating the owner's identity, business information, and registered domain name, a trusted CA generates a public key certificate for the online business. The business owner stores the certificate in the server. Now, a client wants to establish a secure (SSL/TLS) communication channel with the server to send payment to the business. Therefore, the client needs to ensure the authenticity of the server. The server sends its public key certificate to the client. Since all trusted CAs' certificates are already installed into the system, the client can validate the server's authenticity using the received certificate.

In certificate authority (CA)-based PKI, the CAs are arranged in a hierarchical structure extending up to several levels (e.g., top-level/root CA and several levels of intermediate CAs). Any CAs except the root CA are called the intermediate CAs. The root CA certifies the next level of intermediate CAs, often called the regional CAs. These regional CAs certify the next levels of intermediate CAs and so on. Any of these intermediate CAs can generate the end-point certificates. Since the certificates are all signed, anyone can verify this chain of certificates (also called the chain-of-trust) tracing back to the root CA. Over the course, the number of such intermediate CAs has increased significantly. It gives rise to the possibility that the mis-issuance of certificates or the disclosure of any such trusted CAs' private keys can cause serious problems to the security of internet communications [5–7,11,13,17,20,21,23].

Moreover, these CAs have ample powers to maliciously or erroneously issue duplicate certificates or revoke the existing certificates without the owner's consent [5–7,11,13,17,20,21,23]. Therefore, this CA-based approach is not always able to address the challenges in secure internet communications. Furthermore, revoking an issued certificate before the end of its validity period is a difficult and cumbersome task. A certificate can be revoked for different reasons, such as the entity's private key or the CA's private key is compromised, or the CA improperly issued such certificates. To revoke such certificates, the issuing CA or any other trusted authority needs to generate and publish a certificate revocation list (CRL) [4]. This CRL is valid for a specific timeframe and needs to be updated and re-published in a timely manner.

The major problem with CRL is that the revoked certificates can still be accepted where the subjected certificate is not validated against the current CRL. There is no proper way to invalidate the revoked certificate. Also, the CRL has increased in size (up to megabytes) over time. Therefore, doing such validations become cumbersome and cannot be enforced everywhere. To cope with this, an alternative online certificate status protocol (OCSP) [19] is implemented that requires less time and less network bandwidth. However, it has a little or no advantage over CRL. Because, a revoked certificate can still be accepted if the OCSP is not used or unavailable. In short, it requires tremendous efforts to stop rogue certificates in the existing CA-based PKI.

In this paper, we propose a distributed key server (DKS) architecture for public key infrastructure (PKI) that can solve these major problems in the existing CA-based PKI. The proposed architecture provides certificate registration/issuance, storage, distribution, and revocation mechanisms. It does not rely on such hierarchical intermediate CA structures where CAs cannot restrict their subordinate CAs from issuing rogue certificates. Instead, it utilizes distributed authority nodes to reach consensus for issuing or revoking any certificates. Each issued certificate is associated with a 256-bit (32 Bytes) unique identifier (UID). The issued certificates, their associated UIDs, and certificate owners' identity information are securely stored in a permissioned distributed storage system. In this way, this architecture ensures transparency and accountability of the certificate issuers (authority nodes).

The issued certificates and their UIDs are also securely transmitted and stored in the key-server nodes (KSNs) which are the client-facing nodes in this architecture. The KSNs manage the certificate distribution mechanism and participate in the authentication process of a secure communication. These key-server nodes (KSNs) extend the central key-server (CKS)-based authentication presented in the Graphene architecture [9,10]. This mechanism is able to solve the two major problems with the existing CA-based PKI authentication. Also, the revocation of any certificate is effective immediately as soon as the revocation transactions are approved by the network. No extra CRL or OCSP-based mechanisms are required.

The major contributions of this paper can be summarized as follows:

- A distributed key server architecture called DKS-PKI that provides public key infrastructure (PKI) for authentication in secure internet communications. This DKS-PKI can replace the existing certificate authority (CA)-based PKI.
- It utilizes a consensus-based distributed network of authority nodes, permissioned storage nodes, and publicly accessible key-server nodes to ensure that the certificate registration/issuance, storage, distribution, and revocation mechanisms are secure, transparent, and fault-tolerant. All the certificates (registered public keys) in DKS-PKI are accessible using their associated unique identifiers (UIDs) through the key-server nodes.
- This architecture solves the two major problems with the existing CA-based PKI and eliminates the need for having any hierarchical intermediate CAs that can issue any certificates to anyone. It ensures accountability of the certificate issuers and allows the system to detect any mis-issuance of certificates as well as any revocation of certificates promptly.

The rest of the paper is organized as follows. Section 2 discusses the most prominent research on different PKI approaches. Section 3 describes the proposed distributed key server architecture for PKI in detail. Section 4 presents the evaluation of the proposed architecture. It provides the security analysis against the possible attack vectors in DKS-PKI. Then, it describes the implementation and the experimental environment. It also presents the performance analysis of DKS-PKI certificate distribution mechanism. Finally, Sect. 5 summarizes the paper.

2   Related Work

Public key infrastructure (PKI) offers the necessary authentication mechanism to guarantee the participants' identity and maintain integrity in any untrusted internet communications. In spite of different problems, the certificate authority (CA)-based PKI is the most popular arrangement for authentication in the present times. Researchers proposed different PKI approaches to establish authentication in internet communications. These approaches suffer from different security, deployment, and scalability issues. Some approaches [1,8,12,18,25] are attempted but not fully deployed due to different issues.

Web of trust [1] (WoT, also known as peer-to-peer PKI) is a decentralized approach driven by the peers in the network where one peer can generate/issue certificates for the other peers. However, it is very difficult for new users to get certificates from such peers. Also, all peers are not equally trusted to the other peers in the network. This may result in rejection of certificates even though they are valid. Moreover, WoT does not have any certificate revocation mechanism. This makes it almost impossible to revoke generated certificates before their validity periods expire.

Another PKI approach is proposed, called simple public key infrastructure (SPKI) [8,25] to bind privileges or rights (access control) to the public key. However, this approach is never finalized and later merged with the simple distributed security infrastructure (SDSI) [18] that deals with groups and group-membership certificates. These PKI approaches attempted to enhance the existing PKI approach. However, they are still in the draft stage and does not solve the stated problems with the CA-based PKI approach.

Alternative approaches, such as log-based PKI [12] and PKI Safety Net (PKISN) [22] are also proposed. The log-based PKI approach is basically an enhancement to the existing CA-based PKI approach. It follows the same CA-based certificate issuance and revocation mechanisms. However, it provides transparency and accountability by creating publicly available logs for the generated certificates. This approach greatly suffers from deployment challenges and certificate revocation issues [14,16]. Also, it cannot be guaranteed that each CA would play fair in the log generation.

The PKISN [22] also follows the same footsteps as in log-based PKI. However, they propose an approach to solve the certificate revocation problem when a trusted CA's private key is compromised. This approach claims that maintaining a log of issued certificates would help determine when the private key compromise happened and only the certificates issued after that event are deemed malicious and require revocation. However, this approach as well suffers from the same deployment issues and depends on the CAs to maintain such logs.

To deal with this problems, Matsumoto and Reischuk [14,15] proposed an automated platform called "IKP" that incentivize certificate authorities (CAs) for properly issuing certificates and detectors for quickly reporting CA misbehaviors and unauthorized certificates. IKP uses Ethereum smart contracts to incentivize participating CAs and detectors. However, it again depends on a new third party called detectors. The detectors may not properly report any unauthorized certificates and gain advantage from the issuing CAs of such certificates. All CAs may not be a part of this incentivized approach and try to collude the participating CAs to maliciously issue certificates.

Similar to log-based PKI, Yakubov et al. [24] proposed a blockchain-based PKI that actually follows the same hierarchical CA-based PKI. Instead of generating logs for the generated certificates, this approach stores the generated certificates in the blockchain ledger. It offers transparency and accountability for the CAs' operations. However, it does not solve the major problems of the CA-based PKI discussed above.

In our prior work [9,10], we implemented a central key-server (CKS)-based authentication in our secure communication architecture called Graphene. In Graphene, the participants are authenticated using their public key certificates already registered with the CKS. This CKS-based authentication is able to solve the CA trust issues and the certificate revocation problem of the CA-based PKI.

The above discussed PKI approaches suffer from different problems that prevent their adoption into secure internet communications. Most of these approaches are enhancements over CA-based PKI and often suffer from deployment and/or scalability issues. They do not necessarily address the above mentioned problems of CA-based PKI. Also, the growing demand of internet communications require a distributed PKI approach that can decentralize the power of the CAs and handle the certificate mis-issuance problems in a robust way. The issued certificates and their sensitive identity information should be stored in a permissioned distributed storage system. Thus, these approaches may not be appropriate for establishing secure internet communications. Therefore, a distributed key server architecture is required that can address the above stated problems and offer a better, transparent, and accountable PKI mechanism for secure internet communications.

3   DKS-PKI Architecture

The proposed distributed key server (DKS) architecture provides public key infrastructure (PKI) for authentication in secure internet communications. It provides registration/issuance, storage, distribution, and revocation of public key certificates. These public key certificates are often referred to as "digital certificates" or simply "certificates". In DKS-PKI, these certificates are also addressed as "registered public keys" interchangeably and each certificate is associated with a 256-bit unique identifier (UID). This architecture consists of four types of nodes as shown in Fig. 1, namely – (i) authority nodes (ANs), (ii) transaction repository nodes (TxRNs), (*iii*) broadcasting nodes (BNs), and (*iv*) key-server nodes (KSNs).

All four types of nodes play important roles in the certificate registration/issuance, storage, and revocation mechanisms. However, the certificate distribution mechanism that enables entities to authenticate each other in a secure communication, is provided by the KSNs. The proposed architecture does not use hierarchical intermediate CA structure for certificate issuance and revocation as observed in CA-based PKI. Instead, it uses authority nodes (ANs) that perform consensus to register/issue or revoke any certificates. This ensures transparency and accountability of the certificate issuers (ANs) in DKS-PKI. Unlike the CA-based approach where the top-level CAs cannot restrict the subordinate CAs from issuing certificates (original as well as duplicate) literally for any entities (people or organizations).

The key aspects of DKS-PKI architecture are discussed in detail in the following subsections.

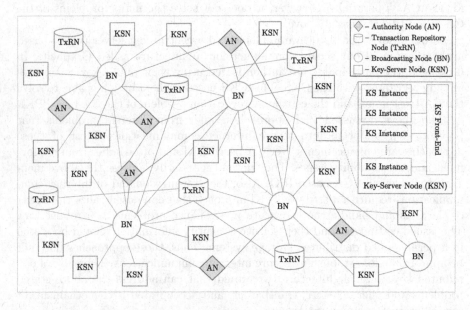

Fig. 1. The proposed distributed key server (DKS) architecture for PKI.

3.1   Overview

In the proposed architecture, the authority nodes (ANs), the transaction repository nodes (TxRNs), and the key-server nodes (KSNs) communicate to each other through the broadcasting nodes (BNs) only. However, the same type of nodes may have direct communication channels (e.g., AN–AN, TxRN–TxRN, BN–BN) between them for data synchronization. All node-to-node communications must be signed by the sender node. All the nodes need to be distributed and can subscribe to their nearest one or more BNs to provide better network stability. Only the authenticated nodes can subscribe to any BNs for receiving specific messages from the other nodes. When the BNs receive an incoming message from a subscribed node, they publish this message to the other subscribed nodes only. Each AN validates certificate registration and revocation requests submitted to it. For each registration request, it generates a public key certificate and its associated 256-bit unique identifier (UID). Then, the AN generates a temporary transaction enclosing these information.

This 256-bit UID is generated by performing hash operation on the validated entity information, and the generated public key certificate. For any authentication, the generated certificates are not usable and the revoked certificates are not invalid until the ANs perform consensus to register/issue or revoke the subjected certificates into the DKS-PKI network. After validating registration/revocation requests, the ANs broadcast temporary transactions enclosing entity information and their signed public key certificates to the other ANs and the TxRNs. After successful consensus between the ANs, the TxRNs generate the sealed transactions from these temporary transactions.

Then, the TxRNs store these sensitive entity information, issued or revoked certificates, and their associated UIDs permanently. The TxRNs also transmit the issued certificates and their associated UIDs to the KSNs. The KSNs provide the certificate distribution mechanism that enables entities to authenticate each other using their associated UIDs. The KSNs store these issued certificates and their associated UIDs locally in the registered certificate store. In case of revocation, the KSNs receive the revoked UIDs from the TxRNs and move the corresponding certificates to the revoked certificate store. These KSNs need to be publicly available at all times and are responsible to manage certificate requests from anywhere in the world.

3.2 Node Operations

Nodes in this architecture operate on three types of transactions, such as register (REG), revoke (RVK), and copy (CPY) transactions. The consensus approach between the ANs uses two types of voting schemes, namely– vote in favor of approval, and vote in favor of rejection. The REG transactions are used to register/issue new certificates into the network. The RVK transactions are used to revoke any existing certificate(s) from the network. The CPY transactions are used to transmit the issued/revoked certificates from the transaction repository nodes (TxRNs) to the KSNs. Each REG transaction corresponds to only one certificate registration request and contains the registering entity information, the generated public key certificate, and the generated 256-bit unique identifier (UID). However, each RVK transaction may contain one or more certificate UID(s) for revocation and their reason(s) of revocation.

The REG and the RVK transactions are generated only by the ANs as temporary transactions (tx'). Each temporary REG/RVK transaction (tx') must be broadcasted to the other ANs and the TxRNs through the BNs. The other ANs verify (duplicity check, mis-issuance check, etc.) the incoming registration/revocation request. Then, the ANs perform consensus and cast their votes on the transaction either in favor of approval or rejection. The TxRNs act as the vote collectors (VCs) during the consensus process. Each transaction requires at least two-third votes in favor of approval to be accepted. However, a single vote in favor of rejection would halt the consensus process and move the subjected transaction to the suspended transaction list. Next, the AN(s) who voted in favor of rejection must present valid reasoning for their actions. On failure to do so, the AN(s) are permanently removed from the network and the suspended transaction is moved to the pending transaction list. An AN may vote in favor of rejection if the registering entity's identity or domain information cannot be verified.

After that, the consensus process resumes with the remaining ANs in the network. After receiving at least two-third votes in favor of approval from the ANs, the temporary transaction (tx') is transformed into a sealed transaction (tx) by the TxRNs. The sealed transaction is signed by the TxRNs and contains the temporary transaction, the received voting information, and the hashed value of all these information. For certificate registration, the TxRNs generate a signed CPY transaction with the issued certificate and its associated UID, and broadcast it to the nearby KSNs. For certificate revocation, the signed CPY transaction only contains the revoked UID(s). Once the CPY transaction is broadcasted, the ANs are notified with a notice-of-approval. After that, the newly issued certificate is available and the revoked certificate(s) are removed for entity authentication. The registering entity receives its 256-bit UID from the corresponding AN.

3.3 Authoritative Signing Keys (ASKs)

The proposed architecture uses only *three* trusted authoritative signing keys (ASKs), such as root/master ASK (RASK), node ASK (NASK), and issuer ASK (IASK). These ASKs differ from the traditional certificate authorities (CAs). The ASKs do not belong to any specific authority or organization. Instead, they are used to maintain the trust value of the network nodes and prevent man-in-the-middle (MITM) attacks from happening at all steps of the node operations. Each ASK is essentially a keypair that consists of a public key certificate and its corresponding private key. The RASK is the master public-private keypair of this DKS-PKI architecture and securely stored offline.

The public key certificates in NASK and IASK are signed using the RASK private key. The NASK private key is only used to generate/issue the public key certificates for the broadcasting nodes (BNs), the transaction repository nodes (TxRNs), and the key-server nodes (KSNs). However, the IASK private key is used to generate the public key certificates for the ANs only. The NASK certificate and the IASK certificate play key roles in DKS-PKI. They are also called the *trusted* Node certificate and the *trusted* DKS certificate, respectively. These certificates must be installed (trusted) into these node systems, all modern browsers, and operating systems. They are used to validate the authenticity of the node-to-node communications and the entity certificates. In case of any private key disclosure, using different ASKs provides better control in separating the node systems (BNs, TxRNs, KSNs) and the entity certificate issuance mechanism.

The *trusted* DKS certificate is used to prove the trustworthiness of the entity certificates (also called the end-user certificates) issued by the ANs. Each entity certificate carries the entity information and its public key, issuer's (AN's) signature, 256-bit unique identifier (UID), and the AN's certificate. This AN's certificate is signed by the IASK private key. Therefore, the AN's certificate can be validated using the IASK certificate, also referred to as the *trusted* DKS certificate in the end-user systems. Once the AN's certificate is validated using the *trusted* DKS certificate, it becomes trusted for the current authentication session. Then, this AN's certificate can be used to validate the entity certificates signed by this AN. This double validation reduces the number of trusted certificates in the end-user systems significantly.

3.4   Certificate Registration/Issuance and Storage

The authority nodes (ANs) receive public key registration applications from different types of entities (e.g., people, businesses, organizations). Each AN is responsible to validate the identity information associated with the applications submitted to them. After successful validation, the AN generates a certificate and a 256-bit unique identifier (UID) for the registering entity. This UID is generated by performing hash operations on the validated entity information and the generated certificate. Next, the AN generates a temporary REG transaction (tx'_{reg}) enclosing these information and broadcasts this tx'_{reg} to the other ANs and the TxRNs. The other ANs verify (duplicity check, mis-issuance check, etc.) this newly generated certificate and the entity information.

After verification, the ANs start casting their votes in favor of approval or rejection for this transaction. The TxRNs wait till they receive at least two-third votes in favor of approval for this transaction. Here, one key difference with the other consensus-based systems is that if a transaction receives a single vote in favor of rejection, that transaction is moved to the suspended transaction list. The AN(s) who voted in favor of rejection must present valid reasoning for casting such vote(s). On failure to do so, the AN(s) are permanently removed from the network and the consensus process resumes by moving the suspended transaction to the pending list.

Once the TxRNs receive two-third votes in favor of approval and there is no vote in favor of rejection, the TxRNs generate a sealed REG transaction (tx_{reg}) from the temporary transaction and store it permanently in the repository. The issued certificate is placed in the registered certificate store until the entity certificate is revoked or expired. Also, the TxRNs synchronize their current state to make sure that there is no discrepancies. After that, the TxRNs generate a CPY transaction (tx_{cpy}) with only the issued certificate and its associated UID and broadcast this transaction using the broadcasting nodes (BNs). The BNs push updates to the listening KSNs. Then, the TxRNs broadcast a notice-of-approval to the ANs. The registering entity receives its 256-bit UID from the corresponding AN. At this point, the issued certificate is registered into the network and can be accessed using its associated 256-bit UID.

3.5   Certificate Distribution

In DKS-PKI, the key-server nodes (KSNs) are responsible to manage the certificate distribution mechanism. This mechanism enables entity authentication in secure communications using the proposed architecture. The issued certificates and their associated 256-bit unique identifiers (UIDs) are transmitted to these KSNs using CPY transactions and stored in their registered certificate store until they are revoked or expired. Similarly, when any certificate(s) are revoked or expired, they are moved to the revoked certificate store. The registering entities do not receive their public key certificates unlike CA-based PKI. Instead, they receive their 256-bit UIDs. In this proposed architecture, entities do not present their certificates to each other for authenticating themselves. Rather, they present their 256-bit UIDs.

These UIDs are used to request their associated registered certificates from the KSNs. To deal with these certificate requests, each KSN runs one or more key-server instance(s) (KSIs). Each KSI is essentially a Hypertext Transfer Protocol (HTTP) service. Therefore, these KSNs accept HTTP requests (e.g., /public-key/?id={UID}) from participating entities and respond with one of four HTTP responses, such as "200 OK", "410 Gone", "404 Not Found", and "400 Bad Request" where the response codes carry their usual meanings. When the requested KSN finds a registered/issued certificate with the requested UID, it responds with a "200 OK" HTTP response attaching the certificate to it. If the requested UID is associated with a revoked certificate, the KSN responds with a "410 Gone" HTTP response. A "404 Not Found" HTTP response is sent when the requested UID does not belong to any of the issued or revoked certificates. In case of any invalid/malformed request URI, the KSN responds with a "400 Bad Request" HTTP response.

Therefore, the availability of these KSNs is crucial for this PKI architecture to succeed in providing certificates for authentications during secure communications. The distributed design used for the KSNs would help improve the availability of these KSNs and reduce the impact of denial-of-service (DoS) or distributed denial-of-service (DDoS) attacks on these KSNs. Since these KSNs serve public key certificates, encrypting the data-in-transit is not necessary. However, all responses must be signed by the KSN's private key to prevent man-in-the-middle (MITM) attacks and accompany the KSN's certificate which is signed by the NASK private key as stated in Sect. 3.3. This KSN certificate can be validated using the *trusted* Node certificate. Then, the validated KSN certificate can be used to validate the response signature.

3.6 Certificate Revocation

In the proposed architecture, the revocation mechanism for the issued certificate(s) is straightforward. When one or more certificate(s) need to be revoked, the request is submitted to an authority node (AN). The requested AN validates the revocation request and generates a temporary RVK transaction (tx'_{rvk}) enclosing the associated UID(s) of the certificate(s) under revocation request and the reason(s) of revocation. Next, the AN broadcasts the transaction to the other ANs and the transaction repository nodes (TxRNs) through the broadcasting nodes (BNs). After receiving this transaction, the TxRNs wait for the votes in favor of approval or rejection from the ANs.

The other ANs verify (malicious/erroneous check) the certificate(s) and their reason(s) of revocation. Then, the ANs start casting their votes in favor of approval or rejection. If any AN(s) vote in favor of rejection, the consensus process halts and the transaction is moved to the suspended transaction list. The AN(s) who voted in favor of rejection must provide valid reasoning for such voting. Otherwise, they are removed from the network permanently and the consensus process resumes with the subjected transaction. Once the TxRNs receive at least two-third votes in favor of approval and no votes in favor of rejection for this transaction, the TxRNs generate a sealed RVK transaction (tx_{rvk}) from this temporary transaction and store it permanently.

After that, the revoked certificate(s) are moved to the revoked certificate store and the TxRNs synchronize their state to avoid any discrepancies. Next, the TxRNs generate a CPY transaction (tx_{cpy}) with the revoked UID(s) and broadcast it to the key-server nodes (KSNs) through the BNs. The KSNs move the revoked certificates and their associated UIDs to the revoked certificate store. A notice-of-approval is sent to the requesting AN. After that, anyone requesting a certificate associated with any of those revoked UIDs receives a HTTP "410 Gone" response from the KSNs.

3.7   Stored-Data Validation

In terms of DKS-PKI, the stored data incorporates the sealed transactions stored in the transaction repository nodes (TxRNs), the certificates and their associated 256-bit unique identifiers (UIDs) stored in the certificate stores (registered and revoked) of the TxRNs and the key-server nodes (KSNs). Each sealed REG transaction represents a single certificate registration/issuance. It contains the validated entity information, the generated public key certificate, the generated UID, the received voting information, and the hashed value of all these information. However, each sealed RVK transaction may contain one or more revoked UID(s), the reason(s) of their revocation, the received voting information, and the hashed value of all these information. Next, the sealed transaction is signed by the respective TxRN where it is stored and added to an append-only list of transactions. Each certificate store (registered/revoked) in the TxRNs, and the KSNs is essentially a list of {UID, certificate} object indexed by the corresponding UID.

To maintain integrity of the stored data, different nodes perform validation checks on the other nodes of the network. The authority nodes (ANs) perform validation check on the stored data in the TxRNs. The ANs pull randomly selected same portion of the transaction list from different TxRNs. Then, they perform integrity and consistency check on the data received from the TxRNs under consideration. If any TxRN(s) fail to comply with the validation process, they are suspended from the network. The suspended TxRN(s) are required to synchronize their stored data with the other active TxRNs. They remain suspended until they pass this integrity and consistency check. Similarly, the active TxRNs perform integrity and validation check on the KSNs. The KSNs also get suspended from the network if failed to comply with the validation check and need to pass the check to become active again.

4 Evaluation

4.1 Security Analysis

The proposed architecture and all the nodes need to be secured from any types of certificate mis-issuance, certificate cloning/tampering, and compromised private key attacks. It is equally important for all the nodes in this architecture to prevent themselves from man-in-the-middle (MITM), and denial-of-service (DoS) attacks. In this section, we identify the possible attack vectors and present a thorough security analysis of the proposed architecture.

Scenario-1 (Compromised Key-Server Node). The key-server nodes (KSNs) are solely responsible to provide the certificate distribution mechanism that allows entities to authenticate each other using their unique identifiers (UIDs) and registered certificates. Each valid certificate contains entity information, entity public key, authority node's signature, and authority node's certificate. However, a compromised KSN may attempt to tamper any registered certificate(s) and add duplicate or cloned certificates in the local storage. Since the KSNs' certificates are generated (signed) by a different authoritative signing key (ASK) than the ANs' certificates as stated in Sect. 3.3, the KSNs are not able to generate/forge any unauthorized or cloned/tampered certificates that can pass the validation check using the *trusted* DKS certificate.

Scenario-2 (Malicious Authority Node). A malicious authority node (AN) may try to mis-use its power to issue unauthorized or duplicate certificates. However, the AN itself cannot register any certificates to the transaction repository nodes (TxRNs) and the key-server nodes (KSNs) without broadcasting it through the broadcasting nodes (BNs). Also, the subjected certificates can only be accepted into the network after receiving *at least* two-third votes in favor of approval from the other ANs. This makes it fairly difficult to corrupt such significant amount of ANs in the proposed architecture.

Scenario-3 (Any TxRN Tampering a Certificate). No other nodes except the ANs can issue and/or revoke any certificates. The TxRNs store the sealed transactions, the issued and the revoked certificates, and their UIDs. Also, they act as the vote collectors (VCs) during the consensus process. If any TxRN is compromised and trying to tamper an approved certificate or publish a tampered certificate to the KSNs, it is readily detected by the other TxRNs and the KSNs. The TxRNs synchronize their sealed transactions. The KSNs receive the same CPY transactions from multiple TxRNs signed by the sender TxRNs. If there is any mismatch, they can report that to the other network nodes. Also, the stored-data validation process can track such discrepancies.

Scenario-4 (Any Private Key Is Lost or Stolen). Compromised private key(s) always cause serious issues in any PKI systems. Therefore, protecting these private keys is of utmost importance. As described in Sect. 3.3, the certificates of the TxRNs, the BNs, and the KSNs are signed using the node ASK's (NASK) private key. The ANs' certificates are signed using the issuer ASK's (IASK) private key. The end-user certificates are signed by their issuing ANs' private keys. Therefore, if any end-user private key is compromised, that end-user must register for a new certificate. In case of any of the ANs' private keys are lost or stolen, the respective ANs must get their new certificates and re-generate (revoke-then-issue) all the previously issued end-user certificates using their new private keys. If any ASKs' private key is compromised, it would cause a large number of certificates to be re-generated. However, using different ASKs for node certificates and certificate issuance mechanism provides a better control over such situations.

Scenario-5 (In Case of Any Man-In-The-Middle). All the node-to-node communications and the KSNs' HTTP responses are signed using their respective private keys. The TxRNs', the BNs', and the KSNs' signatures can be validated using the *trusted* Node certificate and their own certificates. The ANs' signature can also be validated using the *trusted* DKS certificate and the ANs' own certificates. An adversary may try to perform man-in-the-middle (MITM) attacks on any node-to-node communications or the KSNs' HTTP services to gain access and tamper with any temporary transactions, consensus votings, and/or certificate transmissions. However, the authenticated communication approach can effectively prevent such attacks in this proposed architecture.

Scenario-6 (Any Types of Denial-Of-Service). The KSNs provide the certificate distribution mechanism using HTTP services that allow the entities to request each other's certificates for authentication. Also, the broadcasting nodes (BNs) enable the ANs, the TxRNs, and the KSNs to communicate with each other. The BNs use a publish-subscribe approach and only allow nodes that can prove their authenticity with valid certificates to subscribe for specific messages and publish selective messages to the network. An adversary may try to perform denial-of-service (DoS) or distributed denial-of-service (DDoS) attacks on the KSNs, and/or the BNs. This attack scenario can be prevented by increasing the number of KSNs and BNs and distributing them geographically.

4.2 Implementation

The proposed architecture utilizes a permissioned distributed network of four types of nodes, such as authority nodes (ANs), broadcasting nodes (BNs), transaction repository nodes (TxRNs), and key-server nodes (KSNs). Each type of nodes plays important roles in certificate registration/issuance, storage, distribution, and revocation mechanisms. However, to be fault-tolerant and avoid partial centralization problem, such distributed networks require all types of nodes to be deployed in large numbers. Increasing the number of nodes improves the network operations and the unbiasedness of the consensus process. However, deploying such large number of nodes is a challenge on its own. To tackle this deployment challenge and implement the proposed architecture in a way so that its performance can be measured for the certificate distribution mechanism, we adopt some changes in the node operations.

The certificate registration and revocation mechanisms use consensus approach to register/issue and revoke certificates, respectively. The consensus is based on *at least* two-third votes in favor of approval of the transactions which is a proven Byzantine Fault Tolerant (BFT) approach for distributed systems. Therefore, we focused our implementation on the certificate distribution mechanism of the proposed architecture that enables entities to authenticate each other using their registered certificates and associated 256-bit unique identifiers (UIDs). This mechanism is solely dependent on the KSNs, and the already registered and revoked certificates in them. Therefore, we implemented the AN, the KSN, and a request generator (RG) that generates certificate requests to a KSN continuously.

These nodes are implemented using the Java programming language, Java Cryptography Architecture (JCA), socket programming, multi-threading, and HTTP communication protocol. The National Institute of Standards and Technology (NIST) recommendations are strictly followed at all steps of the implementation [2,3]. The AN implementation is used to generate the sample end-user certificates. These sample certificates are manually stored in the KSN's local file system indexed (renamed) by their UIDs. The KSN implementation provides HTTP services that manage certificate requests from the request generators (RGs). This KSN implementation supports all four possible types of request scenarios as stated in Sect. 3.5. Different types of request scenarios can cause different response times. However, the worst-case scenario for measuring the KSN performance is a complete certificate request-response for a valid UID. The RG is implemented as a single-threaded process to simulate continuous HTTP certificate requests to a specific request URI (/public-key/?id={UID}).

4.3 Experimental Environment

For the experiments, twelve Raspberry Pi 3 Model B+ (RPi) devices are configured with CentOS 8 (minimal version) and one-gigabit Ethernet connections as shown in Fig. 2. Each RPi device has a quad-core processor, and 1 GB LPDDR2 SDRAM. This means each RPi can easily run up to four processes or key-server instances simultaneously without any significant processing time overlap. Java 8 is used to develop the implementation and OpenJDK 11.0.3 is used to execute the experiments in CentOS 8 environment. The reason behind using RPi devices (in spite of being low in CPU and memory) is to deploy the node implementations in a more modular way. Using a faster processing multi-core CPU and larger memory machine would yield running multiple nodes in the same machine sharing the same network interface card (NIC) which does not properly represent the network design required for the certificate distribution mechanism of the proposed architecture.

All public-private keypairs are generated using 2048-bit RSA algorithm. The certificates are generated using 256-bit SHA2 hashing algorithm and RSA

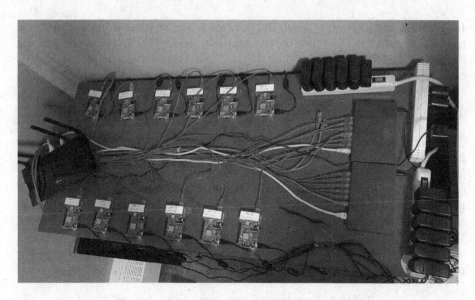

Fig. 2. Experimental environment of the DKS-PKI certificate distribution mechanism.

encryption with PKCS#1 v2.2 padding scheme [2,3]. Three authoritative sign-ing keys (ASKs), such as root ASK (RASK), node ASK (NASK), and issuer ASK (IASK) as stated in Sect. 3.3 are generated using the above algorithms. The *trusted* Node certificate (NASK certificate) and the *trusted* DKS certificate (IASK certificate) are installed into all RPi devices. The KSN certificates are generated using the NASK private key. The AN certificate is generated using the IASK private key. Then, the AN and the KSN certificates and their respective private keys are installed in the same directory where these nodes are deployed.

First, the AN is deployed in a RPi device where all necessary public key certificates and its own private key are installed appropriately. Next, the AN generates 100 sample (test) 2048-bit RSA public-private keypairs, signs these public keys using its own private key, and attaches its own certificate at the end of these test certificates. The AN also generates 256-bit unique identifiers (UIDs) for each of these test certificates. After that, these test certificates are manually stored to a separate directory (presented as the registered certificate store) in each KSN local file system indexed (renamed) by their UIDs. Each KSN is deployed with four key-server instances to manage HTTP requests from the RGs. Therefore, The RPi devices running a KSN does not have any other processing load.

All devices are under the same local network that has no other traffic except the certificate requests generated from the RGs to the KSN(s). Different number of KSNs and RGs are executed in these twelve RPi devices in a distributed manner. The number of KSNs deployed is up to four and the number of RGs deployed is up to 25. Since the RGs are single-threaded processes, each RPi device can run up to four RGs simultaneously. We run up to 25 RGs distributed over eight RPi devices in a round-robin fashion that use three parameters (RG

ID, KSN IP, and KSN port). Each RG instance is executed one minute apart from the last executed RG instance on the next RPi device. For faster execution, we preloaded the RGs with 100 256-bit UIDs. Then, these UIDs are used randomly to generate valid certificate requests to the KSNs.

4.4 Performance Analysis

This section presents the performance analysis for the certificate distribution mechanism of the proposed DKS-PKI architecture. We evaluate the runtime performance and scalability of the key-server nodes (KSNs) in terms of the number of processed requests per second and the average request completion time (in milliseconds) with different number of request generators (RGs). We recorded the request completion time for each request at the RGs and calculated values for the above metrics. We also analyze the implementation with multiple KSNs to show the performance improvement in terms of the number of processed requests per second. Table 1 presents the specification of the experimental environment.

Table 1. Experimental environment specification.

Parameters	Values
Test environment	Raspberry Pi 3 Model B+ (RPi)
RPi processing unit	Cortex-A53 (ARMv8) 64-bit, SoC @ 1.4 GHz quad-core
RPi memory	1 GB LPDDR2 SDRAM
Number of RPi modules	12
Operating system	CentOS 8 (minimal version)
Runtime environment	OpenJDK v11.0.3
Network component	One Gigabit router, Two LAN (Gigabit) switches
Connection type	Ethernet
Network ping time	Less than 1 ms
Number of RGs	1–25

A single KSN is executed in one of the RPi devices. Three more RPi devices are reserved for running three more KSNs later. A new RG instance is executed every one minute in one of the remaining eight RPi devices in a round-robin fashion. Each RG generates a certificate request to the KSN with a valid UID and receives the response. If it is successful (200 OK), then it generates another certificate request with another valid UID and keeps doing this continuously until stopped. In case of a failed request, the RG reports the error and terminates itself. This single KSN experiment is executed with different number of RGs for at least 25 min from the secure shell (SSH) terminal. In this way, we can record the request processing times for one minute duration with different number of RGs sending concurrent requests to the single KSN. Here, our goal is to investigate the performance and scalability of the certificate distribution mechanism.

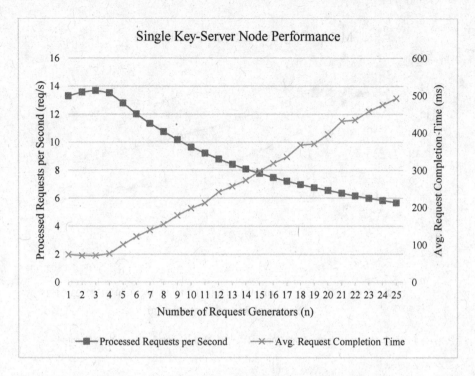

Fig. 3. Performance of the DKS-PKI certificate distribution mechanism using a single key-server node.

Figure 3 shows the runtime performance of the implementation in terms of the number of processed requests per second (viz., ▬ curve) and the average request completion time in milliseconds (viz., ✕ curve) with respect to different number of request generators (RGs) ranging from 1 to 25. The overall runtime performance of the certificate distribution mechanism is reasonable. The performance deteriorates with the increasing number of concurrent certificate requests generated by the RGs. For the first four RG instances, the number of processed requests per second (viz., ▬ curve) and the average request completion time (viz., ✕ curve) are steady and show similar pattern. The reason behind that the KSN is running four key-server instances. Therefore, the number of processed requests per second as well as the average request completion time remains steady.

After that, increasing the concurrent certificate requests (i.e., increasing the RG instances) decreases the number of processed requests per second exponentially and increases the average request completion time linearly. Three times increase in the concurrent certificate requests (12 RGs) results in a 36% decrease in the number of processed requests per second and 340% increase in the average request completion time. Similarly, increasing the concurrent certificate requests by six times (24 RGs) decreases the number of processed requests per second by 60% and increases the average request completion time by almost 700%.

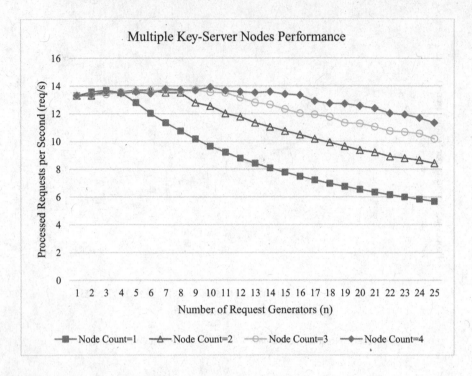

Fig. 4. Performance of the DKS-PKI certificate distribution mechanism using multiple key-server nodes.

Figure 4 presents the performance of the certificate distribution mechanism with multiple KSNs (up to four KSNs) with the increasing number of request generators (RGs). It is readily noticeable that the performance of the KSNs improved significantly with each new KSN. Since each KSN is running four key-server instances, the number of processed requests per second for two KSNs (viz., ─△─ curve) remains steady up to eight RGs. Then, the performance starts deteriorating in the similar way. Similarly, for three KSNs (viz., ─○─ curve) and four KSNs (viz., ─◆─ curve) the performance remains steady up to 12 RGs and 16 RGs, respectively. Therefore, increasing the number of KSN improves the overall performance of the certificate distribution mechanism in DKS-PKI. Using faster processing multi-core CPUs and large memory machines would enhance the scalability of the network even further.

5   Conclusion

The traditional public key infrastructure (PKI) offers entity authentications using trusted third parties called certificate authorities (CAs). All these CAs are organized in a hierarchical structure (e.g., root CA, and several levels of intermediate CAs) and share ample power for issuing any certificate to anyone.

Therefore, this authentication mechanism is largely dependent on the trustworthiness of these CAs. Also, revoking any certificate in the existing CA-based PKI is a difficult and cumbersome job. It is hard to ensure that the revoked certificates cannot be used anymore. When any CA's private key is lost or stolen, this makes it even more complicated to revoke the CA's trusted certificate everywhere and its issued-certificates as well. To solve these problems, a distributed key server architecture for PKI (DKS-PKI) is proposed. This proposed architecture ensures transparency and accountability of the certificate issuers (authority nodes). Any authority node (AN) cannot issue certificates in the network without reaching consensus with the other ANs. This approach solves the certificate mis-issuance problem. Next, certificate revocation is effective as soon as the authority nodes reach a consensus on the revocation transaction. After that, the revoked certificates are separated from the rest of the issued certificates in the TxRNs and the KSNs. This solves the certificate revocation issue as well. In case of any private key disclosure, only the certificates issued by that private key need to be revoked and re-issued. Overall, the performance of the certificate distribution mechanism shows reasonable results with the increasing number of certificate requests. The distributed network of ANs, BNs, TxRNs, and KSNs helps this architecture to prevent DoS/DDoS attacks on any node and improves the availability of the PKI network for authentication.

References

1. Aberer, K., Datta, A., Hauswirth, M.: A decentralised public key infrastructure for customer-to-customer e-commerce. Int. J. Bus. Process Integr. Manag. **1**, 26–33 (2005)
2. Barker, E., Roginsky, A.: Transitioning the use of cryptographic algorithms and key lengths, March 2019. https://doi.org/10.6028/NIST.SP.800-131Ar2
3. Barker, E.B., Dang, Q.H.: SP 800–57 Pt3 R1. Recommendation for Key Management, Part 3: Application-Specific Key Management Guidance, January 2015. https://nvlpubs.nist.gov/nistpubs/SpecialPublications/NIST.SP.800-57Pt3r1.pdf. Accessed 04 Dec 2021
4. Boeyen, S., Santesson, S., Polk, T., Housley, R., Farrell, S., Cooper, D.: Internet X.509 Public Key Infrastructure Certificate and Certificate Revocation List (CRL) Profile. RFC 5280, May 2008. https://doi.org/10.17487/RFC5280. https://www.rfc-editor.org/info/rfc5280
5. Charette, R.: DigiNotar Certificate Authority Breach Crashes e-Government in the Netherlands, September 2011. https://spectrum.ieee.org/riskfactor/telecom/security/diginotar-certificate-authority-breach-crashes-egovernment-in-the-netherlands. Accessed 25 July 2022
6. ComputerWorld.com: To punish Symantec, Google may distrust a third of the web's SSL certificates, March 2017. https://www.computerworld.com/article/3184573/to-punish-symantec-google-may-distrust-a-third-of-the-webs-ssl-certificates.html. Accessed 24 July 2022
7. Constantin, L.: French intermediate certificate authority issues rogue certs for Google domains, December 2013. https://www.computerworld.com/article/2486614/french-intermediate-certificate-authority-issues-rogue-certs-for-google-domains.html. Accessed 25 July 2022

8. Ellison, C.: SPKI Requirements. RFC 2692, September 1999. https://doi.org/10.17487/RFC2692. https://www.rfc-editor.org/info/rfc2692

9. Faisal, A., Zulkernine, M.: Graphene: a secure cloud communication architecture. In: Zhou, J., Deng, R., Li, Z., Majumdar, S., Meng, W., Wang, L., Zhang, K. (eds.) ACNS 2019. LNCS, vol. 11605, pp. 51–69. Springer, Cham (2019). https://doi.org/10.1007/978-3-030-29729-9_3

10. Faisal, A., Zulkernine, M.: A secure architecture for TCP/UDP-based cloud communications. Int. J. Inf. Secur. **20**(2), 161–179 (2020). https://doi.org/10.1007/s10207-020-00511-w

11. Hoogstraaten, H.: Black tulip report of the investigation into the diginotar certificate authority breach. Technical report, Fox-IT BV, August 2012. https://doi.org/10.13140/2.1.2456.7364. Accessed 25 July 2022

12. Laurie, B., Langley, A., Kasper, E.: Certificate Transparency. RFC 6962, June 2013. https://doi.org/10.17487/RFC6962. https://rfc-editor.org/rfc/rfc6962.txt

13. Leyden, J.: 23,000 HTTPS certs will be axed in next 24 hours after private keys leak, March 2018. https://www.theregister.co.uk/2018/03/01/trustico_digicert_symantec_spat/. Accessed 25 July 2022

14. Matsumoto, S., Reischuk, R.M.: IKP: turning a PKI around with blockchains. Cryptology ePrint Archive, Paper 2016/1018 (2016). https://eprint.iacr.org/2016/1018

15. Matsumoto, S., Reischuk, R.M.: IKP: turning a PKI around with decentralized automated incentives. In: 2017 IEEE Symposium on Security and Privacy (SP), pp. 410–426 (2017). https://doi.org/10.1109/SP.2017.57

16. Matsumoto, S., Szalachowski, P., Perrig, A.: Deployment challenges in log-based PKI enhancements. In: Proceedings of the Eighth European Workshop on System Security, EuroSec 2015. Association for Computing Machinery, New York (2015). https://doi.org/10.1145/2751323.2751324

17. Mozilla.org: CA/Symantec Issues. https://wiki.mozilla.org/CA/Symantec_Issues. Accessed 24 July 2022

18. Rivest, R., Lampson, B.: SDSI - a simple distributed security infrastructure, August 1996. https://people.csail.mit.edu/rivest/sdsi10.html. Accessed 24 July 2022

19. Santesson, S., Myers, M., Ankney, R., Malpani, A., Galperin, S., Adams, D.C.: X.509 Internet Public Key Infrastructure Online Certificate Status Protocol - OCSP. RFC 6960, June 2013. https://doi.org/10.17487/RFC6960. https://www.rfc-editor.org/info/rfc6960

20. SecurityIntelligence.com: Symantec's SSL Certificate May Get Cut Off by Chrome, March 2017. https://securityintelligence.com/news/symantecs-ssl-certificate-gets-cut-off-by-chrome/. Accessed 25 July 2022

21. Symantec: Test Certificates Incident Final Report v3, October 2015. https://bug1214321.bmoattachments.org/attachment.cgi?id=8852862. Accessed 24 July 2022

22. Szalachowski, P., Chuat, L., Perrig, A.: PKI safety net (PKISN): addressing the too-big-to-be-revoked problem of the TLS ecosystem. In: 2016 IEEE European Symposium on Security and Privacy (EuroS P), p. 407–422 (2016). https://doi.org/10.1109/EuroSP.2016.38

23. Williams, O.: Google to drop China's CNNIC Root Certificate Authority after trust breach, April 2015. https://thenextweb.com/insider/2015/04/02/google-to-drop-chinas-cnnic-root-certificate-authority-after-trust-breach/. Accessed 25 July 2022

24. Yakubov, A., Shbair, W.M., Wallbom, A., Sanda, D., State, R.: A blockchain-based PKI management framework. In: NOMS 2018–2018 IEEE/IFIP Network Operations and Management Symposium, pp. 1–6, April 2018
25. Ylonen, T., Thomas, B., Lampson, B., Ellison, C., Rivest, R.L., Frantz, W.S.: SPKI Certificate Theory. RFC 2693, September 1999. https://doi.org/10.17487/RFC2693. https://www.rfc-editor.org/info/rfc2693

Generating-Set Evaluation of Bloom Filter Hardening Techniques in Private Record Linkage

Karin Mortl and Rinku Dewri[⊠]

Department of Computer Science, University of Denver, Denver, CO, USA
karin.mortl@du.edu, rdewri@cs.du.edu

Abstract. Private record linkage is an active field of research targeted towards linking data sets from two or more sources, while preserving the privacy of contained sensitive content. With computation and communication efficiency as other two important requirements in such a process, much attention has been given to use Bloom filters for fast encoding of data records, while maintaining privacy of the records at the same time. A number of techniques to modify a typical Bloom filter have also appeared and addresses the need to harden them against known attacks. However, the field significantly lacks quantitative measures of the privacy level introduced by such techniques. In this work, we motivate and propose the *generating-set amplification factor* measure to bridge some of this gap. This privacy measure aims to capture the level of uncertainty that a hardening technique introduces between its output and the input used to create a Bloom filter. We provide algorithms to compute the measure and provide an empirical assessment of the state-of-the-art Bloom filter hardening techniques with respect to the measure. Our assessment shows that current techniques may still be retaining much of the characteristics of the input, although attacks to exploit them are yet to appear.

Keywords: Private record linkage · Bloom filter · Generating set · Privacy evaluation

1 Introduction

Private record linkage is the process of linking records of individuals in the absence of unique identifiers, with a high accuracy, and while preventing access to clear text information about an individual. Quasi-identifiers built from demographic information are often used in such a process. Further, clear text access to such information is prevented through the use of different encoding techniques [13,21,26] or secure protocols [6,17,27]. Due to the possible presence of data entry errors, a record linkage method must be able to link records based on approximated similarity rather than exact matching.

Bloom filter based methods have become actively researched and adopted mechanisms in this domain [1,7,11,22,28]. Bloom filters provide a succinct representation of a data record and can be tailored to provide indirect measurements

© The Author(s), under exclusive license to Springer Nature Switzerland AG 2022
V. R. Badarla et al. (Eds.): ICISS 2022, LNCS 13784, pp. 44–63, 2022.
https://doi.org/10.1007/978-3-031-23690-7_3

of the similarity of two data records. However, their vulnerability to many attacks [4,15,16,18,19,31–33] have also resulted in a number of hardening techniques [14,20,23–25]. A hardening technique operates on a Bloom filter encoding with the objective of diffusing frequency information. Unfortunately, hardening techniques themselves have been shown to be vulnerable, raising the need to have better evaluation of the privacy preserving capabilities of proposed methods.

Quantitative privacy measures for Bloom filters in record linkage are rare. While there exists techniques that are yet to be shown vulnerable to an attack, there also does not exist much assessment on why hardening methods can resist an attack. Recent studies have used measures based on the frequency distribution of bits in a Bloom filter, but they are mostly useful in a comparative setting [10]. In this work, we propose a privacy measure that can inform whether a hardening technique can produce an output that detaches the relationship between a data record and its Bloom filter representation. More specifically, we analyze if the output of a standard hardening technique can be generated from a Bloom filter created from a much larger input set than was actually used. To this end, we make the following contributions in this work. We introduce the notion of a *generating-set amplification factor* that indicates the extent to which a Bloom filter's input set can be amplified and still result in the same hardened output. We then provide algorithms to compute this measure for standard hardening techniques such as balancing [23], XOR-folding [24], Rule90 [25], and random noise addition [8,20,23]. This is detailed in Sect. 3. Since the efficacy of these methods often depend on parametric choices (e.g. probability of distortion), we supplement our work with a theoretical analysis on when probabilistic methods are likely to fare well in terms of maintaining high linkage quality (Sect. 4). Finally, we provide empirical evidence using real world data records that, except for a select few scenarios, most hardening techniques still retain a strong correlation between the input set of a filter and the hardened output (Sect. 5). For the ones that do provide some level of privacy (in terms of the amplification factor), we show that a high linkage quality can be obtained, but requires careful setup of the similarity matching thresholds. Besides the aforementioned sections, Sect. 2 provides a brief background on record linkage using Bloom filters and hardening techniques, and puts related work in context, and Sect. 6 concludes the paper with references to future work.

2 Background and Related Work

A private record linkage aims to join two databases of records without clear text access to the attributes of either database [12,29]. The presence of typographic errors in data records creates an additional challenge in this task. Therefore, the standard approach is to follow approximate matching principles where a record is converted into multiple q-grams (q sized sequences of contiguous characters), and the q-gram sets are instead compared privately to obtain a similarity score [5]. Bigrams ($q = 2$) and trigrams ($q = 3$) are typically used. Approximate matching relies on a provided similarity scoring function and a similarity threshold, and matches are considered valid only if the similarity score crosses the threshold.

The use of Bloom filters to perform private comparison of two q-gram sets has received much attention due to their low communication and computation costs. A Bloom filter is a m-bit binary array, initialized with all zeros. An element is inserted into it using k pseudo-random hash functions, each of which maps the element to one of the m positions, which is then set to one. An element can therefore be tested for membership in the Bloom filter by checking if the bits at its hashed positions are set or not. Bloom filters can have false positives (an element passes the membership test although it was not inserted), but the rate can be controlled by proper choice of m and k. For a Bloom filter B, we use the notation $B[i]$ to indicate the bit at position $i = 0...m - 1$ of the binary array.

2.1 Linkage with Bloom Filters

A Bloom filter can be used to obtain an encoding of the q-gram set of a record by treating each q-gram as an element to be inserted in the filter [21]. Similarity comparisons are then performed on the Bloom filters instead of the q-gram sets. The primary objective here is to hide the exact q-grams of a record, and yet be able to determine the extent of overlap between two such sets. A frequently used similarity function is the Dice coefficient metric, given as

$$\text{Dice}(B, B') = \frac{2 \times \text{bitsum}(B \text{ AND } B')}{\text{bitsum}(B) + \text{bitsum}(B')}, \tag{1}$$

where AND is the bitwise-AND operation, and bitsum is the sum of all bit values in a binary array. A Dice score always falls in $[0, 1]$, where a score of zero implies that there are no positions where the bit is set in both filters, while a score of one implies that the two filters have the same bit value in all positions. Another used measure is the Jaccard coefficient, which is related to the Dice coefficient as $\text{Dice}(B, B')/(2 - \text{Dice}(B, B'))$. Similarity thresholds are often set in an ad-hoc manner, with a value such as 0.8 being a common choice [2,10]. It is often assumed that data set holders will create the Bloom filters from their records using an agreed upon configuration (m, k, hash functions, and hardening method), and send it to a third party for the scoring and final matching.

2.2 Hardening Bloom Filters

Although Bloom filters are efficient constructions and have been found to be useful in capturing the q-gram similarities, they are also vulnerable to frequency attacks. Frequency attacks often leverage the distribution of the set bits across the multiple Bloom filters created from a data set [3,16]. Therefore, a number of hardening methods have been proposed to obfuscate or distort a Bloom filter further. We focus on the following common techniques in this work.

Balancing. A balanced Bloom filter is created by doubling its size, copying the original bits into the additional positions, inverting the extended bits, and then applying a permutation on the extended filter [23]. Balancing produces a filter with equal number of zeros and ones.

XOR-Folding. XOR-folding performs a bitwise XOR operation using the two halves of a Bloom filter, and outputs the resulting bit string [24]. This results in a string that is half the size of the input Bloom filter, and scoring is performed on the XOR-folded strings. We refer to the locations of two XOR-ed bits as *dual locations* of each other, and use the notation $\bar{i}$ to imply the dual location of position i. XOR-folding can lose set bit information if two XOR-ed bits are both one.

RULE90. RULE90 also creates a resulting bit string using an XOR operation, but uses positions $(i-1) \mod m$ and $(i+1) \mod m$ to obtain the resulting bit for position i [25]. As such, the output of RULE90 is of the same length as the original Bloom filter.

The above three methods are deterministic in nature and always produce the same output for a given Bloom filter. The following methods are probabilistic, and parameterized by a probability value p. These methods independently transform each bit of a Bloom filter to obtain a distorted version.

Random Bit Set (RBS). Irrespective of the original bit value at a position, RBS sets a position with probability p and retains the original value with probability $(1 - p)$ [20]. RBS can therefore increase the number set bits in a Bloom filter, possibly creating more false positives.

Random Bit Flip (RBF). At each position, RBF inverts the existing bit with probability p and retains it with probability $(1 - p)$ [23]. If a Bloom filter is set in more than half the positions, RBF can be expected to reduce the number of total set bits in a filter.

Permanent Randomized Response (RAPPOR). At each position, RAPPOR sets the bit to zero with probability $\frac{p}{2}$, sets it to one with probability $\frac{p}{2}$, and retains it with probability $(1 - p)$ [8]. RAPPOR is proven to be able to provide ϵ_∞-differential privacy, with $\epsilon_\infty = 2k\ln(\frac{2}{p} - 1)$, with respect to two different Bloom filters producing the same output string. However, small p values must be used with a small number of hash functions (as small as $k = 1$) to obtain reasonable differential privacy guarantees in this method.

2.3   Privacy Measures

While a number of hardening methods have been proposed for use with Bloom filters, metrics that evaluate their efficacy in preserving the privacy of the records are rare [30]. Bloom filter hardening methods are mostly relied upon based on a "test of time" where modifications are proposed after a method is found to be vulnerable to an attack. We list here two metrics based on the frequency distribution of set bits that have been used in a recent study [10]. Both of these metrics operate on a set of bit strings, possibly generated by a hardening method from records in a data set. Given a set of bit strings, each of length l, we use t_i to denote the total number of ones at position i across all the strings. Further, let $t = \sum_i t_i$ and $q_i = t_i/t$. We also include a distortion measure based on the number of set bits before and after a Bloom filter transformation.

Normalized Shannon Entropy. Normalized Shannon entropy compares the entropy in each position relative to the maximum entropy possible if each position is equally used in the strings. It is computed as

$$1 + \frac{\sum_{i=0}^{l-1} q_i \log_2(q_i)}{\log_2(l)}, \tag{2}$$

and falls between zero (uniform distribution) and one (set bits only in one position).

Jensen-Shannon Distance. Jensen-Shannon distance provides a distance measure between two probability distributions, namely the observed bit frequencies at different positions and an uniform distribution in our case. It is computed as

$$\left(\frac{1}{2l} \sum_{i=0}^{l-1} \log_2 \left(\frac{\frac{1}{l}}{\frac{1}{2}(q_i + \frac{1}{l})} \right) + \frac{1}{2} \sum_{i=0}^{l-1} q_i \log_2 \left(\frac{q_i}{\frac{1}{2}(q_i + \frac{1}{l})} \right) \right)^{0.5}, \tag{3}$$

and produces a value of zero when the distributions are identical, or one at the other extreme.

Mean Distortion Ratio. The distortion ratio of a Bloom filter is computed as the ratio of the number of bits set in the filter after transformation, relative to the number before transformation by a probabilistic hardening method. The mean distortion is obtained from the distortion ratios of a given set of Bloom filters and their hardened output.

3   Generating-Sets and Amplification

Let $\mathcal{U}$ be the universe of elements that can be potentially inserted into a Bloom filter. In the case of private record linkage, $\mathcal{U}$ is composed of all possible q-grams that can be created from letters, numbers and select punctuation symbols. Let $G \subseteq \mathcal{U}$ be the set of elements that is inserted into a Bloom filter B of size m. In other words, every element $g \in G$ is hashed using k hash functions $\mathcal{H}_i$, $i = 1...k$, to k positions in the Bloom filter and those positions are set to one. We then refer to G as the *generating-set* of the filter B, denoted as $\mathcal{GS}(B) = G$. When the hash functions choose positions uniformly at random, the size of the generating-set and the number of bits set in the filter (b_{set}) are approximately related as

$$|\mathcal{GS}(B)| \approx -\frac{m}{k} \log \left(1 - \frac{b_{set}}{m} \right). \tag{4}$$

Bit-frequency based measures of privacy for Bloom filters attempt to capture the distribution of set bits in a filter. They serve as an indirect evaluation of the existence or non-existence of frequently occurring bit patterns, which forms the basis for most known attacks against Bloom filters in private record linkage. A common approach in such methods is to identify frequently occurring bit patterns in a set of Bloom filters (resulting from a data set), and map them in full or parts to actual q-grams based on their known common usage frequencies. It is therefore expected that filters that do not carry much information on frequent bit patterns, in other words, have a more uniform distribution of bits, are likely to be difficult to attack. However, such measures are only useful when comparing hardening approaches [10], and have difficulty in informing us about the difficulty introduced in attacks. If the bit-frequency measures of two hardened Bloom filters are "close," it is not known if they are similarly effective in disrupting a frequent pattern attack. In other words, the sensitivity of a specific measure to the elimination of specific patterns by a hardening method is yet to be analyzed. Some measures can in fact produce values indicating a near-uniform distribution for multiple hardening techniques, thereby making it difficult to assess their effectiveness. In the light of these observations, and that the primary purpose of a Bloom filter in private record linkage is to hide the elements used to create the filter, we seek an alternative measure of privacy that can inform us on the level of uncertainty that a standalone Bloom filter (with or without hardening) introduces in terms of inferring its generating-set.

3.1 Generating-Set Amplification Factor

The objective of an attack on a Bloom filter is to infer its generating-set with best possible accuracy. A typical Bloom filter B has a false positive rate that depends on its size m, the number of hash functions k, and its generating-set size $s = |\mathcal{GS}(B)|$, and approximated as

$$\psi(m, k, s) \approx \left(1 - e^{-ks/m}\right)^k. \tag{5}$$

A false positive element implies that the element is not in the generating-set G, but the bit positions in the filter that would have been set by the element, if present, happens to be already set by a combination of elements in the generating-set. Hence, an element $u \in \mathcal{U}/G$ is a false positive when $\forall i = 1...k, B[\mathcal{H}_i(u)] = 1$. Although the rate of false positives can be controlled by choosing appropriate values for k and m, without knowledge of the generating-set, it is not possible to determine if an element is a true positive or a false positive. Therefore, a perfect attack targeted towards determining the elements used to create a Bloom filter (based on frequent patterns or otherwise) will produce the generating-set of the filter and the false positives. Note that we are not focusing on the attack methodology, but on the output producible by an attack of such nature. Effectively, this set is the largest set of elements that can produce a given Bloom filter B, denoted by $\mathcal{GS}_{max}(B)$, whose size can be approximated as

$$|\mathcal{GS}_{max}(B)| \approx |\mathcal{GS}(B)| + \psi(m, k, |\mathcal{GS}(B)|)|\mathcal{U}|. \tag{6}$$

Therefore, a generating-set may undergo amplification when one tries to infer it from a given Bloom filter. We capture this amplification as a factor, termed the *generating-set amplification factor*, and represented as

$$A_f(B) = \frac{|\mathcal{GS}_{max}(B)|}{|\mathcal{GS}(B)|}. \tag{7}$$

As an example, a 1024-bit Bloom filter created from 50 unique elements using 25 hash functions and a universe of size 5000 has an amplification factor of 1.016. The amplification factor can be used as an indicator of a hardening technique's effectiveness in obfuscating the generating-set. A value of 1 (or close to 1) would indicate that the hardening technique failed to disrupt the relationship between the generating-set and its Bloom filter representation, effectively retaining statistical correlations between the two, open for exploitation in an attack. As the amplification factor increases, the correlations are expected to disperse since multiple generating-sets may produce the same Bloom filter. We therefore use the amplification factor as a measure of the privacy preserving effectiveness of a hardening technique. Although we are not proposing a new attack in this work, we do not make assumptions on the secrecy of parameters used to create the Bloom filters (size, number of hash functions, and the hash functions themselves) since attacks already exist that do not need knowledge of these parameters [33]. In fact, we work under an oracle-supported model where the attacker can query the hash output of any element in the universe.

Equation (6) can be used to estimate the amplification factor for a standard Bloom filter, but does not lend itself well for hardening techniques that remap the filter or modify it with randomization. For example, the XOR-folding technique may produce a filter representation that can be obtained from multiple combinations of bit values in specific positions of the original Bloom filter. Randomization methods such as RBS, RBF and RAPPOR generate probabilistic outputs that can be obtained from any Bloom filter. In the following subsections, we provide algorithms to determine the amplification factor for common hardening methods, and an alternative formulation for probabilistic methods.

3.2 Amplification Factor in Deterministic Methods

Besides the standard non-hardened Bloom filter, we consider three deterministic methods to harden Bloom filters, namely BALANCED, XOR-folding and RULE90. For a non-hardened Bloom filter, $\mathcal{GS}_{max}$ can be obtained by checking if each element $u \in \mathcal{U}$ is present in the filter. Unless the filter's false positive rate is high, or the universe size is comparatively quite large, we do not expect a non-hardened Bloom filter to have an amplification factor much larger than 1. In our experimental evaluation, we use 1024-bit filters with 25 hash functions, to effectively have a false positive rate of 0.00005. With 4761 possible bigrams in the universe set, the average amplification factor in the non-hardened method is practically 1! The BALANCED hardening method uses a negative duplicate of a filter and performs a deterministic permutation on those bits. Since the steps of this method are reversible (reverse the permutation and take first half of the output), any element found to be in $\mathcal{GS}_{max}$ for the non-hardening method will also be found for BALANCED, and vice versa. The amplification factor for BALANCED will therefore be equal to that of the non-hardening method.

The XOR-folding and RULE90 methods generate their final output using an XOR operation on bits from different positions in the original Bloom filter. Since an XOR output of zero can be obtained either as $0 \oplus 0$ or $1 \oplus 1$, and an output of one can be obtained either as $0 \oplus 1$ or $1 \oplus 0$, an element alone may affect the final output, but may not do so when grouped with other elements.

XOR-Folding. Consider a Bloom filter B with the generating-set G, whose XOR-folded bit string is B_{xor}, with $B_{xor}[i] = B[i] \oplus B[\bar{i}], i = 0...\lceil m/2 \rceil - 1$. Recall that $\bar{i}$ represents the dual location of position i in the filter. A brute force method to find $\mathcal{GS}_{max}$ of B is to take every possible superset of G from $\mathcal{U}$, create a Bloom filter from it, and then test if its XOR-folding equals B_{xor}; the largest superset of G that passes the test will give $\mathcal{GS}_{max}$. The method is exponential in size of the universe (less the size of G). However, we can prune the search using an impossibility condition. If $B_{xor}[i] = 1$, then the bit at position i or $\bar{i}$ must be zero, while the other position is one. If an element sets the zero position, then $B_{xor}[i]$ will become zero. Since a bit's value in B cannot be reverted back to zero once set, irrespective of how many other elements we add, $B_{xor}[i]$ can never become one again. Therefore, any element $u \in \mathcal{U}/G$ that would set a zero value position in B, and that position contributes to an already set bit in B_{xor}, cannot be present in $\mathcal{GS}_{max}$. On the other hand, if $B_{xor}[i] = 0$, then both positions i and $\bar{i}$ have the same value in B. When both positions are one, an element $u \in \mathcal{U}/G$ setting one or both of the positions have no effect on B_{xor}. When both positions are zero, $B_{xor}[i]$ may change to one if u sets only one of the two positions. However, in such a case, there could be another element that sets the other zero value position, thereby reverting $B_{\bar{x}or}[i]$ back to its original value of zero. Hence, when $B_{xor}[i]$ is zero, elements may be added in groups to B without affecting the XOR-folding output.

We incorporate the above observations into a depth-first-search (DFS) of the set $\mathcal{U}/G$ to identify subsets that can be added to B without changing B_{xor}. As the first step, we remove all elements from $\mathcal{U}/G$ that would create the impossibility condition for any position i in B_{xor} with $B_{xor}[i] = 1$. With a *base set* of G, for each remaining candidate u, we initiate a DFS by creating a temporary Bloom filter B' from $G \cup \{u\}$ and obtain its XOR-folded version B'_{xor}. Due to the handling of the impossibility condition in the first step, mismatches between B_{xor} and B'_{xor} can only happen in positions with $B_{xor}[i] = 0$ and $B'_{xor}[i] = 1$, and not the other way. For every such mismatch position, we identify all elements (not already added) that when added to B' can reset the bit in B'_{xor} at the mismatch position back to zero. Note that while such elements can reset the bit in a mismatch position, they may also create further mismatches in other positions. Hence, the search continues into the next level with the set used to create B' as the base set, and the identified elements as candidates. If no mismatches exist between B_{xor} and B'_{xor} at any point of this recursive procedure, then the set of elements used to create the corresponding B' is noted, and the specific search branch is terminated. Effectively, when all elements from a noted set exist in a Bloom filter, its XOR-folded bit string equals the original folded string B_{xor}. We take the union of all the noted sets as $\mathcal{GS}_{max}$ of B.

RULE90. The approach used to find $\mathcal{GS}_{max}$ for a Bloom filter hardened with RULE90 is similar to that for XOR-folding. The distinction is in how dual locations are defined in the two methods. RULE90 uses the neighboring bits at a

Table 1. Probability of transformation of bit values. $p_{ij} = \Pr(i \rightarrow j)$.

RBS				RBF				RAPPOR			
p_{00}	p_{01}	p_{10}	p_{11}	p_{00}	p_{01}	p_{10}	p_{11}	p_{00}	p_{01}	p_{10}	p_{11}
$1-p$	p	0	1	$1-p$	p	p	$1-p$	$1-\frac{p}{2}$	$\frac{p}{2}$	$\frac{p}{2}$	$1-\frac{p}{2}$

position for the XOR operation, and produces an output equal in length to the Bloom filter. While the principles are the same, care should be taken when implementing the algorithm for RULE90. In XOR-folding, a bit position serves as the dual location of exactly one other position, while in RULE90, a bit position i serves as the dual location of two positions, $(i-2) \mod m$ and $(i+2) \mod m$. In XOR-folding, during the impossibility condition check in the first step, we can use a loop variable $i = 0...m-1$ to check if $B[i] = 0$ and $B[\bar{i}] = 1$, and eliminate elements that set the location i. When the loop variable reaches $\bar{i}$, the reverse condition gets checked by symmetry. For RULE90, if $B[i] = 1$ and $B[(i+2) \mod m] = 0$, then the location to avoid setting is $(i+2) \mod m$, otherwise it is i. When the loop variable reaches $(i+2) \mod m$, note that the locations being tested are now $(i+2) \mod m$ and $(i+4) \mod m$.

3.3 Amplification Factor in Probabilistic Methods

Unlike in deterministic methods, probabilistic methods such as RBS, RBF and RAPPOR are parameterized by a probability value p that determines how a Bloom filter is transformed. Due to the probabilistic nature, even a Bloom filter with all bits set can get transformed to any given bit string, albeit with varying probabilities. Therefore, we use an alternative formulation for $\mathcal{GS}_{max}$ in such methods. A probabilistic transformation method parameterized by p effectively gives us the probability of transforming a zero bit to a one, and vice versa. We use p_{ij} to denote the probability of transforming a bit value i to a bit value j. Table 1 lists these probabilities for RBS, RBF and RAPPOR, in terms of the parameter p.

Any element $u \in \mathcal{U}$ when added to a Bloom filter B would set the bits at positions $l_i = \mathcal{H}_i(u), i = 1...k$. Given a transformed version of the filter, B_{trf}, we calculate the probability that the element was present in B as

$$\Pr(u \in B | B_{trf}) = \prod_{i=1}^{k} p_{1 B_{trf}[l_i]}. \tag{8}$$

Given $G = \mathcal{GS}(B)$, we consider the probabilities corresponding to all elements $g \in G$ to be significant, no matter how small they are. In other words, any attack that successfully retrieves G using B_{trf} cannot discard these probabilities to be small; otherwise the attack fails. Under such a condition, all elements that have higher probabilities than elements in G will be retained as well. Therefore, we define $\mathcal{GS}_{max}$ as the set of all elements whose probabilities are greater or equal to the minimum probability of elements in G.

$$\mathcal{GS}_{max}(B|B_{trf}) = \{u \in U | \Pr(u \in B|B_{trf}) \geq \min_{g \in G} \Pr(g \in B|B_{trf})\} \quad (9)$$

It is also possible to define $\mathcal{GS}_{max}$ under a different requirement wherein retrieving a specific fraction f of the elements in G may be considered sufficient under some attack. In such a case, we can change the inequality to be with respect to a quantile value instead of the minimum.

$$\mathcal{GS}_{max}(B|B_{trf}) = \{u \in U | \Pr(u \in B|B_{trf}) > Q(1 - f)\}, \quad (10)$$

where $Q(q)$ returns a threshold value such that q fraction of values in $\{\Pr(g \in B|B_{trf})|g \in G\}$ are less than or equal to the returned value. This variation can be useful in evaluating if a hardening method can provide amplification when the entire generating-set is not an attack target.

4 Parameter Selection in Probabilistic Methods

Probabilistic methods distort a Bloom filter based on a parameter for bit manipulation, such as the probability parameter p. Higher values of p are likely to provide better privacy, but it comes at the expense of poor linkage quality. Earlier studies have reported on this where p values as small as 0.1 can lead to significant degradation in linkage quality [10]. However, we believe that choice of the parameter is linked with the threshold chosen for similarity acceptance. Nonetheless, it is not known how large of a p value can be accommodated for acceptable linkage quality even with a properly chosen similarity threshold. In this section, we seek to generate some guidance around this issue.

Consider two Bloom filters B and B' of size m, with their transformed versions as B_{trf} and B'_{trf}. For a given number of set bits $b_{set} > 0$ in the two original filters, the probability that the two filters have $b_{common} \in \{0, 1, .., b_{set}\}$ number of common positions where the bits are set can be obtained as

$$\Pr(b_{common}|b_{set}) = \frac{\binom{b_{set}}{b_{common}} \binom{m - b_{set}}{b_{set} - b_{common}}}{\binom{m}{b_{set}}}. \quad (11)$$

When $b_{set} = 0$ or $b_{common} > b_{set}$, this probability is zero. Since the number of set bits cannot be more than m, we normalize this probability as

$$\Pr(b_{common}|b_{set}, m) = \frac{\Pr(b_{common}|b_{set})}{\sum_{b_s=0}^{m} \sum_{b_c=0}^{b_s} \Pr(b_c|b_s)}. \quad (12)$$

If the filters B and B' have $b_{common\text{-}before}$ common bits, then the expected number of set bits in each filter, $b_{set\text{-}before}$, can be obtained as

$$b_{set\text{-}before} = \frac{\sum_{b=0}^{m} b \Pr(b_{common\text{-}before}|b, m)}{\sum_{b_s=0}^{m} \Pr(b_{common\text{-}before}|b_s, m)}. \quad (13)$$

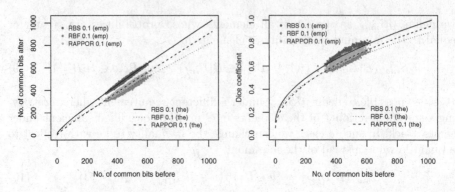

Fig. 1. Comparison of theoretical (the) and empirical (emp) computations for common bits in two Bloom filters (before and after transformation) and Dice coefficient values on the transformed filter. Filter size $m = 1024$ bits.

The denominator is necessary since we are conditioning on the event that the set bits result in exactly $b_{common-before}$ common bits. During transformation, these set bits remain set with a probability p_{11} and clear bits get set with a probability p_{01}. Therefore, the expected number of set bits in a transformed filter, $b_{set-after}$, is obtained as

$$b_{set-after} = p_{11}b_{set-before} + p_{01}(m - b_{set-before}). \tag{14}$$

We can then obtain the expected number of common bits between B_{trf} and B'_{trf} as

$$b_{common-after} = \frac{\sum_{b=0}^{m} b \Pr(b|b_{set-after}, m)}{\sum_{b_c=0}^{m} \Pr(b_c|b_{set-after}, m)}. \tag{15}$$

Figure 1 (left) shows $b_{common-before}$ and $b_{common-after}$ computed from the above equations for RBS, RBF and RAPPOR with $p = 0.1$, and $m = 1024$ bits. For accuracy check, we also show 10,000 sample points for each method, obtained from Bloom filter ($m = 1024, k = 25$) encodings of real name and address strings (average of 46 bigrams in a string). The figure (right) also shows the Dice coefficient values computed from the estimated counts of the set and common bits after the transformation. This is effectively $b_{common-after}/b_{set-after}$. While the Dice coefficients are slightly underestimated, the trends follow accurately and relative differences across different methods are maintained.

The box-plots in Fig. 2 show the distribution summary of Dice coefficients for non-hardened Bloom filter pairs and ones where different transformations have been performed. Each summary is obtained from Dice coefficient values corresponding to a varying number of common set bits. Non-hardened Bloom filter pairs can have Dice coefficient values as low as zero (no common bits) and as high as one (all set bits are common). The middle 50% (interquartile range) of Dice scores fall in the range of $[0.5002, 0.8661]$, with a median score of 0.7072. Depending on the hardening method and extent of distortion (choice of the parameter p), the range of scores become less dispersed. For example, with RBF

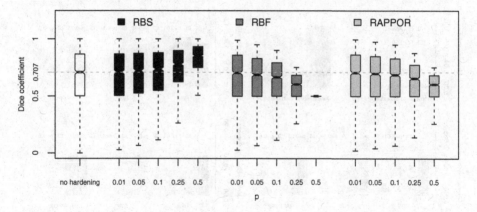

Fig. 2. Distribution (range and quantiles) of theoretically estimated Dice coefficient values.

and $p = 0.5$, the Dice scores are expected to become 0.5, irrespective of the number of common bits in the original Bloom filters. In other cases, such as RBS 0.5, RBF 0.25 and RAPPOR 0.5, the scores become significantly less dispersed than in the original Bloom filters. Good dispersion of scores is important to preserve a good linkage quality as it can provide for stronger distinction between matching and non-matching input pairs. We therefore need a quantitative method to assess if the range of Dice scores can become significantly compressed under a hardening method. We use a heuristic based on the interquartile range of Dice scores, wherein a method is deemed unsuitable for record linkage if the entire interquartile range of resulting scores fall above or below the median score in a non-hardened setting. The condition is effectively met if the first quartile value of the scores from a hardening method is greater than the median score in a non-hardened case, or if the third quartile value is smaller than the non-hardened median. Under this heuristic, we expect RBS 0.5, RBF 0.25, RBF 0.5 and RAPPOR 0.5 to be unsuitable for acceptable record linkage. Note that the tests are done on theoretically estimated Dice score distributions since the parametric decision is to be made before Dice scores on an actual data set are calculated. In a real use case, the number of common bits between two Bloom filters will fall in a much narrower range, compressing the distributions further.

5   Empirical Evaluation

In this section, we show an empirical evaluation of different hardening methods and their effectiveness with respect to the generating-set amplification factor measure. We also perform a sample linkage of two data sets and demonstrate that linkage quality can be retained for high probabilistic distortions by properly setting the similarity threshold.

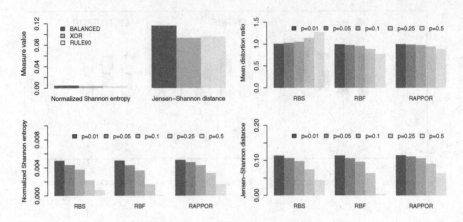

Fig. 3. Bit frequency based measures of privacy.

5.1 Setup

We use the North Carolina Voter Registration (NCVR) data set to create the data sets for our evaluation (www.ncsbe.gov). NCVR contains more than 7 million records with demographics data on individuals. We combine the attributes related to the name and address of an individual to form a single string representing a record in the data set. We create three data sets for use in the evaluation: (i) a data set of 10,000 records to assess the amplification factor induced by different methods (Sect. 5.2 and Sect. 5.3), and (ii) two separate data sets, each with 10,000 records, but having an overlap of 1,000 records, to assess linkage quality under different methods (Sect. 5.4). Records are sampled uniformly at random from the entire NCVR data set.

Each record is converted to uppercase symbols and then split into a set of bigrams (46 bigrams on average in a record). Bloom filters of size $m = 1024$ bits are created from the bigram sets of the records, often referred to as record level filters [22], using $k = 25$ hash functions. Each hash function is instantiated using HMAC-SHA56, but uses a separate randomly generated 32-bit hash key [19]. A hash function's output is mapped to a position in a Bloom filter using the mod m operator on the hash output. Considering all uppercase letters, numbers and punctuations, we have a universe set of $69^2 = 4761$ bigrams.

We explore BALANCED, XOR-folding and RULE90 for deterministic hardening methods, and RBS, RBF and RAPPOR for probabilistic methods, with p values of 0.01, 0.05, 0.1, 0.25 and 0.5. Record linkage is performed by computing the Dice coefficient scores for all pairs of filters after applying a hardening method. For each record in one data set, we find the record in the other data set with the highest Dice coefficient score, and consider them a match if the score crosses a set threshold. Ties are broken randomly. Typically, blocking approaches are used to reduce the number of score comparisons to be performed, especially for large data sets [9]. We choose a threshold of $\mu + 6\sigma$ for each method, where μ and σ are respectively the mean and standard deviation of the computed Dice

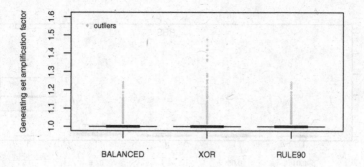

Fig. 4. Distribution of generating-set amplification factor for deterministic methods.

scores. While this method of threshold setting may not produce the best link-age in all cases, it gives us the platform to evaluate the linkage quality under an unbiased and uniform methodology. Linkage quality is then evaluated using the measures of precision (fraction of correct matches in identified matches) and recall (fraction of true matches correctly identified).

5.2 Bit Frequency Measures

Figure 3 shows the different bit frequency based measures of privacy. For all methods, the normalized Shannon entropy measure is near zero, indicating an "almost" uniform distribution of bits. Even for the non-hardened case, the entropy value is close to zero (0.005). This observation aligns with observations made in other data sets in earlier studies [10]. The Jensen-Shannon distance reduces (indicating closer to uniform) when an obfuscation is applied to the original Bloom filters (e.g. XOR and RULE90) or when the level of distortion is increased in a probabilistic method. The non-hardened Jensen-Shannon distance is similar to the BALANCED method, at 0.116. RBF 0.5 has a near zero Jensen-Shannon distance, which conforms to the observation that Dice scores are uniform as per the theoretical analysis in Sect. 4. In terms of distortion ratio, the number of bits set is expected to increase in RBS with higher p values. However, the number reduces for RBF and RAPPOR. Both cases lead to more compression of the range of Dice scores; the probability of having a given number of common bits reduces/increases as the number of set bits reduce/increase.

5.3 Generating-Set Amplification Factor

Figure 4 shows the distribution of amplification factors when using the three deterministic methods. Recall that the amplification factor of a non-hardened case is same as that of the BALANCED method. While some outliers are present in all cases, the amplification factors are close 1 in all three methods, implying that most of the produced bit strings are unique to the generating-set of the filter. While this is not unexpected for a non-hardened method and BALANCED (due

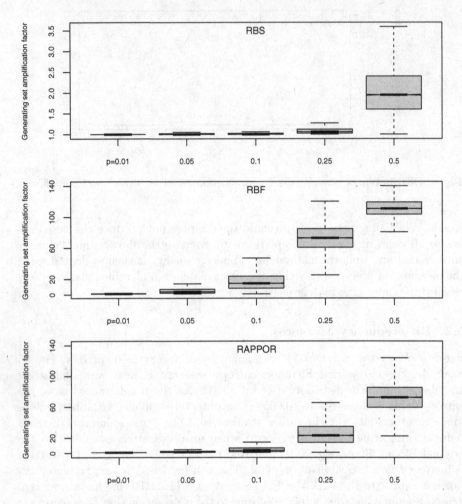

Fig. 5. Distribution of generating-set amplification factor for probabilistic methods. Outliers are not shown.

to the small false positive rate), XOR-folding and RULE90 also produce unique mappings between generating-sets and output strings.

Figure 5 shows the distribution of amplification factors for the three probabilistic methods. The amplification factors here are generated based on Eq. (9). The results here are more promising than deterministic methods, especially with higher p values. However, recall from Sect. 4 that we do not expect RBS 0.5, RBF 0.25, RBF 0.5 and RAPPOR 0.5 to be able to produce reasonable linkage quality. With this consideration, the RBS method is unable to provide amplification of the generating-set at $p < 0.5$. RBF with $p = 0.1$ has a mean amplification factor of 17.89, which implies that the bit flipping successfully mixes the probability values of the generating-set elements and approximately 777 elements outside

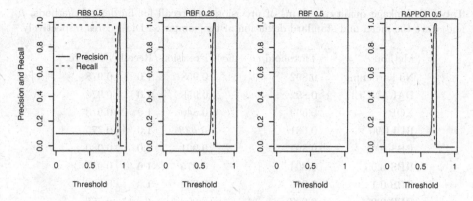

Fig. 6. Precision and recall curves for methods that are not expected to provide reasonable linkage quality per the theoretical analysis (Sect. 4).

the set (16.3% of the universe). RAPPOR with $p = 0.25$ can provide a slightly higher amplification, but it needs to be able to retain the linkage quality at that level of distortion. Note that, for a given value of p, the probability of flipping a bit in RAPPOR is half that in RBF (Table 1). As such, the amplification we see in RBF 0.1 is similar to as in RAPPOR 0.25. p values lower than 0.1 fail to produce much amplification in all three methods. It is important to point that if Eq. (10) is instead used for determining the amplification factor, say with $f = 0.25$, even RBF 0.1 and RAPPOR 0.25 cannot generate high amplification factors. This is concerning since an attack that can recover 75% of the bigrams in the generating-set could be often sufficient to recreate the entire string.

5.4 Linkage Quality

Figure 6 shows the precision and recall curves for RBS 0.5, RBF 0.25, RBF 0.5, and RAPPOR 0.5, which are scenarios that lead to significant compression of the range of Dice scores as per our determination heuristic (Sect. 4). The curves are obtained by computing the precision/recall values for varying thresholds between 0 and 1, at 0.01 increments. It is evident that an acceptable balance between precision and recall is not possible in these scenarios, irrespective of the threshold. RBF 0.5 leads to heavy loss of variability in the scores, and hence matched pairings fail to be correct for all strings.

Table 2 lists the precision, recall and F1-score (harmonic mean of precision and recall) for the remaining methods. Recall that the thresholds are set using a computational method ($\mu + 6\sigma$). With the set thresholds, in most cases, the methods are able to retrieve all the overlapping records, with a precision above 95%. The thresholds are found to adjust based on the distribution of the Dice scores; in RBS, Dice scores increase with more distortion, hence the threshold increases as well, while in RBF and RAPPOR, the scores decrease, leading to lowering of the threshold. RBS 0.25 has a significantly lower recall at the set

Table 2. Linkage quality in terms of precision and recall for hardening methods. μ and σ are the mean and standard deviation of the computed Dice scores respectively.

Method	Threshold ($\mu + 6\sigma$)	Precision	Recall	F1-score
No hardening	0.892	0.958	1.0	0.978
BALANCED	0.892	0.958	1.0	0.978
XOR	0.669	0.840	1.0	0.913
RULE90	0.631	*0.633*	1.0	0.775
RBS 0.01	0.893	0.961	1.0	0.980
RBS 0.05	0.894	0.975	1.0	0.987
RBS 0.1	0.896	0.992	1.0	0.996
RBS 0.25	0.907	0.998	*0.624*	0.768
RBF 0.01	0.884	0.964	1.0	0.982
RBF 0.02	0.854	0.989	1.0	0.994
RBF 0.1	**0.817**	**0.995**	**1.0**	**0.997**
RAPPOR 0.01	0.888	0.961	1.0	0.980
RAPPOR 0.05	0.873	0.976	1.0	0.988
RAPPOR 0.1	**0.853**	**0.980**	**1.0**	**0.990**
RAPPOR 0.25	**0.797**	**0.998**	**0.965**	**0.981**

threshold. Since the precision is high, it is expected that reducing the threshold can produce improvement in the recall without affecting the precision. For example, at a slightly higher threshold of 0.91, RBS 0.25 has a precision of 96% and recall of 96.9%. Similarly, a threshold of 0.7 can increase the precision of RULE90 to 94.3% while maintaining the recall at 100%.

5.5   Discussion

The Shannon entropy measure is not sensitive to changes created in a Bloom filter by the hardening methods. As such, this measure in not suitable for privacy evaluation in record linkage. Comparatively, the Jensen-Shannon distance measure reacts more to changes. Nonetheless, all values we obtained for the measure are typically low, which could lead to a misinterpretation of a method's effectiveness when viewed alone. Distortion ratio shows a change of $\pm20\%$ at most, even at high p values such as 0.5. In summary, measures based on bit frequencies are generally not very sensitive to differences in the hardening methods. When viewed through the use of amplification factors, we see more prominent changes in the metric's value as more distortion is introduced in a Bloom filter. We also see that typically used small values of p in probabilistic methods are in fact not advisable due to their inability to diffuse the probabilistic relationship between generating-set elements and a transformed Bloom filter. In deterministic methods such as XOR-folding and RULE90, generating-set amplification is almost non-existent. Both methods use two bit positions in a Bloom filter to derive a resulting bit, which seems to be insufficient. Use of low false positive rates and good pseudo-random hash functions appear to create issues for such methods in mixing the Bloom filter bits. While variants exist to include more bit positions in the operation, they have a detrimental effect on the linkage quality.

Although we show the linkage quality for different methods, note that most of the scenarios do not fare well in terms of the generating-set amplification factor measure. Nonetheless, methods such as RBF and RAPPOR do have few niche parameter settings (e.g. $p = 0.1$) that can provide both quality linkage and high amplification factors. However, getting these methods to perform well in record linkage is dependent on the choice of the set threshold. We showed two cases (RULE90 and RBS 0.25) where a small change in the set threshold significantly improves the obtained precision and recall. In general, linkage quality can be highly sensitive to the threshold when a hardening method compresses the range of similarity scores.

The amplification factor can provide general guidance on the difficulty of obtaining the exact generating-set of a Bloom filter. However, attacks can leverage additional filtering to eliminate elements that cannot sensibly be part of a record. For example, a hardening method may provide a high amplification factor, but most of the false q-grams that it introduces may not be combinable to form record strings. Therefore, it may not be sufficient for a method to introduce a high amplification factor, but the false elements have to be able to introduce uncertainty in terms of record reconstruction.

6   Conclusion and Future Work

A number of Bloom filter hardening methods have appeared in the past two decades, and have also been found to be insufficient for privacy protection. In this work, we explored the issue of quantifying the privacy guarantees of current Bloom filter hardening methods. Using the proposed generating-set amplification factor measure, we found that most methods generate output representations of Bloom filters that are unique to the input set of elements. Few probabilistic methods can offer an amplification of the input set with higher levels of distortion than traditionally performed. However, such methods can significantly compress the range of similarity scores, and require careful setting of the similarity cut-off to be able to produce a good linkage output. We also provided a heuristic to determine if a probabilistic hardening method can provide acceptable linkage quality for a specific level of distortion of the Bloom filters.

We have identified multiple gaps in the current research. Besides the need for hardening methods that can provide better generating-set amplifications, it is important to design guidelines for the choice of similarity thresholds with respect to the methods. Adhoc amplification may also not be useful and effort should be directed at creating hardening methods that can guarantee desired levels of amplification and with sensible false positive elements. Of course, equal effort is needed to ensure that these methods can retain a high linkage quality. Bloom filter based methods also require more theoretical assessments, primarily because their adoption is outpacing our understanding of their privacy assurances. Finally, more work in needed in the field of privacy measures for Bloom filters in record linkage to reveal different privacy related aspects of a Bloom filter.

References

1. Baker, D.B., Knoppers, B.M., Phillips, M., van Enckevort, D., Kaufmann, P., Lochmuller, H., Taruscio, D.: Privacy-preserving linkage of genomic and clinical data sets. IEEE/ACM Trans. Comput. Biol. Bioinform. **16**(4), 1342–1348 (2019)
2. Brown, A.P., Randall, S.M., Boyd, J.H., Ferrante, A.M.: Evaluation of approximate comparison methods on Bloom filters for probabilistic linkage. Int. J. Popul. Data Sci. **4**(1), 1095 (2019)
3. Christen, P., Ranbaduge, T., Vatsalan, D., Schnell, R.: Precise and fast cryptanalysis for Bloom filter based privacy-preserving record linkage. IEEE Trans. Knowl. Data Eng. **31**(11), 2164–2177 (2019)
4. Christen, P., Schnell, R., Vatsalan, D., Ranbaduge, T.: Efficient cryptanalysis of Bloom filters for privacy-preserving record linkage. In: 2017 Pacific-Asia Conference on Knowledge Discovery and Data Mining, pp. 628–640 (2017)
5. Churches, T., Christen, P.: Blind data linkage using n-gram similarity comparisons. In: 2004 Pacific-Asia Conference on Knowledge Discovery and Data Mining, pp. 121–126 (2004)
6. Dewri, R., Ong, T., Thurimella, R.: Linking health records for federated query processing. Proc. Priv. Enhanc. Technol. **2016**(3), 4–23 (2016)
7. Durham, E.A., Kantarcioglu, M., Xue, Y., Toth, C., Kuzu, M., Malin, B.: Composite bloom filters for secure record linkage. IEEE Trans. Knowl. Data Eng. **26**(12), 2956–2968 (2014)
8. Erlingsson, U., Pihur, V., Korolova, A.: RAPPOR: randomized aggregatable privacy-preserving ordinal response. In: 2014 21st ACM Conference on Computer and Communications Security, pp. 1054–1067 (2014)
9. Franke, M., Sehili, Z., Rahm, E.: Parallel privacy-preserving record linkage using LSH-based blocking. In: 2018 3rd International Conference on Internet of Things, Big Data and Security, pp. 195–203 (2018)
10. Franke, M., Sehili, Z., Rohde, F., Rahm, E.: Evaluation of hardening techniques for privacy-preserving record linkage. In: 2021 24th International Conference on Extending Database Technology, pp. 289–300 (2021)
11. Guesdon, M., Benzenine, E., Gadouche, K., Quantin, C.: Securizing data linkage in French public statistics. BMC Med. Inform. Decis. Mak. **16**(1), 129 (2016)
12. Hall, R., Fienberg, S.E.: Privacy-preserving record linkage. In: 2010 International Conference on Privacy in Statistical Databases, pp. 269–283 (2010)
13. Karakasidis, A., Verykios, V.: Privacy preserving record linkage using phonetic codes. In: 2009 4th Balkan Conference in Informatics, pp. 101–106 (2009)
14. Kirsch, A., Mitzenmacher, M.: Less hashing, same performance: building a better bloom filter. In: Azar, Y., Erlebach, T. (eds.) ESA 2006. LNCS, vol. 4168, pp. 456–467. Springer, Heidelberg (2006). https://doi.org/10.1007/11841036_42
15. Kroll, M., Steinmetzer, S.: Automated cryptanalysis of bloom filter encryptions of health records. In: German Record Linkage Center, Working Paper Series. No. WP-GRLC-2014-05 (2014)

16. Kuzu, M., Kantarcioglu, M., Durham, E., Malin, B.: A constraint satisfaction cryptanalysis of Bloom filters in private record linkage. In: Privacy Enhancing Technologies, pp. 226–245 (2011)
17. Lazrig, I., Ong, T.C., Ray, I., Ray, I., Jiang, X., Vaidya, J.: Privacy preserving probabilistic record linkage without trusted third party. In: 2018 16th Annual Conference on Privacy, Security and Trust, pp. 1–10 (2018)
18. Mitchell, W., Dewri, R., Thurimella, R., Roschke, M.: A graph traversal attack on Bloom filter-based medical data aggregation. Int. J. Big Data Intell. 4(4), 217–226 (2017)
19. Niedermeyer, F., Steinmetzer, S., Kroll, M., Schnell, R.: Cryptanalysis of basic Bloom filters used for privacy preserving record linkage. J. Priv. Confid. 6(2), 59–79 (2014)
20. Schnell, R.: Privacy-preserving record linkage. In: Methodological Developments in Data Linkage, pp. 201–225 (2015)
21. Schnell, R., Bachteler, T.: Privacy-preserving record linkage using Bloom filters. BMC Med. Inform. Decis. Mak. 9(1), 41 (2009)
22. Schnell, R., Bachteler, T., Reiher, J.: A novel error-tolerant anonymous linking code. SSRN Electron. J. (2011). https://doi.org/10.2139/ssrn.3549247
23. Schnell, R., Borgs, C.: Randomized response and balanced Bloom filters for privacy preserving record linkage. In: 2016 16th International Conference on Data Mining Workshops, pp. 218–224 (2016)
24. Schnell, R., Borgs, C.: XOR-folding for Bloom filter-based encryptions for privacy-preserving record linkage. SSRN Electron. J. (2016). https://doi.org/10.2139/ssrn.3527984
25. Schnell, R., Borgs, C.: Hardening encrypted patient names against cryptographic attacks using cellular automata. In: 2018 International Conference on Data Mining Workshops, pp. 518–522 (2018)
26. Smith, D.: Secure pseudonymisation for privacy-preserving probabilistic record linkage. J. Inf. Secur. Appl. 34, 271–279 (2017)
27. Stammler, S., et al.: Mainzelliste SecureEpilinker (MainSEL): privacy-preserving record linkage using secure multi-party computation. Bioinformatics 38(6), 1657–1668 (2022)
28. Vatsalan, D., Christen, P., Rahm, E.: Scalable privacy-preserving linking of multiple databases using counting Bloom filters. In: 2016 16th International Conference on Data Mining Workshops, pp. 882–889 (2016)
29. Vatsalan, D., Christen, P., Verykios, V.: A taxonomy of privacy-preserving record linkage techniques. Inf. Sys. 38(6), 946–969 (2013)
30. Vatsalan, D., Sehili, Z., Christen, P., Rahm, E.: Privacy-preserving record linkage for big data: current approaches and research challenges. In: Zomaya, A.Y., Sakr, S. (eds.) Handbook of Big Data Technologies, pp. 851–895. Springer, Cham (2017). https://doi.org/10.1007/978-3-319-49340-4_25
31. Vidanage, A., Christen, P., Ranbaduge, T., Schnell, R.: A graph matching attack on privacy-preserving record linkage. In: 2020 29th ACM International Conference on Information & Knowledge Management, pp. 1485–1494 (2020)
32. Vidanage, A., Ranbaduge, T., Christen, P., Randall, S.: A privacy attack on multiple dynamic match-key based privacy-preserving record linkage. Int. J. Popul. Data Sci. 5(1) (2020)
33. Vidanage, A., Ranbaduge, T., Christen, P., Schnell, R.: Efficient pattern mining based cryptanalysis for privacy-preserving record linkage. In: 2019 35th International Conference on Data Engineering, pp. 1698–1701 (2019)

SHIELD: A Multimodal Deep Learning Framework for Android Malware Detection

Narendra Singh[1], Somanath Tripathy[1(✉)], and Bruhadeshwar Bezawada[2]

[1] Department of Computer Science and Engineering,
Indian Institute of Technology Patna, Bihta, India
{narendra_2021cs21,som}@iitp.ac.in
[2] Indian Institute of Technology Jammu, Jammu, India
bez.bru@iitjammu.ac.in

Abstract. The widespread adoption of Android OS in recent years is due to its openness and flexibility. Consequently, the Android OS continues to be a prime target for serious malware attacks. Traditional malware detection methods are ineffective as Android malware use sophisticated obfuscation and adapt to the anti-virus defenses. In this paper, we present a multimodal deep learning framework, for unseen Android malware detection, called *SHIELD*, which employs Markov image of opcodes and dynamic APIs. *SHIELD* uses multimodal autoencoder (MAE) technique, which cuts down the dependency on feature engineering and automatically discovers the relevant features for malware detection. We validate our approach of unseen malware detection using the CICandMal2020 and AMD benchmarks datasets while achieving detection rates of 94% and 87%, respectively. Further, we created 500 obfuscated backdoor applications to evaluate the effectiveness of *SHIELD* with respect to other existing mobile anti-malware programs. Existing anti-malware programs fail to detect obfuscated backdoor, while *SHIELD* successfully flagged the obfuscated backdoor as a malicious application. *SHIELD* exhibits state-of-the-art performance for traditional malware detection, with an accuracy of 99.52%.

Keywords: Malware detection · Unseen android malware · Hybrid analysis

1 Introduction

Android operating system developed by Google is used in over 2.5 billion devices globally [2], including smartphones, smartwatches, and automobiles. Consequently, it has also been a prime target for malware developers to create new Android malware. Malicious applications that successfully compromise a device can result in significant financial losses [21,22], sensitive information leakage, and identity theft. Since many apps are available on the market, it is impossible to

© The Author(s), under exclusive license to Springer Nature Switzerland AG 2022
V. R. Badarla et al. (Eds.): ICISS 2022, LNCS 13784, pp. 64–83, 2022.
https://doi.org/10.1007/978-3-031-23690-7_4

verify their legitimacy individually. In previous research, machine learning (ML) algorithms were employed to automate detection at scale. However, a deep understanding of Android malware is typically required to hand-craft the necessary features in such detection mechanisms. Therefore, they are vulnerable to malware attacks until the new malware is detected and then reverse-engineered. The anti-malware features are updated in order to detect them. This paper discusses a method that can separate domain knowledge from input features by learning mechanisms and demonstrates that our approach is potentially beneficial in real-world situations. In case of unseen malware detection, signature-based solutions would fail since no signature could be derived to identify the unknown threat. Furthermore, Machine Learning based mechanisms could suffer from failure to detect unknown malware if they have not been trained on the type of malware.

Malware visualization methods are designed to enable humans to visualize the characteristics of a malicious application. In previous works, researchers have created greyscale images from malware binaries [17] images, entropy graphs [8], and hashing algorithms that have used image-processing algorithms for malware analysis [6]. These algorithms help to visually represent the features that distinguish malware from benign files and to differentiate between diverse families of malware with less domain-specific knowledge. Generally, image-based features are fed into neural networks to build decision models for malware detection. In spite of the variety of malware visualization methods, some difficulties persist, such as real-time detection of malware, inaccurate detection, and failure to detect unseen malware in real-time.

In our work, to utilize visualization features for malware detection, we target the generation of Markov Images from two raw input features -machine opcodes and dynamic API calls, each of which is extracted from the Android application. The generated Markov images combine and fuse into multimodal latent features or concatenate the hidden representations by learning multimodal autoencoder (MAE) and mapping them to a common space. Finally, the fused features are given as input to five different convolutional neural network models for detection. The fused features were found to be effective in identifying unknown malware families and making it harder for new threats to escape detection. CNN models reported accuracy ranging from 92.01% to 99.52%. The proposed method outperforms the state-of-the-art for a previously unseen malware family detection, arguably the most challenging test of a proposed method, and in conventional detection cases.

The main contributions of our work are as follows.

– This work proposes a Android malware detection framework named *Shield*. Shield uses a multimodal autoencoder to deal with multimodality of data types that discovers key malware features and fuses to common features space which enables it to detect unknown Android malware applications.
– The proposed framework shows a detection performance of 94% and 87% on the CICandMal2020 and AMD datasets, respectively, for unknown malware. Further, The *SHIELD* also exhibits state-of-the-art performance in traditional detection cases with an accuracy of 99.40% and 99.52% on the CICandMal2020 and CICAndMal2017 datasets, respectively.

– We developed 500 obfuscated backdoors by embedding malicious payload into benign applications. We observed that the 57 mobile anti-malware programs in Virustotal are unable to detect created obfuscated backdoors. Fortunately, *SHIELD* is successfully able to detect those backdoors.

The remaining part of this paper is organized as follows: In Sect. 2, the existing research work on Android malware detection are discussed. Our proposed method is described in Sect. 3. Section 4 discusses the experimental results. Section 5 concludes this work and discusses future work (Table 1).

Table 1. Summary of existing malware detection methods

Similar work	Analysis	Features	Datasets	Algorithm	UMDR
[3]	Static	Permission API calls Seq.	AndroZoo Contagio MalShare	RF, DT	✗
[7]	Static	HWD Comp. Restric. API call	Drebin	SVM	✓
[25]	Static	XML resources bytecode	G. Play store-VirusShare MassVet	LSTM	✗
[12]	Static	Perm. Opcode API, String Shared library	VirusShare G. Play Store Malgenome	Multimodal DNN	✗
[15]	Static	Pack., Perm. certs, intents	Comodo Cloud Sec. Center	DBN	✗
[16]	Static	Perm. source code	Malgenome Drebin	Classification Clustering	✗
[20]	Dynamic	Network Traffic	✗	One class SVM	✗
[18]	Dynamic	Wildfire Activity	Drebin Kharon	LSTM BERT	✗
[23]	Dynamic	Network Traffic	Drebin	Multilevel network	✓
[13]	Dynamic	Memory CPU battery	Drebin VirusShare AndroZoo	ML classifier	✗
[11]	Dynamic	HTTP Info.	Trust. Repo.	✗	✗
[26]	Hybrid	Perm. Behaviors	✗	DBN	✗
[5]	Hybrid	Perm. APIs	McAfee Labs	DL classifier	✓
[9]	Hybrid	APIs, cert. Perm.	VirusShare Contagio	✗	✓

UMDR: Unseen Malware Detection Rate.

2 Related Work

2.1 Static Analysis Based Android Malware Detection Techniques

Most static analysis-based mobile antivirus solutions detect malicious applications by analyzing the static features of the Manifest.xml and Classes. dex file such as permissions, opcode sequence, App component, string information, or a combination of these. Alazab et al. [3] proposed a static analysis-based classification method that integrates permission and API calls sequence as input features. It maximizes the likelihood of detecting Android malware apps by making three different grouping strategies (The ambiguous groups, the risky groups, and disruptive groups), which effectively-identified android malware with 94.3% F-Score. DREBIN [7] performed a comprehensive static analysis for android malware detection and collected eight different features such as hardware components, network address, used permission, app components, and many more. These features are combined in a single feature vector, and these common patterns effectively identify android malware. Only DREBIN [7] has attempted to simulate a zero-day scenario. DeepRefiner [25] proposed a neural network that incorporates an LSTM. However, it has 18 million parameters in just three hidden layers. There is a concern about how well it might generalize since the number of training samples was so much smaller, and no zero-data experiments were performed. A deep learning-based framework was proposed by Kim et al. [12] that includes multi-modal features (String, method opcode, method API, shared library functions, app component, environmental feature), and feature selection approach based on similarity-based extraction was employed to produce the most effective representation of the feature. However, there is no significant difference between the results and their baseline model. Lee et al. [15] used stacked CNN and RNN and jointly learned to extract relevant information from several features such as packages, permissions, intent, etc. Nikola el at. [16] employed classification and clustering algorithm to determine malicious Android apps based on the permissions and source code analysis. Permission-based mechanisms have 89% F-1 Score, while source code analysis indicates the F-1 Score is 95.1%. MalDozer [10] uses raw API call sequences as features to detect Android malware efficiently. It evaluated Malgenome, Drebin, and their MalDozer dataset. Results show MalDozer successfully detects and attributes malware to its actual families with an F1-Score up to 99% and a false positive rate of up to 2%.

2.2 Dynamic Analysis Based Android Malware Detection Techniques

The detection of Android malware can be accomplished through dynamic analysis, which evaluates the app's behavior in real-time. The Shabtai et al. [20] dynamic analysis-based system analyzes network traffic to detect malicious behavior. It is accomplished by logging the network traffic patterns for each app and identifying harmful potential deviations. They evaluated their model using the C4.5 algorithm, achieving an accuracy of up to 94%. Oak et al. [18] employed LSTM and BERT model for Android malware detection. However, dynamic analysis logs were captured by Palo Alto Networks using their Wildfire tool [1]. These dynamic characteristics are difficult to capture, as Wildfire is not an open-source tool. Wang et al. [23] proposed a lightweight framework for android malware classification using network traffic analysis, data analysis is performed on the server by mirroring wireless access points to generate network work traffic. Extract behavior feature from network characteristic and feed them into the C4.5 machine learning model that can identify Android malware. Koliaridis et al. [13] proposed the Mal-warehouse, they designed an open-source tool called MIET to extract features such as memory, CPU, battery, and network traffic over a period of time. A detection module was implemented in Mal-warehouse that was evaluated using a traditional machine learning classifier and achieved an AUC score of 85.4%. Kelkar et al. [11] proposed a framework for detecting Android malware applications that exfiltrate data via HTTP and their analysis focused on the leaked data, and the locations where it was exfiltrated, and the correlation between these factors and sensitive data. The disadvantage of these methods is that there has been no comprehensive testing of these methods in an actual unknown malware detection, which is perhaps the most difficult of all.

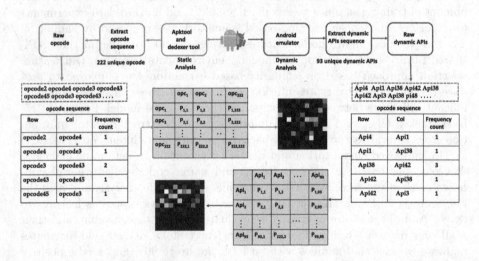

Fig. 1. Feature extraction and image generation

2.3 Hybrid Analysis Based Android Malware Detection Techniques

The hybrid analysis combines static and dynamic analysis. It is a method or technology for detecting malicious behavior or suspicious functionality that integrates behavior-based features from dynamic analysis combined with static features that can be obtained while analyzing the application's source code. Droid-Detector [26] extracts permissions, sensitive APIs, and dynamic behaviors from each application and uses series of autoencoders in a deep belief network to classify Android malware. The DL-Droid [5], DL-based android malware detection system employed code of input generation method with the commonly used stateless approach. Stateless approaches obtained an accuracy of 97.8%, while combined dynamic and static features obtained an accuracy of 98.82%. Jang et al. [9] designed Andro-AutoPsy, a malware detection engine based on similarity matching of Android malware. They collected malware information from anti-malware threat reports, malware datasets, and third-party websites. They used five different features, including API call sequence, a digital certificate serial number, permissions, intents, and system commands to train their proposed model. Andro-Autopsy can detect and classifies malware accurately with low false positives and false negatives and can detect zero-day mobile malware.

3 *SHIELD:* The Proposed Framework

A multimodal deep learning framework is proposed in the *SHIELD* for Android malware detection as shown in Fig. 2. It would be able to detect unknown malware cases in addition to the existing malware samples. It implements multimodal autoencoder (MAE) and learns from Markov images of low-level opcodes and the dynamic API as run time behavior of the malicious applications. These features fuse into multimodal latent features or concatenating the hidden representations and mapping them to a common space. Further, fused features are fed as input to five different CNN models for detection.

3.1 Feature Extraction

Privacy and data leakage in Android devices are generally directly related to application execution sequence at runtime. Hence, the opcode sequence and dynamic APIs sequence consider in the analysis.

Dex Files Extraction. An Android application comprises a (Dalvik Executable) .dex file called Classes.dex that contains code related to application execution at runtime. Therefore, each application is submitted into apktool[1] via command-line interface. It performs reverse engineering on android applications. The decompiled app contains *AndroidManifest.xml, classes.dex, resources.arsc*, and many subfolders such *assets, res, and META-INF*, etc. The file structure of an Android application contains necessary information related to the Android application. Further, Classes.dex file consists of executable code for each application. Now, each application of dex file is uploaded to dedexer[2] disassembler tool and gets dex.log file, which contains relevant information about the various segments of dex files, extract all opcode sequences by filtering the code section of dex.log files. Every dex file that contains an android application must be processed in the same way.

---

[1] https://ibotpeaches.github.io/Apktool/.
[2] https://sourceforge.net/projects/dedexer/.

Dynamic API Extraction. Frida[3] is a dynamic instrumentation framework for monitoring APIs during the app execution. The user can choose to monitor a predefined list of APIs see Table 2 divided into several categories (e.g., Device Data, Device Info, SMS) or a custom list of APIs passed through the command line to the script. It stores the invoked API, classes, methods, the return value, and the file from where it was called. For this, we use the latest version of 'frida-server'[4] for the arm64 architecture. This file is extracted, and pushed to the genymotion emulator, made executable, and run.

In order to fetch dynamic APIs, each Android app install into the genymotion emulator using ADB command, fetch package name of installed application. Following that, Push Frida server into the emulator, change the permissions frida-server file, and execute it. Now, Start importing the Frida library and retrieve genymotion emulator device id. Then, invoke the spawn() function to start the massager in order to determine the installed application PID. Finally, create a Frida session using attached PID. It allows hooking JavaScript code[5] inside the main activity of a running application. It read class name[6] and method for each 18 category of Dynamic API and monitor them. At the end of the process, we uninstall android application from emulator environment.

Table 2. Dynamic API listed under various categories.

Sno.	Dyanmic API	# of API	Sno.	Dynamic API	# of API
1	Device data	12	10	DeviceInfo	9
2	Shared preferences	14	11	IPC	6
3	SMS	2	12	Database	19
4	System manager	4	13	SharedPreferences	3
5	Base64 encode/decode	3	14	WebView	11
6	Dex class loader	6	15	Java Native Interface	2
7	Network	8	16	Command	3
8	Crypto - Hash	4	17	Process	3
9	Binder	3	18	FileSytem - Java	4

3.2   Markov Image Generation

We extracted opcode and dynamic APIs sequence from each Android application. The Markov image generation is provided by Algorithm 1. The input to the algorithm are pairs of N-gram features and then determines the frequency of

---

[3] https://frida.re/.

[4] https://github.com/frida/frida/releases.

[5] https://github.com/Dado1513/PAPIMonitor/blob/master/api-android-monitor/frida_script_template.js.

[6] https://github.com/Dado1513/PAPIMonitor/blob/master/api-android-monitor/api-monitor.json.

occurrence of consecutive N-gram pairs such as n_i followed by $n_i + 1$ and $n_i + 1$ followed by $n_i + 2$ where $1 \le i \le 93$ or 222. Further, calculate the probability of N-gram pairs that n_i followed by $n_i + 1$. Finally, calculate the pixel values of Markov images as shown in Fig. 1. Pixels in Markov model-based images are expressed mathematically as follows. Where PM[i][j] represents the probability matrix that N-gram pairs n_i followed by $n_i + 1$, and MV represents the maximum probability calculated from the matrix of transition probabilities PM.

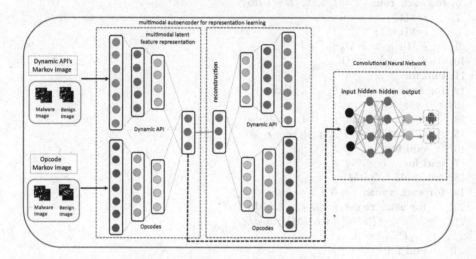

Fig. 2. *SHIELD:* the proposed framework

3.3   Network Construction

Autoencoders are unsupervised neural networks that are trained to encode an input $X \in R^d$ by computing the reconstruction error between X and the decoded output $X' \in R^d$. The autoencoders have the advantage of learning the constructive representation of the data, which is often expressed in a compressed format, where the input X is converted into a latent representation $Z \in R^k$. Where k. The encoder module of the AE network mappings from X to Z. Decoder modules of AE networks mapping Z to the reconstruction X'.

AE can reconstruct outputs similar to their inputs but cannot handle multimodal information (i.e., information originating in different data types). Although, a traditional supervised learning algorithm is limited to learning from intersecting samples that are labeled and clean. Contrary to this, Multimodal Autoencoders (MAE) encoder weights are learned from Markov images of dynamic APIs and Opcode sequences.

Algorithm 1. Markov Image Generation

1: Input $N \quad = \quad n_1, n_2, n_3...n_m$, where N_i, N-gram featrue extarcted from Opcode and Dynamic APIs Sequence.

2: Ouput $P = p_1, p_2, p_3...p_m$, where P_i, Pixel value for Markov image.

3: $L = LENGTH(x)$, Get Length of vector

4: The matrix PM, Initialized with $L \times L$ zeroes;

5: The Array $F_q.$, Initialized with $L \times 1$ zeroes;

6: for each round $t = 1, 2, ..., L - 1$ do

7:     r=N[t];

8:     c=N[t+1];

9:     $PM[r][c] = PM[r][c] + 1$

10:     $F_q[r] = F_q[r] + 1$

11: end for

12: for each round $i = 0, 1, ..., L$ do

13:     vs= $F_q[i]$;

14:     for each round $j = 0, 1, ..., L$ do

15:         $PM[i][j] = PM[i][j]/vs$;

16:     end for

17: end for

18: $MV = MAX(PM)$;

19: for each round $i = 0, 1, ..., L$ do

20:     for each round $j = 0, 1, ..., L$ do

21:         $p = ((PM[i][j] * L)/MV)modL$;

22:. $P[i][j] = p$;

23:     end for

24: end for

25: END

A multimodal Autoencoder is analogous to a three-stage autoencoder. First, each type of feature category is represented by a specific modality, while the subsequent stage reflects the cross-modality. This paper demonstrates the construction of a Multimodal Autoencoder (MAE) as a bi-modal Autoencoder. An AE for each modality is not just a single-layer Autoencoder but multilayer and continuously shrinking encoder with a variable number of layers. By default, the Multimodal Autoencoder model fuse Dynamic APIs and Opcode modalities, containing several layers with ReLU that are fully connected. The cross-modality Autoencoder is a multilayer continuously shrinking Autoencoder with different output layers for different predictions. Nevertheless, the encoder and decoder networks are symmetrical in terms of the number of hyperparameters per layer.

In the third stage, we use five different Convolution Neural Network (CNN) models, as shown in Table 3, that are smart enough to learn from fuses information of Markov images (Dynamic APIs and Opcode). It consists of configurable kernels performing convolutional over the fuses feature. CNN's typically consist combination of four layers: convolutional layer, max-pooling layer, dropout layer, and dense layer. The convolutional layer is responsible for loading the fuses features into the network. It enhances signal qualities to decrease noise, the max-pooling layer compresses the data while retaining relevant information, convolutional neural networks use the Dropout Layer to avoid complicated co-adaptation of training data, and the dense layer of CNN network that has 'softmax' as its activation function.

Formal Description. *SHIELD* first transformes input Dynamic APIs and Opcode Sequence to Markov images as vector of X_d and X_o respectively to hidden representations

$$h_d = f(W_d * X_d + b_d) \tag{1}$$
$$h_o = f(W_o * X_o + b_o) \tag{2}$$

Concatenating the hidden representations and mapping them to a common space

$$h_{mae} = f(W_{mae} * [h_d; h_o] + b_{mae}) \tag{3}$$

The multimodal autoencoder (MAE) is trained to reconstruct the hidden representations of two different modalities h_{mae}.

$$[\hat{h}_d; \hat{h}_o] = f(W'_{mae} * h_{mae} + \hat{b_{mae}}) \tag{4}$$

$$\alpha = [W_d, W_o, W'_d, W'_o, W_{mae}, W'_{mae}] \tag{5}$$

and finally, reconstruction of original representations of various modalities such as Markov image of Dynamic APIs and Opcode Sequence input.

$$\hat{x_d} = f(W'_d * \hat{h}_d + \hat{b}_d) \tag{6}$$
$$\hat{x_o} = f(W'_o * \hat{h}_o + \hat{b}_o) \tag{7}$$

where x'_d, x'_o are the reconstruction of input vectors x_d, x_o, and $\hat{h}_d$, $\hat{h}_o$ are the reconstruction of hidden representations h_d, h_o. The hyperparameters as shown in Eq. 5, $W_d, W_o, W'_d, W'_o, W_{mae}, W'_{mae}$ are weight matrices, $b_d, b_o, \hat{b}_d, \hat{b}_o, b_{mae}, \hat{b_{mae}}$ are bias vectors. Here $[\cdot \, ; \cdot]$ indicate the vector concatenation, and f indicate ReLU(.) function.

According to Serban et al. [19], noise distributions are considered using bregman divergences, which correlate to normal distributions. Each modality has its own loss function and bregman divergence, therefore assuming a specific noise distribution for output.

Before training the Multimodal Autoencoder (MAE) model, we used the entire dataset for training with 20% for the validation set. AE training involves optimizing the hyperparameter to minimize reconstructions loss, as defined below:

$$\min_{\alpha} \sum_{k=1}^{n} (||x_d^k - \hat{x_d^k}||)^2 + (||x_o^k - \hat{x_o^k}||)^2 \tag{8}$$

where k represents the kth features, and the $\alpha = [W_d,\ W_o,\ W_d',\ W_o',\ W_{mae},$ $W_{mae}', b_d,\ b_o,\ \hat{b_d},\ \hat{b_o},\ b_{mae},\ \hat{b_{mae}}]$ are MAE parameter. Autoencoders can be stacked to create deep networks. In order to improve the quality of semantic representations, we use a multimodel autoencoder (MAE) that consists of multiple hidden layers that are stacked together.

Table 3. Different CNN model used in proposed method

Models	Architectures	Best Hyperparameter
M-I	Con. + Conv. + Maxpool + Dense + Dense	Epochs = 100, LR = 0.00001
M-II	Con.+ Maxpool+ Dense + Dense	Epochs = 100, LR = 0.0001
M-III	Con.+ Maxpool + Conv.+ Dense + Dense	Epochs = 100, LR = 0.00001
M-IV	Con. + Maxpool + Dropout+Dense + Dense	Epochs = 100, LR = 0.001
M-V	Con. + Maxpool + Dropout+ Con.+Dense + Dense	Epochs = 100, LR = 0.0001

Table 4. Detection performance for Opcode (Op.) Markov and dynamic (APIs) image separately.

Model	Dataset used	Pre.		Re.		F1-Sc.		Acc.	
		Op.	APIs	Op.	APIs	Op.	APIs	Op.	APIs
M-I	CICAndMal2017	0.9255	0.9444	0.9802	0.9842	0.9075	0.9639	0.9201	0.9640
M-II	CICAndMal2017	0.9432	0.9429	0.8758	0.9842	0.9175	0.9664	0.9306	0.9664
M-III	CICAndMal2017	0.9685	0.9793	0.8830	1	0.9238	0.9895	0.9359	0.9896
M-IV	CICAndMal2017	0.9893	0.9740	0.8878	0.9260	0.9358	0.9556	0.9464	0.9642
M-V	CICAndMal2017	0.9323	0.9842	0.9212	0.9842	0.9267	0.9842	0.9359	0.9850
M-I	CICandMal2020	0.9197	0.9685	0.9494	0.9736	0.9370	0.9711	0.9432	0.9711
M-II	CICandMal2020	0.9746	0.9684	0.9164	0.9684	0.9446	0.9684	0.9527	0.9690
M-III	CICandMal2020	0.9669	0.9792	0.9069	0.9947	0.9359	0.9869	0.9453	0.9872
M-IV	CICandMal2020	0.9872	0.9740	0.9260	0.9894	0.9556	0.9819	0.9612	0.9820
M-V	CICandMal2020	0.9776	0.9735	0.9403	0.9685	0.9586	0.9709	0.9642	0.9720

CNN Classifiers. CNN is a deep learning-based technique that have extremely effective in dealing with problems such as image classification and recognition [14]. Table 3 presents the five different CNN models implemented in the proposed work. Markov images of Dynamic APIs and Opcode Sequence fuse into multimodal latent features using Multimodal Autoencoder (MAE) or concatenating the hidden representations and mapping them into a common space. These semantic feature representations h_{mae} are applied to different CNN architectures. CNN hyperparameters are tuned while experimenting to achieve more accurate results. The optimizer used in all the models is Adam, with different learning rates, as shown in Table 3. The convolutional layer comprises 32 learnable kernels of size 4×4 for each model. Since android malware detection is a classification problem, either benign or malign, Z can be denoted as:

$$Z = ReLu(W_h * [h_{mae}] + b_h) \tag{9}$$

Here, W_h and b_h represent the weights and biases of the hidden layer. When vector Z is passed to SoftMax's classification layer, the probability of the application belonging to each class is determined.

$$P(Y = j|Z) = \frac{\exp(W_j^T * Z + b_j)}{\sum_{j'} \exp(W_{j'}^T * Z + b_{j'})} \tag{10}$$

Here, W_j and b_j represent the trainable weights and biases. The output layer predicted for each of the j classes, $W_j^T * Z$ is the inner product of W_j and Z, where Y represents the predicted class.

4   Experimental Evaluation

4.1   Dataset

In this study, three datasets are used - (1) We leveraged the Androzoo repository to select a benign application [4]. It contains more than 15 million Android samples from 18 app vendors, including the Genome project and Google Play Store, which are available on Androzoo with information like name, size, checksum, and VirusTotal score. Further, we assumed that Google Play Store apps did not exhibit malicious behavior. Therefore, selected 26780 Android samples from Google Play Store were rated benign by VirusTotal. Additionally, the database was optimized based on the target SDK Version of the android apps, i.e., API level 22 or greater, which resulted 22398 benign apps. For the malware dataset, Argus Lab's Android Malware Database(AMD) is used, which comprises over 24,500 android malware samples from 2010 to 2019, categorized into 135 variants across 71 android malware families [24].

(2) CICandMal2020[7] dataset contains 200K benign and 200K malicious samples. It contain 13 malware family groups, including adware, backdoors, file infectors, no categories, potentially unwanted applications (PUAs), ransomware, riskware, scareware, trojans, trojan-droppers, trojan-sms, and trojan-spy. In addition, malarious applications have 147 different malware families. Further, 24980 android samples are randomly selected where 11678 benign applications and 13302 malicious applications.

(3) CICAndMal2017[8] dataset comprised 1555 pieces of malware. The malware samples consisted of 42 different malware families with 416 applications,

---

[7] https://www.unb.ca/cic/datasets/andmal2020.html.
[8] https://www.unb.ca/cic/datasets/andmal2017.html.

while the benign samples had 1139 apps and consisted of popular app genres, including life, leisure, and social commerce.

These datasets have been continuously used in the Android malware detection domain, enabling direct comparisons between the proposed approach and existing methods. The dataset is split into 70:20:10 ratios for training, testing, and validation. The combined Androzoo and AMD dataset is only used to construct the baseline architecture and tune the hyperparameters. The benchmark datasets CICAndMal2017 and CICandMal2020 are used for the evaluation and state-of-the-art comparison, but neither training nor validation is conducted using these datasets.

Table 5. Detection performance for combined Markov image

Model	Features used	Pre.		Re.		F1-Sc.		Acc.	
		2017	2020	2017	2020	2017	2020	2017	2020
M-I	Opcode+Dynamic API	0.9742	0.9916	0.9947	0.9888	0.9843	0.9902	0.9845	0.9930
M-II	Opcode+Dynamic API	0.9843	1	0.9947	0.9843	0.9895	0.9921	0.9896	0.9934
M-III	Opcode+Dynamic API	0.9842	0.9907	0.9894	0.9925	0.9868	0.9916	0.9871	0.9940
M-IV	Opcode+Dynamic API	0.9844	0.9907	1	0.9843	0.9921	0.9875	0.9922	0.9910
M-V	Opcode+Dynamic API	1	0.9935	0.9896	0.9861	0.9948	0.9898	0.9952	0.9926

4.2 Evaluation Environment

The programs that carried out the experiment were written in Python using anaconda-2021.05, sckit-learn, Keras-2.6.1, and TensorFlow-2.8.0 libraries. The anaconda[9], Keras[10], and TensorFlow[11] The installation guide describes how to install the software. We configured Window 10 with Processor Intel®Core^{TM}i7-1185G7 Processor 12M Cache, up to 4.80 GHz, with IPU and 16 GB RAM with 500 GB SSD.

4.3 Performance Analysis Based Markov Images Separately

Initially, we assess the effectiveness of different Convolutional Neural Network architecture learning from only one of the generated Markov image features set. It creates a baseline model which compares to our proposed model and allows us to assess the contribution of each of these features individually. Each Convolutional Neural Network model is individually trained using the training data for CICAndMal2017 and CICandMal2020 and then evaluated against unseen testing data.

---

[9] https://docs.anaconda.com/anaconda/install/index.html.
[10] https://anaconda.org/conda-forge/keras.
[11] https://docs.anaconda.com/anaconda/user-guide/tasks/tensorflow/.

Markov Image of Opcode Sequence. We performed an experiment on the Markov Image of Opcode Sequence. From Table 4, it can be observed that the model M-IV (convolutional layers, max pool layer, dropout layer, and dense layer) on the CICAndMal2017 dataset obtained a 94.64% accuracy, and Precision, Recall, and F-Measure values of 0.9893, 0.8878, and 0.9358, respectively, while model M-I (two convolutional layers, max pool layer followed by dense layer) shows poor performance: 92.01% of accuracy and Precision, Recall, and F-Measure values of 0.9255, 0.9802, and 0.9075, respectively. Similarly, as shown in Table 4 for CICandMal2020, the model M-V (convolutional layer, max pool layer, dropout layer, convolutional layer, and dense layer) has an improvement in accuracy by 1.80% compared to the best performing model M-IV (convolutional layers, max pool layer, dropout layer, and dense layer) on CICAndMal2017.

Markov Image of Dynamic APIs. Similarly, we performed experiments on Markov images of Dynamic APIs. From Table 4 it can be observed that for the CICAndMal2017 dataset, the model M-III (convolutional layer, max-pool layer followed by convolutional layer and, dense layer) reports the best result with 98.96% accuracy and Precision, Recall, and F-Measure values of 0.9793, 1 and 0.9895 respectively. For the CICandMal2020 dataset, The Model M-III (convolutional layer, max-pool layer followed by convolutional layer and, fully connected layer) again reports the highest performance with 98.72% accuracy and Precision, Recall, and F-Measure values of .9792, 0.9947 and 0.9869 respectively. The model M-III has run for 100 epochs on both CICAndMal2017 and CIC-andMal2020, respectively, with learning rates of 0.001 and 0.000001.

4.4 Performance Analysis Based on Multimodal Latent Features

There are two distinct modalities in the Markov images (Dynamic APIs and Opcode Sequences). A modality-specific Autoencoder is not only a single-layer Autoencoder but also a multilayer and gradually diminishing encoder with varying layers for each modality due to the changes in their dimensions. The Autoencoder model fuse dynamic APIs and Opcode modalities, The cross-modality Autoencoder(AE) is also a multilayer gradually shrinking Autoencoder with different sizes of output layer for each prediction. Now, multimodal latent feature representation from different modalities is derived from the Multimodal Autoencoder (MAE) model. It uses an input feature to different CNN models to assess how performance is affected versus using only a single modality set. The performance of models obtained using multimodal latent features on CICAndMal2017 and CICandMal2020 is depicted in Table 5. It can be observed that from both datasets, multimodal latent feature sets always improve performance. The model M-V (convolutional layer, max-pool layer, dropout layer, convolutional layer followed by full connected layer) exhibited improved (99.52% accuracy and 0.9948 F F-measure) results compared to all other models on CICAndMal2017. In contrast, the model M-III (convolutional layer, max-pool layer followed by convolutional layer, and fully connected layer) produced 99.40% of accuracy and 0.9921 F F-measure on the CICandMal2020 dataset.

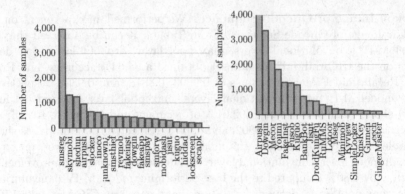

Fig. 3. Top 20 malware families from both CICandMal2020 and ADM dataset

4.5   Unknown Malware Family Detection

An experiment was conducted in Drebin's original paper, where the top 20 most important families were selected from the benchmark dataset. Then each of them was excluded from the training process, and testing was conducted with the same unknown family. Therefore, a similar experiment is performed on the CICandMal2020 and AMD datasets by separating each family from training to use as test data. A state-of-the-art comparison is carried out by comparing Drebin detectors and Maldozers. The experiment is extended by evaluating the top 20 largest families and all families in the CICandMal2020 and AMD datasets. We use accuracy, precision, recall, and F1-score as a metric to evaluate the performance of our proposed model. In order to report results for all families, we also use a weighted average detection rate because the number of data points varies across families as per Figs. 3A and 3B. Consequently, the results could be considerably skewed, likely why Drebin's paper presented data from only 20 of the most important families. The detection accuracy for each family is further weighted by the ratio of the number of data points in the dataset to the number of data points available for each family. To facilitate comparison with previously reported results, we use the weighted average detection rate for the top 20 largest families.

Table 6. Detection performance in zero day scenario

Average	Dataset	Drebin	Maldozer	SHIELD
Top 20 families	Mal-2020	52.3%	89.4%	93.2%
All families (wt.)	Mal-2020	58.8%	88%	94%
Top 20 families	AMD	86%	81.99%	86.2%
All families (wt.)	AMD	74%	75.66%	87%

The results for the CICandMal2020 dataset can be seen in Table 6, where the detection performance is shown for the top 20 largest families and all 147 families. The proposed model outperforms Drebin and Maldozer for the most prominent 20 families, with 93.2% of the weighted average detection rate. Furthermore, our proposed model performs best when the variation in family size is taken into account by using weighted averages when we extend this experiment to all 147 families.

Table 6 shows detection results for the 20 most prominent families in the AMD dataset along with the weighted average result and overall of 71 families. The *SHIELD* achieves a detection rate of 86.2% for the 20 largest families, significantly higher than the Drebin and Maldozer detectors. The performance improvement is still evident when all 71 families in the AMD dataset are considered, the proposed model scoring 87% weighted detection rate as opposed to 74% and 75.66% for Drebin and Maldozer, respectively. Based on the performance of our proposed method, we can conclude *SHIELD* extracts higher quality, more accurate features during training with less overfitting. As a result, the proposed approach can generalize more effectively against unknown malware families and threats that have not been encountered before. In contrast, signature-based systems are most likely to fail.

4.6   Backdoor Analysis

In order to evaluate the effectiveness of *SHIELD* and other existing mobile anti-malware programs, we created 500 obfuscated backdoor applications using Msfvenom[12]. Msfvenom is a command-line instance of Metasploit, and it is used to generate Android meterpreter payloads in reverse_https format and encrypt them with additional encoder modules. A targeted app was downloaded from the Google Play Store. Both malicious payload and target app are decoded using the apktool[13]. Inject malicious payload code into decoded target app and add

Table 7. Backdoor analysis

AV	D-rate		AV	D-rate		AV	D-rate		AV	D-rate	
	Conn.	W. Conn.		Conn.	W. Conn.		Conn.	W. Conn.		Conn.	W. Conn
AhnLab-V3	59%	54%	eScan	27%	29%	NANO-Antivirus	0%	0%	Arcabit	41%	34%
Avast	51%	56%	ESET-NOD32	41%	45%	Rising	0%	0%	Emsisoft	22%	20%
Avast-Mobile	43%	45%	F-Secure	5%	10%	TACHYON	0%	0%	Panda	0%	0%
Avira	42%	39%	Gridinsoft	29%	29%	Trend	0%		AVG	61%	61%
AdAware	3%	2%	GData	28%	30%	Tencent	0%	0%	Fortinet	49%	49%
Alibaba	0%	0%	Jiangmin	0%	0%	FireEye	18%	12%	TrendMicro	0%	0%
ALYac	0%	0%	K7GW	49%	47%	Trustlook	0%	0%	Antiy-AVL	0%	0%
BitDefenderFalx	61%	53%	K7AntiVirus	0%	0%	Sophos	46%	42%	Kaspersky	55%	54%
Baidu	0%	0%	Kingsoft	0%	0%	Symantec Mobile	0%	0%	Sangfor Engine Zero	34%	37%
CAT-QuickHeal	43%	45%	MAX	0%	0%	VirIT	0%	0%	BitDefenderTheta	5%	2%
Cynet	67%	64%	MaxSecure	0%	0%	VBA32	0%	0%	Lionic	0%	0%
Cyren	0%	0%	Microsoft	0%	0%	ViRobo	0%	0%	SUPERAntiSpyware	0%	0%
Comodo	0%	0%	McAfee	0%	0%	Zillya	0%	0%	ClamAV	0%	0%
DrWeb	40%	33%	McAfeeEdition	0%	2%	ZoneAlarm	7%	2%	Yandex	0%	0%
Malwarebytes	0%	0%	*SHIELD (Our method)*	100%	97%						

---

[12] https://www.offensive-security.com/metasploit-unleashed/msfvenom/.
[13] https://ibotpeaches.github.io/Apktool/.

meterpreter hook. The required permissions are injected into the manifest file of the target app. Then, Re-build the target app via apktool. Finally, Sign the target app apk with jarsigner and zipalign. The target app is installed on an android device via social engineering methods.

The created backdoor is uploaded to VirusTotal, providing a JSON report from 57 different mobile antiviruses. The generated backdoors[14] successfully bypass all antivirus programs in VirusTotal. Further, start the msfconsole reverse handler and run the target app on the victim's phone. It creates metasploit session between the victim and attacker, compromising android device security. Fortunately, *SHIELD* successfully flagged the generated backdoor as a malicious application.

We carried out four different experiments based on backdoor connections and dangerous Permission. First, backdoor connection with dangerous Permission, The backdoor analysis report is listed in Table 7. It can be observed that the backdoor detection rates of existing mobile antivirus vendors are nearly half of the proposed approach. Second, without backdoor connection with dangerous Permission, we don't provide LHOST and LPORT information (without connection) to the backdoor during the backdoor creation. These backdoor applications can not exploit android security because they can not create a Metasploit session. From Table 7, It can be observed that the existing mobile antivirus vendor flag malicious applications while *SHIELD* predicted the generated backdoor correctly as a benign application with 97% detection rate. Finally, existing mobile antivirus vendors and the proposed approach are showing benign applications for backdoor connections with no permission and without backdoor connections with no permission.

Table 8. Performance comparison

Model	Strategy	Malign	Benign	Pre.(%)	Re.(%)	F1(%)	Acc.(%)
[5] (S.L)	H	19620	11505	95.31	97.19	96.24	95.42
[5] (S.F)	H	19620	11505	98.09	99.56	98.82	98.50
[23]	D	5560	8312	—	—	—	97.89
[16]	S	—	—	95.8	95.8	—	95.6
[12]	S	21260	20000	98.0	99.0	98.0	98.0
[26]	H	840	840	96.76	96.76	96.76	96.76
SHIELD (M-V)	H	24,500	22398	1	98.96	99.48	99.52

4.7 Comparison with State-of-the-Art Work

A multimodal approach is proposed in this paper for detecting Android malware. To evaluate *SHIELD* performance, we compared *SHIELD* with recent exiting work. From Table 8 it can be observed that DL-Droid hybrid approach

[14] md5 hash: 9428c569daddeaf815d48768e259ee27.

with stateful analysis achieved 98.50% accuracy compared to *SHIELD* which has 99.52% accuracy while utilizing the more number of samples for the experiments. *SHIELD* outperformed DL-Droid [5] in all other metrics except recall. In DL-Droid stateful analysis has slightly more recall compared to our mechanism. *SHIELD* also outperforms DL-Droid [5] stateless analysis, S. Wang et al. [23], Shabtai et al. [16], Kim et al. [12] and Droid detector [26] in all metrics.

5   Conclusion and Future Work

This paper presents *SHIELD* for Android malware detection and classification learning from Markov image of low-level opcodes and dynamic APIs. Several relevant conclusions can be drawn from our experiments. Firstly, using multimodal autoencoder (MAE) techniques suitable for malware detection and classification problems allows us to achieve state-of-the-art results in Android malware detection while minimizing the requirement of feature engineering and domain expertise. Secondly, using *SHIELD* compared to models where Markov image of Opcodes and Dynamic APIs feed alone. It improves performance since the model fuses into multimodal latent features or concatenates the hidden representations and maps them to a common space by learning a multimodal autoencoder(MAE) capable of handling various attacks. Third, *SHIELD* shows an impressive detection rate compared to the Maldozer and Drebin detectors, which shows that this architecture is more effective than standard ones at detecting unknown malware families. Finally, to evaluate the effectiveness of *SHIELD* and other existing mobile anti-malware programs, we created 500 obfuscated backdoor applications; the experiment shows that most existing mobile antivirus solutions fail to detect obfuscated back doors compromising the Android device security. *SHIELD* also exhibits state-of-the-art performance in the traditional detection cases of Android malware detection.

Our future work will focus on detecting the presence of zero-day malware, ransomware, and in-memory malware in computing systems. The data pertinent to zero-day malware is extremely difficult to obtain. However, we aim to enhance our methods to learn the possible set of features that might result due to malware evolution. Usually, malware exhibits generational nature, and changing malware significantly requires time and serious effort. On the other hand, Ransomware and in-memory malware are found to share some features with existing malware patterns. However, the data in these scenarios is not widely available to make any significant conclusions. We will attempt to resolve these issues.

Acknowledgment. We acknowledge the Government of India, Ministry of Home Affairs, Bureau of Police Research and Development for funding this research.

References

1. Palo alto networks, wildfire malware analysis service. https://docs.paloaltonetworks.com/wildfire.html
2. Stephanie cuthbertson - director, android - google google i/0 2019 keynote speech. https://www.youtube.com/watch?v=lyRPyRKHO8M
3. Alazab, M., Alazab, M., Shalaginov, A., Mesleh, A., Awajan, A.: Intelligent mobile malware detection using permission requests and API calls. Future Gener. Comput. Syst. **107**, 509–521 (2020)
4. Allix, K., Bissyandé, T.F., Klein, J., Le Traon, Y.: AndroZoo: collecting millions of android apps for the research community. In: 2016 IEEE/ACM 13th Working Conference on Mining Software Repositories (MSR), pp. 468–471. IEEE (2016)
5. Alzaylaee, M.K., Yerima, S.Y., Sezer, S.: DL-droid: deep learning based android malware detection using real devices. Comput. Secur. **89**, 101663 (2020)
6. Arefkhani, M., Soryani, M.: Malware clustering using image processing hashes. In: 2015 9th Iranian Conference on Machine Vision and Image Processing (MVIP), pp. 214–218. IEEE (2015)
7. Arp, D., Spreitzenbarth, M., Hubner, M., Gascon, H., Rieck, K., Siemens, C.: DREBIN: effective and explainable detection of android malware in your pocket. In: Ndss, vol. 14, pp. 23–26 (2014)
8. Han, K.S., Lim, J.H., Kang, B., Im, E.G.: Malware analysis using visualized images and entropy graphs. Int. J. Inf. Secur. **14**(1), 1–14 (2015)
9. Jang, J.w., Kang, H., Woo, J., Mohaisen, A., Kim, H.K.: Andro-autopsy: anti-malware system based on similarity matching of malware and malware creator-centric information. Digit. Investig. **14**, 17–35 (2015)
10. Karbab, E.B., Debbabi, M., Derhab, A., Mouheb, D.: MalDozer: automatic framework for android malware detection using deep learning. Digit. Investig. **24**, S48–S59 (2018)
11. Kelkar, S., Kraus, T., Morgan, D., Zhang, J., Dai, R.: Analyzing http-based information exfiltration of malicious android applications. In: 2018 17th IEEE International Conference on Trust, Security and Privacy in Computing and Communications/12th IEEE International Conference On Big Data Science And Engineering (TrustCom/BigDataSE), pp. 1642–1645. IEEE (2018)
12. Kim, T., Kang, B., Rho, M., Sezer, S., Im, E.G.: A multimodal deep learning method for android malware detection using various features. IEEE Trans. Inf. Forensics Secur. **14**(3), 773–788 (2018)
13. Kouliaridis, V., Barmpatsalou, K., Kambourakis, G., Wang, G.: Mal-warehouse: a data collection-as-a-service of mobile malware behavioral patterns. In: 2018 IEEE SmartWorld, Ubiquitous Intelligence & Computing, Advanced & Trusted Computing, Scalable Computing & Communications, Cloud & Big Data Computing, Internet of People and Smart City Innovation (SmartWorld/SCALCOM/UIC/ATC/CBDCom/IOP/SCI), pp. 1503–1508. IEEE (2018)
14. Krizhevsky, A., Sutskever, I., Hinton, G.E.: ImageNet classification with deep convolutional neural networks. In: Advances in Neural Information Processing Systems 25 (2012)
15. Lee, W.Y., Saxe, J., Harang, R.: SeqDroid: obfuscated android malware detection using stacked convolutional and recurrent neural networks. In: Alazab, M., Tang, M.J. (eds.) Deep Learning Applications for Cyber Security. ASTSA, pp. 197–210. Springer, Cham (2019). https://doi.org/10.1007/978-3-030-13057-2_9

16. Milosevic, N., Dehghantanha, A., Choo, K.K.R.: Machine learning aided android malware classification. Comput. Electr. Eng. **61**, 266–274 (2017)
17. Nataraj, L., Karthikeyan, S., Jacob, G., Manjunath, B.S.: Malware images: visualization and automatic classification. In: Proceedings of the 8th International Symposium on Visualization for Cyber Security, pp. 1–7 (2011)
18. Oak, R., Du, M., Yan, D., Takawale, H., Amit, I.: Malware detection on highly imbalanced data through sequence modeling. In: Proceedings of the 12th ACM Workshop on Artificial Intelligence and Security, pp. 37–48 (2019)
19. Serban, I.V., Ororbia II, A.G., Pineau, J., Courville, A.: Multi-modal variational encoder-decoders (2016)
20. Shabtai, A., Tenenboim-Chekina, L., Mimran, D., Rokach, L., Shapira, B., Elovici, Y.: Mobile malware detection through analysis of deviations in application network behavior. Comput. Secur. **43**, 1–18 (2014)
21. Tang, M., Alazab, M., Luo, Y.: Big data for cybersecurity: vulnerability disclosure trends and dependencies. IEEE Trans. Big Data **5**(3), 317–329 (2017)
22. Venkatraman, S., Alazab, M.: Use of data visualisation for zero-day malware detection. Secur. Commun. Netw. **2018** (2018)
23. Wang, S., Chen, Z., Yan, Q., Yang, B., Peng, L., Jia, Z.: A mobile malware detection method using behavior features in network traffic. J. Netw. Comput. Appl. **133**, 15–25 (2019)
24. Wei, F., Li, Y., Roy, S., Ou, X., Zhou, W.: Deep ground truth analysis of current android malware. In: Polychronakis, M., Meier, M. (eds.) DIMVA 2017. LNCS, vol. 10327, pp. 252–276. Springer, Cham (2017). https://doi.org/10.1007/978-3-319-60876-1_12
25. Xu, K., Li, Y., Deng, R.H., Chen, K.: DeepRefiner: Multi-layer android malware detection system applying deep neural networks. In: 2018 IEEE European Symposium on Security and Privacy (EuroS&P), pp. 473–487. IEEE (2018)
26. Yuan, Z., Lu, Y., Xue, Y.: Droiddetector: android malware characterization and detection using deep learning. Tsinghua Sci. Technol. **21**(1), 114–123 (2016)

Samyukta: A Unified Access Control Model using Roles, Labels, and Attributes

B. S. Radhika[1]([⊠])[iD], N. V. Narendra Kumar[2], and R. K. Shyamasundar[3]

[1] Indian Institute of Information Technology Dharwad, Dharwad, India
radhikabs184@gmail.com
[2] Institute for Development and Research in Banking Technology, Hyderabad, India
nvnarendra@idrbt.ac.in
[3] Indian Institute of Technology Bombay, Mumbai, India

Abstract. Access control is one of the key mechanisms used for protecting system resources. While each of the existing access control models has its own benefits, it is difficult to satisfy all the requirements of a contemporary system with a single model. In this paper, we propose a unified model by combining three existing well-known models – Role-based Access Control (RBAC), Mandatory Access Control (MAC), and Attribute-based Access Control (ABAC) – in a novel way. The proposed model, named Samyukta, combines these three models in a modular way and uses them in a specific order so that the modules complement each other and we gain benefits of all three models. The widely used RBAC, with its roles, provides scalability, auditability, and easy management. With its labels, MAC provides Information Flow Control (IFC), and ABAC, with its attributes, provides flexible, context-aware, fine-grained access control. Along with these benefits, Samyukta also has advantages with respect to expressiveness, performance, and verifiability. We provide a relative comparison of our model with an existing model and also present a prototype implementation of Samyukta and demonstrate its efficiency.

Keywords: Access control · Role-based access control ·
Mandatory-based access control · Attribute-based access control ·
RBAC · MAC · ABAC

1 Introduction

Over the years, several access control models have been proposed, each with its own benefits and shortcomings. While adopting an access control model, features like usability, flexibility, auditability, ease of administration, scalability, etc., are considered.

While the existing models satisfy some of the requirements, no individual model can provide a comprehensive solution.

V. R. Badarla et al. (Eds.): ICISS 2022, LNCS 13784, pp. 84–102, 2022.
https://doi.org/10.1007/978-3-031-23690-7_5

RBAC is one of the most widely used models where access permissions are assigned to users through roles. It provides several benefits such as scalability, ease of administration, and auditability [23,32]. However, RBAC also suffers from shortcomings such as complex role-engineering, coarse-grained access control, lack of flexibility, and lack of support for dynamic-parameters such as time, location, etc. [15].

MAC is another well-known traditional model where access policy is specified in terms of subject and object labels. MAC supports information flow control which is essential in realizing properties like confidentiality, integrity, and privacy. However, MAC models are generally less flexible, coarse-grained, and lack support for dynamic attributes.

ABAC is an emerging model that specifies access rules in terms of attributes. This makes it a flexible and fine-grained model [15]. More importantly, its support for dynamic parameters based authorization is very useful. However, as the number of attributes and policy size increase, it becomes challenging to keep track of the permission assignments and ensure the enforcement of the intended access control.

From the above discussion, it is evident that each of the three popular models has its own advantages but fails to meet all the security requirements of contemporary systems. With the growing demand for more effective access control, numerous attempts have been made to enhance the existing models in various ways to achieve better authorization.

Several works have focused on integrating RBAC and ABAC. There are three broad ways of combining these two models [23]: (1) Dynamic roles: using attributes to dynamically map users to roles [2,17], (2) Attribute-centric: treating role as just another attribute, and (3) Role-centric: using attributes to constrain the permissions given by roles [20,30]. Among these classes, attribute-centric, loses the benefits of RBAC since it treats roles as attributes (and hence removing the abstraction provided by roles). The dynamic-roles approach simplifies the RBAC configuration and automates user-role mapping. However, by using attributes only during configuration (and not at run-time), it fails to capture the full benefits of the dynamic nature of attributes. The role-centric approach manages to benefit from both RBAC and ABAC by constraining permission of roles using dynamic attribute values. However, the existing role-centric works [20,30] require significant modifications to the RBAC model and have high performance overhead.

Attempts have also been made to combine RBAC and MAC [22,26,28,31]. Among them, some [22,26,31] emulate MAC using RBAC, some emulate RBAC using MAC [22]. The resulting configurations in these emulations are often too complex and unintuitive and therefore not practically viable for large systems. Works on unifying frameworks [3,19] generally focus on common specification of access control requirements rather than gaining benefits during deployment.

Thus, the current efforts to enhance the existing models are not adequate to provide effective access control. Most of them provide only ad-hoc solutions and therefore have limited applications. Moreover, many of these hybrid solutions fail to capture their component models' advantages to the full extent. This is mainly because, most of these methods try to capture one model using the other and in the process lose the benefits of the original model. While combining multiple models, it is essential to retain the characteristic features of the component models in order to retain their inherent benefits. This paper proposes a unified model called Samyukta to address these problems. It uses a modular approach and provides an elegant way of combining the three models – RBAC, MAC, and ABAC – that is useful both at a specification and at implementation level. Our contributions in the paper include:

- Presenting a unified model referred to as, Samyukta,(which means *unified* in Sanskrit) that combines RBAC, MAC, and ABAC in such a way that we can essentially unify the benefits of each of the models.
- Developing a prototype implementation of Samyukta and demonstrated its efficiency.

The remainder of the paper is organized as follows: In Sect. 2, we present a brief description of the MAC model used in Samyukta. Section 3 reviews the related works. In Sect. 4, we present the motivation, followed by details of Samyukta in Sect. 5. In Sect. 6, we discuss the effectiveness of Samyukta and Sect. 7 discusses the experimental analysis. Finally, Sect. 8 concludes the paper.

2 Related Work

In this section, we highlight some of the important works that use RBAC, MAC, and ABAC in various combinations.

Kuhn et al. [23] and Cyne and Weil [9] have discussed different ways of combining RBAC and ABAC. As discussed in Sect. 1, the role-centric approach is more effective in integrating the benefits of these two models. RABAC [20] and AERBAC [30] are two such role-centric solutions. RABAC uses Permission Filtering Policy (PFP) to constrain the permissions of the roles. AERBAC adds attribute-based conditions to the RBAC authorization. Both the methods require modification to the standard RBAC. Several RBAC extensions such as temporal [25], spatial [10], and spatio-temporal [1] have been proposed to include dynamic parameters like time and location in RBAC authorization. Researchers have also worked on converting RBAC policies to ABAC [8] and ABAC policies to RBAC [4] in order to gain benefits of the target model. C-ABAC [12] proposes a formal model of ABAC using category- based meta-model of access control (CBAC) [3]. Here permissions are assigned to categories of users rather than to individual users. For this, along with the principal, resource, and environment attributes, it also uses category attributes and access decision is taken based on these attribute values. Although, grouping users into categories (which is similar to RBAC) is an improvement over regular ABAC, it doesn't provide all the benefits of RBAC and also doesn't provide information flow control. The latter is crucial for privacy.

Works have also been proposed to combine RBAC and MAC. Sandhu [31] proposed a method to emulate lattice-based access control using role hierarchies and constraints. Osborn [27], Gofman et al. [14], and Stambuli et al. [33] have worked on information flow control in RBAC to achieve the benefits of MAC using RBAC configuration. Tuval and Gudes [34] attempt to analyze the information flows in a given RBAC configuration and resolve flow conflicts. These solutions work for only smaller systems with few roles and objects. As the number of roles and objects increase, the analysis becomes complex and cumbersome.

Jin et al. [19] propose a unified attribute-based model that can help specify DAC, MAC, and RBAC policies using ABAC. However, once MAC labels and RBAC roles are represented as attributes, their inherent benefits such as auditability and easy management will be lost. Barker [3] has proposed a unified meta-model that aims to provide a basis for a common specification of access control requirements. Based on this model, Kafura and Gracanin [21] have proposed a meta model for information flow control. Jajodia et al. [18] proposed a unified framework that can enforce multiple access control policies. These models and frameworks are flexible and can model various existing systems. However, they focus only on the specification of requirements rather than ways to achieve effective authorization.

Thus, we can see that several attempts have been made to integrate the existing models for better access control. However, the current solutions are not adequate to support an effective and practical implementation. In the next section, we illustrate the need for an unified model with an example.

3   Need for a Unified Model

In this section, we motivate the need for a unified model through a simple example.

Example 1. Consider an organization with two types of users: *clerk* and *manager*. There are two users: *cl*, a *clerk* and *mg*, a manager. A clerk is responsible for bookkeeping of financial transactions that are stored in a file named *txnFile* and therefore has read and write permissions for the file. A manager is responsible for handling business management and has read and write permissions for a management file named *mgmtFile*. The *mgmtFile* contains sensitive business information that should not be revealed to a *clerk*. When needed, a *manager* can also perform the *clerk's* tasks and therefore has all the associated permissions. Furthermore, the organization has two constraints on the permissions (i) a transaction file can be written only during the working hours of working days, (ii) a management file can be written only from within the office.

The above example includes various security requirements that are commonly seen in organizations. It has access permissions based on the user's job or position in the organization. It needs to protect sensitive information against leaks. It also needs to control certain permissions based on various characteristics of the entities involved in the access and access environment.

The requirements based on the users job description can be well captured by RBAC. A simple RBAC configuration for the above example includes two users {cl, mg}, two objects {txnFile, mgmtFile}, two roles {clerk, manager}. The role *manager* is higher up in the role hierarchy and therefore inherits all the permissions assigned to *clerk*. The complete configuration with user-role assignment (UA), permission-role assignment (PA), and role hierarchy (RH) is shown in Fig. 1. This configuration is easy to understand as it clearly represents the organizations structure. The organization can easily add any new employees by simply assigning them to the suitable role. Also, the organization can easily find the set of permissions available to a user simply by first getting the active roles of the user and then by finding the set of permissions mapped to those roles. This makes auditing easy.

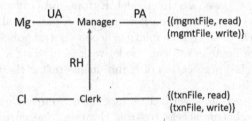

Fig. 1. RBAC configuration

However, this configuration doesn't prevent leak of information from *mgmtFile* to *cl*. The leak is possible through indirect information flow caused when *mg* (as *manager*) reads *mgmtFile* and writes the content to *txnFile* which can then be read by *cl* (with role *clerk*). This indirect information flow is shown in Fig. 2.

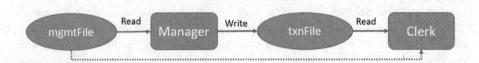

Fig. 2. Indirect information flow

Also, the above configuration has not covered the constraints specified in terms of time, day, and location. RBAC fails to support authorizations based on such dynamic values easily. Since all the permissions are mainly decided statically during role creation and user-role mapping, one way to support such parameters is to create multiple roles for each of the values of these parameters. Thus, for considering all the three parameters (time, day, location), each with two possible values (working hour, non-working hour, working day, non working day, office, out-of-office), in the worst case, we may need to create 8 roles each for *manager* and *clerk*, leading to role-explosion. Moreover, any slight change in these constraints may require changes in the role configuration making the authorization system cumbersome to manage.

The requirements related to confidentiality and integrity that involve information flow control are generally captured by MAC models. Let us consider a simple MAC configuration for Example 1 using a classic multi-level security (MLS) model, BLP. It would involve using two labels, l_1 and l_2 where $l_2 > l_1$. l_1 is assigned to the *txnFile* and *cl* and l_2 is assigned to *mgmtFile* and *mg* (since *mgmtFile* is confidential and is at a higher security level). BLP allows only information flows from lower to higher levels through its *no-read-up* and *no-write-down* rules. As a result, the manager *mg* with level $l2$ will not be allowed to write to *txnFile*. Thus preventing flow from *mgmtFile* to *cl*. However, notice that this configuration doesn't really capture the job descriptions and organization's structure. Also, such basic MAC models are not flexible enough for practical usage in mainstream systems. Furthermore, similar to RBAC, MAC models also don't support dynamic parameters.

ABAC is known for its fine-granularity and flexibility. An ABAC configuration for Example 1 can be created by using the attributes *role, object_type, location, time, day*. With these attributes, a policy can be defined as shown in Fig. 3. Note that we can also use an attribute *level* to capture the simple MLS rules discussed above. However, to keep the policy simple and intuitive, we have not included it in the policy.

ABAC Policy 1

1. $(read, (object\_type(o) = transaction \wedge level(o) \leq level(s)))$
2. $(write, (object\_type(o) = transaction \wedge level(s) \leq level(o) \wedge day = working\_day \wedge time = working\_hour))$
3. $(read, (role = manager \wedge object\_type(o) = management \wedge level(o) \leq level(s)))$
4. $(write, (role = manager \wedge object\_type(o) = management \wedge level(s) \leq level(o) \wedge location = office))$

Fig. 3. ABAC policy for Example 1

With such attribute-based policy, we can specify precise access rules. These rules are easy to change as per the changing requirements. However, notice that it is not easy to understand the organization's structure and retrieve permissions assigned to a user (auditing) easily from the policy, especially when the policy size increases.

Thus, as the policies get larger, their management and auditing (involves enumerating over all the rules) becomes very difficult.

Table 1. Advantages and shortcomings of RBAC, MAC, and ABAC

	Advantages	Shortcomings
RBAC [9,23,32]	– Captures organization's structure – Scalable – Easy to manage – Auditable	– Complex role engineering – Role explosion – Coarse-grained – Lack of flexibility – Lack of support for dynamic parameters
MAC [16,24]	– Provides IFC – Scalable	– Lack of flexibility – Lack of support for dynamic parameters – Coarse-grained
ABAC [9,15]	– Fine-grained – Flexible – Supports dynamic parameters	– Difficult to audit – Difficult to scale

Note that the above configurations are the straightforward, intuitive usage of each of the three models.

The RBAC, MAC, and ABAC models are expressive enough to emulate the other models and capture the aspects that are not attributed to them in the above description. For example, RBAC can be configured to support IFC [31,33] and finer-grained access [2,20,30], ABAC can be configured to support roles and IFC [19], MAC can emulate RBAC [22]. However, such configurations are unintuitive and cumbersome to manage. Using three models instead of a single model naturally incurs performance overhead. On of our major goals is to minimize this overhead caused while combining these models.

Table 1 summarizes the benefits and shortcomings of each of the three models. From the table, it is evident that while each of the three models has its own strengths, it is difficult to cover all the requirements using any one of them effectively. Trying to capture all the requirements with any one of these models will result in unintuitive and hard-to-manage policies. Using three different policies help in separating the requirements based on their nature and create modular policies. So it would be more effective to use these models without changing their inherent characteristics and combine them in such a way as to we gain best of each of the component models without significant performance overhead. In this paper, we combine these three models – RBAC, MAC, and ABAC– using a modular approach to get the best of each of the models and provide comprehensive access control.

4 Preliminaries

Basic authorization concepts of RBAC [32] and ABAC [15] are well-known. Hence, for the purpose of brevity, we refer the reader to standard expositions. In this section, we briefly describe a relatively new lattice-based MAC model called Readers-Writers Flow Model (RWFM) that is used in Samyukta.

4.1 Readers-Writers Flow Model

Readers-Writers Flow Model (RWFM) [24] is a decentralized information flow model. It is complete with respect to the Denning's model [11,24] and can be used to provide both confidentiality and integrity. It supports dynamic labeling and downgrading. Also, it can capture several well-known models such as Bell-LaPadula (BLP) [5], Biba [6], Chinese Wall [7]. These features make RWFM better suited for mainstream application. So, in Samyukta, we use RWFM as the MAC module. Its labeling and access rules are provided below:

Labeling: Let S and O be the set of subjects and objects in the system respectively. An RWFM label (RW $Class$) is defined as a triplet (s, R, W). Where $s \in S$ denotes the owner of the information in the class. $R \in 2^S$ denotes the set of subjects which can read the objects of the class. $W \in 2^S$ denotes the set of subjects that can write or have influenced the class.

Since objects are passive entities, in the RWFM implementation their labels are static, i.e., once a label is assigned to an object, it remains unchanged. Whereas in the case of subjects, which are dynamic in nature, the labels can change. When a subject is created, it has gained no information. Such a subject is positioned at the bottom of the lattice. Which means, the readers of the newly created subject includes all the subjects in the system and the only writer is just the subject itself (as no other subject has yet influenced it). Thus, on creation, a subject's *readers* (R) is set to S and *writers* (W) is set to the subject itself. After this initialization, the label can change according to the information gain as the subject performs various operations.

Access Rules: With the above labeling model in place, access rules of RWFM are specified as follows:

- *Read(slabel, olabel)*- RWFM provides flexibility by supporting reading-up i.e a subject s can read an object o that is higher up in the lattice provided $owner(s) \in R(o)$. Before allowing the access, the label of the subject is modified and moved up the lattice to reflect the information gain. So, when a subject s_1 with label *slabel* of the form (s_1, R_1, W_1) reads an object o_1 with label *olabel* of the form (s_2, R_2, W_2), its label is changed as follows: $(s_1, R_1, W_1) \bigoplus (s_2, R_2, W_2) = (s_1, R_1 \cap R_2, W_1 \cup W_2)$.
- *Write(slabel, olabel)*- A subject s_1 with label *slabel*:(s_1, R_1, W_1) is allowed to write an object o_1 with label *olabel*:(s_2, R_2, W_2) if $s_1 \in W_2$ and $R_1 \supseteq R_2$ and $W_1 \subseteq W_2$.

5   Samyukta: A Unified Access Control Model

In this section, we present our unified model Samyukta. We first discuss the model's formal specification. We then describe the request flow in Samyukta and its authorization procedure.

5.1   Formal Specification

The specification of Samyukta consists of basic access control components and components relevant to RBAC, MAC, and ABAC models. The basic components include:

- $U-$ a set of authorized users in the system.
- $S-$ a set of subjects/sessions in the system.
- $O-$ a set of objects in the system.
- $Op-$ a set of operations (actions) that can be performed on the objects.
- $owner(e : S \cup O) \to U$ is a function that maps an entity e (subject or object) to its corresponding owner.

Components relevant to RBAC are:

- $R-$ denotes a set of roles where a role represents a job function in the organization.
- $RH \subseteq R \times R$ is a partial order on R that denotes the role hierarchy where $(r_1, r_2) \in RH$ implies that r_1 is higher up in the hierarchy and therefore inherits all the permissions of r_2. It can also be denoted as $r1 > r2$.
- $PERMS \subseteq O \times Op$ is the set of permissions that are allowed in the system.
- $UA \subseteq U \times R$ is a many to many mapping from users to roles.
- $PA \subseteq PERMS \times R$ is a many to many mapping from permissions to roles.
- $active\_roles(s : S) \to 2^R$ is a function that maps session s to a set of roles that are active in the session.
- $avail\_session\_perm(s : S) \to 2^{PERMS}$ is function that maps a session s to the set of permissions available in that session.
- C represents the constraints used with respect various RBAC configuration components such as UA, PA, RH, etc.

Components relevant to MAC are:

- L represents the set of security labels.
- $\leq \subseteq L \times L$ represents permissible information flows. $l1 \leq l2$ where $l1, l1 \in L$ indicates that information in $l1$ can flow to $l2$.
- $\bigoplus : L \times L \to L$ represents the label combination (Least Upper Bound) operation.
- $\lambda : S \cup O \to L$ is a function that assigns labels to subjects and objects.
- $FlowDirection : Op \to \{in, out, both, none\}$ is a function that denotes the type of information flow caused by an operation $op \in Op$. Here in denotes information flow from object to subject (as in case of $read$), out denotes flow from subject to object (as in case of $write$), $both$ denotes flow in both the directions, and $none$ denotes no information flow.

Finally, components of the ABAC module are as follows:

- $UAtt$ represents the set of user attribute names.
- $SAtt$ represents the set subject attribute names.
- $OAtt$ represents the set of object attribute names.
- $EAtt$ represents the set of environment attribute names.
- $Range(a)$ denotes a function that maps an attribute $a \in UAtt \cup SAtt \cup OAtt \cup EAtt$ to the set of all possible values for a.
- $\forall ua \in UAtt,\ \exists f_{ua} : U \to Range(ua)$ represents a function that maps a user to its value for attribute ua.
- $\forall sa \in SAtt,\ \exists f_{sa} : S \to Range(sa)$ represents a function that maps a subject to its values for attribute sa.
- $\forall oa \in OAtt,\ \exists f_{oa} : O \to Range(oa)$ represents a function that maps an object to its value for attribute oa.
- $\forall ea \in EAtt,\ \exists ea \mapsto Range(ea)$ represents a mapping from environment attribute ea to its current value.
- $Access\_Rules$ denotes a set of rules of the form $(op, Cond)$ where $op \in Op$ and $Cond$ corresponds to conditions specified in terms of attributes of users, subjects, objects, and environment.

This specification encompasses all the components necessary for RBAC, MAC, and ABAC models. We can divide the security requirements among the three models and specify three policies. Though we have the overhead of specifying three different policies, we get the benefits offered by each of these policies and having a modular policy gives the advantage of modifying one policy without affecting the other. Note that as per security requirements, we can also omit the components that are not needed in a specific system. For example, if a system does not require IFC, we can omit the MAC components, if a system requires separate roles for *working hours* and *non working hours*, then we can omit the *time* attribute. Thus with this generic and expressive specification, we can encode several of the existing access control models.

5.2   Request Flow in Samyukta

As mentioned, we use a modular approach where the modules are independent of each other so that they can be configured and managed separately. The three modules are ordered i.e., an access request is sent to the component modules in the specific order of RBAC$\longrightarrow$ MAC $\longrightarrow$ ABAC as shown in Fig. 4. The RBAC module specifies the maximum set of permissions available to a subject. The MAC module, which follows the RBAC module, allows the subset of accesses that satisfy the MAC rules and therefore are flow-secure. Here we use RWFM for MAC and in the rest of the paper we use RWFM and MAC interchangeably. The accesses that are allowed both by RBAC and MAC are forwarded to ABAC module which further applies constraints based on the attribute values.

The order in which the modules are used plays a vital role in harnessing the benefits of the individual modules. We use RBAC as the first modules as it is

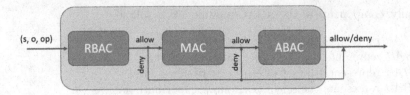

Fig. 4. Request flow through the modules

easy and straightforward to capture the organization's structure with it. It also provides easy management, scalability, and auditability. Hence we use RBAC to assign maximum set of permissions to the users and once RBAC captures the organization's structure through its roles and role hierarchies, MAC and ABAC modules are used to fine-tune these authorizations based on information flow and attribute based requirements. To reap the full benefits of fine-granularity, and dynamic nature of ABAC, it is used as the last module. Thus, MAC serves as the second module. Using MAC after RBAC enables use of the RBAC policy as the basis for labelling of subjects/objects for RWFM. This helps in keeping track of information flows and prevent information leaks caused by RBAC permissions.

The RBAC configuration in Fig. 1 clearly captures the job-based requirements of Example 1. However, as discussed, it fails to protect the sensitive information in *mgmtFile*. Using RWFM after RBAC helps in fulfilling such requirements by identifying and preventing indirect flows while providing adequate flexibility. The RWFM labels for objects of Example 1 would be (note that here we use the labels at the granularity of roles instead of subjects):

- *mgmtFile*: $\{manager, \{manager\}\{manager\}\}$ The *mgmtFile* can be read and written by only *manager*. Therefore, the *readers* and *writers* components of the label have single element.
- *txnFile*: $\{clerk, \{manager, clerk\}\{manager, clerk\}\}$ Since the *txnFile* can be read and written by both *manager* and *clerk*, both are part of the *readers* and *writers* components of the label.

When a subject s corresponding to Mg is created, its label will be initialized to $\{manager, \{manager, clerk\}\{manager\}\}$. With these labels set, when s reads *mgmtFile*, as per the RWFM read rule, its label changes to $\{manager, \{manager\}, \{manager\}\}$. Now when s tries to write to *txnFile*, RWFM write rule fails ($R(s) \not\supseteq R(txnFile)$) preventing the transitive flow, and thereby fulfilling the requirement. Thus, with dynamic labeling, RWFM effectively prevents indirect information flows and also proves to be more flexible than the traditional models like BLP [24].

Finally, the ABAC module deployed at the end provides authorization at a finer granularity. For Example 1, with most of the requirements covered by RBAC and MAC, the ABAC has to cover only the two constraints on write operation. This can be easily specified by using the attributes *object_type*, *location*, *time*, and *day*. With these attributes, a policy can be defined as shown Fig. 5. ABAC module is useful especially in systems where access decisions need to be taken based on continuous-valued attributes such as time, temperature, etc., mainly because it is difficult capture such authorization with other models.

ABAC Policy

1. $(write, (object\_type(o) = transaction \land day = working\_day \land time = working\_hour))$
2. $(write, (object\_type(o) = management \land location = office)$

Fig. 5. ABAC policy in Samyukta

Using the ABAC model as the last model is also useful with respect to performance. Compared to RBAC and MAC, ABAC is performance intensive. As ABAC is used mainly to constrain the earlier models' permissions, its policy size would be significantly smaller (compared to a standalone ABAC policy such as the policy in Fig. 3) and therefore requires less computation. Also, as ABAC processes only those requests allowed by the previous two models, it avoids unnecessary evaluations of ABAC rules for all the requests and helps achieve good performance.

Thus, whether an access is permitted by Samyukta, depends on whether the subject's role is authorized to perform the access, whether the information flow caused by the action is permitted, and finally, whether all the dynamic and fine-grained constraints are satisfied.

Samyukta also aids the models to complement one another effectively. The fine-grained access control of ABAC overcomes the coarse-granularity in RBAC and RWFM. RBAC's drawbacks of role explosion, lack of flexibility, and dynamic parameters are overcome with the flexible and dynamic ABAC. Lack of information flow control in RBAC is overcome with MAC. ABAC's drawbacks in terms of scalability, policy management, and performance are overcome with RBAC and MAC.

As discussed above, the order of models used in Samyukta has several benefits that are useful in most of the cases. However, in certain cases, depending on the granularity of the attribute, and the access requirements, we can also use ABAC before RBAC. For example, in the scenario discussed in Example 1, if all the accesses are allowed only within the office, then we can check the *location* attribute first. We can check other modules only if value of the attribute *location* is *office*. This way, we can avoid evaluation of other modules and speed of the authorization.

5.3   Authorization Procedure

Now, we describe how an access request is processed by Samyukta. Given a Samyukta configuration and an access request of the form (s, o, op) where s is a subject id, o is an object id, and op is an operation, Samyukta first sends the request to the RBAC module followed by the MAC and ABAC modules. If any of these modules denies the access, the request is not forwarded to the next modules, and it is denied by Samyukta. A request is authorized only if it is authorized by all three modules. This procedure is described in Algorithm 1. The authorization in the individual modules are described below:

Algorithm 1: SamyuktaAuthorization

Input : A Samyukta configuration and an access request *Req* of the form
            (s, o, op)
Output: Authorization decision of Samyukta: ALLOW or DENY
if *RBAC_Authorization(Req)* then
│   if *MAC_Authorization(Req)* then
│   │   if *ABAC_Authorization(Req)* then
│   │   │   return ALLOW
│   │   end
│   end
end
return DENY

RBAC Authorization: The authorization of RBAC is simple. When an access request is received, the module extracts the subject's active roles and checks if any of these roles have the requested permission. If so, the access is allowed else denied. As the procedure is fairly straightforward, we omit the algorithm for brevity.

MAC Authorization: Here we first extract the RWFM labels of subject and object using the corresponding IDs and then depending on the direction of the information flow, we apply the RWFM access rules discussed in Sect. 4. The authorization procedure used in this module is given in Algorithm 2. Here, *Read()* and *Write()* functions apply the RWFM read and write rules respectively and return *True* (success) or *False* (failure).

ABAC Authorization: When the ABAC module receives a request, it extracts the associated attributes and then evaluates the access rules applicable for the requested operation (this is done by *eval()* function that evaluates the conditions of the rule with respect the extracted attributes). If the conditions are satisfied, the access is allowed otherwise denied. This procedure is described in Algorithm 3. Note that since ABAC is mainly used to constrain the permissions given by the previous modules, if no rule applies to a request, the request will be permitted by ABAC. Therefore, if there are no constraints on an operation (as in case of the read operation in Example 1), then we do not have to specify any ABAC rules for it and such operations can be allowed without evaluating any ABAC rules.

Algorithm 2: MAC_Authorization

Input : An access request *Req* of the form (s, o, op)
Output: Authorization decision: ALLOW or DENY
slabel = getSubjectLabel(s)
olabel = getObjectLabel(o)
flow_dir = getFlowDirection(op)
if *flow_dir = none* **then**
  | return ALLOW
else if *flow_dir = in* **then**
  | **if** *Read(slabel, olabel)* **then**
  | | return ALLOW

end
else if *flow_dir = out* **then**
  | **if** *Write(slabel, olabel)* **then**
  | | return ALLOW

end
else if *flow_dir = both* **then**
  | **if** *Read(slabel, olabel) AND Write(slabel, olabel))* **then**
  | | return ALLOW

end
return DENY

Algorithm 3: ABAC_Authorization

Input : An access request *Req* of the form (s, o, op)
Output: Authorization decision of: ALLOW or DENY
u = owner(s)
uatt = getUAttributes(u)
satt = getSAttributes(s)
oatt = getOAttributes(o)
eatt = getEAttributes()
foreach *(op, cond) in AccessRules* **do**
  | **if** *not eval(cond)* **then**
  | | return DENY
  | **end**
end
return ALLOW

---

6 Effectiveness of Samyukta

Here, we demonstrate the effectiveness of Samyukta by comparing it with the existing RBAC-ABAC hybrid model called RABAC [20]. RABAC is a role-centric model that extends the NIST RBAC model [13,32] with attributes and permission filtering policies (PFP). PFPs constrain the available set of permissions based on user and object attributes. Conceptually, it is similar to the way

Samyukta combines RBAC and ABAC, albeit with MAC in between them and different enforcement techniques.

In [20], the authors use a hospital example with two main roles, Doctor, and VisitDoc (visiting Doctor). Doctors are allowed to read their patients' records at any time. VisitDoc is only allowed to read authorized documents which are revealed for collaboration purpose with other hospitals and the request will only be approved during working hours and if made from any certified devices. In addition, visiting doctors from other hospitals are only allowed to view authorized documents pertaining to the projects they participate in. For the illustration, we use three objects $\{o1, o2, o3\}$ where $\{o1, o2\}$ are patient records and $o3$ is an *AuthorizedDoc*. To configure this example, RABAC uses two filtering functions, one for patient records and one for authorized docs. These filters are applied to all the requests, irrespective of whether the basic RBAC rules allow the request or not.

In case of Samyukta, the RBAC module uses PA to assign the maximum set of permissions to roles. ABAC applies its *Access_Rules* on the requests authorized by RBAC to constrain the permissions of RBAC. Some of the important components of Samyutka for this scenario are given in Fig. 6. Here we use three user attributes, *doctorof* which represents the patients of a doctor, *uproj* which represents the projects that a user is associated with, and *device* which corresponds to the device used by the user. It also uses three object attributes, *object_type*, which specifies the type of the object, *recordof*, which specifies the patient to whom the record belongs, and *oproj*, which represents the project (where object is a project file). Finally, it uses an environmental attribute *time* that indicates the time at which an access request has been made.

From the above illustration, we can observe that RABAC requires modifications to the standard RBAC model and requires processing attribute-based rules for every access request incurring performance overhead. Whereas in case of Samyukta, we can use the standard RBAC without any modification and therefore get the benefits that are inherent to the model and use attribute-based rules for only those requests that satisfy the RBAC rules which leads to better performance.

Note that here we have not used components related to the MAC model as there is no explicit IFC requirement in the example.

Configuration 1: Configuration for Hospital Scenario using Samyukta

- $PA : \{(doctor, (o1, view)), (doctor, (o2, view)), (visitDoc, (o3, view))\}$
- $UAtt = \{doctorof, uproj, device\}$ $OAtt = \{object\_type, recordof, oproj\}$ $EAtt = \{time\}$
- $Range(object\_type) = \{PatientRecord, AuthorizedDoc\}$
- $Range(uproj) = Range(oproj) = Projects$
- $Range(recordof) = Range(doctorof) = Patients$
- $Access\_Rules = \{(view, (object\_type(o) = PatientRecord \land recordof(o) \in doctorof(s)), (view, (object\_type = AuthorizedDoc \land device(s) = certified \land oproj(o) \in uproj(u) \land time = working))\}$

Fig. 6. Configuration for the hospital scenario

6.1   Merits of Samyukta

Some of the major advantages of Samyukta are briefed below:

- It is modular and hence supports independent configuration and management of each of the models.
- Since we don't modify the component models, it is possible to effectively use the existing standards, best-practices, verification techniques/tools for the modules.
- It gains benefits of all the component models.
- It is generic and can capture a spectrum of existing models.

7   Experimental Analysis

In this section, we demonstrate the performance of the prototype implementation of Samyukta. We have implemented Samyukta using Python 3.8 on a system running Ubuntu 20.04 with 16 GB RAM. RBAC and MAC implementations follow from existing implementations using simple data structures and set operations. ABAC implementation follows from a XACML-based design [29] and uses JSON for request and access rules specification.

As discussed, using the modules in the specified order where each module filters out the requests that it authorizes has a performance advantage. This is especially useful with respect to the ABAC module as evaluating attribute-based rules incur relatively high performance overhead. Unlike in previous works such as [20] and [30], Samyukta evaluates the attribute-based rules only for the requests that are permitted by both RBAC and MAC module and therefore saves significant computation.

To demonstrate the performance benefit of filtering the requests, we perform the following two executions and compare their execution times: (1) Without filtering: here we pass a set of requests *Reqs* to the three modules separately so that each module processes all the requests in *Reqs* (2) With filtering: here we process the requests in *Reqs* using Samyukta which uses the modules in sequence and requests are filtered out at each step.

We perform the experiment on three synthetic datasets (DS) shown in Table 2. We run each experiment 10 times and record the average time taken. We have set $|Reqs| = 200$ in each run to get a good mix of requests that go through all the modules when we pass them through the modules in sequence. The experiments' results for the three datasets for with and without request filtering are given in Table 3. From the results, it is evident that Samyukta gains significant performance by using the filtering approach.

Table 2. Datasets

	DS1	DS2	DS3
Users	5	10	20
Subjects	50	100	200
Objects	50	100	200
Roles	5	10	20
UAtt	5	10	20
SAtt	5	10	20
OAtt	5	10	20
EAtt	5	10	20

Table 3. Execution times for with and without request filtering

Dataset	Execution time (in microseconds)	
	Without filtering	With filtering
DS1	2879.51	23.37
DS2	3727.87	77.85
DS3	3794.10	98.30

Table 4. Execution times for different module orderings

Dataset	Execution time (in microseconds)					
	Samyukta	MRA	RAM	MAR	AMR	ARM
DS1	23.37	23.52	34.24	1248.26	2821.56	2893.72
DS2	76.05	77.85	132.12	1888.55	3741.21	3721.30
DS3	95.17	98.30	136.89	179.19	3795.56	3304.41

Also, among the 6 possible orderings of the modules possible, the order used by Samyukta provides better performance. We demonstrate this by comparing their execution times for processing the three datasets in Table 2 by Samyukta, MRA (MAC-RBAC-ABAC), RAM (RBAC-ABAC-MAC), MAR (MAC-ABAC-RBAC), AMR (ABAC-MAC-RBAC), and ARM (ABAC-RBAC-MAC). The execution times for different module orderings are shown in Table 4 (the approach used is same as that of the previous experiment). From the table it is clear that the order used by Samyukta provides better performance than the other orderings.

8 Conclusions

Providing easy-to-use, effective access control is crucial in protecting system resources from intended or unintended misuse. It is difficult to achieve all the desired authorization requirements in a contemporary system with a single access control model. In this paper, we have presented a unified model, Samyukta, that combines RBAC, MAC, and ABAC in such a way that the user can benefit from the best of all these models. The proposed solution is simple, elegant, and flexible so that the user can implement the solution as per their security requirements. Our experimental analysis has demonstrated that the filtering approach and the ordering of the modules used in the proposed model significantly improve its performance making it viable for practical usage.

Acknowledgement. The work presented in this paper was done at the Indian Institute of Technology Bombay and was supported by the Information Security Research and Development Centre, Ministry of Electronics and Information Technology, Government of India.

References

1. Abdunabi, R., Al-Lail, M., Ray, I., France, R.B.: Specification, validation, and enforcement of a generalized spatio-temporal role-based access control model. IEEE Syst. J. **7**(3), 501–515 (2013)
2. Al-Kahtani, M.A., Sandhu, R.S.: A model for attribute-based user-role assignment. In: CSAC, pp. 353–362 (2002)
3. Barker, S.: The next 700 access control models or a unifying meta-model? In: SACMAT Proceedings, pp. 187–196 (2009)
4. Batra, G., Atluri, V., Vaidya, J., Sural, S.: Deploying ABAC policies using RBAC systems. J. Comput. Secur. **27**(4), 483–506 (2019)
5. Bell, D.E., LaPadula, L.J.: Secure computer systems: mathematical foundations. Technical report MTR-2547-VOL-1, MITRE Corp., Bedford, MA (1973)
6. Biba, K.J.: Integrity considerations for secure computer systems. Technical report. MTR-3153-REV-1, MITRE Corp., Bedford, MA (1977)
7. Brewer, D.F.C., Nash, M.J.: The Chinese wall security policy. In: Proceedings of IEEE Symposium on Security and Privacy, pp. 206–214 (1989)
8. Chakraborty, S., Sandhu, R., Krishnan, R.: On the feasibility of RBAC to ABAC policy mining: a formal analysis. In: SKM, Proceedings, pp. 147–163 (2019)
9. Coyne, E., Weil, T.R.: ABAC and RBAC: scalable, flexible, and auditable access management. IT Prof. **15**(3), 14–16 (2013)
10. Damiani, M.L., Bertino, E., Catania, B., Perlasca, P.: GEO-RBAC: a spatially aware RBAC. ACM Trans. Inf. Syst. Secur. **10**(1), 2 (2007)
11. Denning, D.E.: A lattice model of secure information flow. Commun. ACM **19**(5), 236–243 (1976)
12. Fernández, M., Mackie, I., Thuraisingham, B.M.: Specification and analysis of ABAC policies via the category-based metamodel. In: Proceedings of the Ninth ACM Conference on Data and Application Security and Privacy, CODASPY 2019, pp. 173–184. ACM (2019)
13. Ferraiolo, D.F., Sandhu, R.S., Gavrila, S.I., Kuhn, D.R., Chandramouli, R.: Proposed NIST standard for role-based access control. ACM Trans. Inf. Syst. Secur. **4**(3), 224–274 (2001)
14. Gofman, M.I., Luo, R., Solomon, A.C., Zhang, Y., Yang, P., Stoller, S.D.: RBAC-PAT: a policy analysis tool for role based access control. In: Proceedings TACAS, pp. 46–49 (2009)

15. Hu, V.C., Ferraiolo, D., Kuhn, R., Friedman, et al.: Guide to attribute based access control (ABAC) definition and considerations. NIST Spec. Pub. 800 (162) (2013)
16. Hu, V.C., Kuhn, D.R., Xie, T., Hwang, J.: Model checking for verification of mandatory access control models and properties. Int. J. Softw. Eng. Knowl. Eng. $21(1)$, 103–127 (2011)
17. Huang, J., Nicol, D.M., Bobba, R., Huh, J.H.: A framework integrating attribute-based policies into role-based access control. In: SACMAT, pp. 187–196 (2012)
18. Jajodia, S., Samarati, P., Sapino, M.L., Subrahmanian, V.S.: Flexible support for multiple access control policies. ACM Trans. Database Syst. $26(2)$, 214–260 (2001)
19. Jin, X., Krishnan, R., Sandhu, R.S.: A unified attribute-based access control model covering DAC, MAC and RBAC. In: DBSec 2012 Proceedings, pp. 41–55 (2012)
20. Jin, X., Sandhu, R.S., Krishnan, R.: RABAC: role-centric attribute-based access control. In: MMM-ACNS Proceedings, pp. 84–96 (2012)
21. Kafura, D.G., Gracanin, D.: An information flow control meta-model. In: Conti, M., Vaidya, J., Schaad, A. (eds.) 18th ACM Symposium on Access Control Models and Technologies, SACMAT, pp. 101–112. ACM (2013)
22. Kuhn, D.R.: Role based access control on MLS systems without kernel changes. In: Proceedings of the 3rd ACM Workshop on RBAC, pp. 25–32 (1998)
23. Kuhn, D.R., Coyne, E.J., Weil, T.R.: Adding attributes to role-based access control. IEEE Comput. $43(6)$, 79–81 (2010)
24. Kumar, N.V.N., Shyamasundar, R.K.: A complete generative label model for lattice-based access control models. In: SEFM, Proceedings, pp. 35–53 (2017)
25. Mitra, B., Sural, S., Vaidya, J., Atluri, V.: Migrating from RBAC to temporal RBAC. IET Inf. Secur. $11(5)$, 294–300 (2017)
26. Osborn, S.L.: Mandatory access control and role-based access control revisited. In: Proceedings of the 2nd Workshop on RBAC, pp. 31–40 (1997)
27. Osborn, S.L.: Information flow analysis of an RBAC system. In: SACMAT Proceedings, pp. 163–168 (2002)
28. Phillips, C., Demurjian, S., Ting, T.: Towards information assurance in dynamic coalitions. IEEE IAW, USMA (2002)
29. pyABAC: Attribute Based Access Control (ABAC) for python. https://py-abac.readthedocs.io. Accessed Dec 2020
30. Rajpoot, Q.M., Jensen, C.D., Krishnan, R.: Attributes enhanced role-based access control model. In: TrustBus Proceedings, pp. 3–17 (2015)
31. Sandhu, R.S.: Role hierarchies and constraints for lattice-based access controls. In: Computer Security - ESORICS 96, Proceedings, pp. 65–79 (1996)
32. Sandhu, R.S., Ferraiolo, D.F., Kuhn, D.R.: The NIST model for role-based access control: towards a unified standard. In: Fifth ACM Workshop on RBAC, Berlin, Germany, 26–27 July 2000, pp. 47–63 (2000)
33. Stambouli, A., Logrippo, L.: Data flow analysis from capability lists, with application to RBAC. Inf. Process. Lett. 141, 30–40 (2019)
34. Tuval, N., Gudes, E.: Resolving information flow conflicts in RBAC systems. In: DBSec Proceedings, pp. 148–162 (2006)

Efficient and Effective Static Android Malware Detection Using Machine Learning

Vidhi Bansal$^{(\boxtimes)}$ ⓘ, Mohona Ghosh ⓘ, and Niyati Baliyan ⓘ

Department of Information Technology, Indira Gandhi Delhi Technical University for Women, New Delhi, India
vidhi015mtit20@igdtuw.ac.in

Abstract. The increasing use of android, its openness and lack of security checks have led to an alarming increase in malware applications. The traditional signature-based detection methods are inefficient against sophisticated malware, and lack scalability resulting in lingering concerns about their reliability. Given the state of affairs, there is an urgent need for a reliable and scalable alternative to signature-based techniques. In this work, we present an effective and reliable machine learning based approach for static android malware detection. We also propose an efficient and effective feature set consisting of 25 features. We achieve an accuracy of 94.68% using Random forest classifier on 20% test size. High recall of 94.67%, precision of 94.68% and f1 score of 94.68% were achieved. We implemented various existing android malware detection schemes and a detailed comparison reveal that the proposed scheme outperforms them all in all classification metrics.

Keywords: Malware detection · Machine learning · Security · Android security · Binary classification

1 Introduction

Android has emerged as the most popular operating system for smartphones. Android users have increased exponentially from 122 million in 2007 to 1535 million users in 2021[1]. In 2020 2.56 million applications were recorded on Google Play Store[2]. This astonishing growth rate in android market, open android ecosystem, vague permission management system, invoking of third-party code makes it a lucrative target for malware developers [14]. Every 10 s a new malware sample is fed to the android market [13]. Pegasus[3] is a well documented cases of Android malware. It is of the trojon horse family capable of tracking location, calls, reading SMS, and passwords of the victim.

---

[1] https://www.statista.com/statistics/263437/global-smartphone-sales-to-end-users-since-2007.

[2] https://www.statista.com/statistics/276623/number-of-apps-available-in-leading-app-stores.

[3] https://en.wikipedia.org/wiki/Pegasus_(spyware).

© The Author(s), under exclusive license to Springer Nature Switzerland AG 2022
V. R. Badarla et al. (Eds.): ICISS 2022, LNCS 13784, pp. 103–118, 2022.
https://doi.org/10.1007/978-3-031-23690-7_6

Signature based techniques extract the signature of an application from its APK and compare it against the existing known malware database signature. However, such techniques have proved to be ineffective on new malware samples. The high volume of new applications makes manual examination difficult. There is an urgent need for highly reliable and scalable android malware detection mechanism. Current malware applications employ polymorphic and obfuscation techniques to bypass different detection software. They encrypt the malicious payload, and insert dead code concealing the malicious piece of code making it difficult for signature based techniques to detect the malware. Zero-day detection of such malware is almost impossible [32, 35].

Researches in machine learning based techniques reveals that they can detect previously unseen or new malware and provides high detection rate [14]. Android malware detection technology can be divided into three categories: static, dynamic, and hybrid. Static detection identifies malware by scanning the APK without running it. It creates a feature set without executing the application. Its primary focus is on the API calls, permissions and library functions used by an application. [3, 7, 10, 11, 19, 30, 31, 33] use different techniques to perform static analysis for android malware detection. Dynamic detection extracts the features by running the Android application. Dynamic analysis identifies the network state, file input/output and other information leaks while the application is in a running state. [26] and [20] perform dynamic analysis of android, they have extracted features by running the applications in a sand-boxed environment. Static analysis is faster and more scalable than dynamic analysis. Hybrid detection combines both [16]. [18] employs a hybrid approach for android malware classification. In this work, we focus on the static analysis.

In this paper we analyse a set of static features obtained from the APK. Android applications are deployed in the form of APK. We decompile the APK to obtain the permissions, Android version, library and services called and used by an application. The permissions requested by an application should follow the principle of *least-privilege*. They tell the data flow revealing a lot about its runtime behaviour. Any exception to *least-privilege* indicates a malicious intent [13]. We selected 25 features and trained them on various Machine learning algorithms.

Contribution. The major contributions of this work are:

– An efficient and effective feature set of size 25.
– A reliable android malware detection mechanism with high accuracy of 94.68%, along with high precision of 94.68% and recall of 94.67%.
– Detailed comparative analysis of the work with existing techniques establish the supremacy of our work.

Organisation. Section 2 summarizes the previous and related Android malware detection techniques built around machine learning. Section 3 contains the detailed description of the approach, experimental framework, dataset description and evaluation of the current scheme. Section 4 compares the proposed work with existing techniques. In Sect. 5 we discuss the rationale of using 25 features. Section 6 concludes the paper.

2 Related Work

In this section we present the previous and related Android malware detection techniques built around machine learning.

[37] used permission features like $INTERNET, WRITE\_SMS, SEND\_ SMS, CALL\_PHONE, CHANGE\_CONFIGURATION$ to distinguish between malware and benign samples. Highest accuracy achieved by them was 91.75%. However, the dataset used by them consisted of only 200 samples. In [33] a parallel classification approach using applied machine learning clustering and heterogeneous machine learning algorithms, including Naïve Bayes, Decision Tree, Simple Logistic Regression is used. Their feature set consists of permissions, commands-related, and API call-related features. SIGPID [13] used a set of 22 significant permissions with Support Vector Machine as a classifier for malware detection. A permission pruning method was used to reduce the number of permissions from 135 to 22. Their classification accuracy is 93.62% on 2000 malware samples. [29] used dynamic analysis to construct the feature set for malware detection. They used the APIMonitor tool to record the APIs called by the malware at runtime. Android Virtual Device (AVD) was used for collecting application logs. Each apk was executed in DroidBox- a tool for dynamic android application analysis. Dataset used by them consisted of 34000 samples. Accuracy was 92.5%. In [21], the authors evaluated the performnace on CICInvesAndMal2019 dataset and obtained accuracy of 96.05%. They used Principal Component Analysis (PCA) as the feature reduction technique. [20] claimed that runtime behavior modelling is an effective approach towards Android malware classification. The authors used machine learning-based classification method with the runtime behavior of an executable for building feature vector. In [27] PCA-Relief is used for feature reduction with SVM classifier. [8] received an accuracy of 81% on sample size of 5902. The feature set was constructed using manifest permissions. The reliability of current machine learning based detection techniques is questionable owing to less sample size and moderate classification results.

3 Methodology

In this section we summarize the dataset, machine learning classifiers used, and evaluation parameters used to assess the performance of the proposed method. Figure 1 presents schematic diagram of the proposed Static Android malware detection.

In Table 1 system configurations on which experiments were performed are given.

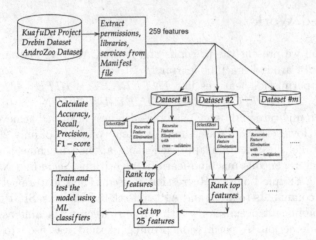

Fig. 1. Proposed static android malware detection

Table 1. System configuration

RAM	8 GB
Hard disk	1 TB
Operating System	Windows 10

3.1 Dataset Description

In this work, we used following three standard datasets-

- KuafuDet Project[4] [6]
- Drebin Dataset[5] [2]
- AndroZoo Dataset[6] [1]

Table 2 summarises the datasets used. The KuafuDet and Drebin datasets are used to collect 2,000 and 4,000 malicious samples, respectively. For collecting 6,000 latest benign samples, AndroZoo is used.

Table 2. Dataset description

Source	No. of APKs	Benign/Malicious
AndroZoo	6000	Benign
Drebin	4000	Malicious
KuafuDet	2000	Malicious

---

[4] https://nsec.sjtu.edu.cn/kuafuDet/download.html.
[5] https://www.sec.cs.tu-bs.de/~danarp/drebin/index.html.
[6] https://androzoo.uni.lu.

3.2 Feature Set

In this subsection we explain the process of extraction and selection of the Feature set.

Each APK was decompiled to fetch the permissions, services, libraries used by an Android application. Initially, 259 features were extracted.

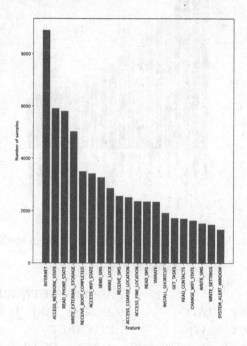

Fig. 2. Top 20 features present in most instances

Figure 2 shows the Top 20 features present in most instances. INTERNET is accessed by almost all the applications. Figure 3 depicts the top 20 features present in most benign instances and Fig. 4 shows the top 20 features present in most malware instances. Following features appear in the top 20 features of malware but not in benign applications CALL_PHONE, CAMERA, com.google.android.maps, RECEIVE, READ_EXTERNAL_STORAGE.

To reduce the time and memory complexity the 259 feature set was reduced to feature set of top 25 features. The rationale of using 25 features is discussed in Sect. 5. We selected the features using omni-ensemble toolkit- OptimalFlow[7]. It performs feature permutation and rescaling before creating various subsets of dataset. Subsets are created using horizontal partitioning. Each subset then extracts features using SelectKBest, Recursive Feature Elimination, Recursive Feature Elimination using Cross Validation. Top features are ranked for getting the best features. Final feature set used is given in Table 3.

---

[7] https://optimal-flow.readthedocs.io/en/latest/index.html.

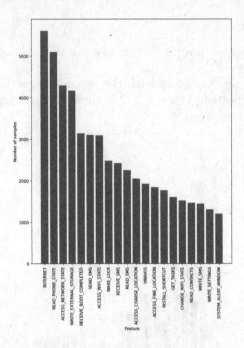

Fig. 3. Top 20 features present in most benign instances

Table 3. Feature set

'SEND_SMS'	'ACCESS_NETWORK_STATE'
'READ_PHONE_STATE'	'ACCESS_FINE_LOCATION'
'ACCESS_WIFI_STATE'	'INTERNET'
'WRITE_EXTERNAL_STORAGE'	'ACCESS_COARSE_LOCATION'
'WRITE_SETTINGS'	'READ_CONTACTS'
'RECEIVE_BOOT_COMPLETED'	'INSTALL_SHORTCUT'
'WAKE_LOCK'	'VIBRATE'
'READ_HISTORY_BOOKMARKS'	'READ_SETTINGS'
'GET_TASKS'	'GCMBroadcastReceiver'
'READ_SMS'	'SYSTEM_ALERT_WINDOW'
'CHANGE_WIFI_STATE'	'BootReceiver'
'UNINSTALL_SHORTCUT'	'CALL_PHONE'
'GET_ACCOUNTS'	

3.3 Machine Learning Classifier

We trained and tested the feature set on the following machine learning classifiers at test size of 10%, 20%, 30%, and 40%.

Decision Tree. Decision Tree transforms the dataset into an inverted tree using the decision rule [23] and is well suited for large and complicated datasets [22].

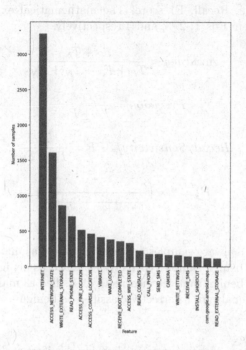

Fig. 4. Top 20 features present in most malware instances

Random Forest. Random forests constructs multiple decision tree and merge them giving more stable and accurate prediction overcoming the problem of overfitting [9].

K Nearest Neighbours. k-NN works on the assumption that *"similar things exist in proximity"*. Distance between training data and test data is computed. Data points are sorted in ascending order. Top k points are picked and the most frequent class is assigned to the test point [24].

Logistic Regression. Logistic Regression uses a probabilistic approach [28]. It uses a logistic model with given parameters and then computes the data from coefficients.

Naive Bayes. Naive Bayes assumes independence between features and uses a probabilistic approach to predict the class [4].

Support Vector Machines. Support Vector Machine constructs a hyperplane in a multi-dimensional space for differentiating and separating data points with maximum possible distance and least error [5].

3.4   Evaluation

In this work, following metrics were used to evaluate the model's performance-accuracy, Precision, Recall, F1 score. The mathematical expression for these metrics are stated in Eqs. 1, 2, 3, and 4 respectively.

$$Accuracy = \frac{T_P + T_N}{T_P + F_P + T_N + F_N} \tag{1}$$

$$Precision = \frac{T_P}{T_P + F_P} \tag{2}$$

$$Recall/Sensitivity/TPR = \frac{T_P}{T_P + F_N} \tag{3}$$

$$F1 = 2 \times \left(\frac{1}{\frac{1}{Precision} + \frac{1}{Recall}} \right) \tag{4}$$

where,

- T_P: number of malware samples correctly classified as malicious
- T_N: number of benign samples correctly classified as benign
- F_P: number of benign samples incorrectly classified as malicious
- F_N: number of malware incorrectly classified as benign

Table 4. Accuracy of various machine learning classifiers at different test size

Test size (in %)	Random forest	KNN	SVM	Naive Bayes	Decision Tree	Logistic Regression
10	0.9327	0.9385	0.9277	0.8588	0.9336	0.9219
20	0.9468	0.9306	0.9427	0.8671	0.9252	0.9132
30	0.9402	0.9310	0.9324	0.8607	0.9294	0.9211
40	0.9346	0.9186	0.9337	0.8529	0.9298	0.9211

Table 5. Precision of various machine learning classifiers at different test size

Test size (in %)	Random forest	KNN	SVM	Naive Bayes	Decision Tree	Logistic Regression
10	0.9331	0.9388	0.9281	0.8622	0.9339	0.9222
20	0.9468	0.9318	0.9438	0.8704	0.9259	0.9133
30	0.9403	0.9318	0.9336	0.8668	0.9297	0.9214
40	0.9350	0.9185	0.9340	0.8569	0.9304	0.9212

We evaluated the above mentioned machine learning classifiers on test size of 10%, 20%, 30%, and 40%. The results are presented in Tables 4, 5, 6, and 7. Following are the observations from them:

Table 6. Recall of various machine learning classifiers at different test size

Test size (in %)	Random forest	KNN	SVM	Naive Bayes	Decision Tree	Logistic Regression
10	0.9325	0.9383	0.9276	0.8548	0.9330	0.9215
20	0.9467	0.9301	0.9419	0.8654	0.9247	0.9131
30	0.9400	0.9304	0.9316	0.8600	0.9295	0.9209
40	0.9341	0.9187	0.9336	0.8522	0.9294	0.9209

Table 7. F1 score of various machine learning classifiers at different test size

Test size (in %)	Random forest	KNN	SVM	Naive Bayes	Decision Tree	Logistic Regression
10	0.9328	0.9385	0.9279	0.8585	0.9335	0.9219
20	0.9468	0.9310	0.9428	0.8679	0.9253	0.9132
30	0.9402	0.9311	0.9326	0.8634	0.9296	0.9212
40	0.9345	0.9186	0.9338	0.8546	0.9299	0.9211

- Table 4 shows that all classifiers gave high accuracy except Naive Bayes which assumes independence amongst features. Random forest gave the highest classification accuracy of 94.68% for 20% test size. Random Forest being an ensemble method use the rule of majority for classification. 35 classifiers were used in Random Forest. We used *'Rbf'* kernel for SVM. SVM, Decision Tree, and KNN also gave high accuracy. In KNN we chose $n = 5$.
- In Table 5 precision values are presented. As shown in Eq. 2 it shows the ability of the classifier to detect the True positives amongst the total values classified as positives. Random Forest had the highest recall. For standard 20% test size recall value is 0.9467 i.e. amongst the total samples classified as malware, 94.67% were correctly classified.
- Table 6 depicts the Precision value of the classifiers. As given in Eq. 3 it shows the ability of the classifier to detect the True positives amongst the total positives. Random Forest had the highest Precision. For standard 20% test size Precision value is 0.943 i.e. amongst the total malware samples, 94.3% malware were correctly classified.
- Table 7 shows the F1 score. Highest F1 score for 20% test size was 0.9468.

4   Comparison with Existing Approaches

We compared the feature set proposed by other researches with our work. We evaluated their feature sets on our dataset for ensuring uniformity of experiments. Following schemes were used for comparison.

- Mazlan and Hamid (2017) [15]: This work proposed 2 feature sets using TF-IDF method and Weighted-based Feature Selection mechanism. Each set consisted of 10 items.
- Li et al. (2018) [13]: In this paper the authors reduced the permission set to 22. They proposed 2 sets using Multi-Level Data Pruning (MLDP) and Mutual information method.

- Yildiz and Doğru (2019) [34]: The authors propose 16 features reduced using genetic algorithm.
- Pehlivan et al. (2014) [17]: In this work, the authorS propose 34 features. They reduced the feature set using 7 different feature selection algorithms.
- Wang et al. (2014) [25]: In this work the authors used Corrcoef, T-test, Mutual Information to propose 3 feature sets each of size 40.
- Kyaw and Kham (2019) [12]: In this scheme, a three level data pruning technique is used to reduce the feature set to 22 permissions.

Table 8. Comparison of proposed work with existing schemes

Metric	Propo-sed Work	Pehl-ivan et al. (2014)	Yildiz and Doğru (2019)	Kyaw and Kham (2019)	Mazlan and Hamid (2017) Weight-ed based	Mazlan and Hamid (2017) TF-IDF	Li et al. (2018) MLDP	Li et al. (2018) Mutual Inform-ation	Wang et al. (2014) Corr-coef	Wang et al. (2014) Mutual Inform-ation	Wang et al. (2014) T-test
Accuracy	**0.9468**	0.9360	0.9024	0.9231	0.8966	0.7673	0.9306	0.8999	0.9285	0.9273	0.9269
Recall	**0.9467**	0.9354	0.9024	0.9229	0.8959	0.7643	0.9302	0.8999	0.9283	0.9273	0.9269
Precision	**0.9468**	0.9362	0.9024	0.9233	0.8973	0.7975	0.9310	0.8998	0.9286	0.9275	0.9271
F1 score	**0.9468**	0.9358	0.9024	0.9230	0.8963	0.7599	0.9305	0.8998	0.9285	0.9273	0.9269

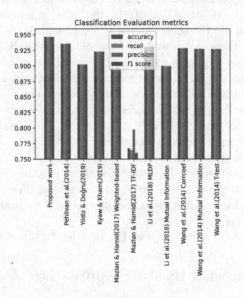

Fig. 5. Comparison of proposed work with existing schemes

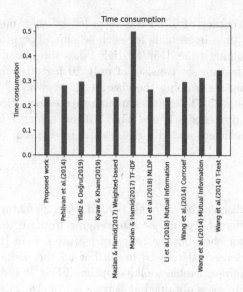

Fig. 6. Time comparison of proposed work with existing schemes

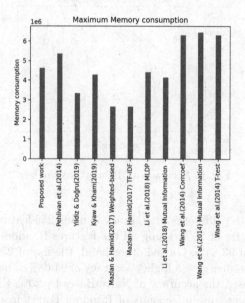

Fig. 7. Memory comparison of proposed work with existing schemes

Figure 5 and Table 8 shows the Comparison of proposed work with existing schemes based on Accuracy, Recall, Precision, and F1 score. It is evident that the proposed methodology outperforms the existing schemes in all the parameters establishing the reliability of proposed mechanism. Poorest results were recorded by [15] TF-IDF. Accuracy of 0.763 was recorded by their mechanism. Figure 6 shows the training time in seconds for each scheme. The proposed work takes least amount of training time. [15] TF-IDF takes the maximum training time even though their feature set consists of only 10 features. In Fig. 7 maximum memory consumption in training the classifier is shown. [17,25] Corrcoef, [25] Mutual Information, [25] T-test the maximum memory block required them is higher than the proposed scheme. They all use a bigger feature set. In the proposed work, an efficient and effective feature set is used.

5   Discussion

In this section, we discuss the rationale behind using 25 features. Figure 8 shows the accuracy at different feature set size ranging from 10 to 40. We leveraged the related works for choosing the range of feature set. In [12,13,15,17,25,34] range of feature set used is from 10 to 40. For all the sizes, we computed the feature set using omni-ensemble toolkit- OptimalFlow. It is evident from Fig. 8 that maximum accuracy is obtained at feature set of size 25.

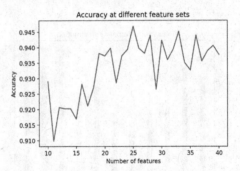

Fig. 8. Accuracy at different feature sets

Figure 9 shows the difference in accuracy in using 259 features and 25 selected features on a test size of 20%. Using all the features Random features gave the highest accuracy of 93.64%. On the other hand, the use of 25 features with the Random Forest classifier gave a higher accuracy of 94.68%. The use of 25 features significantly increased the accuracy of Naive Bayes by 20%. Figure 10 shows the difference in training time in seconds of Random Forest in using 259 features and 25 features. The use of 25 features uses less training time. The proposed feature set is also memory efficient as shown in Fig. 11. The maximum block of memory required by 25 features is far less than required by 259 features.

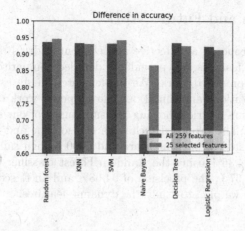

Fig. 9. Difference in accuracy in using 259 features and 25 features

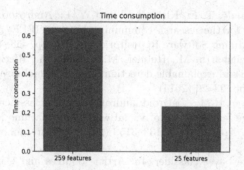

Fig. 10. Difference in training time of SVM in using 259 features and 25 features

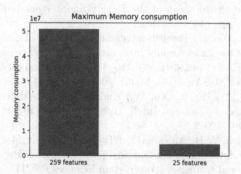

Fig. 11. Difference in maximum memory consumption of Random Forest in using 259 features and 25 features

6   Conclusion and Future Work

In this work, we proposed an effective and efficient android malware detection technique using 25 features. We provided a detailed comparison of the existing schemes with our proposed work. We implemented many existing techniques under uniform conditions and found out the proposed work outperforms them all in all classification metrics showing the supremacy of our scheme over state of art mechanisms. The proposed technique is also time and memory efficient. Dataset used consisted of 6000 malware and 6000 benign samples. We achieve high accuracy of 94.35% using the Random Forest classifier on 20% test size. A high recall of 94.67%, the precision of 94.68% and an f1 score of 94.68% was obtained. In future we plan to study the dynamic features.

References

1. Allix, K., Bissyandé, T. F., Klein, J., Traon, Y. L.: Androzoo: collecting millions of android apps for the research community. In: 2016 IEEE/ACM 13th Working Conference on Mining Software Repositories (MSR), pp. 468–471 (2016)
2. Arp, D., Spreitzenbarth, M., Hubner, M., Gascon, H., Rieck, K., Siemens, C.: Drebin: effective and explainable detection of android malware in your pocket. In: NDSS, vol. 14, pp. 23–26 (2014)
3. Bakour, K., Ünver, H.M.: VisDroid: android malware classification based on local and global image features, bag of visual words and machine learning techniques. Neural Comput. Appl. **33**(8), 3133–3153 (2020). https://doi.org/10.1007/s00521-020-05195-w
4. Bayes, T.: Naive bayes classifier. In: Article Sources and Contributors, pp. 1–9 (1968)
5. Boser, B.E., Guyon, I.M., Vapnik, V.N.: A training algorithm for optimal margin classifiers. In: Proceedings of the Fifth Annual Workshop on Computational Learning Theory, pp. 144–152 (1992)
6. Chen, S., Xue, M., Xu, L.: Towards adversarial detection of mobile malware: poster. In Proceedings of the 22nd Annual International Conference on Mobile Computing and Networking, MobiCom 2016, pp. 415–416. Association for Computing Machinery, New York, NY, USA (2016). https://doi.org/10.1145/2973750.2985246
7. Ding, Y., Zhang, X., Hu, J., Xu, W.: Android malware detection method based on bytecode image. J. Ambient Intell. Hum. Comput. (2020). https://doi.org/10.1007/s12652-020-02196-4.
8. Herron, N., Glisson, W.B., McDonald, J.T., Benton, R.K.: Machine learning-based android malware detection using manifest permissions. In: Proceedings of the 54th Hawaii International Conference on System Sciences (2021)
9. Ho, T.K.: Random decision forests. In: Proceedings of 3rd International Conference on Document Analysis and Recognition, vol. 1, pp. 278–282. IEEE (1995)
10. Huang, T.H.-D., Kao, H.-Y:.R2-d2: color-inspired convolutional neural network (CNN)-based android malware detections. In: 2018 IEEE International Conference on Big Data (Big Data), pp. 2633–2642 (2018). https://doi.org/10.1109/BigData.2018.8622324

11. Karimi, A., Moattar, M.H.: Android ransomware detection using reduced opcode sequence and image similarity. In: 2017 7th International Conference on Computer and Knowledge Engineering (ICCKE), pp. 229–234 (2017). https://doi.org/10.1109/ICCKE.2017.8167881

12. Kyaw, M.T., Kham, N.S.M.: Machine learning based android malware detection using significant permission identification. In: Seventeenth International Conference on Computer Applications (ICCA 2019)(2019)

13. Li, J., Sun, L., Yan, Q., Li, Z., Srisa-An, W., Ye, H.: Significant permission identification for machinelearning-based android malware detection. IEEE Trans. Industr. Inf. **14**, 3216–3225 (2018)

14. Liu, K., Xu, S., Xu, G., Zhang, M., Sun, D., Liu, H.: A review of android malware detection approaches based on machine learning. IEEE Access **8**, 124579–124607 (2020)

15. Mazlan, N.H., Hamid, I.R.A.: Using weighted based feature selection technique for android malware detection. In: Kim, K.J., Joukov, N. (eds.) ICMWT 2017. LNEE, vol. 425, pp. 54–64. Springer, Singapore (2018). https://doi.org/10.1007/978-981-10-5281-1_7

16. Pan, Y., Ge, X., Fang, C., Fan, Y.: A systematic literature review of android malware detection using static analysis. IEEE Access **8**, 116363–116379 (2020)

17. Pehlivan, U., Baltaci, N., Acartürk, C., Baykal, N.: The analysis of feature selection methods and classification algorithms in permission based android malware detection. In: 2014 IEEE Symposium on Computational Intelligence in Cyber Security (CICS), pp. 1–8. IEEE (2014)

18. Pektaş, A., Acarman, T.: Ensemble machine learning approach for android malware classification using hybrid features. In: Kurzynski, M., Wozniak, M., Burduk, R. (eds.) CORES 2017. AISC, vol. 578, pp. 191–200. Springer, Cham (2018). https://doi.org/10.1007/978-3-319-59162-9_20

19. Singh, A.K., Jaidhar, C.D., Kumara, M.A.A.: Experimental analysis of Android malware detection based on combinations of permissions and API-calls. J. Comput. Virol. Hacking Tech. **15**(3), 209–218 (2019). https://doi.org/10.1007/s11416-019-00332-z

20. Pektaş, A., Çavdar, M., Acarman, T.: Android malware classification by applying online machine learning. In: Czachórski, T., Gelenbe, E., Grochla, K., Lent, R. (eds.) ISCIS 2016. CCIS, vol. 659, pp. 72–80. Springer, Cham (2016). https://doi.org/10.1007/978-3-319-47217-1_8

21. Sangal, A., Verma, H.K.: A static feature selection-based android malware detection using machine learning techniques. In: 2020 International Conference on Smart Electronics and Communication (ICOSEC), pp. 48–51. IEEE (2020)

22. Song, Y.-Y., Ying, L.: Decision tree methods: applications for classification and prediction. Shanghai Arch. Psychiatry **27**, 130 (2015)

23. Swain, P.H., Hauska, H.: The decision tree classifier: design and potential. IEEE Trans. Geosci. Electron. **15**, 142–147 (1977)

24. Varmuza, K.: K-nearest neighbour classification (knn-method). In: Pattern Recognition in Chemistry, pp. 62–71. Springer, Heidelberg (1980). https://doi.org/10.1007/978-3-642-93155-0

25. Wang, W., Wang, X., Feng, D., Liu, J., Han, Z., Zhang, X.: Exploring permission-induced risk in android applications for malicious application detection. IEEE Trans. Inf. Forensics Secur. **9**, 1869–1882 (2014)

26. Wei, L., Luo, W., Weng, J., Zhong, Y., Zhang, X., Yan, Z.: Machine learning-based malicious application detection of android. IEEE Access **5**, 25591–25601 (2017). https://doi.org/10.1109/ACCESS.2017.2771470

27. Wen, L., Yu, H.: An android malware detection system based on machine learning. In: AIP Conference Proceedings, vol. 1864, p. 020136. AIP Publishing LLC (2017)

28. Wright, R.E.: Logistic regression. In: Grimm, L.G., Yarnold, P.R. (eds.), Reading and Understanding Multivariate Statistics, pp. 217–244. American Psychological Association, Washington, DC (1995)

29. Wu, W.-C., Hung, S.-H.: Droiddolphin: a dynamic android malware detection framework using big data and machine learning. In: Proceedings of the 2014 Conference on Research in Adaptive and Convergent Systems, pp. 247–252 (2014)

30. Yang, M., Wen, Q.: Detecting android malware by applying classification techniques on images patterns. In: 2017 IEEE 2nd International Conference on Cloud Computing and Big Data Analysis (ICCCBDA), pp. 344–347 (2017). https://doi.org/10.1109/ICCCBDA.2017.7951936

31. Yen, Y.-S., Sun, H.-M.: An android mutation malware detection based on deep learning using visualization of importance from codes. Microelectr. Reliab. **93**, 109–114 (2019). https://doi.org/10.1016/j.microrel.2019.01.007

32. Yerima, S.Y., Sezer, S., Muttik, I.: Android malware detection using parallel machine learning classifiers. In: 2014 Eighth International Conference on Next Generation Mobile Apps, Services and Technologies, pp. 37–42. IEEE (2014)

33. Yerima, S.Y., Sezer, S., Muttik, I.: Android malware detection using parallel machine learning classifiers. In: 2014 Eighth International Conference on Next Generation Mobile Apps, Services and Technologies, pp. 37–42 (2014b) . https://doi.org/10.1109/NGMAST.2014.23

34. Yildiz, O., Doğru, I.A.: Permission-based android malware detection system using feature selection with genetic algorithm. Int. J. Softw. Eng. Knowl. Eng. **29**, 245–262 (2019)

35. You, I., Yim, K.: Malware obfuscation techniques: a brief survey. In: 2010 International Conference on Broadband, Wireless Computing, Communication and Applications, vol. 85, pp. 297–300 (2010). https://doi.org/10.1109/BWCCA.2010

36. Yuan, Z., Lu, Y., Wang, Z., Xue, Y.: Droid-sec: deep learning in android malware detection. In: Proceedings of the 2014 ACM Conference on SIGCOMM, pp. 371–372 (2014)

37. Zarni Aung, W.Z.: Permission-based android malware detection. Int. J. Sci. Technol. Res. **2**, 228–234 (2013)

Attacks on ML Systems: From Security Analysis to Attack Mitigation

Qingtian Zou[1]([✉]), Lan Zhang[1], Anoop Singhal[2], Xiaoyan Sun[3], and Peng Liu[1]

[1] The Pennsylvania State University, State College, USA
{qzz32,lfz5092,px120}@psu.edu
[2] National Institute of Standards and Technology, Gaithersburg, USA
anoop.singhal@nist.gov
[3] California State University, Sacramento, USA
xiaoyan.sun@csus.edu

Abstract. The past several years have witnessed rapidly increasing use of machine learning (ML) systems in multiple industry sectors. Since security analysis is one of the most essential parts of the real-world ML system protection practice, there is an urgent need to conduct systematic security analysis of ML systems. However, it is widely recognized that the existing security analysis approaches and techniques, which were developed to analyze enterprise (software) systems and networks, are no longer very suitable for analyzing ML systems. In this paper, we seek to present a **vision** on how to address two unique ML security analysis challenges through ML-system-specific security analysis. This paper intends to take the initial step to bridge the gap between the existing computer security analysis approaches and an 'ideal' ML system security analysis approach.

Keywords: Machine learning · Deep learning · Security analysis

1 Introduction

The development and use of machine learning (ML) systems is significantly increased in the past several years. Autonomous cars are using object detection systems to process the images or videos from their cameras to understand the real-time traffic around them [12]; machine translation has been deployed in many languages [3]; Companies such as Mozilla [33], Google [5], IBM [2], and so on, have developed deep learning-based audio products. Even in art and entertainment, there exist "AI artists" that can compose poetry, sing songs, and draw [58].

As the usage of ML systems is on the rise, they are also attracting more and more attackers. One of the earliest famous attacks to ML system is Microsoft's Twitter chat-bot, Tay [1]. Built with online machine learning, Tay was led astray by some users, who ask Tay to repeat potentially harmful or inappropriate contents. In the end, Microsoft shut down Tay in short order due to its negatively impactful communicative behavior. This security incident indicates that it is increasingly more important to protect ML systems.

V. R. Badarla et al. (Eds.): ICISS 2022, LNCS 13784, pp. 119–138, 2022.
https://doi.org/10.1007/978-3-031-23690-7_7

Since security analysis is one of the most essential parts of the real-world ML system protection practice, there is an urgent need to conduct systematic **security analysis** of ML systems. However, it is widely recognized in the security community that the existing security analysis approaches and techniques, which were developed to analyze enterprise (software) systems and networks, are no longer very suitable for analyzing ML systems that are introducing new kinds of computations and adversarial behaviors. There are at least three main reasons for this. First, the security vulnerabilities of ML systems are different from the traditional enterprise networks. While the security vulnerabilities of traditional enterprise information systems are mainly associated with program logic and software implementation bugs, the vulnerabilities of ML systems are associated with not only traditional security bugs, but also some fundamental limitations of ML algorithms/models. For example, the existence of universal adversarial perturbations [30] is one of the fundamental limitations of deep learning algorithms. These fundamental limitations introduce a variety of adversarial attacks such as adversarial examples, data poisoning, and model backdoors.

Second, the architecture of a ML system and the architecture of a traditional enterprise information system are no longer similar. Besides the traditional software engineering perspective, ML systems also have other perspectives. In this paper, we present the ML perspective, the platform perspective, and the supply chain perspective, detailed in Sect. 2. These new perspectives and unique components introduce new challenges for security analysis.

Third, the above-mentioned two reasons introduce new kinds of causality relationships which are unable to be sufficiently handled by current approaches for security analysis. For example, attack graphs [21,45] are fundamental tools for enterprise security analysis but mainly focus on causal relationships between security vulnerabilities (such as CVEs - Common Vulnerabilities and Exposures [10]) and exploits (which mainly focus on newly gained permissions/accesses). In contrast, a good foundation for analyzing security issues in ML systems must also capture the causality relationships involved in adversarial attacks. It is clear that such causality relationships are not really relevant to traditional attacks that involve CVEs.

The adversarial consequences of ML systems are in many cases measured by the **severity** (e.g. the impact and damage) of these consequences. Here adversarial consequences include but are not limited to ML model output manipulation [25], model extraction [54] and membership inference [53]. The causal events must be systematically analyzed to understand how these adversarial consequences are generated. Below, we show a variability in the causal events encountered from attack scenarios - with some being straightforward and others being complex. This helps describe the necessity for a new approach for ML security analysis.

Example 1: Simple Causality Relation. In the autonomous driving scenario, a traffic sign recognition (TSR) system is used to recognize various traffic signs (e.g. speed limits, stop signs, cross roads, etc.). For practical usage, the TSR system is expected to recognize traffic signs correctly on a near real-time basis.

However, it has been verified that carefully spoofed traffic signs, though easily observed by humans, can still fool the TSR system [15, 27, 32, 35]. As shown in Fig. 1, the attacker can use a projector to project a crafted image on one stop sign and cause the sign to be misclassified as a "speed limit 50" sign by an approaching vehicle [27]. In this example, the causal events and their relationships are very clear: the image crafting attack action enables the projection event to fool the TSR system. Such attacks can lead to serious consequences such as paralyzed traffics and even injuries or worse.

Fig. 1. Stop sign attack [27]

Example 2: Complicated Causality Relation. As shown in Fig. 2, the attacker intends to trigger a neural network to translate a newly constructed English word into a specific meaning within another language (e.g. Spanish) [44]. In Fig. 2, each ellipse node represents a causal event, the rounded rectangle node represents the production, and each edge represents causality. The word-to-word translation ML system takes an English word as the input, and outputs the word with the same meaning in another language. It uses English Wikipedia as the training data source. Because Wikipedia is publicly editable, the attacker can post his/her pre-designed contents there. If those contents are gathered by the ML developers, then the training data is poisoned, which eventually results in a tainted ML model that acts wrongly to certain words. That is, if this word is given, instead of the correct word, the tainted model will output an arbitrary word of the attacker's choice. Although the attack sounds simple, it already involves multiple causal events and quite complicated causality relationships. Although we will not explain the individual causality relationships until Section IV, we note that the complexity is mainly caused by the logic of machine learning. In particular, (a) word embeddings (i.e., using a low-dimensional vector to represent a word) encode word "meaning" in such a way that distances between words' vectors correspond to their semantic proximity. (b) Instead of directly applying deep learning against the Wikipedia public data, the ML system firstly performs unsupervised learning to get the semantic embeddings. (c) Instead of directly poisoning the training data used by the deep learning agent, the attacker poisons the data used by the unsupervised learning agent, since an attack on the semantic embeddings can affect diverse downstream tasks.

Besides the "complicated causality relationships" challenge shown in Example 2, we find that ML system security analysis faces another daunting challenge, which is the rapid-changing deep learning techniques. Although the computing platform and the data supply chain are relatively stable for a particular ML-based application, new variants of ML models, like convolutional neural network

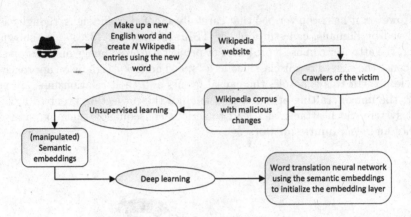

Fig. 2. Word-to-word translation attack

(CNN), recurrent neural network (RNN), and graph neural network (GNN), and ML methods, like supervised, semi-supervised, and self-supervised ML, keep on emerging, and the existing ML-based applications keep on evolving through adopting these new variants. Accordingly, new variants of adversarial attacks may keep on emerging. As a result, the set of causality relationships for the particular ML-based application may dynamically change from time to time, and this makes security analysis hard to keep pace with the changes. The causality relationships needs to be updated constantly in order to ensure the accuracy and validity of security analysis.

In this paper, we seek to present a **vision** on how one could address these daunting challenges - the complicated causality relationships and the constant changes of such relationships - through a ML-system-specific security analysis approach. This paper intends to take the initial step to bridge the gap between the existing cyber-attack security analysis approaches and an 'ideal' ML system security analysis approach. Specifically, we first review prior works which study ML system security from different aspects. Then, we identify the (quantitative) security analysis requirements of ML systems. Next, we propose a preliminary ML security analysis approach. Lastly, we present a case study showing how one could analyze the security associated with the word-to-word translation attack (see Fig. 2), and how the preliminary approach could be leveraged to mitigate security issues in ML systems. It should be noticed that since this is a vision paper, full development of the preliminary ML security analysis approach is out of the scope of this paper.

This paper is organized as follows. Section 2 provide a brief review of the existing works studying ML system security issues from various aspects. Section 3 identifies the security analysis requirements of ML systems. Section 4 depicts our vision of what the new ML system security analysis approach should be, and discusses a demonstrating use case. Section 5 discusses mitigation strategies in response to security issues of ML systems. Section 6 shows our conclusions.

2   ML Systems and Attacks

2.1   ML Systems Have Three Main Perspectives

Since ML systems are highly sophisticated, it is unlikely to gain a good under-standing of a ML system based on a single perspective view of the system. Rather, we find that ML systems have at least three essential perspectives, which are as follows.

The ML Perspective. The ML pipeline consists of two **sets** of cyclic or non-cyclic workflows. The first workflow *produces* deep learning (DL) models: raw data are processed to feed to a model which can be deployed in production systems. During training phase, the ML pipelines include four main steps. First, given a repository of Raw Data, they manually or semi-automatically annotate each unit of raw data with a label. Second, the data are processed including feature extraction and data structure formation for next step. Third, the Model Training step trains a model using the initial set of training data samples. Lastly, the trained models are deployed for the second workflow. The second workflow *consumes* DL models: they take (newly arrived) raw data as input, and output classification or prediction results. During test phase, when newly arrived unit of raw data needs to be classified, the unit will be sent to the Data Processing component and then be fed into the Deployed Model.

The Platform Perspective. Even for the same ML model, the model training platform is often different from the model deployment platform. For example, while a private cluster (e.g. Kubernetes) is employed to train a model, the trained model could be deployed in a public cloud environment (e.g. AWS). In case the trained model is deployed at the edge of a cloud, the computing resources could be much more restrictive.

The Supply Chain Perspective. We find there are three main supply chains involved in real-world ML systems. The data supply chain involves the data collection, data annotation, data processing, and data consumption. The model supply chain involves the usage of pre-trained models, the adoption of continuous model training, and the usage of foundation models (e.g. GPT-3). The library supply chain is a ML-specific type of software supply chain, since during the model training phase engineers usually use ML libraries provided by a upstream supplier/company.

2.2   Adversarial Attacks

As shown in Table 1, we classify the representative adversarial attacks based on the three supply chains mentioned in the previous section.

Evasion Attacks Through Adversarial Examples. The model supply chain are involved in evasion attacks because the attackers generally take advantage of vulnerabilities in the ML models. Evasion attacks refer to crafting malicious inputs during the test phase in order to evade the ML detection models. The

Table 1. Attack classification

Adversarial attacks	Attack name	Supply chain
Evasion attacks	L-BFGS attack [48]	Model
	FGSM attack [16]	Model
	BIM & ILCM attack [23]	Model
	JSMA attack [40]	Model
	DeepFool attack [31]	Model
	C&W attack [8]	Model
	Universal attack [30]	Model
	Zoo attack [11]	Model
	GAN attack [50,57]	Model
	RL based attack [19,22,56]	Model
Poisoning attacks	Backdoor attack [17,52]	Data & Model
	Trigger attack [24,26,34,36]	Data & Model
	Subpopulation attacks [20]	Data & Model
Exploratory attacks	Model inversion attack [13,14]	Model
	Model extraction attack [49]	Model
	Information inference attack [7,46]	Model
Software attacks	DOS attack [4,51]	Library
	Code execution attack [4,29,51]	Library
	Overflow attack [4,51]	Library
	Memory corruption attack [4,51]	Library

evasion attacks are grouped into two categories based on the access permission of the ML models. In the *white-box* scenario, attackers have access to the neural networks such as the architecture, parameters, training weights, and training data distribution. In the *black-box* scenario, attackers can only access to model information that is publicly available such as input format and classification confidential scores. However, they have no clue regarding the internal structure, parameters, and training datasets.

Since white-box attacks obtain detailed knowledge of the ML models, those attacks take advantage of the gradient of the network to generate perturbation on the inputs. Szegedy et al. [48] first identified the blind spot in deep learning models using small perturbations to the images. They proposed a box constrained L-BFGS algorithms to generate a small perturbation on original image so that it is misclassified by the models. Goodfellow et al. [16] proposed the Fast Gradient Sign Method (FGSM) algorithm to obtain an optimal max-norm constrained perturbation using the gradient of the cost function with respect to the input. Basic Iterative Method (BIM) and Iterative Least Likely Class Method (ILCM) developed by Kurakin et al. [23] extended and improved FGSM by iteratively generate adversarial samples in small step size. Jacobian-based Saliency Map Attack (JSMA) proposed by Papernot et al. [40] leveraged the saliency map to select critical features to modify the original binaries. Su et al. [47] perturbed the original image by using Differential Evolution. Moosavi-Dezfooli et al. [31]

proposed DeepFool algorithm that utilizes distance metric to measure the decision boundary of the target neural networks to perturb the image in an iterative manner. Carlini and Wagner [8] proposed gradient-based attacks to generate adversarial samples by calculating one back-propagation step. Moosavi-Dezfooli et al. [30] designed a universal perturbation that can be added to any image to evade the detection model. Yuan et al. [55] injected voice commands into songs to control the automatic speech recognition system without being noticed.

The black-box attacks generate an implicit approximation to the gradient of the networks using limited information. Papernot et al. [39] designed a substitute model to attack against the black-box models and then generated adversarial examples with the gradient of the substitute model. Zeroth order optimization based black-box attack estimates the approximate gradient using a finite difference method [11]. Generative Adversarial Network(GAN) is introduced to generate adversarial examples directly from the generative adversarial network [50,57]. Guo et al. [18] proposed an attack based on a greedy local-search technique. Reinforcement learning are also introduced to generate adversarial examples by adding small perturbations with the gradient of the loss function or the confidential score of the models [19,22,56].

Evasion attacks are very often conducted towards TSR systems. Nassi et al. [35] conducted a real-world experiment to fool advanced driver assistance systems using a drone equipped with a portable projector. The projector projected an incorrect traffic sign, e.g. speed limit sign, to a wall and the TSR system of a drive-by car was misled to classify the spoofed sign as a real sign. Gnanasambandam et al. [15] proposed a projector-camera system that transform the adversarial samples in the real metallic stop sign, and the TSR system misclassified it as a Speed 30 sign. Lovisotto et al. [27] proposed Short-Lived Adversarial Perturbations (SLAP) to generate physically robust real-world adversarial examples by using a projector in a variety of light conditions (including outdoors), and against state-of-the-art object detectors Yolov3 and Mask-RCNN and traffic sign recognizers Lisa-CNN and Gtsrb-CNN.

Poisoning Attacks and Backdoors. The goal of poisoning attacks is to craft malicious examples during the model training phase to plant a backdoor or vulnerability in the network models for future attacks. Both the data supply chains and model supply chains are involved in poisoning attacks because 1) attackers manipulate the training data, 2) the tainted data will affect the produced ML models, and 3) the affected ML models will be used for detection later.

Visible backdoor triggers, which are easily identified by humans, are first injected to the ML models by introducing a trigger including a pixel pattern and its target label. Gu et al. [17] demonstrated the potential vulnerabilities in the deep learning supply chain. If the model is trained with poisoned data, or if the model is based on a malicious pre-trained models, the attacker can leverage the backdoor in the ML models to evade detection. Xu et al. [52] investigated the backdoored DNN and proposed an effective defense method that can decrease the attack success rate and also correctly classify the clean images. Liu et al. [26] proposed a trojan trigger generation algorithm that takes the gradient of a cost function to generate masks on the initial images.

Invisible backdoor triggers proposed by Li et al. [24] used the gradient of loss function and saliency map to generate invisible triggers. Ning et al. [36] proposed an invisible poisoning attack in the black-box scenarios. Muñoz-González et al. [34] proposed a new algorithm based on back-gradient optimization for multiclass problems. Jagielski et al. [20] proposed subpopulation attacks that can misclassify a subpopulation in the data and maintain the performance of points outside this subpopulation. Patel et al. [42] introduced a method to inject spurious concepts that degrade the performance of the system.

Exploratory Attacks. The goal of exploratory attacks is to obtain the information about ML models so the model supply chain are affected. For example, model inversion attacks [13,14] can extract private and sensitive features and recover facial images with the outputs of ML model. Model extraction attacks via APIs [49] learn to extract parameters of popular model classes including logistic regression, neural networks, and decision trees. Inference attacks [7,46] gather relevant information from ML models, i.e., whether a given data belongs to the training set of the model.

Software Attacks. Software attacks are related to library supply chain, which leverage the vulnerability of dependency package to attack the ML systems. More than 10 new software bugs and their dependency packages, which cause heap overflow, integer overflow, crash, and denial-of-service (DoS) in several deep learning frameworks, have been reported [51]. [4] lists 299 vulnerabilities of Google Tensorflow reported since 2019. Products built on PyTorch versions below 2.3.24 [29] use unsafe YAML loading, which causes the embedded malicious code designed by attackers to be run locally.

3 Security Analysis Requirements of ML Systems

3.1 ML System Security Analysis Requirements

We envision that to successfully perform ML security analysis, a (quantitative) analysis approach should demonstrate the following:

- **R1:** The approach should address the "complicated causality relationships" challenge (see Example 2) through a systematic, largely automated approach.
- **R2:** The approach should help security analysts avoid common mistakes in keeping pace with changes due to ML system evolution and new variants of ML models and methods.
- **R3:** Since ML systems have three main perspectives, isolated component-level security analysis is very limited. The approach should be able to conduct synthesized security analysis at the ML system level.
- **R4:** Security analysis results should be explainable.
- **R5:** If a defense measure could result in notable attack mitigation effects, the defense measure and/or the mitigation effects should be able to be explicitly modeled in the approach.
- **R6:** Newly discovered ML system security issues does not need any methodological changes of the approach itself.

3.2   Limitations of Prior Work on ML Security Analysis

We divide the prior works into three groups: those that focus on individual attacks, those that do qualitative systematic analysis, and those that focus on traditional security analysis.

Individual Adversarial Attacks: Recently, a substantial amount of work has been done on analyzing individual adversarial attacks. Such works focus on a particular adversarial attack and/or a particular component of a ML system. In Sect. 2, we have already enumerated many such attacks, so we will not discuss such works in detail here. This kind of work shares the same limitation. That is, isolated security analysis provides limited understanding about how the adversary could exploit the dependencies between different components of a ML system. In many cases, simply adding up (e.g. weighted sum) all the individual security (and robustness) scores does not automatically result in very meaningful ML-system-level security analysis. Therefore, another approach at the ML system level is necessary.

Qualitative ML System Security Analysis: Such works [28,38] try to answer the question of how to synthesize the aforementioned individual security analysis results in a meaningful way. They first model the whole ML system, enumerate all possible attack surfaces and impacts, and then try to provide prevention/mitigation suggestions. However, being "qualitative" is not enough. ML system security should be quantified in a meaningful way.

Traditional Security Analysis: Classical security analysis approaches such as attack graphs [21,45] are fundamental for enterprise security analysis. Attack graphs can generate possible attack paths by analyzing the causal relationships between security vulnerabilities (such as CVEs existing in the network) and exploits. However, attack graph analysis is not adequate in analyzing ML systems due to the following reasons. First, attack graph analysis assumes that an attack path usually has several stages, and each stage requires the adversary to take a particular attack action. In addition, attack graph analysis assumes that these attack actions are identified based on the vulnerabilities detected by a network vulnerability scanner. In contrast, although an adversarial attack against a ML system also has one or more stages, it does not require the adversary to take an attack action during each stage. In most cases, it only requires the adversary to take a particular attack action (e.g., data injection) during the first stage. During each of the following stages, certain dependency between the attack action and a benign ML system action is leveraged (by the adversary) to propagate the malicious influence of the attack action, but a ML security analysis tool can no longer use a network vulnerability scanner to identify the dependency and the benign action. In sum, attack graph analysis tools focus on analyzing vulnerabilities, while ML security analysis tools should focus on analyzing dependencies. Second, MulVAL [37], a widely-used attack graph analysis tool, assumes that each security reasoning rule usually matches multiple kinds of vulnerabilities in real enterprise networks. Based on this assumption, new CVEs usually will not require MulVAL to add new rules. However, in the context of ML system security analysis, we find that each security reasoning rule usually only matches one particular type of adversarial attack. This indicates that whenever a new ML-system vulnerability is discovered, the current set of security reasoning rules may have to be extended.

4   Proposed Approach

In order to meet the requirements identified in the previous section, we propose a preliminary ML system security analysis (**ML-SSA**) approach that consists of the following two main parts:

- An **AI Security Causality (AISC) graph** which captures all the causality relationships that play a role in assessing the likelihood of adversarial consequences. Compared to traditional causality graphs such as attack graphs, the AISC graph is unique because it captures the intrinsic causality relations involved in adversarial attacks.
- A two-layer **ML system dependency (MLSD) graph** which not only captures the traditional kinds of dependencies in software systems, but also captures the dependencies introduced by the supply chain perspective of an ML system. A main motivation for the MLSD graph is that the MLSD graph could be used to identify a good portion of the edges and nodes in the AISC graph in a largely automated way.

4.1   The AI Security Causality Graph

The AISC graph is proposed to meet requirement **R1** described in Sect. 3.1. It also plays an essential role in meeting the other requirements. In order to illustrate the causality relationships involved in the word translation attack (see Fig. 2) mentioned in Sect. 1, we craft the corresponding AISC graph which is shown in Fig. 3. This example indicates that AISC graphs have the following characteristics:

- In an AISC graph, each node is a proposition (a.k.a statement) describing a pre-condition or a post-condition for a causal event, and each edge represents a particular causal relationship between two nodes. For example, proposition p_4 ("The Wikipedia corpus is poisoned") is a pre-condition for p_5 ("Unsupervised learning is abused"); and both p_4 and p_5 correspond to the unsupervised learning causal event.
- One causal event could have two or more pre-conditions. For example, only when the calculation result of formula "p_1 AND p_2 AND p_3" is True, post-condition p_4 can become True. More complicated relationships like "OR" can also be defined. Here in our demonstration, we only use the "AND" relationship for simplicity.
- The pre-conditions for one post-condition could include not only propositions about adversarial attacks, but also propositions about traditional software

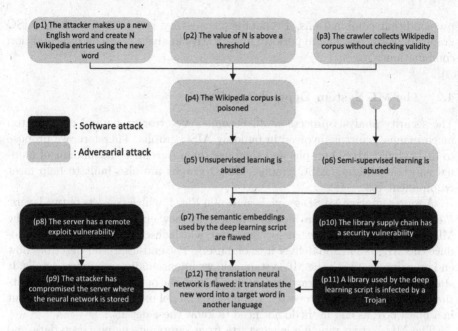

Fig. 3. The causality relationships involved in the word translation attack scenario.

attacks. For example, node p_{12} has three pre-conditions: while p_7 describes the effect of the attacker's data poisoning attack on semantic embeddings, p_9 and p_{11} describe two effects of the attacker's software attacks on the server and a library, respectively.

Regarding why AISC graphs can play an essential role in analyzing the adversarial consequences, we have the following observations. First, in order to avoid ignorance-related mistakes in analyzing adversarial consequences, it is important to gain awareness of all the relevant causality relationships. Following this principle, the ML-SSA approach requires AISC graphs to hold all the identified causality relationships.

Second, we observe that the causality relationships captured by AISC graphs enable logical reasoning through proposition logic. It is clear that such reasoning would play an essential role in analyzing adversarial consequences. Through such reasoning, we can identify alternative attack paths towards a particular adversarial consequence, and compare the different paths.

Third, we observe that AISC graphs make quantitative security analysis possible. For example, when analyzing data-poisoning attack in a ML system, the literature of data-poisoning attack is either focused on worst case analysis (i.e., whether such an attack is possible) or focused on estimating how many (e.g. x%) poisoned data samples are needed to make the attack succeed. In contrast, security analysis usually needs to make all the attack assumptions explicit and analyze not only the individual pre-conditions (of the attack) but also the pre-condition combinations. Probabilistic causality reasoning based on AISC graphs makes it possible to perform quantitative analysis based on pre-condition combinations.

4.2   The ML System Dependency Graph

The security analysis process could become very error-prone and costly if too much manual effort is involved in building AISC graphs. Therefore, we propose to firstly build MLSD graphs and then use them to reduce the amount of manual effort in building AISC graphs. MLSD graphs are also built to help meet requirement **R3**.

A representative MLSD graph is shown in Fig. 4, which consists of two layers: *the end-user layer*, which is intended to describe how end users interact with the ML system, and *the ML system pipeline layer*, which describes how developers produce the ML system and deliver it to end users. The end-user layer describes how end users interact with the ML system, and we intentionally omit many details. It starts with the user input raw data, and ends with the outputs. Other components such as how raw data is processed and how the model uses it for inference are put in a black box, as end users do not need to know these details.

The ML system pipeline layer starts from sampling engineer raw data and ends with an optimized model to be delivered to end users. It should be noted that the engineer raw data is different from that of user input, and we depict it as "engineer raw data pool". The user input raw data may not be collected by the developers, and even if they are collected, such data may not be sampled by the developers. As a result, the engineer raw data pool is usually a subset of all user input data, so we use two different nodes to depict them. The following ML functionalities, datasets, models, and supporting libraries show the pipeline of how the ML system is engineered, and each functionality is supported by the corresponding domain knowledge. For the sake of readability, only some typical domain knowledge is listed.

In the ML system pipeline layer, we define five kinds of nodes, which are ML functionalities (e.g., training, testing), supporting libraries (3rd party libraries helping implement a ML functionality), datasets (data objects involved in ML), models (models involved, no matter downloaded or self-trained), and domain knowledge (e.g., domain-specific features, loss functions), and three kinds of dependencies:

- *Data dependencies* are shown as a solid line in Fig. 4. They show how raw/processed data are transferred among different components. For example, the training dataset is the output of pre-processing, and is the input of model training. Because only data is directly involved, they are connected by data dependency.
- *Model dependencies* are shown as a dashed line in Fig. 4. Model dependencies can start with pre-trained models (if the ML developers do not want to start from scratch) or with model training (if the ML developers don't use existing models but start from scratch). Taking the evaluation node as an

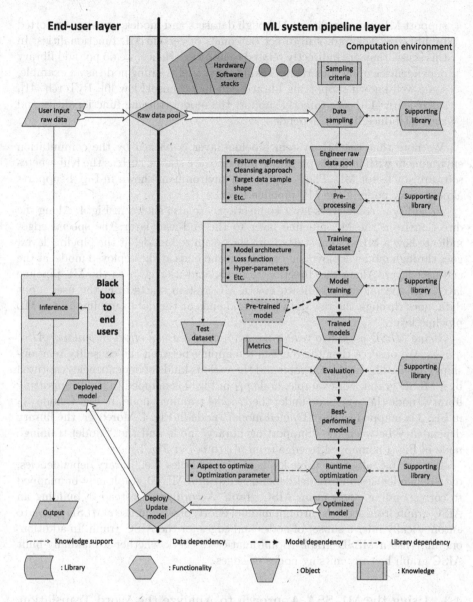

Fig. 4. A representative MLSD graph.

example, it takes all trained models as one of the inputs, and outputs the best-performing model. Among those three nodes, only models are passed, so they are connected by model dependency.

- *Library dependencies* are shown as a dotted line in Fig. 4. They show all the third-party libraries used by ML developers. We only model the dependencies between functionalities and library nodes, because libraries are to support ML functionalities. Although datasets and models are also supported by libraries, they are still direct outcomes of certain ML functionalities. In this sense, they are indirectly related to libraries. Hence, we do not add library dependencies upon such them. Taking the model training node as an example, some well-known supporting libraries, include TensorFlow [6], PyTorch [41], scikit-learn [43], etc., directly support the model training functionalities and thus introduce library dependencies.

We note that the ML system pipeline layer is backed by the computation environment with multiple platforms and software stacks, such as the Kubernetes software stacks for ML. The computation environment shown in Fig. 4 supports almost every node in the ML pipeline layer.

In addition, some cross-layer connections are also shown in Fig. 4. Along the direction from the ML pipeline layer to the end-user layer, the special edges indicate how a ML system starts from the optimized model at the pipeline layer, goes through model deployment/updating, and ends at the deployed model at the end-user layer. Along the direction from the end-user layer to the ML pipeline layer, the special edges indicate how a ML system starts from the user input data, goes through the raw data pool, and ends at the data sampling in the ML pipeline layer.

Using MLSD graphs to reduce the amount of manual effort in building AISC graphs. We observe that there exists a mapping between the causality relationships captured by an AISC graph and the various kinds of dependencies captured by a MLSD graph. For example, node p_{11} in Fig. 3 is mapped to the "Supporting library" node (i.e., the node under the "Model training" node) in Fig. 4; node p_{12} in Fig. 3 is mapped to the "Trained model" node in Fig. 4. Moreover, the library dependency between the "Supporting library" node and the "Model training" node in Fig. 4 is mapped to edge from p_{11} to p_{12} in Fig. 3.

In principle, all of the three kinds of dependencies (i.e., library dependencies, data dependencies and model dependencies) in a MLSD graph may be mapped to corresponding edges in an AISC graph. Accordingly, instead of building an AISC graph from scratch through manual effort, one could use a MLSD graph to automatically infer a subset of nodes and edges for the AISC graph. In addition, one may use a MLSD graph to automatically check whether a manually-built AISC graph has any missing nodes or edges.

4.3 Using the ML-SSA Approach to Analyze the Word Translation Attacks

We use the word translation attack (shown in Fig. 2) again to demonstrate the ML-SSA approach. When the ML-SSA approach is used to conduct security analysis of a ML system, we firstly build the ML system's MLSD graph, and then use the MLSD graph to help build the corresponding AISC graph, as shown in Fig. 3.

As illustrated in this AISC graph, in order to produce a flawed translation neural network the attacker could consider three alternative **attack paths**. The first attack path includes p_8, p_9 and p_{12}; the second attack path includes path p_{10}, p_{11} and p_{12}; the third path includes p_1, p_2, p_3, p_4, p_5, p_7 and p_{12}. In addition to identifying these attack paths, we can also reason the likelihood of each attack path using proposition logic. (Note that the AISC graph is essentially a set of proposition logic formulas.)

5 AI Security Analysis and Attack Mitigation

Regarding the viable attack mitigation strategies and how to properly implement a fine strategy, our main observations are as follows.

First, based on the observation that in many cases the direct effect of an AI attack is *not* the ultimate attack goal, the attacks can often be effectively mitigated by blocking (or slowing down) the propagation of the attack's impact. Usually there exist one or more **impact propagation paths** that leads the AI attack to the ultimate attack goal. If such paths are blocked, the ultimate attack goal won't be achieved. Taking data poisoning attacks as an example, the direct effect of the attack is the corruption of a particular sub-set of training data samples. Through security-aware active learning, a good portion of the corrupted data samples may get excluded from the labelled training set. In this way, the attack impact on the trained model will be significantly reduced. Nevertheless, we note that the defense mechanisms for blocking (or slowing down) the propagation paths of AI attacks are still under-investigated in the research community.

Second, instead of blocking (or slowing down) the propagation paths of AI attacks, the attacks could also be mitigated by preventing a propagation path from being formed. Taking the data poisoning attack as an example again, in some close-loop deployment environments (e.g. a factory) of a ML system, it is actually feasible to certify all the data providers. This can make it very difficult for the attacker to corrupt enough data samples.

Third, in addition to the above two categories of attack mitigation strategies, the attacks could also be effectively mitigated by confusing the attackers through moving target defenses. For example, a) fake propagation paths could be created to mislead the attacker; b) decoy ML models could be deployed; c) some ML models could serve as a honeypot; d) the ML models could be trained with randomized samples or adversarial examples.

Fourth, as soon as impact propagation is detected, the attack impact could be substantially reduced by taking a (proactive) quarantine and isolation strategy. For example, if training data from external sources (e.g. twitter comments, customer reviews, user-provided images etc.) are used, we could isolate the data collection process to prevent malicious data from entering the training/deployment process. Also, before the collected the data is used for model training, the developers can check the validity of the data through semantics or outlier detection.

Fifth, in-depth analysis of the AISC graphs and the ML system's causality relationships can help identify the actionable strategies of mitigating attacks. In particular, we observe that 1) evasion attacks and exploratory attacks are often related to the model supply chain, so the integrity of the model's publishers should be checked to make sure the models are not intentionally poisoned or compromised; 2) protecting data supply chain including training data and test data is the key to prevent poisoning attacks; 3) keeping software up-to-date helps to protect the library supply chain; 4) if public ML models from GitHub or PyTorch Hub are used (for transfer learning, fine-tuning, or other reasons), it's better to put them in a isolated environment to make sure the downloaded models are free of malicious components, in both the ML security and the software security aspects. Therefore, the proposed approach can help with blocking the propagation paths by 1) firstly constructing the propagation path; and then 2) identifying key components in the propagation path that can be isolated or enhanced.

5.1 Using the Example Word-to-Word Translation ML System to Illustrate Relevant Mitigation Strategies

To mitigate the potential attacks towards the word-to-word translation ML system, we also consider how the attacker can impact the three supply chains. As a data poisoning attack, this attack is mostly related to the data supply chain. The attacker's action happens at a very early stage and usually taints the raw data gathered by the ML developers. Therefore, one immediate mitigation approach is to validate the gathered raw data (eliminating possibility of p_3 in Fig. 3), so that any attacker tainted content will not get into the corpus, or that the amount of tainted content getting into the corpus will be decreased. In addition to validating collected data, there are also training data fault mitigation techniques to mitigate data poisoning [9], such as label smoothing, label correction, robust loss, etc. By assuming the collected data is faulty, these techniques can protect the ML models at an early stage. Another possible mitigation method is to conduct extensive model testing before deploying the model, with the hope that the strange behavior of the trained model can be uncovered.

6   Conclusion and Future Directions

Since the existing security analysis approaches and techniques were mainly developed to analyze traditional security issues in enterprise networks, they are no longer very suitable for analyzing ML systems. Therefore, we seeks to present a vision on how to address two unique ML security analysis challenges through a new security analysis approach. This paper intends to take the initial step to bridge the gap between the existing cyber security analysis approaches and an ideal ML system security analysis approach.

The proposed ML-SSA approach is preliminary and may present the following future research opportunities: 1) designing a systematic, largely automated approach to build AISC graphs; 2) investigating approaches for AISC-graph-based probabilistic reasoning; and 3) exploring AISC-graph-based security threat mitigation algorithms and procedures.

Acknowledgment. This work was supported by NIST 60NANB22D144. Xiaoyan Sun is also supported by NSF DGE-2105801.

Disclaimer. Commercial products are identified in order to adequately specify certain procedures. In no case does such identification imply recommendation or endorsement by the National Institute of Standards and Technology, nor does it imply that the identified products are necessarily the best available for the purpose.

References

1. DailyWireless, March 2020. https://dailywireless.org/internet/what-happened-to-microsoft-tay-ai-chatbot. Accessed 8 Feb 2022
2. IBM Watson - Speech to Text, August 2021. https://www.ibm.com/cloud/watson-speech-to-text. Accessed 8 Feb 2022
3. Machine Translation - Microsoft Translator for Business, September 2021. https://www.microsoft.com/en-us/translator/business/machine-translation. Accessed 8 Feb 2022
4. Google TensorFlow: CVE security vulnerabilities, versions and detailed reports, July 2022. https://www.cvedetails.com/product/53738/Google-Tensorflow.html?vendor_id=1224. Accessed 11 July 2022
5. Speech-to-Text: Automatic Speech Recognition | Google Cloud, February 2022. https://cloud.google.com/speech-to-text. Accessed 8 Feb 2022
6. Abadi, M., et al.: TensorFlow: large-scale machine learning on heterogeneous systems (2015). Software available from tensorflow.org. https://www.tensorflow.org/
7. Ateniese, G., Mancini, L.V., Spognardi, A., Villani, A., Vitali, D., Felici, G.: Hacking smart machines with smarter ones: how to extract meaningful data from machine learning classifiers. Int. J. Secur. Netw. **10**(3), 137–150 (2015)
8. Carlini, N., Wagner, D.: Towards evaluating the robustness of neural networks. In: 2017 IEEE Symposium on Security and Privacy (SP), pp. 39–57. IEEE (2017)
9. Chan, A., Gujarati, A., Pattabiraman, K., Gopalakrishnan, S.: The fault in our data stars: studying mitigation techniques against faulty training data in machine learning applications. In: DSN (2022)
10. Cheikes, B.A., Cheikes, B.A., Kent, K.A., Waltermire, D.: Common platform enumeration: Naming specification version 2.3. US Department of Commerce, National Institute of Standards and Technology (2011)
11. Chen, P.Y., Zhang, H., Sharma, Y., Yi, J., Hsieh, C.J.: ZOO: zeroth order optimization based black-box attacks to deep neural networks without training substitute models. In: Proceedings of the 10th ACM Workshop on Artificial Intelligence and Security, pp. 15–26 (2017)
12. Feng, D., Harakeh, A., Waslander, S.L., Dietmayer, K.: A review and comparative study on probabilistic object detection in autonomous driving. IEEE Trans. Intell. Transp. Syst. **23**, 9961–9980 (2021)
13. Fredrikson, M., Jha, S., Ristenpart, T.: Model inversion attacks that exploit confidence information and basic countermeasures. In: Proceedings of the 22nd ACM SIGSAC Conference on Computer and Communications Security, pp. 1322–1333 (2015)
14. Fredrikson, M., Lantz, E., Jha, S., Lin, S., Page, D., Ristenpart, T.: Privacy in pharmacogenetics: an {End-to-End} case study of personalized warfarin dosing. In: 23rd USENIX Security Symposium (USENIX Security 2014), pp. 17–32 (2014)

15. Gnanasambandam, A., Sherman, A.M., Chan, S.H.: Optical adversarial attack (2021). https://doi.org/10.48550/arxiv.2108.06247. https://arxiv.org/abs/2108.06247

16. Goodfellow, I.J., Shlens, J., Szegedy, C.: Explaining and harnessing adversarial examples. arXiv preprint arXiv:1412.6572 (2014)

17. Gu, T., Dolan-Gavitt, B., Garg, S.: BadNets: identifying vulnerabilities in the machine learning model supply chain. arXiv preprint arXiv:1708.06733 (2017)

18. Guo, C., Gardner, J., You, Y., Wilson, A.G., Weinberger, K.: Simple black-box adversarial attacks. In: International Conference on Machine Learning, pp. 2484–2493. PMLR (2019)

19. Huang, S., Papernot, N., Goodfellow, I., Duan, Y., Abbeel, P.: Adversarial attacks on neural network policies. arXiv preprint arXiv:1702.02284 (2017)

20. Jagielski, M., Severi, G., Pousette Harger, N., Oprea, A.: Subpopulation data poisoning attacks. In: Proceedings of the 2021 ACM SIGSAC Conference on Computer and Communications Security. pp. 3104–3122 (2021)

21. Jha, S., Sheyner, O., Wing, J.: Two formal analyses of attack graphs. In: Proceedings 15th IEEE Computer Security Foundations Workshop. CSFW-15, pp. 49–63 (2002). https://doi.org/10.1109/CSFW.2002.1021806

22. Kos, J., Song, D.: Delving into adversarial attacks on deep policies. arXiv preprint arXiv:1705.06452 (2017)

23. Kurakin, A., Goodfellow, I.J., Bengio, S.: Adversarial examples in the physical world. In: Artificial Intelligence Safety and Security, pp. 99–112. Chapman and Hall/CRC (2018)

24. Li, S., Zhao, B.Z.H., Yu, J., Xue, M., Kaafar, D., Zhu, H.: Invisible backdoor attacks against deep neural networks. arXiv preprint arXiv:1909.02742 (2019)

25. Li, Y., Jiang, Y., Li, Z., Xia, S.T.: Backdoor learning: a survey. IEEE Trans. Neural Netw. Learn. Syst. arXiv:2007.08745 (2022)

26. Liu, Y., et al.: Trojaning attack on neural networks (2017)

27. Lovisotto, G., Turner, H., Sluganovic, I., Strohmeier, M., Martinovic, I.: {SLAP}: improving physical adversarial examples with {Short-Lived} adversarial perturbations. In: 30th USENIX Security Symposium (USENIX Security 2021), pp. 1865–1882 (2021)

28. McGraw, G., Figueroa, H., Shepardson, V., Bonett, R.: An architectural risk analysis of machine learning systems: toward more secure machine learning. Berryville Institute of Machine Learning, Clarke County, VA (2020). Accessed 23 Mar 2020

29. MITRE: CVE of Sockeye (2022). https://www.cvedetails.com/cve/CVE-2021-43811/

30. Moosavi-Dezfooli, S.M., Fawzi, A., Fawzi, O., Frossard, P.: Universal adversarial perturbations. In: Proceedings of the IEEE Conference on Computer Vision and Pattern Recognition, pp. 1765–1773 (2017)

31. Moosavi-Dezfooli, S.M., Fawzi, A., Frossard, P.: DeepFool: a simple and accurate method to fool deep neural networks. In: Proceedings of the IEEE Conference on Computer Vision and Pattern Recognition, pp. 2574–2582 (2016)

32. Morgulis, N., Kreines, A., Mendelowitz, S., Weisglass, Y.: Fooling a real car with adversarial traffic signs. arXiv preprint arXiv:1907.00374 (2019)

33. Mozilla: DeepSpeech, February 2022 https://github.com/mozilla/DeepSpeech. Accessed 8 Feb 2022

34. Muñoz-González, L., et al.: Towards poisoning of deep learning algorithms with back-gradient optimization. In: Proceedings of the 10th ACM Workshop on Artificial Intelligence and Security, pp. 27–38 (2017)

35. Nassi, D., Ben-Netanel, R., Elovici, Y., Nassi, B.: MobilBye: Attacking ADAS with camera spoofing (2019). https://doi.org/10.48550/arxiv.1906.09765. https://arxiv.org/abs/1906.09765

36. Ning, R., Li, J., Xin, C., Wu, H.: Invisible poison: a blackbox clean label backdoor attack to deep neural networks. In: IEEE INFOCOM 2021 - IEEE Conference on Computer Communications, pp. 1–10 (2021). https://doi.org/10.1109/INFOCOM42981.2021.9488902

37. Ou, X., Govindavajhala, S., Appel, A.W.: MulVAL: a logic-based network security analyzer. In: USENIX Security (2005)

38. Papernot, N.: A marauder's map of security and privacy in machine learning. arXiv:1811.01134 [cs], November 2018

39. Papernot, N., McDaniel, P., Goodfellow, I., Jha, S., Celik, Z.B., Swami, A.: Practical black-box attacks against machine learning. In: Proceedings of the 2017 ACM on Asia Conference on Computer and Communications Security, pp. 506–519 (2017)

40. Papernot, N., McDaniel, P., Jha, S., Fredrikson, M., Celik, Z.B., Swami, A.: The limitations of deep learning in adversarial settings. In: 2016 IEEE European symposium on security and privacy (EuroS&P), pp. 372–387. IEEE (2016)

41. Paszke, A., et al.: PyTorch: an imperative style, high-performance deep learning library. In: Advances in Neural Information Processing Systems 32, pp. 8024–8035. Curran Associates, Inc. (2019). http://papers.neurips.cc/paper/9015-pytorch-an-imperative-style-high-performance-deep-learning-library.pdf

42. Patel, N., Krishnamurthy, P., Garg, S., Khorrami, F.: Bait and switch: online training data poisoning of autonomous driving systems (2020). https://doi.org/10.48550/arxiv.2011.04065. https://arxiv.org/abs/2011.04065

43. Pedregosa, F., et al.: Scikit-learn: machine learning in Python. J. Mach. Learn. Res. **12**, 2825–2830 (2011)

44. Schuster, R., Shuster, T., Meri, Y., Shmatikov, V.: Humpty dumpty: controlling word meanings via corpus poisoning. In: IEEE S&P (2020)

45. Sheyner, O., Haines, J., Jha, S., Lippmann, R., Wing, J.: Automated generation and analysis of attack graphs. In: Proceedings of 2002 IEEE Symposium on Security and Privacy, pp. 273–284 (2002). https://doi.org/10.1109/SECPRI.2002.1004377

46. Shokri, R., Stronati, M., Song, C., Shmatikov, V.: Membership inference attacks against machine learning models. In: 2017 IEEE symposium on security and privacy (SP), pp. 3–18. IEEE (2017)

47. Su, J., Vargas, D.V., Sakurai, K.: One pixel attack for fooling deep neural networks. IEEE Trans. Evol. Comput. **23**(5), 828–841 (2019)

48. Szegedy, C., et al.: Intriguing properties of neural networks. arXiv preprint arXiv:1312.6199 (2013)

49. Tramèr, F., Zhang, F., Juels, A., Reiter, M.K., Ristenpart, T.: Stealing machine learning models via prediction {APIs}. In: 25th USENIX security symposium (USENIX Security 2016), pp. 601–618 (2016)

50. Xiao, C., Li, B., Zhu, J.Y., He, W., Liu, M., Song, D.: Generating adversarial examples with adversarial networks. arXiv preprint arXiv:1801.02610 (2018)

51. Xiao, Q., Li, K., Zhang, D., Xu, W.: Security risks in deep learning implementations. In: 2018 IEEE Security and Privacy Workshops (SPW), pp. 123–128. IEEE (2018)

52. Xu, K., Liu, S., Chen, P.Y., Zhao, P., Lin, X.: Defending against backdoor attack on deep neural networks. arXiv preprint arXiv:2002.12162 (2020)

53. Yin, H., et al.: Dreaming to distill: Data-free knowledge transfer via DeepInversion. In: Proceedings of the IEEE/CVF Conference on Computer Vision and Pattern Recognition, pp. 8715–8724 (2020)

54. Yu, H., Yang, K., Zhang, T., Tsai, Y.Y., Ho, T.Y., Jin, Y.: CloudLeak: large-scale deep learning models stealing through adversarial examples. In: NDSS (2020)
55. Yuan, X., et al.: {CommanderSong}: a systematic approach for practical adversarial voice recognition. In: 27th USENIX security symposium (USENIX security 2018), pp. 49–64 (2018)
56. Zhang, L., Liu, P., Choi, Y., Chen, P.: Semantics-preserving reinforcement learning attack against graph neural networks for malware detection. IEEE Trans. Depend. Secur. Comput. arXiv:2009.05602 (2022)
57. Zhao, Z., Dua, D., Singh, S.: Generating natural adversarial examples. arXiv preprint arXiv:1710.11342 (2017)
58. Zhou, L., Gao, J., Li, D., Shum, H.Y.: The design and implementation of XiaoIce, an empathetic social chatbot. arXiv:1812.08989 [cs], September 2019

MILSA: Model Interpretation Based Label Sniffing Attack in Federated Learning

Debasmita Manna, Harsh Kasyap[(⊠)], and Somanath Tripathy

Department of Computer Science and Engineering, Indian Institute of Technology
Patna, Patna, India
{debasmita_2121cs18,harsh_1921cs01,som}@iitp.ac.in

Abstract. Federated learning allows multiple participants to come together and collaboratively train an intelligent model. It allows local model training, while keeping the data in-place to preserve privacy. In contrast, deep learning models learn by observing the training data. Consequently, local models produced by participants are not presumed to be secure and are susceptible to inference attacks. Existing inference attacks require training multiple shadow models, white-box knowledge of training models and auxiliary data preparation, which makes these attacks to be ineffective and infeasible. This paper proposes a model interpretation based label sniffing attack called *MILSA*, which does not interfere with learning of the main task but learns about the presence of a particular label in the target (participant's) training model. *MILSA* uses Shapley based value functions for interpreting the training models to frame inference attacks. *MILSA* is evaluated on different datasets and the results show its effectiveness. Further, *MILSA* is evaluated against differentially-private local model updates, and it is observed that *MILSA* could successfully perform the inference attacks. We propose a secure training strategy to address these issues.

Keywords: Federated learning · Label sniffing attack · Model interpretation · Shapley value

1 Introduction

Federated learning (FL) is a collaborative machine learning paradigm which allows training a common model, keeping the training data in-place on local machines [12]. FL allows numerous devices to jointly learn an intelligent model without sharing their training data. FL has shown significant potential in wide range of areas including applications for smartphones, wearable gadgets and sensors (e.g., human activity recognition, heart rate monitoring, and keyboard prediction) as well as other areas, like healthcare (e.g., disease diagnosis online expert systems, and medical insurance registration) [5,7], transportation (vehicular networking technologies) [6] and malware detection [17]. All participants in

D. Manna, H. Kasyap, and S. Tripathy—All authors have equal contribution.

traditional FL train on their locally-held data. In each round, a set of participants are chosen to upload their local model updates to the central curator. This makes FL a promising solution for data-sensitive applications. Still, the security and privacy implications of the FL training process are an intriguing subject. Any feature of a participant's private data must be properly protected because the gradients may leak some sensitive and personal information about the training data. Similarly, attackers want to explore about the private training dataset of participants, *i.e.*, presence of an individual [13,16], whether a particular label appears during the training phase or the amount of a global property in the private training dataset [1,9,18].

This paper investigates whether a particular label, that appears during the training phase, can be inferred from the participant's local model updates. Considering that training data come from various sources, the number of samples may vary among distinct labels, showing the overall characteristics of participants. Malicious attackers could access these numbers illegally and leak personal identifiable information (PII). For example, a global healthcare centre wants to create an online disease prediction system using FL, including thousands of hospitals. Each hospital will train over its locally-held data. The global healthcare centre will aggregate their local model updates to receive a global model that can anticipate the trend of many diseases, not only those that have appeared in a single hospital. An adversary (a participant or the global healthcare centre) wishes to know how many hospitals have treated a specific ailment. It could help them to increase treatment costs and even predict a disease's approximate dispersion scope.

This work identifies the problems in the existing property inference attacks, which requires more knowledge on model and data, as well as training cost. A model interpretation based label sniffing attack (*MILSA*) is presented here which is more effective but requires a few data samples from the similar distribution of private training data. It neither requires training multiple meta-classifiers nor the white-box access of the target model. *MILSA* detects whether a specific label is present in the participant's private training data. Further, we evaluate *MILSA* by adopting a secure (*differentially-private*) training strategy and discuss a possible defence (secure training strategy) to resist against such inference attacks.

Key contributions of this work are summarized as follows:

- This paper presents a black-box model interpretation based label sniffing attack, called *MILSA*, which peculiarly infers the class labels, and their quantity in the client's training data.
- Extensive experiments are carried out with different datasets and distributions, which provide a shred of evidence for the effectiveness of the proposed attack. We also evaluate against a differentially private model, and find that *MILSA* performs a successful inference attack.
- We present a secure training strategy, introducing multiple intermediate servers, to preserve privacy of the participant's local model.

Organization. The rest of the paper is structured as follows: Sect. 2 discusses the background, and the existing inference attacks and defenses. Section 3 discusses the capabilities and knowledge of an adversary. Section 4 presents a model interpretation based label sniffing attack, called *MILSA*. Section 5 describes the experiment setup and results. Section 6 presents a secure training strategy. Section 7 concludes this work.

2   Background and Related Works

2.1   Federated Learning

Federated learning is a machine learning technique that allows the learning model to gain experience from many data sets located at separate locations (e.g., local data centres, a central server) without exchanging training data [12]. This allows personal data to stay on local servers, lowering the risk of data breaches. The global model's parameters are provided to local data centres (users) so that they can train their local models over it. Users train on their locally held datasets. Model parameters are periodically shared between the central server and the users. Samples of local data are not provided, which increases data security and protection.

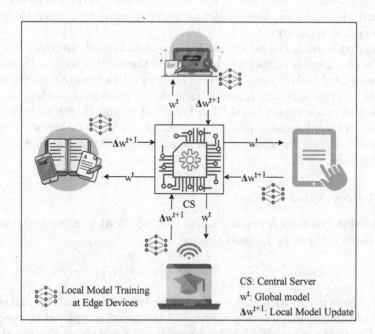

Fig. 1. Federated learning

Figure 1 illustrates a federated learning network. Let there be n participants owning their data D_i, for each participant $i \in n$. There exists a central server $\mathcal{CS}$, which defines the training plan and broadcasts the global model parameters w^t to the participants for local training in iteration t. Further, each participant trains locally as

$$w_i^{t+1} \leftarrow w_i^t - \eta \nabla l(w_i^t; b \in D_i)$$

where η is the local learning rate of clients and b is a batch from local dataset D_i. After completing the local training at the edge, participants send their local model update $\triangle w_i$ to $\mathcal{A}$. Further, $\mathcal{CS}$ collects all the updates to get the plan w^{t+1} for the next iteration. It uses different aggregation algorithms. FedAvg [11] is the most common and popular among them. It does weighted averaging of the shared local model updates (gradient) as

$$w^{t+1} \leftarrow w^t + \sum_{i=1}^{S} \frac{n_i}{\sum_{j=1}^{n} n_j} \triangle w_i^{t+1}$$

where S is the subset of participant selected for iteration t, n_i is the number of private data samples of client i. The whole process runs for several iterations until convergence.

Different machine learning approaches can be used with federated learning models, but data type and context are crucial. Learning actions of mobile phone users, driverless vehicles, and predicting health hazards from wearable gadgets are all possible applications.

Federated learning can benefit the healthcare and health insurance industries since it allows sensitive data to be protected in the original source. To diagnosis rare diseases, federated learning models can collect data from many sources (e.g., hospitals, electronic health record databases) to provide more data diversity. According to a new report titled "The Future of Digital Health with Federated Learning" [14], federated learning can assist overcome data privacy and data governance concerns by allowing machine learning models to be built from non co-located data.

2.2 Shapley Value

Shapley value evaluates a player's payoff (contribution) in a co-operative game with n players. It can be formally defined as

$$\phi_j(\text{val}) = \sum_{S \subseteq \{1,...,p\} \setminus \{j\}} \frac{|S|!(p-|S|-1)!}{p!} (\text{val}(S \cup \{j\}) - \text{val}(S)) \tag{1}$$

The players in this cooperative game are replaced by the features and characteristics of the machine learning model, and the payoff is replaced by the model output (contribution) itself. The Shapley value is defined via a value function val of players in S, where S is a subset of the features used in the machine learning model, x is the vector of feature values with P number of features[1]. $val_x(S)$ is

---

[1] https://christophm.github.io/interpretable-ml-book/shapley.html.

the model prediction for the features in subset S, marginalized over features not present in S.

$$\text{val}_x(S) = \int \hat{f}(x_1, \ldots, x_p) \, d\mathbb{P}_{x \notin S} - E_X(\hat{f}(X)) \tag{2}$$

The Shapley value can be computed without any understanding of the model's internal mechanics, as long as you know its input and output. It has access to the prediction vector $f(x)$ for any input x but not to the model parameters or intermediate calculations of $f(x)$. When each player may have contributed more or less than the others, shapley value can help decide a payoff for all of them. The (weighted) average of marginal contributions is the Shapley value. It is most commonly used in situations where each actor's contribution is unequal, but they work together to achieve the target. It assures that each actor earns as much as or more than they would if they were acting alone.

2.3   Inference Attacks

Because ML algorithms are prone to retaining information from training data, they are subject to a variety of privacy threats [4], such as membership inference attacks [13,16] and property inference attacks [1,9,18].

Existing Attack Techniques: Authors in [1] proposed a white-box inference attack to infer the global properties of the private training data, on a fully connected neural network. Wang et al. [18] categorized PIA into three different types of attacks such as class sniffing, quantity inference and whole determination attack. The goal of class sniffing is to detect whether a specific label appears in the targeted training dataset. Quantity inference attack targets to detect the amount of each label in a single round, which leaves the composition proportion of the training label owned by the selected participant, while, the whole determination attack determines the properties in the training process. Authors in [21] harnessed the fact that gradient variation for every participant has a distinguishable sensitivity for a given label, which helps to expose the participant's preference for that particular class.

Existing Defense Techniques: Many of the existing defenses use cryptographic techniques [2,19,20] and adversarial training [3] to preserve privacy of the participant's local model. Authors in [2] proposed a privacy-enhanced federated learning (PEFL) scheme to prevent leakage of private data, even if multiple participants are colluded. They used Secure Multi-Party Computation, however it costs heavy communication and loss of efficiency. Authors in [3] showed how adversarial training can mitigate inference attacks by not allowing the model to learn specific trends from private training data of participants, and thus guaranteeing privacy. However, it is computationally expensive. Authors in [19] integrated differential privacy to provide privacy, but it costs loss of accuracy. Authors in [20] proposed a double-masking protocol for preserving local models, however it incurs heavy communication overhead for all the participants. Authors in [10] proposed a shapley based poisoning defense, which motivates us for the model interpretation based inference attack.

3   Threat Model

Federated learning promises privacy to the system by bringing the model to data. However, it suffers threats from both the participants and the central server in a traditional federated learning system.

The participants train under the orchestration of a central server. The server can frame inference attacks to learn the membership or property from the local model updates received from the different participants. Besides that, a participant can also frame inference attack to learn the membership or property from the gradients received through different participants.

In this work, the adversary's goal is to determine whether a particular label has been used for training. The adversary has black-box access of the victim's target model. Furthermore, the adversary has knowledge of the data distribution, and has a few auxiliary data points.

4   *MILSA*: The Proposed Attack

Here, we discuss the intuition behind the proposed model interpretation based label sniffing attack (*MILSA*), before presenting the proposed attack. Suppose f be the target model, x be the instance with d features, $f(x)$ is the prediction to be approximated. The explanatory model (g) which calculates the additive feature attribution can be expressed through Eq. 3 in relation to the feature attribution ($\phi_j \in \mathbb{R}$) and prediction ($g(z')$) for every feature $j \in d$ at a given instance x.

$$g\left(z'\right) = \phi_0 + \sum_{j=1}^{M} \phi_j z'_j \qquad (3)$$

where $z'_j \in \{0,1\}^M$ is the coalition vector, M is the maximum size of the coalition vector. The coalition vector is called simplified features, in which the presence of a feature is indicated as, present (1) and absent (0). Thus, given target model f and instance x, Shapley explainer returns attributions matrices $(A_1, A_2, \ldots, A_L)$ for all labels L, where A_i is an attribution matrix which contains ϕ_j for every feature $j \in d$.

$$A_i = \begin{bmatrix} \phi_{11} & \phi_{12} & \cdots & \phi_{1m} \\ \phi_{21} & \phi_{22} & \cdots & \phi_{2m} \\ \cdots & \cdots & \cdots & \cdots \\ \phi_{n1} & \phi_{n2} & \cdots & \phi_{nm} \end{bmatrix}$$

Figure 2 illustrates the model interpretation results on a target model which has been trained on MNIST dataset[2], with and without label 4 separately. The

---

[2] http://yann.lecun.com/exdb/mnist/.

observations drawn from them become the basis of our proposed attack. It can be clearly seen in Fig. 2a and 2b, f which has not seen label 4 in training, has zero attributions for label 4. In contrary to this, label 4 has a mix of positive and negative attributions as the model has seen all labels for training, as shown in Fig. 2c and 2d. It satisfies the dummy property of Shapley, which tells that a feature $j \in d$ of any instance x with no effect on the predicted value $f(x)$, regardless of the coalition of feature values, should have zero attribution.

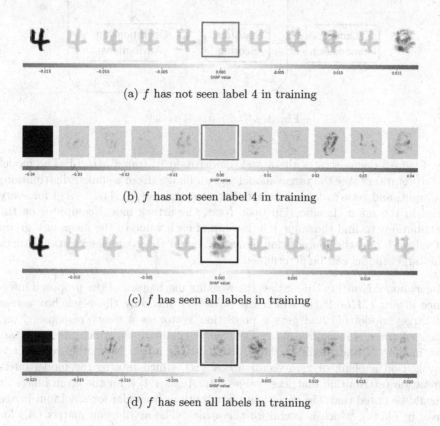

(a) f has not seen label 4 in training

(b) f has not seen label 4 in training

(c) f has seen all labels in training

(d) f has seen all labels in training

Fig. 2. Model interpretation analysis on target model f

MILSA: The goal of our proposed attack *MILSA* (**M**odel **I**nterpretation based **L**abel **S**niffing **A**ttack) is to detect whether a particular label has been used to train a model. The adversary has black-box access to the participant local model, *i.e.*, the target model, which is considered for the attack. In addition to this, the adversary has some auxiliary data, similar to that of the original distribution. We use Shapley value based DeepShapExplainer to interpret the model.

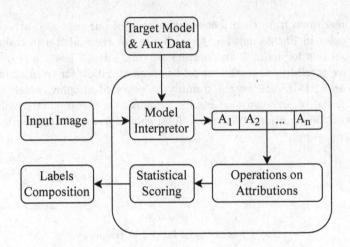

Fig. 3. *MILSA* attack model

Figure 3 demonstrates the attack model used to frame *MILSA*. The model interpretation takes the target model and an image (from a similar distribution) as input, and returns label-wise attribution matrices $(A_1, A_2, \ldots, A_L)$ for every level in the main classification task. Next, the attack model computes on the attributions to find the value relationship of each value to the mean of a group of values. Thus, the composition of every label in the main classification task of the target model can be determined.

Algorithm: Algorithm 1 describes the working mechanism of the proposed inference attack (*MILSA*), in which the adversary has only the black box access of target model (f) and gets a prediction vector as a query response. Now, the *explainer* is initialized using DeepShapExplainer[3] [8], which takes the target model (f) and auxiliary data (*aux_data*) as input. Next, the explainer is invoked on a blank or zero-vector image (B), which returns the model interpretation (attribution matrices) values $(A_1, A_2, \ldots, A_L)$, for the given image. It should be noted that, the variation in attributions is similar for any input image (real or blank), which is useful for the attack. The attribution matrix (A_i) for each label is flattened. Each attribution score (ϕ_j) in the one-d attribution vector (A_i), which impacts the prediction positively, is aggregated for every label $l \in L$ and *z_score* is computed as stated in Eq. 4.

$$z\_score = \frac{x - \mu}{\sigma} \qquad (4)$$

where x is the aggregated value, μ and σ are the mean and standard deviation of group values, respectively. *z_score* is a statistical method to compare a value to a normal population which tells about the composition of a given label in the

---

[3] https://github.com/slundberg/shap.

Algorithm 1. Proposed Model Interpretation based Label Sniffing Attack

Require: f (Target model), L (Labels), aux_data (Auxiliary data)
Ensure: $l \in L$ present or not

1: /*Model Interpretation*/
2: $B \leftarrow$ initialize a blank image
3: $explainer \leftarrow$ DeepShapExplainer(f, aux_data)
4: $A_1, A_2, \ldots, A_L \leftarrow explainer$.shap_values($B$)   //Shapley values for B in reference to f.

5: /*Label-wise positive attributions*/
6: $sum\_pos\_attrs \leftarrow [0$ for each $l \in L]$ //sum of positive attributions.
7: **for** each A_i in $A_1, A_2, \ldots, A_L$ **do**
8:    $A_i \leftarrow flatten(A_i)$ //convert to one-d matrix.
9:    **for** each attribution $\phi_j \in A_i$ **do**
10:       **if** $\phi_j > 0$ **then**
11:          $sum\_pos\_attrs[l] \leftarrow sum\_pos\_attrs[l] + \phi_j$
12:       **end if**
13:    **end for**
14: **end for**

15: /*Label Sniffing*/
16: $\mu =$ mean(sum_pos_attrs)
17: $\sigma =$ std.deviation(sum_pos_attrs)
18: $z\_scores \leftarrow \left(\frac{sum\_pos\_attrs - \mu}{\sigma}\right)$ //Z-score, $\forall\ l \in L$.
19: **for** each label l in L **do**
20:    $z\_score \leftarrow z\_scores[l]$
21:    **if** $z\_score > 3.\sigma$ or $z\_score < -3.\sigma$ **then**
22:       Label l is not present.
23:    **else if** $z\_score > 2.\sigma$ or $z\_score < -2.\sigma$ **then**
24:       Label l is partially present.
25:    **else if** $z\_score > 1.\sigma$ or $z\_score < -1.\sigma$ **then**
26:       Label l is present.
27:    **else**
28:       Label l is equally present to any other label.
29:    **end if**
30: **end for**

private training dataset of a participant. This is a numerical measurement used to describe the relationship between a value and the mean of a group of values. An analyst can determine whether a score is typical for a specific data set or atypical by calculating z_score. If z_score is greater than 3σ or less than -3σ, then the particular label appears very less frequently in the private training data in the training phase. If z_score is greater than 2σ or less than -2σ, then the particular label appears partially (around 25–50%). If z_score is greater than σ or less than $-\sigma$, then the particular label appears significantly (around 50–75%). Otherwise, the label appears most frequently in the private training data while training.

5   Experiments and Results

5.1   Experimental Setup

MILSA is evaluated with different datasets and distributions. It is also evaluated against secure (*differentially-private*) training strategy. We performed these experiments on the federated testbed using PyTorch scripts. In order to run these experiments, we used a Docker setup with an Ubuntu image. Installation and migration were made easier by using it. The container was deployed on a host machine equipped with an Intel Xeon(R) CPU E5-2650 v4 @ 2.20 GHz processor.

Evaluation Datasets: We considered four datasets MNIST[4], Fashion-MNIST[5], MedNIST[6], CIFAR-10[7] for evaluating model interpretation based label sniffing attack (*MILSA*).

MNIST: MNIST is a dataset of handwritten grayscale digits ranging from 0–9, with a training set of 60,000 training images each of size 28×28 and 10,000 test samples distributed across all ten categories. Each image is of size 28×28. It is a 10-class classification problem and one of the benchmarking datasets for evaluating deep learning algorithms.

Fashion-MNIST: Fashion-MNIST dataset contains 70000 images of grayscale fashion products distributed evenly among ten classes, each of size 28×28.

MedNIST: MedNIST is a collection of medical images. It has a total of 58954 standardized images, belonging to 6 classes (not perfectly balanced). Each image is of size 64×64.

CIFAR-10: CIFAR-10 is considered as a complex dataset, which consists of 60000 training images each of size 32×32 colour images in 10 classes, with a training set of 50,000 training and 10,000 test samples.

Learning Classifiers: The client device was trained locally with CNN (Convolution Neural Network). Its architecture consists of two convolution layers with 32 and 64 kernels of size 3×3, followed by a max-pooling layer, and two fully connected layers with 9216 and 128 neurons. Each layer uses ReLU activation with a dropout of 0.25. We used this architecture to train MNIST and Fashion-MNIST datasets. Similarly, we tuned the same architecture to train MedNIST dataset. We used the complex (ResNet-101) model architecture to train the complex CIFAR-10 dataset.

FL Settings: We considered 50 participants. Each participant trains locally for 1 round with a batch size of 32 before submitting an update to the server.

---

[4] http://yann.lecun.com/exdb/mnist/.
[5] https://github.com/zalandoresearch/fashion-mnist.
[6] https://github.com/Project-MONAI/MONAI-extra-test-data/releases/download/0.8.1/MedNIST.tar.gz.
[7] https://www.cs.toronto.edu/~kriz/cifar.html.

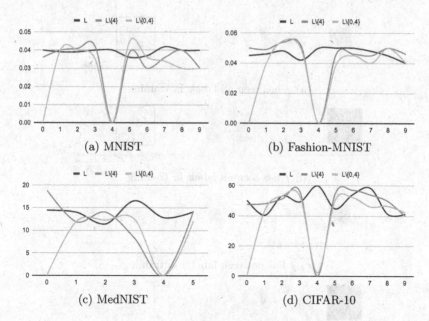

Fig. 4. Model interpretation results for *MILSA* on target model (f) trained over different datasets. $L : f$ has seen all labels, $L\backslash\{4\} : f$ has not seen label 4, and $L\backslash\{0,4\} : f$ has not seen labels 0 and 4.

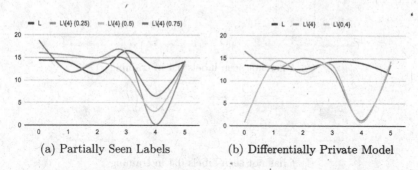

Fig. 5. Results for *MILSA* on different target models (f) over MedNIST (medical image dataset).

The server runs for a total of 50 epochs. For carrying out label sniffing attack (*MILSA*) on (MNIST, Fashoin-MNIST, MedNIST and CIFAR-10) datasets, we assumed the victim model to train without labels of 0, 4, 0 and 4 both.

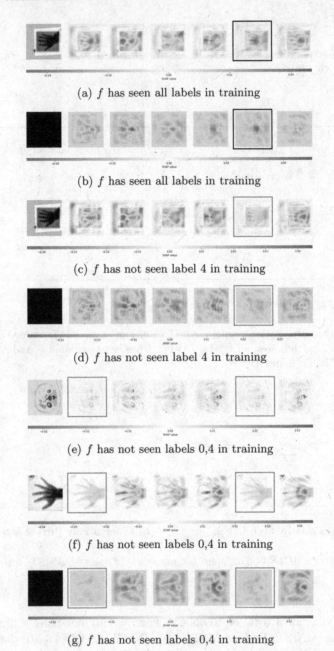

(a) f has seen all labels in training

(b) f has seen all labels in training

(c) f has not seen label 4 in training

(d) f has not seen label 4 in training

(e) f has not seen labels 0,4 in training

(f) f has not seen labels 0,4 in training

(g) f has not seen labels 0,4 in training

Fig. 6. Model interpretation results for *MILSA* on target models (f) trained over MedNIST

5.2   Results

We evaluated *MILSA* on MNIST, Fashion-MNIST, MedNIST and CIFAR-10 datasets. Figure 4 illustrates the result for three cases: 1) L : Target model (f) has seen all the labels in training phase; 2) $L\backslash\{4\}$: Target model (f) has not seen label 4 in training phase; 3) $L\backslash\{0,4\}$: Target model (f) has not seen labels 0 and 4 in training phase. Y-axis plots the sum of positive attributions score, X-axis plots the approximate number of labels. It can be clearly observed that the graph touches the bottom for label 4 ($L\backslash\{4\}$) in all the cases. Similarly, it touches bottom for labels 0 and 4 ($L\backslash\{0,4\}$) in all the cases.

Partially Seen Labels in Training Phase: We also evaluated the target models which have seen few labels partially (0.25, 0.50, 0.75). We could observe that z_score for respective scenarios falls in ($3\sigma, 2\sigma, \sigma$) region of the normal distribution graph. Figure 5a illustrates the result for all these cases, where the sum of positive attributions of label 4 lie in different regions with different proportions of label 4 present in the private training data.

Label Sniffing on Differentially Private Target Models: We evaluated the proposed attack on a differentially private target model f, which has not seen a particular label. It can be observed that, f both impacts the accuracy of all labels and leaks privacy as any other model. Figure 5b illustrates result for a differentially private model f, for $L\backslash\{4\}$ and $L\backslash\{0,4\}$.

Detailed Analysis on MedNIST Dataset: Figure 6 illustrates the model interpretation results for *MILSA* on MedNIST dataset. Figure 6a takes a label 4 image as input to interpret, against a target model f, which has seen all labels in the training phase. It can be observed that, there is a homogeneous distribution of attributions. Similarly, a homogeneous distribution of attributions can be observed in Fig. 6b, where a blank image is interpreted against f, trained with all labels. Figure 6c and 6d illustrate the scenario where f has not seen label 4 in training phase, hence, the attributions are nearly zero for label 4. Figure 6e, 6f and 6g illustrate the scenario where f has not seen label 0 and 4 in training phase, hence, the attributions are nearly zero for label 0 and 4. We obtain the same result with an input image of any other class or a blank image.

6   The Proposed Defense

Here, we discuss a secure training strategy, to mitigate the above-discussed inference attack. Figure 7 illustrates training with multiple participants, by introducing a few intermediate servers (IS). The participants train locally and split their locally trained model into the numbers of intermediate servers. In the given figure, participant $P1$ trains local model w_1 and splits it into three components, such that, $w_{11} + w_{12} + w_{13} = w_1$. Further, $P1$ adds a random number (ϕ_{xy}) to every component after split, before sharing it to any of the intermediate server. $P1$ shares $\hat{w_{11}} = w_{11} + \phi_{11}$ to IS-1, $\hat{w_{12}} = w_{12} + \phi_{12}$ to IS-2

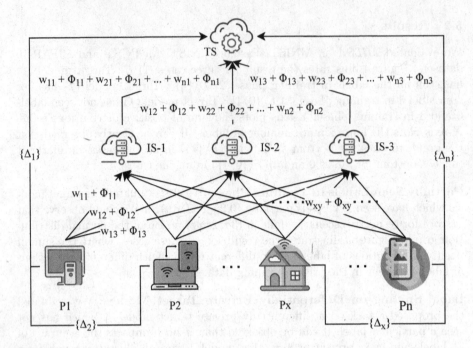

Fig. 7. Secure training strategy with intermediate servers TS: trusted server, IS: intermediate server, P: participant

and $\hat{w_{13}} = w_{13} + \phi_{13}$ to *IS-3*, such that, $\phi_{11} + \phi_{12} + \phi_{13} = \triangle_1$. Similarly, other participants send their shares of locally trained model to the intermediate servers. Each intermediate server performs addition of the received shares from individual participants. *IS-1* computes $\hat{w_{11}} + \hat{w_{21}} + \ldots + \hat{w_{n1}}$, which equals to $w_{11} + \phi_{11} + w_{21} + \phi_{21} + \ldots + w_{n1} + \phi_{n1}$. Similarly, *IS-2* and *IS-3* perform addition over the received shares. Next, all the intermediate servers send their local computation results to the central trusted server (*TS*).

Once *TS* receives the updates from the intermediate servers, it sums all those updates to get $\hat{w}$, which is equal to $w_1 + \triangle_1 + w_2 + \triangle_2 + \ldots + w_n + \triangle_n$. Now, each participant (i) sends $\{\triangle_i\}$ to *TS* in a secure channel. This saves us from heavy communication, where all the participants mutually agree for a perturbation vector which adds to zero. *TS* subtracts all $\triangle_i$ from $\hat{w}$, to compute w. However, this approach suffers the dropping out of participants, which can be taken care by utilizing the Shamir's *t-out-of-N* secret sharing protocol [15]. In last, it can be observed that, none of the intermediate server or intruder can get raw access to the participant's local model to infer from. This approach also prevents any inference attack, even considering sniffing from the channel or multiple collusions.

Discussion: The proposed defense mitigates *MILSA* including the existing inference attacks. It does not expose the raw local model update to the central server, to infer from. The intermediate servers do not have the access to the raw update. Taking strong assumptions that, all the intermediate servers collude, then also, they can not get the access of the raw update, as it contains noise $(w_{11} + \phi_{11} + w_{12} + \phi_{12} + w_{13} + \phi_{13})$. The central server can not access an individual raw update, it has only access to a noisy aggregated model.

$$[w_{11} + \phi_{11} + w_{12} + \phi_{12} + w_{13} + \phi_{13}+$$

$$w_{21} + \phi_{21} + w_{22} + \phi_{22} + w_{23} + \phi_{23}+$$

$$\ldots +$$

$$w_{n1} + \phi_{n1} + w_{n2} + \phi_{n2} + w_{n3} + \phi_{n3}]$$

The noise $(\triangle_1 = \phi_{11} + \phi_{12} + \phi_{13})$ is cancelled out, only when all the participants send the accumulated noise $(\triangle_1, \triangle_2, \ldots, \triangle_n)$ in a separate channel to the central server. Thus, neither the intermediate servers nor the central server can access the raw model update of an individual participant.

7   Conclusion

This paper presented a model interpretation based label sniffing inference attack, called *MILSA*. It highlighted the issues in the machine learning as well as traditional FL-assisted applications. *MILSA* achieved improved attack results, without raw access to the target model, or calibrating any shadow models. It is also evaluated against differentially private target models, and successfully carried out the attack. Further, we proposed a secure training strategy, which preserved the privacy of the participant's local updates, and avoided any chance for inference attacks.

Acknowledgement. We acknowledge the Ministry of Education, Government of India, for providing fellowship to complete this work.

References

1. Ganju, K., Wang, Q., Yang, W., Gunter, C.A., Borisov, N.: Property inference attacks on fully connected neural networks using permutation invariant representations. In: Proceedings of the 2018 ACM SIGSAC Conference on Computer and Communications Security, pp. 619–633 (2018)
2. Hao, M., Li, H., Luo, X., Xu, G., Yang, H., Liu, S.: Efficient and privacy-enhanced federated learning for industrial artificial intelligence. IEEE Trans. Ind. Inform. **16**(10), 6532–6542 (2019)
3. Hayes, J., Ohrimenko, O.: Contamination attacks and mitigation in multi-party machine learning. In: Advances in Neural Information Processing Systems 31 (2018)
4. Jere, M.S., Farnan, T., Koushanfar, F.: A taxonomy of attacks on federated learning. IEEE Secur. Priv. **19**(2), 20–28 (2020)

5. Kasyap, H., Tripathy, S.: Privacy-preserving decentralized learning framework for healthcare system. ACM Trans. Multimedia Computi. Commun. Appl. (TOMM) **17**(2s), 1–24 (2021)
6. Kong, X., Gao, H., Shen, G., Duan, G., Das, S.K.: FedVCP: a federated-learning-based cooperative positioning scheme for social internet of vehicles. IEEE Trans. Comput. Soc. Syst. **9**, 197–206 (2021)
7. Kulkarni, P.P., Kasyap, H., Tripathy, S.: DNet: an efficient privacy-preserving distributed learning framework for healthcare systems. In: Goswami, D., Hoang, T.A. (eds.) ICDCIT 2021. LNCS, vol. 12582, pp. 145–159. Springer, Cham (2021). https://doi.org/10.1007/978-3-030-65621-8_9
8. Lundberg, S.M., Lee, S.I.: A unified approach to interpreting model predictions. In: Advances in Neural Information Processing Systems, pp. 4765–4774 (2017)
9. Luo, X., Wu, Y., Xiao, X., Ooi, B.C.: Feature inference attack on model predictions in vertical federated learning. In: 2021 IEEE 37th International Conference on Data Engineering (ICDE), pp. 181–192. IEEE (2021)
10. Manna, A., Kasyap, H., Tripathy, S.: *Moat*: model agnostic defense against targeted poisoning attacks in federated learning. In: Gao, D., Li, Q., Guan, X., Liao, X. (eds.) ICICS 2021. LNCS, vol. 12918, pp. 38–55. Springer, Cham (2021). https://doi.org/10.1007/978-3-030-86890-1_3
11. McMahan, B., Moore, E., Ramage, D., Hampson, S., y Arcas, B.A.: Communication-efficient learning of deep networks from decentralized data. In: Artificial Intelligence and Statistics, pp. 1273–1282. PMLR (2017)
12. McMahan, H.B., Moore, E., Ramage, D., y Arcas, B.A.: Federated learning of deep networks using model averaging. CoRR abs/1602.05629 (2016). http://arxiv.org/abs/1602.05629
13. Nasr, M., Shokri, R., Houmansadr, A.: Comprehensive privacy analysis of deep learning: passive and active white-box inference attacks against centralized and federated learning. In: 2019 IEEE Symposium on Security and Privacy (SP), pp. 739–753 (2019). https://doi.org/10.1109/SP.2019.00065
14. Rieke, N., et al.: The future of digital health with federated learning. NPJ Digit. Med. **3**(1), 1–7 (2020)
15. Shamir, A.: How to share a secret. Commun. ACM **22**(11), 612–613 (1979)
16. Shokri, R., Stronati, M., Song, C., Shmatikov, V.: Membership inference attacks against machine learning models. In: 2017 IEEE Symposium on Security and Privacy (SP), pp. 3–18. IEEE (2017)
17. Singh, N., Kasyap, H., Tripathy, S.: Collaborative learning based effective malware detection system. In: Koprinska, I., et al. (eds.) ECML PKDD 2020. CCIS, vol. 1323, pp. 205–219. Springer, Cham (2020). https://doi.org/10.1007/978-3-030-65965-3_13
18. Wang, L., Xu, S., Wang, X., Zhu, Q.: Eavesdrop the composition proportion of training labels in federated learning. arXiv preprint arXiv:1910.06044 (2019)
19. Wei, K., et al.: Federated learning with differential privacy: algorithms and performance analysis. IEEE Trans. Inf. Forensics Secur. **15**, 3454–3469 (2020)
20. Xu, G., Li, H., Liu, S., Yang, K., Lin, X.: VerifyNet: Secure and verifiable federated learning. IEEE Trans. Inf. Forensics Secur. **15**, 911–926 (2019)
21. Zhou, C., et al.: PPA: preference profiling attack against federated learning. arXiv preprint arXiv:2202.04856 (2022)

IoTInDet: Detecting Internet of Things Intrusions with Class Scatter Ratio and Hellinger Distance Statistics

N. G. Bhuvaneswari Amma[✉][iD] and P. Valarmathi[iD]

Vellore Institute of Technology, Chennai, Tamil Nadu, India
ngbhuvaneswariamma@gmail.com
{bhuvaneswariamma.ng,valarmathi.sudhakar}@vit.ac.in

Abstract. Technology evolution has attracted hackers to launch cyber-attacks on Internet of Things (IoT) devices. Smart devices must be protected against these attacks by identifying anomalies in IoT communications. Intrusions in IoT traffic can often be detected using statistical methods. The problem with current statistical intrusion detection methods is that these methods suffer from curse of dimensionality and are unable to identify intrusions with a low false positive rate when choosing to change the statistical assumptions. In order to deal with these issues, a method called **IoT Intrusion Detection** (**IoTInDet**) is proposed. The IoTInDet identifies intrusions based on how well a set of features correlates with one another after selecting intrusion relevant features. Class Scatter Ratio (CSR) selects the features by calculating the weights of the features and ranking them. Using the Hellinger Distance Chart (HDC), the correlation between the chosen features is calculated. By calculating the HDC of the new traffic with the produced IoT normal traffic description, the intrusion is discovered. It is clear from the experiments on benchmark UNSW Bot-IoT dataset that the proposed IoTInDet method is providing promising results.

Keywords: Class scatter ratio · Statistical method · Hellinger distance · Intrusion detection · IoT traffic

1 Introduction

Nowadays, smart environment uses IoT devices extensively. IoT security issues are exacerbated by the accretion of IoT devices that generate noteworthy amounts of data [6]. Due to their Internet connectivity and lack of security mechanisms, IoT devices are easily targeted by attackers. By gaining control of smart devices, an attacker can quickly hack IoT devices. Any activity that differs from the normal is referred to as an intrusion [5]. The methodologies used by the intrusion detection mechanisms are statistical, machine learning, and data mining. These strategies all have two phases: training and testing. By linking

© The Author(s), under exclusive license to Springer Nature Switzerland AG 2022
V. R. Badarla et al. (Eds.): ICISS 2022, LNCS 13784, pp. 155–168, 2022.
https://doi.org/10.1007/978-3-031-23690-7_9

the characteristics to the class labels during the training phase, the model grasps from training data. The tested model is used to categorise untrained data [15].

Pattern-based detection and anomaly-based detection are the two basic types of detection systems [11]. Because not all attributes may be beneficial for the detection system, it is important to select an appropriate subset of features for intrusion detection. A feature selection algorithm is also necessary to select the pertinent features. The two main feature selection methods are the filter approach and the Wrapper approach [3]. The filter strategy selects the features using ranking techniques. By adding and eliminating features, the wrapper technique uses the classifier to create a subset of candidate features. Utilizing feature extraction techniques improves the efficacy of the intrusion detection system [13]. The majority of feature extraction approaches used in the existing systems are based on the class labels that is afflicted by the curse of dimensionality problem.

Due to the undefined structure of network traffic, statistical-based detection algorithms are needed. Statistical methods-based detection systems are very quick when it comes to detection times. By using these techniques, we can determine if the traffic differs from normal profiles by calculating the average, variance, and standard deviation. When compared to machine learning and data mining techniques, these methods take less time to detect and require less cost to compute [4]. The key benefit of using these methods is that prior knowledge of attack records is not necessary. The key contributions of this study include the following propositions:

1. A Hellinger distance-based class scatter ratio method is used to determine the most appropriate set of features.
2. Hellinger distance chart for extracting correlations between selected features.
3. Hellinger distance chart to build the normal IoT traffic description.
4. IoTInDet approach for intrusion detection in IoT traffic.

The remainder of the study is structured as follows: The literature pertaining to this study are discussed in Sect. 2. The proposed IoTInDet statistical technique is described in Sect. 3. The performance evaluation of the suggested strategy is covered in Sect. 4. The conclusion and recommendations for additional research are described in Sect. 5.

2   Related Works

The possibility for integrating smart gadgets into our daily lives over the Internet grows as a result of technological advancement, which opens the door to several cyber-attacks. Intrusion detection is required in these situations to thwart these attacks. The Intrusion Detection System (IDS) keeps an eye on the network and notifies the administrator of any unusual network traffic behaviour [7].

The literature has covered a number of feature extraction and selection algorithms. There are two types of feature selection techniques: filter techniques and wrapper methods. Because it only constructs one model, the filter-based method is quicker than wrapper-based methods. This approach finds statistical relationships between features. Two forms of filter-based feature selection algorithms include correlation coefficient-based algorithms and mutual information-based algorithms. The simplest correlation coefficient-based method is the Pearson correlation coefficient, which is based on the linear interdependence between two variables [2]. CSR is utilized in the proposed study to select the best set of features.

Techniques for feature extraction change the features to draw association between them [12]. The triangle area map approach was utilised to improve the attack detection procedure. The drawback is that the final cluster centres of the k-means clustering are used as the two points for each triangle [14]. Principal component analysis was used by the geometric area analysis based IDS to extract the features [10]. This approach of feature extraction cannot detect recent attacks, which results in a high proportion of false alarms. In contrast to the methods mentioned above, the proposed method uses the Hellinger Distance (HD) measure to determine the distance between each and every feature, and then it chooses the transformed features that are located above the diagonal of the HD space to create HDC. To expedite and enhance the intrusion detection process, the chosen features are converted into a different form.

There are numerous intrusion detection methods listed in the literature. One such group includes concepts like Mahalanobis distance, Earth movers distance, Euclidean distance, etc., that are based on multivariate correlation analysis [1]. The detection system's accuracy was increased by these methods, but the computing complexity was also increased. Data mining and machine learning methods are the foundation of a different class of IDS [8]. These techniques have a longer learning curve and a higher level of computational complexity. The proposed solution, which is based on the HD metric, is different from the aforementioned existing IDS.

3   IoTInDet Methodology

IoTInDet is a statistical intrusion detection approach proposed to overcome the curse of dimensionality problem by providing low false positive rate. This approach selects the best set of features using CSR based feature selection. The detection mechanism is enhanced by extracting the interrelationship between features using HDC method. The IoT normal traffic description is built using HD measure and deviation if any from the normal profile is detected as intrusion. Figure 1 depicts the architecture of the proposed IoTInDet approach. The proposed approach consists of CSR based feature selection, HDC generation, IoT normal traffic description, and IoT traffic intrusion detection modules.

IoT traffic dataset is represented as $Tr_{IoT} = [Ir_1, Ir_2, Ir_3, \ldots, Ir_m]$, where $Ir_j = [Tf_{1j}, Tf_{2j}, Tf_{3j}, \ldots, Tf_{mj}]$, $(1 \leq j \leq m)$, the jth IoT traffic record. Each

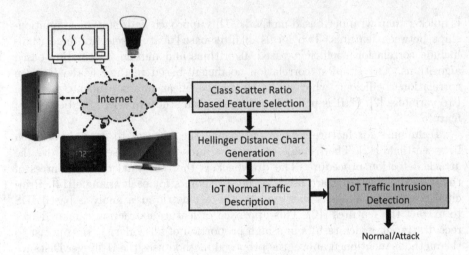

Fig. 1. Architecture of proposed IoTInDet approach

record contains y features. The dataset is displayed as follows:

$$
Tr_{IoT} = \begin{bmatrix} Tf_1^1 & Tf_2^1 & Tf_3^1 & \cdots & Tf_y^1 \\ Tf_1^2 & Tf_2^2 & Tf_3^2 & \cdots & Tf_y^2 \\ \vdots & \vdots & \vdots & \ddots & \vdots \\ Tf_1^n & Tf_2^n & Tf_3^n & \cdots & Tf_y^n \end{bmatrix} \tag{1}
$$

The bias in the data is removed using a min-max normalisation procedure. By determining min_{fi} and max_{fi}, respectively, the raw data is normalised in the range [0,1]. The normalised value is then determined using (2).

$$
nf_i^j = \frac{Tf_j^y - min_{fj}}{max_{fj} - min_{fj}} \tag{2}
$$

where Tf_{jv} is the data to normalize. The following is a representation of the normalised training dataset:

$$
Tr_{IoT_N} = \begin{bmatrix} Tnf_1^1 & Tnf_2^1 & Tnf_3^1 & \cdots & Tnf_y^1 \\ Tnf_1^2 & Tnf_2^2 & Tnf_3^2 & \cdots & Tnf_y^2 \\ \vdots & \vdots & \vdots & \ddots & \vdots \\ Tnf_1^n & Tnf_2^n & Tnf_3^n & \cdots & Tnf_y^n \end{bmatrix} \tag{3}
$$

The most advantageous set of features is chosen using this normalised data.

3.1 Class Scatter Ratio Based Feature Selection

The proposed CSR based feature selection approach uses the Hellinger distance-based classifier and CSR to choose a subset of features [3]. To improve the performance, the features that matter most are chosen. The flow diagram of CSR

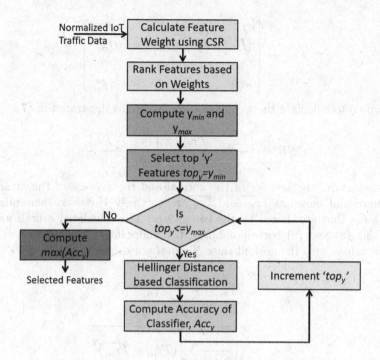

Fig. 2. Flow diagram of CSR based feature selection

based feature selection is depicted in Fig. 2. The normalised training dataset is used to compute the feature weights, and CSR is used to rank the features according to the computed weights. The distance-based classifier receives the top y features, which have been chosen. The top y features are chosen once the classifier's performance has been assessed and found to be satisfactory. Otherwise, $y + 1$ features are chosen, and the performance of the classifier is assessed. If the performance is adequate, the feature's inclusion is ended.

The training dataset is made up of p records of regular traffic and q records of attack traffic, as shown in (4).

$$Tr_{IoT_N} = Tr_{n_p} \| Tr_{a_q} \tag{4}$$

The description of normal IoT traffic records and attack IoT traffic records are given in (5) and (6), respectively.

$$Tr_{n_p} = \begin{bmatrix} nf_1^1 & nf_2^1 & nf_3^1 & \cdots & nf_m^1 \\ nf_1^2 & nf_2^2 & nf_3^2 & \cdots & nf_m^2 \\ \vdots & \vdots & \vdots & \ddots & \vdots \\ nf_1^p & nf_2^p & nf_3^p & \cdots & nf_m^p \end{bmatrix} \tag{5}$$

$$Tr_{a_q} = \begin{bmatrix} nf_1^{p+1} & nf_2^{p+1} & nf_3^{p+1} & \cdots & nf_m^{p+1} \\ nf_1^{p+2} & nf_2^{p+2} & nf_3^{p+2} & \cdots & nf_m^{p+2} \\ \vdots & \vdots & \vdots & \ddots & \vdots \\ nf_1^n & nf_2^n & nf_3^n & \cdots & nf_m^n \end{bmatrix} \tag{6}$$

CSR is used to calculate the weight of each feature as illustrated in (7).

$$CSR_i = \frac{\left(\overline{Tr_{n_i}} - \overline{Tr_i}\right)^2 \times \left(\overline{Tr_{a_i}} - \overline{Tr_i}\right)^2}{Sig_{n_i} - Sig_{a_i}} \tag{7}$$

For each feature, the average of the normal and the average of the attack are determined and shown as $\overline{Tr_{n_i}}$ and $\overline{Tr_{a_i}}$, respectively. However, there might be some values that are shared by the two groups. The calculated overall mean is $\overline{Tr_i}$. Using (8) and (9) correspondingly, the midpoint of each feature and the range of values with the desired class $Normal$ are calculated.

$$\overline{Tr_{n_i}} = \frac{1}{p} \sum_{i=1}^{p} Tr_{n_i} \tag{8}$$

$$Sig_{n_i} = \sqrt{\frac{1}{p-1} \sum_{i=1}^{p} \left(Tr_{n_i} - \overline{Tr_{n_i}}\right)^2} \tag{9}$$

where Tr_{n_i} is the ith feature in Tr_{n_p}. The middle point of each feature and the spread of values with the target class $Attack$ are computed using (10) and (11) respectively.

$$\overline{Tr_{a_i}} = \frac{1}{q} \sum_{i=1}^{q} Tr_{a_i} \tag{10}$$

$$Sig_{a_i} = \sqrt{\frac{1}{q-1} \sum_{i=1}^{q} \left(Tr_{a_i} - \overline{Tr_{a_i}}\right)^2} \tag{11}$$

where Tr_{a_i} is the ith feature in Tr_{a_p}. The overall mean is calculated using (12).

$$\overline{Tr_i} = \frac{\overline{Tr_{n_i}} + \overline{Tr_{a_i}}}{2} \tag{12}$$

$\overline{Tr_i}$ represents the middle point of $\overline{Tr_{n_i}}$ and $\overline{Tr_{a_i}}$.

The features are ranked using the feature weights that were derived using formula (7). The feature with the highest weight is the one that is most relevant to the detection process, while the feature with the lowest weight is the one that is least relevant. The top y rated features are chosen from the ranked features and provided to the HD classifier for evaluation.

The classification procedure performs poorly because the current classifiers cannot reliably categorise the traffic as normal or malicious. In order to categorise the traffic, a classifier employing HD calculated using (13) and (14) is proposed in this study.

$$HD_{n_{FS_j}} = \sqrt{\frac{1}{2} \sum_{j=1}^{y} \left(Tr_{N^{y_j}} - \overline{Tr_{n^{y_j}}} \right)^2} \tag{13}$$

$$HD_{a_{FS_j}} = \sqrt{\frac{1}{2} \sum_{j=1}^{y} \left(Tr_{N^{y_j}} - \overline{Tr_{a^{y_j}}} \right)^2} \tag{14}$$

where $Tr_{N^{y_j}}$ represents j^{th} normalized training record with y's selected according to the rank order. Using the minimum of $HD_{n_{FS_i}}$ and $HD_{a_{FS_j}}$, each record's class is determined as in (15).

$$Cl_{FS_j} = Cl \left(Min \left(HD_{n_{FS_j}}, HD_{a_{FS_j}} \right) \right) \tag{15}$$

In order to compute the mean with the y selected features, the following formula has been used:

$$\overline{Tr_{IoT_n^{y_j}}} = \frac{1}{p} \sum_{j=1}^{p} Tr_{IoT_n^{y_j}} \tag{16}$$

where $Tr_{IoT_N^{y_j}}$ represents the normal traffic records with y chosen features. Using the y selected features, we compute the mean of the attack traffic records:

$$\overline{Tr_{IoT_a^{y_j}}} = \frac{1}{q} \sum_{j=1}^{q} D_{a^{y_j}} \tag{17}$$

where $Tr_{IoT_A^{y_j}}$ represents the attack traffic records with y selected features. In order to represent the top y selected features, the classifier is trained using the training data as follows:

$$Tr_{IoT_{NFS}} = \begin{bmatrix} Tnf_1^1 & Tnf_2^1 & Tnf_3^1 & \cdots & Tnf_k^1 \\ Tnf_1^2 & Tnf_2^2 & Tnf_3^2 & \cdots & Tnf_k^2 \\ \vdots & \vdots & \vdots & \ddots & \vdots \\ Tnf_1^n & Tnf_2^n & Tnf_3^n & \cdots & Tnf_k^n \end{bmatrix} \tag{18}$$

$Tr_{IoT_{NFS}}$ is given as input to the Hellinger distance chart generation process.

3.2   Hellinger Distance Chart Generation

To hasten the detection process, an internal connection between the selected features is retrieved. For the statistical technique, knowledge of the attack history is not required. So, just the regular network traffic logs are used to create the HD Chart (HDC). Assume that the dataset consists of y records of typical network traffic in the following format:

$$Tr_n = \begin{bmatrix} nf_1^1 & nf_2^1 & nf_3^1 & \cdots & nf_m^1 \\ nf_1^2 & nf_2^2 & nf_3^2 & \cdots & nf_m^2 \\ \vdots & \vdots & \vdots & \ddots & \vdots \\ nf_1^y & nf_2^y & nf_3^y & \cdots & nf_m^y \end{bmatrix} \tag{19}$$

HD is used to compute distances between features and is as follows:

$$D_{HD}\left(nf_i, nf_j\right) = \sqrt{\frac{1}{2}\sum_{i=1}^{n}\left(\sqrt{nf_i} - \sqrt{nf_j}\right)^2} \tag{20}$$

The HDC of record i is calculated as follows:

$$D_{HDC} = \begin{bmatrix} nf_{11}^1 & nf_{12}^1 & nf_{13}^1 & \cdots & nf_{1m}^1 \\ nf_{21}^2 & nf_{22}^2 & nf_{23}^2 & \cdots & nf_{2m}^2 \\ \vdots & \vdots & \vdots & \ddots & \vdots \\ nf_{m1}^y & nf_{m2}^y & nf_{m3}^y & \cdots & nf_{mm}^y \end{bmatrix} \tag{21}$$

The distance between two identical features is always zero. The diagonal elements are always 0 as a result. The values in HDC are the same above and below the diagonal. In order to create HDC, the values that are either below or above the diagonal are removed to represent it in vector form. The HDC's mean is calculated as follows:

$$HDC_{n_i} = \begin{bmatrix} nf_{12}^i & nf_{13}^i & \cdots & nf_{1m}^i f_{23}^i & \cdots & nf_{2m}^i & \cdots & nf_{(m-1)m}^i \end{bmatrix} \tag{22}$$

3.3   IoT Normal Traffic Description

The HD between the normal traffic HDC and that of the usual traffic is computed in order to determine the normal traffic profile. This is depicted as follows:

$$HD\left(HDC_{n_i}, \mu_{HDC_{n_i}}\right) = \sqrt{\frac{1}{2}\sum_{i=1}^{n}\left(\sqrt{HDC_{n_i}} - \sqrt{\mu_{HDC_{n_i}}}\right)^2} \tag{23}$$

The method used to determine HD's mean is as follows:

$$\mu_{HD_n} = \frac{1}{n}\sum_{i=1}^{n}HD_i \tag{24}$$

The method used to determine HD's standard deviation is as follows:

$$\sigma_{HD_n} = \sqrt{\frac{1}{n-1}\sum_{i=1}^{n}\left(HD_i - \mu_{HD_n}\right)} \tag{25}$$

The mean and standard deviation of HD make up the typical traffic profile, which is utilised to calculate thresholds.

3.4 IoT Traffic Intrusion Detection

To detect the intrusion, the threshold is calculated as follows:

$$IoT_{Thresh} = \mu_{HD_n} \pm \sigma_{HD_n} \times \alpha \tag{26}$$

where the significance level *alpha* of a normal distribution is defined as having a range of 1 to 3. It describes the range in which the HD learned during the creation of the IoT normal traffic description that classifies the IoT traffic records as normal. The intrusion is detected by calculating the HD between the mean of the HD_n and the HDC of the test data. If the test traffic's distance falls under the threshold, it is classified as normal; if not, it is considered intrusive.

4 Experimental Results

Windows 10 was used to analyse the trials on an Intel(R) Core(TM) i7-6700 CPU with 16 GB of RAM. The effectiveness of the intrusion detection system was tested using experiments with the Bot-IoT dataset from UNSW [9]. The distribution of the Bot-IoT dataset is displayed in Table 1. The IoT traffic records were created utilising smart home devices, such as thermostats, refrigerators, motion-activated lights, garage doors, and weather stations. Tables 2 and 3 show the categories and sub-categories of IoT traffic, respectively.

Table 1. Binary class data distribution

IoT traffic	Training data	Test data
Normal	1018	477
Attack	3036915	3668045

Table 2. Multi-class data distribution

IoT traffic	Training data	Test data
Normal	1018	477
DDoS	2027166	1926624
DoS	894463	1650260
Reconnaissance	115167	91082
Theft	119	79

The characteristics of the Bot-IoT dataset are shown in Table 4. The experiment took into account the selected features, the top 10 features, and all features to gauge how well the suggested technique performed.

The effectiveness of the suggested technique was examined using performance metrics including true negative (TN), false positive (FP), false negative (FN), and

Table 3. Subcategories of traffic in dataset

IoT traffic		Samples	
Category	Sub-category	Training	Test
Normal	Normal	1018	477
DDoS	TCP	1471635	977380
	HTTP	4576	989
	UDP	550955	948255
DoS	TCP	165412	615800
	HTTP	7298	1485
	UDP	721753	1032975
Reconnaissance	OS_Fingerprint	25846	17914
	Service_Scan	89321	73168
Theft	Data_Exfiltration	21	6
	Keylogging	98	73

Table 4. List of dataset features

Features	Feature names
Selected features	*seq, stddev, N_IN_Conn_P_SrcIP, state_number, mean, N_IN_Conn_P_DstIP, drate, srate*
Best 10	*seq, stddev, N_IN_Conn_P_SrcIP, min, state_number, mean, N_IN_Conn_P_DstIP, drate, srate, max*
All	*pkSeqID, Stime, flgs, flgs_number, Proto, proto_number, saddr, sport, daddr, dport, pkts, bytes, state, state_number, ltime, seq, dur, mean, stddev, sum, min, max, spkts, dpkts, sbytes, dbytes, rate, srate, drate, TnBPSrcIp, TnBpDstIP, TnP_PSrcIP, TnP_PDstIP, TnP_perProto, TnP_Per_Dport, AR_P_Proto_P_SrcIp, AR_P_Proto_DstIP, N_IN_Conn_P_SrcIP, N_IN_Conn_P_DstIP, AR_P_Proto_P_Sport, AR_P_Proto_P_Dport, Pkts_P_State_P_Protocol_P_DestIP, Pkts_P_State_P_Protocol_P_SrcIP*

true positive (TP). In Table 5, the contingency table for binary class classification is presented. The performance measures for binary class classification are tabulated in Table 6 including precision, recall, F-measure, FPR, accuracy, and error rate (ER), were calculated using Eqs. (27), (28), (29), (30), (31), and (32), respectively. According to the experimental findings, the selected features using the proposed methodology perform prominently better than the rest of the features.

$$Precision = \frac{TP}{TP + FP} \times 100 \tag{27}$$

$$Recall = \frac{TP}{TP + FN} \times 100 \tag{28}$$

$$F - measure = 2 \times \frac{Precision \times Recall}{Precision + Recall} \tag{29}$$

$$FPR = \frac{FP}{FP + TN} \times 100 \tag{30}$$

$$Accuracy = \frac{TP + TN}{TP + FP + TN + FN} \times 100 \tag{31}$$

$$ER = \frac{FN + FP}{TP + FP + TN + FN} \times 100 \tag{32}$$

Table 5. Contingency table for binary class

Features	TN	FP	FN	TP
Selected features	429	48	8912	3659133
Best 10	417	60	8938	3659107
All	403	74	8964	3659081

Table 6. Performance of binary class

Features	Precision	Recall	F-measure	FPR	Accuracy	ER
Selected features	99.9987	99.7570	99.8777	10.0629	99.7558	0.2442
Best 10	99.9984	99.7563	99.8772	12.5786	99.7547	0.2453
All	99.9980	99.7556	99.8767	15.5136	99.7536	0.2464

Table 7 represents the contingency table for multi-class classification. In Table 8, the effectiveness of the suggested approach for multi-class categorization is tabulated. Results are promising, with the exception of normal and theft traffic. These traffic under-performed because they had less training samples than other traffic. It is also clear that tests with the selected features using the proposed approach performed better than those with all features. Figure 3 depicts the performance of the proposed approach with existing statistical approaches and it is evident that the FPR of the proposed approach is less in all the IoT traffic classes except theft traffic class as the theft class contains less number of training data compared to other traffic classes.

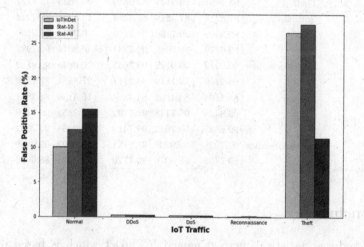

Fig. 3. IoT traffic vs. false positive rate

Table 7. Contingency table for multi-class

Features	Traffic	Normal	DDoS	DoS	Reconnaissance	Theft
Selected features	Normal	429	13	30	5	0
	DDoS	13	1921116	5232	263	0
	DoS	30	3211	1646948	71	0
	Reconnaissance	5	23	42	91011	1
	Theft	0	9	8	4	58
Best 10	Normal	417	19	35	6	0
	DDoS	19	1921107	5234	264	0
	DoS	35	3212	1646941	72	0
	Reconnaissance	6	29	44	91002	1
	Theft	0	9	9	4	57
All	Normal	403	22	36	12	4
	DDoS	22	1921129	5057	414	2
	DoS	36	2963	1646863	397	1
	Reconnaissance	12	19	31	91019	1
	Theft	4	2	2	1	70

Table 8. Performance of multi-class

Features	Traffic	Precision	Recall	F-measure	FPR	Accuracy	ER
Selected features	Normal	89.9371	89.9371	89.9371	10.0629	89.9371	10.0629
	DDoS	99.8308	99.7141	99.7724	0.2859	99.7141	0.1692
	DoS	99.6785	99.7993	99.7389	0.2007	99.7993	0.3215
	Reconnaissance	99.6245	99.9220	99.7731	0.0780	99.9220	0.3755
	Theft	98.3051	73.4177	84.0580	26.5823	73.4177	1.6949
Best 10	Normal	87.4214	87.4214	87.4214	12.5786	87.4214	12.5786
	DDoS	99.8301	99.7136	99.7719	0.2864	99.7136	0.1699
	DoS	99.6779	99.7989	99.7384	0.2011	99.7989	0.3221
	Reconnaissance	99.6212	99.9122	99.7665	0.0878	99.9122	0.3788
	Theft	98.2759	72.1519	83.2117	27.8481	72.1519	1.7241
All	Normal	84.4864	84.4864	84.4864	15.5136	84.4864	15.5136
	DDoS	99.8438	99.7148	99.7792	0.2852	99.7148	0.1562
	DoS	99.6897	99.7942	99.7419	0.2058	99.7942	0.3103
	Reconnaissance	99.1028	99.9308	99.5151	0.0692	99.9308	0.8972
	Theft	89.7436	88.6076	89.1720	11.3924	88.6076	10.2564

5 Conclusion

In this study, a statistical method named IoTInDet which is based on CSR and HD is suggested to detect intrusions in IoT traffic. In order to improve the attack detection system's accuracy and decrease false alarms, it is necessary to solve the curse of dimensionality problem. The CSR with HD based method was used to choose the best set of characteristics. The correlation between the features was extracted using the recommended HDC method. The HD metric was used to detect attacks. Using the UNSW Bot-IoT benchmark dataset, the performance of IoTInDet was assessed. The results exhibit that the suggested system has a 99.7558% accuracy rate. Comparing the suggested approach to the statistical attack detection systems, promising results are obtained. The FPR, however, declines as the accuracy rises. Still there is room for improvement in the reduction of FPR. Therefore, the development of a component to increase true positive rate while keeping low FPR could be the extension of this work.

References

1. Ambusaidi, M.A., He, X., Nanda, P., Tan, Z.: Building an intrusion detection system using a filter-based feature selection algorithm. IEEE Trans. Comput. **65**(10), 2986–2998 (2016). https://doi.org/10.1109/TC.2016.2519914
2. Bhuvaneswari Amma, N.G., Subramanian, S.: Feature correlation map based statistical approach for denial of service attacks detection. In: 2019 5th International Conference on Computing Engineering and Design (ICCED), pp. 1–6. IEEE (2019). https://doi.org/10.1109/ICCED46541.2019.9161080
3. Amma, N.B., Selvakumar, S., Velusamy, R.L.: A statistical approach for detection of denial of service attacks in computer networks. IEEE Trans. Netw. Serv. Manag. **17**(4), 2511–2522 (2020). https://doi.org/10.1109/TNSM.2020.3022799
4. Bhuvaneswari Amma, N.G., Selvakumar, S.: A statistical class center based triangle area vector method for detection of denial of service attacks. Cluster Comput. **24**(1), 393–415 (2020). https://doi.org/10.1007/s10586-020-03120-3
5. Denning, D.E.: An intrusion-detection model. IEEE Trans. Softw. Eng. **13**(2), 222–232 (1987). https://doi.org/10.1109/TSE.1987.232894
6. Douiba, M., Benkirane, S., Guezzaz, A., Azrour, M.: Anomaly detection model based on gradient boosting and decision tree for IoT environments security. J. Reliab. Intell. Environ., 1–12 (2022). https://doi.org/10.1007/s40860-022-00184-3
7. Gangula, R.: Network intrusion detection system for Internet of Things based on enhanced flower pollination algorithm and ensemble classifier. Concurr. Computa. Pract. Exp., e7103 (2022). https://doi.org/10.1002/cpe.7103
8. Iglesias, F., Zseby, T.: Analysis of network traffic features for anomaly detection. Mach. Learn. **101**(1–3), 59–84 (2015). https://doi.org/10.1007/s10994-014-5473-9
9. Koroniotis, N., Nour, M., Elena, S., Benjamin, T.: UNSW Bot-IoT dataset (2018). https://www.unsw.adfa.edu.au/unsw/canberra/cyber/cybersecurity/ADFA-NB15-Datasets/bot-iot.php
10. Moustafa, N., Slay, J., Creech, G.: Novel geometric area analysis technique for anomaly detection using trapezoidal area estimation on large-scale networks. IEEE Trans. Big Data (2017). https://doi.org/10.1109/TBDATA.2017.2715166
11. Bhuvaneswari Amma, N.G., Selvakumar, S.: Anomaly detection framework for Internet of Things traffic using vector convolutional deep learning approach in fog environment. Future Gener. Comput. Syst. **113**, 255–265 (2020). https://doi.org/10.1016/j.future.2020.07.020

12. Tan, Z., Jamdagni, A., He, X., Nanda, P., Liu, R.P.: Multivariate correlation analysis technique based on Euclidean distance map for network traffic characterization. In: Qing, S., Susilo, W., Wang, G., Liu, D. (eds.) ICICS 2011. LNCS, vol. 7043, pp. 388–398. Springer, Heidelberg (2011). https://doi.org/10.1007/978-3-642-25243-3_31

13. Tan, Z., Jamdagni, A., He, X., Nanda, P., Liu, R.P.: A system for denial-of-service attack detection based on multivariate correlation analysis. IEEE Trans. Parallel Distrib. Syst. **25**(2), 447–456 (2014). https://doi.org/10.1109/TPDS.2013.146

14. Tsai, C.F., Lin, C.Y.: A triangle area based nearest neighbors approach to intrusion detection. Pattern Recogn. **43**(1), 222–229 (2010). https://doi.org/10.1016/j.patcog.2009.05.017

15. Weller-Fahy, D.J., Borghetti, B.J., Sodemann, A.A.: A survey of distance and similarity measures used within network intrusion anomaly detection. IEEE Commu. Sur. Tutor. **17**(1), 70–91 (2015). https://doi.org/10.1109/COMST.2014.2336610

Detecting Cloud Originated DDoS Attacks at the Source Using Out-Cloud Attack Detection (OCAD)

Gulshan Kumar Singh and Gaurav Somani[✉]

Department of Computer Science and Engineering, Central University of Rajasthan, Ajmer, India
gaurav@curaj.ac.in

Abstract. DNS/NTP amplification and reflection attacks are few important forms of massive DDoS attacks. In this paper, we argue that such DDoS attacks which are originated from a cloud platform can be easily detected at the boundary of the source cloud platform. We design an out-cloud attack detection (OCAD) mechanism which monitors the traffic at the level of virtual network interfaces in the hypervisors or cloud physical servers. The traffic direction and the virtual network interfaces based monitoring help us in effective attack detection of DNS and NTP based reflection and amplification attacks. To show the effectiveness of our proposed detection mechanism, we conducted a set of real-time attack experiments on a small scale cloud prototype and observed the performance of our proposed mechanism, OCAD. We observe that our proposed mechanism detects the DNS/NTP reflection attacks in minimal time without getting much affected by the attack amplification factor and benign request rates.

Keywords: Cross-VM attacks · Amplification attacks · DDoS

1 Introduction

Cloud security has already been an important question in cloud adopters mind. Additionally, in many attack incidents, cloud services are used as attack infrastructure. Attackers used Amazon EC2 [10] instances to launch a DDoS attack by exploiting the vulnerability in the Elasticsearch. Therefore, both cloud provider and consumer may become the target of the attacker. A recent incident on GitHub[1] broke all the earlier records of DDoS attacks and touched the peak attack rate of 1.35 Tbps. This attack was a reflection based amplification attack which used Memcached server to reflect the traffic towards the victim. There are more significant breaches[2] in the cloud which affected organizations like Microsoft, Dropbox, LinkedIn, Yahoo, and Apple iCloud in the recent past.

Most attacks target cloud services to extort money or gain business benefits by affecting the availability and the fraudulent resource consumption. Similarly,

---

[1] https://www.wired.com/story/github-ddos-memcached/.
[2] https://blog.storagecraft.com/7-infamous-cloud-security-breaches/.

© The Author(s), under exclusive license to Springer Nature Switzerland AG 2022
V. R. Badarla et al. (Eds.): ICISS 2022, LNCS 13784, pp. 169–185, 2022.
https://doi.org/10.1007/978-3-031-23690-7_10

cloud resources are also used as attack infrastructure and provide on-demand resources for on-demand attacks. Booters[3] is a service type which uses malware driven bots and spoofing driven machines/infrastructure and bots to perform DDoS attacks.

Our proposed approach, OCAD (out-cloud attack detection) provides two-way monitoring of network traffic at the level of hypervisors in the cloud. The first monitoring point of traffic is towards the VMs to search for the amplification/reflection and the second point of monitoring is from VMs to check whether attack traffic is generated from the VMs. OCAD leverages the virtual interfaces and network monitoring to detect the malicious behaviour in the network traffic. Despite varying the rate of attacks, the packet detection time is almost same for all the cases. OCAD produces no performance overhead on VMs as monitoring and detection are done at the level of hypervisors.

The rest of this paper is organized as follows: Sect. 2 describes related work. Section 3 details cloud based DDoS attacks and Sect. 4 describes attack scenarios. Section 5 details the proposed detection method. Section 6 details the analysis and experimental results. In Sect. 7, we discuss the performance of our approach. We conclude our work in Sect. 8.

2   Related Work

There is a large amount of work related to DDoS attacks and its variants such as reflection and amplification attacks in traditional non-cloud environments. There are also a range of solutions based on cloud environments which cater to the detection and characterization of DDoS attacks for cloud environments [18]. In this work, we only focus on solutions dealing with the problem related to detecting reflection/amplification attacks at the source. While going through the past solutions, we observed a few other categories of solutions that overlap with the detection of amplification and reflection attacks and DDoS attacks in general. These categories are resource abuse in the cloud [5,14], IP spoofing [9], BotCloud detection [11], co-residency attacks [4], reflection/amplification detection at the target cloud [13], and the out-cloud attacks [1,2,8,12,17]. For a comprehensive coverage to the state of the art, we also discuss a few contributions in these categories.

IP spoofing has been a very important obstacle while designing solutions to combat DDoS attacks. The authors in [6] describe challenges with IP spoofing and showcase solutions working either in the network or at the target end. A basic technique to prevent IP spoofing is employed by filtering the spoofed packets where filtering can be ingress or egress filtering.

Cloud resource abuse is one of the top threats in cloud computing [5]. In [5], the authors proposed an anomaly detection system for the IaaS cloud built upon the neural network. Cloud resources can be abused either by a cloud user or an attacker who gained access to the cloud resources. Cloud resources are mostly

---

[3] https://booter-toplist.com.

abused by using botnets on cloud resources. The authors in [14] proposed an intrusion detection system to determine the malicious behaviour of the VMs. They used the Smith-Waterman algorithm to collect GPU usages data of VMs and analyze it to determine the malicious behaviour of the VMs.

Amplification and reflection attacks use multiple infected machines to target a victim service. Internet of Things (IoT) devices are gaining a lot of popularity and with the increase in the number of internetworking devices, we see an expansion in the attack surface. Authors in [7] analyzed four protocols SNMP, SSDP, NTP, and DNS and showed how they could be used in a reflection attack without sustaining the maximum amplification rate.

Apart from the DDoS attack, co-residency attacks in cloud infrastructure are also prevalent, which target sensitive data such as private keys of the victim. In [16], the authors presented the taxonomy of various shared resources and possible attacks in cloud infrastructure and a set of solutions to mitigate these attacks. In [4], the authors devised a method for co-residing VM in the Amazon EC2 instance and some guidelines to minimize the time for co-residing a VM.

Out-cloud attacks are the attacks originating from a cloud computing infrastructure. Attackers abuse cloud resources to generate heavy attack traffic towards the victim. Authors in [1,2,8,12,17] detailed the out-cloud attack and possible solutions to detect these types of attacks at the origin itself. In [1], the authors derived a method to detect cloud-based DDoS attacks at the origin using IP Spoofing detection. They used traffic flow behaviour and flow count to detect the high and low rate DDoS attack.

Similarly, in [17], the authors used hypervisor-based ingress filtering to detect the DNS amplification attack. The authors targeted Any, RRSIG, NS, DNSkey query of DNS to filter out malicious packets. The authors in [8] designed a machine learning based approach to filter out malicious network packets at the source. This approach uses both hypervisor and VM to study the packets and then filter them out at the hypervisor level. In [2], the authors proposed an approach using the graphical turing test and TTL to update the white and black lists of IPs to mitigate EDoS. In [12], the authors proposed a learning-based security method to monitor the cloud network and virtualization layer from outside of the cloud. They scan the packets for IP and MAC spoofing and pass filtered packets through the network.

Based on the above discussion over the state-of-the-art, we see very few solutions that cater to the need to detect amplification or reflection attacks originating or getting reflected or amplified from a public cloud platform. In this work, we address the out-cloud attacks having an attacker or a reflector in the cloud and accordingly design a solution that can effectively combat such attacks and stop the abuse of cloud resources.

3   Cloud-Based DDoS Attacks

Cloud provides profound resources so that the request of cloud customers can be fulfilled with a promise to provide on-demand resources. Primary launch method of DDoS attack is to spoof the source IP addresses, so that determination of attacker sources and subsequent filtering is falsified. An attacker can utilize the on-demand resources of the cloud to launch massive DDoS attacks utilizing spoofing, reflection, and amplification based methods. Figure 1 depicts how cloud resources can be utilized to generate massive attack traffic. Due to cloud's profound resources attack strength is also increased.

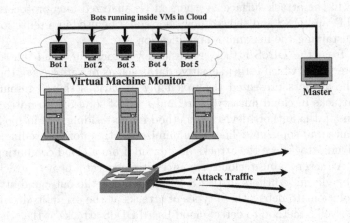

Fig. 1. Cloud-based DDOS attack scenario

An efficient defense and monitoring mechanism for cloud computing should help the cloud to monitor and detect the incoming and outgoing attacks. In this paper, we focus on an important class of DDoS refection and amplification attacks which are originated from the cloud. We discuss these attacks with a focus on how reflection/amplification and spoofing enabled attacks should be handled when they are generated or assisted by a cloud infrastructure.

4   Out-Cloud Attack Cases in Cloud

DDoS originating from the cloud can be classified into two categories. In the first category of attacks, the attacker is inside the cloud. In the second category of attacks, a VM hosted in the cloud may be used as a reflector in the reflection and amplification attacks. Besides these two cases, there is one more possibility where a victim host is hosted inside the cloud. We primarily focus on detecting DDoS amplification and reflection attacks originating from the cloud.

A cloud-hosted VM has a set of network configuration parameters which are known to cloud service providers. Some of these parameters include IP address, MAC address, hostname, and virtual interface name. These parameters are mostly available to the cloud provider to perform many management activities such as resource allocation, fault tolerance, load balancing, and resource billing. We leverage the above network parameters to monitor the network and find the anomaly in the network traffic. By utilizing these already available parameters, we argue that this scheme can always be offered by a CSP without having the knowledge of additional information related to the traffic flows. This would also help cloud consumers to trust such a solution from a CSP. Whenever a VM instance is created, cloud service provider initializes the VM with various configuration parameters including the network parameters such as address information and the interface names on the physical servers. Virtual interfaces created by cloud service provider for VMs are the virtual network interface in the hypervisor. The hypervisor can see these virtual interfaces and can monitor the network traffic passing through these virtual interfaces in both incoming and outgoing directions. Now, we discuss a set of attack scenarios which are important to understand the dynamics of the cloud originated attacks.

4.1   An Attacker in the Cloud

This is the scenario where an attacker owns a VM in the cloud and use the cloud infrastructure to launch an attack. In the case of DDoS attack, an attacker sends spoofed reflection packets to the amplification/reflection servers which are hosted outside or inside the cloud. In Fig. 2, we see this scenario where an attacker hosted inside a cloud is sending attack traffic to the amplifier server hosted outside the cloud. In this scenario, the attack traffic is found in the outgoing traffic of the attacker VM. The attacker VM plans the attack in a manner such that the response to the attack goes to the spoofed identity as a victim identity. We spot an opportunity to monitor the outgoing traffic to detect attacker VM present in the cloud.

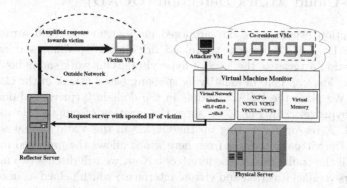

Fig. 2. Attack scenario (attacker in cloud)

4.2   A Reflector Server in the Cloud

In this scenario, the reflector or amplifier server (VM) is hosted inside the cloud. The attacker uses this server to reflect the attack traffic towards the victim. The attacker sends the spoofed reflection packet to the amplification server which is hosted inside the cloud. In Fig. 3, we see the scenario where an amplification server is hosted inside the cloud and is used by the attacker as an amplifier. In this, the attack traffic is found in the incoming traffic of the amplifier server. We argue that monitoring the incoming traffic of the amplification server may help in detection of these attacks.

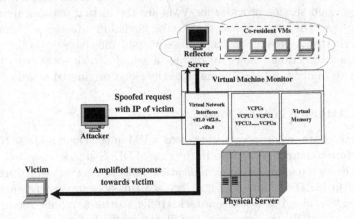

Fig. 3. Attack scenario (reflector in cloud)

5   Out-Cloud Attack Detection (OCAD)

In this section, we describe our proposed mechanism out-cloud attack detection (OCAD). OCAD detects the cloud originating spoofing and amplification/reflection attacks at the level of hypervisors. Our work shows how a cloud service provider can help in identifying spoofing based attack in the cloud environment. We place the OCAD module in the domain 0 (privileged domain) of the Xen hypervisor. In Fig. 4, we show the location of our OCAD module in the VMM. A reason for setting up the OCAD in the VMM is that we get to access all the virtual interfaces from here which allows the proposed module to monitor all the traffic from these interfaces. Now, we will discuss two important parameters (traffic direction and virtual interfaces) which helped us in collecting network traffic data and to detect the attacker/reflector in the cloud.

5.1   Traffic Directions

The direction of network traffic helps in detecting whether the network packet is from attacker hosted in the cloud or it is a request from an attacker to amplifier server hosted in the cloud. We give following outputs by tcpdump to showcase the network direction.

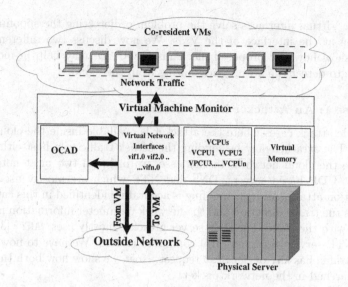

Fig. 4. Out-Cloud Attack Detection (OCAD) module in cloud

```
16:43:35.394854 IP 10.0.101.229.43887 > 10.0.96.101.123:
```

Above output shows that the direction of traffic is from port number 43887 of 10.0.101.229 to port number 123 of 10.0.96.101. It suggests that traffic is from client to server which is NTP server (port 123) is this case.

```
11:50:09.819525 IP 10.0.96.101.123 > 10.0.13.192.48523:
```

Above output shows the direction of traffic is from port number 123 of 10.0.96.101 to port number 48523 of 10.0.013.192 which suggests that the traffic direction is from the server towards a client.

5.2 Virtual Interfaces vs Real Interfaces

Virtual interfaces are the interfaces used by VMs for network connectivity. These interfaces are created by the CSP to manage the VMs. Each virtual interface created for the VMs follow a nomenclature to name the virtual interfaces. If a VM is hosted on a cloud where domain ID of VM is 3 and hosted on a cloud server with ID 0, then the virtual interface name for the VM is vif3.0. The name of the virtual interface is assigned as:

$$Virtual\ Interface\ Name = DomainID.hostID$$

In this way, we find which traffic flow is from which source by finding the name of the domain ID in the virtual interface name. In the case of real interfaces, these are the interfaces on the individual's physical machine and identifiers/names of such interfaces are not readily available to the network edges. Therefore, we cannot determine the spoofed traffic generated from machines using real interfaces. Virtual interfaces solve the problem of detecting the spoofing attack by looking at the interface of the VMs. We now discuss two different attack cases to show how our proposed mechanism, OCAD, may help in monitoring the traffic to detect the attacks originating from the cloud.

5.3 Case 1: An Attacker in the Cloud

We include attack cases where the attacker is available inside the cloud infrastructure. The attacker may be sending the attack traffic to a host either inside or outside the cloud network. In this case, we included two most notable and important UDP based servers, DNS and NTP which are mostly used for the amplification attack. Address spoofing is accurately identified in this category of attacks as the traffic direction and the network parameter information is already available with the cloud. For DNS server attacker mostly uses "ANY" [3] request and for NTP server "monlist" [15] command is used. We have to now monitor whether traffic has ANY or monlist request. Now, we show how both the queries can be searched in the network packet.

DNS Protocol Enabled Attack. The attacker uses ANY query to amplify the request. To capture the packets with ANY request, we have to first look at the packet format of the DNS shown in Fig. 5. The first line in the Fig. 5 is showing the request type with IP address of both the parties. First IP is of the sender and the second IP is of the server. We can see the word ANY? in the first line which shows that the query is of ANY type. Searching "ANY" in the packet header with IP addresses is easy for detection of DNS ANY requests.

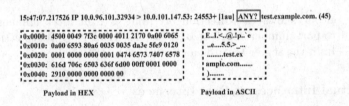

15:47:07.217526 IP 10.0.96.101.32934 > 10.0.101.147.53: 24553+ [1au] ANY? test.example.com. (45)

0x0000: 4500 0049 7f3c 0000 4011 2170 0a00 6065	E..I.<..@.!p.. e
0x0010: 0a00 6593 80a6 0035 0035 da3e 5fe9 0120	..e....5.5.>_...
0x0020: 0001 0000 0000 0001 0474 6573 7407 6578	.........test.ex
0x0030: 616d 706c 6503 636f 6d00 00ff 0001 0000	ample.com.......
0x0040: 2910 0000 0000 0000 00	)........

Payload in HEX   Payload in ASCII

Fig. 5. Network packet format - DNS ANY query

NTP Protocol Enabled Attack. In the case of NTP packets, the attacker uses monlist command to amplify the response generated by the NTP server. We can see the packet format of the NTP monlist request in Fig. 6. The first line in the packet format of the NTP monlist shows the IP address of both the parties. First IP address belongs to the sender and the second IP is of the NTP server. We are not able to see details showing it as a monlist request in the first line. We have to look into the payload of the packet to see the monlist request. In the payload part of the packet, we can see that "2a" in HEX payload and "*" in ASCII payload which stands for the monlist request.

11:54:22.164600 IP 10.0.96.101.55603 > 134.75.239.2.123: NTPv2, Reserved, length 160

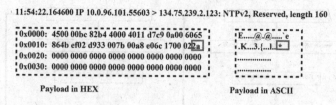

Payload in HEX   Payload in ASCII

Fig. 6. Network packet format - NTP `monlist` command

5.4   Case 2: A Reflector Server in the Cloud

In this case, reflector or amplifier server is hosted in the cloud and helps the attacker in launching massive DDoS attacks. The attacker sends amplification query to the server to amplify the response. Similar to attack case in Sect. 5.3, we considered two amplification servers, i.e., DNS and NTP. In this case, we need to monitor the incoming traffic instead of outgoing traffic. Reason for monitoring incoming traffic is that attacker sends the spoofed query to the server hosted inside the cloud. In this case, the server will not be able to identify whether packets are spoofed or not as the attack source is outside the network under administration. We provide a detection mechanism which by using a fixed threshold, can detect that the victim server (reflector) is forced to participate in an amplification or reflection attack. As discussed in Sect. 5, we employ a similar monitoring mechanism for DNS and NTP traffic. The packet format for the incoming traffic is same for both servers as shown in Fig. 5 and Fig. 6. In Fig. 5, the first IP is the source IP address which is spoofed.

5.5   OCAD Modules

Now, we discuss all the four modules used in OCAD. We detailed the steps involved in detecting out-cloud attacks in Fig. 7. First, we monitor the incoming traffic for detecting amplifier server or outgoing traffic to detecting attacker using DNS amplification attack. The second step is to match the packets with attack features available with the cloud provider. After that, the OCAD filters out all identified attack packets. If the frequency is greater than the threshold, an alert will be generated for the cloud provider about the attack. Same steps are being followed for detection of NTP server; we search for the `monlist` request instead of `ANY` request.

6   Experimental Evaluation

In order to ascertain the applicability and efficacy of our proposed mechanism, we conduct a set of real attack experiments in an experimental setup.

6.1   Experimental Setup

In this section, we discuss our experimental setup used for evaluation of our proposed approach. For this purpose, we set up a small cloud prototype to perform

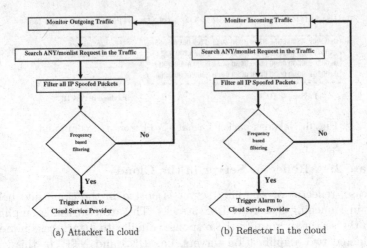

(a) Attacker in cloud   (b) Reflector in the cloud

Fig. 7. Flowchart for detection (a) attacker sending reflection packets from the cloud (b) attacker using DNS/NTP server as amplifier

real attack experiments. For this purpose, we setup following servers/machines. We detail the overall experimental setup in Fig. 8 and Table 1 and Table 2.

1. **Attacker Machine (External Network):** This machine sends attack traffic using reflector and amplification servers using external NTP/DNS servers.
2. **Victim Machine (External Network):** This machine represents a machine outside the cloud network which gets the reflected and amplified traffic from the cloud.
3. **DNS and NTP Server (External Network):** These servers represent the servers which are reflectors and amplifiers used by the attacker inside the cloud.
4. **A cloud server (Cloud Network):** This server represents the cloud network which has two kinds of VMs
   (a) **Attacker VM:** Sending attack traffic from a cloud network.
   (b) **Reflector VM:** Reflecting/amplifying the traffic from a cloud network.

Table 1. Configurations used for experimental analysis

Configuration	Attacker/victim (outside cloud)	Server (DNS and NTP) (outside cloud)	Cloud server
Processor	Intel Core i5-2500, 4 CPUs	Intel Core i5-2500, 4 CPUs	Intel Core i7-4770, 8 CPUs
Memory	2 GB DDR3	2 GB DDR3	8 GB DDR3
Disk	500 GB	500 GB	500 GB
Operating System	Ubuntu 17.04 Desktop Edition	Ubuntu 17.04 Desktop Edition	Ubuntu 14.04 Server Edition
DNS Server Version	–	bind9 version 9.10.3	–
NTP Server Version	–	ntp version 4.2.8.p10	–
Hypervisor Version	–	-	Xen hypervisor version 4.5

Figure 8 shows our experimental setup. Similarly, in Table 2 we can see the configurations of the VMs used for experimentation.

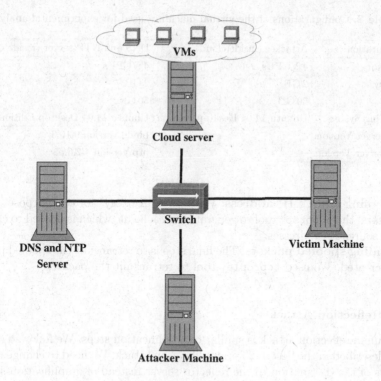

Fig. 8. Experimental setup

6.2 Amplification Attack

In this section, we discuss the steps involved to perform amplification attack for the different scenarios we discussed in Sect. 5.3. We explain the attack experiment setup in the following:

1. **Establishing DNS server:** We used bind9[4] utility to establish a DNS server. We use the TXT entry to generate the response of 4038 bytes.
2. **Establishing NTP server:** We used ntp[5] utility to establish a NTP server. We enabled monlist query and added 200 entries to get the amplification factor of 100.
3. **Packet generation for DNS ANY query:** We used dig[6] command of Linux to generate ANY query.
4. **Packet generation for NTP monlist query:** We use ntpdc command to generate NTP monlist query.
5. **Packet capturing:** We captured the packet using the tcpdump[7] tool.

---

[4] https://linux.die.net/man/2/bind.
[5] https://manpages.ubuntu.com/manpages/xenial/man8/ntpd.8.html.
[6] https://linux.die.net/man/1/dig.
[7] https://www.tcpdump.org/tcpdump_man.html.

Table 2. Configurations of the virtual machines used for experimental analysis

Configuration	Attacker (inside cloud)	DNS and NTP server (inside cloud)
Processor	4 VCPUs	4 VCPUs
Memory	2 GB	2 GB
Disk	50 GB	50 GB
Operating System	Ubuntu 14.04 Desktop Edition	Ubuntu 14.04 Desktop Edition
DNS Server Version	–	bind9 version 9.10.3
NTP Server Version	–	ntp version 4.2.6.p5

6. **Spoofing source IP address:** We used `tcpreplay`[8] for our purpose. First, we used the `tcpprep`[9] tool to generate the cache file which is needed to change the source IP addresses.
7. **Sending spoofed packets:** The final step is to retransmit the spoofed packet we created. We used `tcpreplay` tool to retransmit the packet.

6.3   Reflection Attack

Performing reflection attack is similar to amplification steps. We followed all the steps described in the Sect. 6.2 for amplification attack. We need to change the IP address of the destination to the reflector server instead of amplification server. In next section, we discuss the attack experiment results using our proposed mechanism.

6.4   Experimental Results

In this section, we detail the experimental results of five different experiments.

1. **MAC/IP Spoofing:** First, we created a module to detect the IP or MAC spoofing attacks originating from cloud-hosted VMs. This module utilizes the known parameters of VMs like IP address, MAC address, and direction of the network traffic flow to detect the IP/MAC spoofing attacks.
   The direction of the network traffic helped us to easily get all the source IPs and MACs in the same column (discussed in Sect. 5.1). Figure 9 shows the screenshot of our live experimentation to find the source IP and MAC address in the network traffic. The first column in the Fig. 9 is showing the frequency of the packets, the second column shows the source MAC address of the VM, and the third column displays the source IP address of the VM.
2. **Out-Cloud Attack: Attacker inside cloud (DNS Amplification):** On top of the MAC/IP spoofing module, we created a higher level module which reads the packets to detect the desired request sent by the VM. We transmitted the spoofed packet with different frequencies and tried to detect them in

---

[8] https://linux.die.net/man/1/tcpreplay.
[9] https://linux.die.net/man/1/tcpprep.

Table 3. Attack detection time for DNS server when attacker inside cloud.

Req./sec.		Total packets received	Attack packets detected	Detection time (in sec.)		
Benign	Attack			$AF=20$	$AF=45$	$AF=90$
10	100	6482	5887	0.084	0.076	0.072
10	200	12817	11704	0.128	0.136	0.120
10	500	29878	29282	0.288	0.272	0.268
10	1000	58880	58276	0.588	0.576	0.586
10	2000	117177	116576	1.112	1.032	1.140
20	100	6678	5892	0.079	0.081	0.076
20	200	12732	11813	0.121	0.127	0.120
20	500	29803	29326	0.291	0.289	0.282
20	1000	58923	58334	0.601	0.592	0.590
20	2000	117342	116813	1.123	1.120	1.114
50	100	6692	5884	0.081	0.078	0.080
50	200	12756	11823	0.109	0.121	0.119
50	500	29812	29334	0.301	0.299	0.286
50	1000	58876	58341	0.588	0.591	0.589
50	2000	118125	116892	1.121	1.120	1.119

the VMM. For normal traffic, we used `dig` command to generate A, AAAA, and MX request with three different rates of 10, 20, and 50 requests per seconds. The result of our detection mechanism is detailed in Table 3 and 4. We monitored traffic in the slots of 60 s each, for this reason we added an additional time of 60 s to the observed attack detection time.

We observe that there is no effect on detection time when benign request rate or amplification factor is increased. Our method is independent of benign request rate and amplification factor because we are not monitoring the amplified requests and only monitoring the packets which lead to the amplification.

3. **Out-Cloud Attack: DNS amplifier inside cloud:** Table 3 shows the case where DNS server is hosted inside the cloud and attacker is using this server as an amplifier server. The attacker sends amplification query to this server to get the amplified response. Therefore, we have to monitor the incoming traffic to detect whether the server is forced to be used as an amplifier server.

4. **Out-Cloud Attack: Attacker inside cloud (NTP Amplification):** In this case, the attacker is sending amplification requests to the NTP server. We have to monitor outgoing traffic in this case to detect whether NTP amplification request is transmitted or not. We discussed in Sect. 4. how `monlist` command helps attackers. The `monlist` command returns the last 600 host

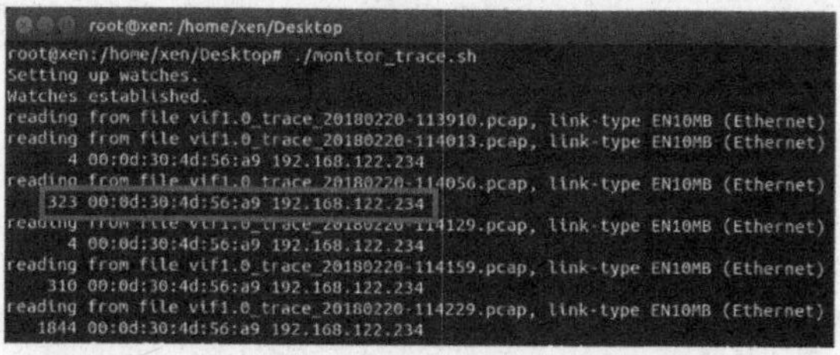

Fig. 9. Monitoring source IP and MAC address

Table 4. Attack detection time for DNS server when reflector inside cloud.

Req./sec.		Total packets received	Attack packets detected	Detection time (in sec.)		
Benign	Attack			AF = 20	AF = 45	AF = 90
10	100	8546	5898	0.068	0.068	0.060
10	200	14901	11799	0.112	0.116	0.132
10	500	32532	29497	0.264	0.232	0.224
10	1000	62540	58990	0.472	0.448	0.488
10	2000	121224	118841	0.948	1.020	0.976
20	100	8558	5888	0.071	0.069	0.066
20	200	14953	11813	0.122	0.119	0.120
20	500	32541	29502	0.258	0.249	0.251
20	1000	62567	58987	0.463	0.471	0.474
20	2000	121326	118861	0.962	1.013	0.976
50	100	8543	5886	0.072	0.068	0.067
50	200	14961	11823	0.119	0.123	0.121
50	500	32533	29512	0.260	0.256	0.254
50	1000	62559	58977	0.461	0.469	0.470
50	2000	121332	118858	0.965	1.002	0.984

entries which connected to the NTP server in the past. We also discussed in Sect. 5.3 how to detect the `monlist` request in the network packet. We have to search for "*" in HEX output or "2a" in ASCII output. In this manner, we can find whether NTP amplification request is transmitted or not from the VM hosted in the cloud. We show the attack detection time for NTP server in Tables 5 and 6.

Table 5. Attack detection time for NTP server when attacker inside cloud.

Req./sec.		Total packets received	Attack packets detected	Detection time (in sec.)		
Benign	Attack			AF = 25	AF = 50	AF = 100
10	100	6487	5884	0.144	0.148	0.147
10	200	12351	11753	0.376	0.324	0.332
10	500	29837	29276	0.648	0.664	0.668
10	1000	58525	57935	1.472	1.448	1.548
10	2000	116583	115981	3.464	3.220	3.340
20	100	6479	5886	0.141	0.144	0.147
20	200	12351	11753	0.334	0.329	0.331
20	500	29845	29281	0.658	0.661	0.660
20	1000	58532	57941	1.451	1.449	1.547
20	2000	116579	115978	3.346	3.339	3.342
50	100	6483	5881	0.139	0.143	0.145
50	200	12362	11758	0.335	0.331	0.331
50	500	29856	29279	0.656	0.659	0.661
50	1000	58543	57949	1.449	1.447	1.551
50	2000	116582	115984	3.349	3.338	3.336

5. **Out-Cloud Attack: NTP amplifier server inside the cloud:** In this case, attacker is using NTP server hosted in the cloud for the amplification attack. Attacker sends amplification query to the server with spoofed source IP address. We have to monitor the incoming traffic to detect the NTP amplification query. We discussed the case of an attacker in the cloud where the attacker is sending NTP amplification query to a server hosted outside the

Table 6. Attack detection time for NTP server when reflector inside cloud

Req./sec.		Total packets received	Attack packets detected	Detection time (in sec.)		
Benign	Attack			AF = 25	AF = 50	AF = 100
10	100	8766	5898	0.220	0.228	0.224
10	200	14233	11798	0.424	0.432	0.412
10	500	33005	29495	0.876	0.812	0.848
10	1000	62981	59807	1.812	1.804	1.720
10	2000	123986	119305	3.472	3.542	3.520
20	100	8774	5892	0.222	0.227	0.226
20	200	14242	11791	0.425	0.431	0.430
20	500	33012	29493	0.868	0.854	0.862
20	1000	62989	59812	1.817	1.809	1.721
20	2000	123979	119314	3.469	3.551	3.548
50	100	8786	5896	0.219	0.228	0.223
50	200	14251	11789	0.422	0.430	0.428
50	500	33023	29487	0.865	0.858	0.862
50	1000	62984	59821	1.821	1.819	1.745
50	2000	123981	119323	3.463	3.559	3.553

cloud in the above point. Similarly, we followed the same procedure in the incoming traffic to find "*" in HEX and "2a" in ASCII to determine the amplification query. By this mechanism, we detect the cloud-hosted NTP server used for amplification attack.

We can see that by varying amplification factor, it does not affect the detection time of our mechanism OCAD. The reason behind this is the traffic we monitor, for detection of an attacker in the cloud we monitor outgoing packets which is not amplified. Similarly, we monitor incoming packets for detecting amplification server in the cloud which is also is not an amplified packet.

7   Discussion

In this Section, we detail some additional aspects related to our solution.

1. **Detection Accuracy:** We showed that our approach is good at detecting spoofing and spoofing driven attacks (amplification, reflection and DDoS in general). In the current set of experiments, we used a count based filtering mechanism which filters a source as the attacker when sees 100 number of similar request packets in a time period. Other more sophisticated schemes may be also be employed to overcome the performance and false negative issues related to the count based filtering mechanisms.

2. **Amplification Factor:** Amplification factor plays an important role in amplification attack. Amplification factor decides the rate at which victim receives the network traffic. We can understand this with some examples. For request size 16 bytes and amplification factor 145, we can get the received traffic size by multiplying the request size and amplification factor.

$$Received\ Size = 16 \times 145 = 2320\ bytes$$

We can see that how amplification factor give the advantage to attacker for generating the traffic beyonds its bandwidth.

3. **Amplification Factor vs Detection Time:** We study the amplification factor and its relevance in the DDoS attack. Amplification factor increases the bandwidth of the DDoS attack, but amplification factor does not affect the detection time of our mechanism. Our mechanism, OCAD, monitors incoming traffic for amplifier servers and outgoing traffic for attackers. In both the cases, we monitor the request which is not amplified yet, that's why our mechanism is not affected by the amplification factor.
4. **Non-intrusive detection:** OCAD sees the traffic which is coming out of the virtual network interfaces and detects the malicious activities. Security is an important cloud adoption issue and many cloud consumers expect security as an additional product/service from a cloud infrastructure. The network configuration information available with the hypervisor or the cloud service provider actually helps in the performing the out-cloud attack detection even in the presence of much-difficult spoofing enabled attacks.
5. **Cloud Scale Attacks:** The proposed methods can be extended to see the cloud scale data from multiple hypervisors and take decisions which involved collusive attacks and attacks affecting multiple servers in the cloud etc.

8   Conclusions

DNS/NTP amplification are some of the important DDoS attack variants which produce massive attack traffics towards the victim. In this paper, we proposed OCAD mechanism which detects out-cloud attacks at the origin of the attacks that is cloud infrastructure. We argue that detecting IP spoofed packets originating from cloud platform is easy to detect at the source. We show that the detection efficacy of our proposed mechanism, with the help of real-time attack experiments in a small-scale cloud prototype in the lab setting. Our mechanism detects IP spoofing enabled amplification and reflection attack at the level of hypervisors. We also show that our mechanism is independent of amplification factor and rate of the benign requests. Our module effectively detected NTP amplification in 1.223 s and DNS amplification in 0.458 s on the average.

Acknowledgments. This research work is partially supported by the DST-SERB, Government of India with the help of a Core Research Grant number CRG/2020/005759.

References

1. Agrawal, N., Tapaswi, S.: A lightweight approach to detect the low/high rate IP spoofed cloud DDoS attacks. In: 2017 IEEE 7th International Symposium on Cloud and Service Computing (SC2), pp. 118–123. IEEE (2017)
2. Al-Haidari, F., Sqalli, M.H., Salah, K.: Enhanced EDOS-shield for mitigating EDOS attacks originating from spoofed ip addresses. In: 2012 IEEE 11th International Conference on Trust, Security and Privacy in Computing and Communications, pp. 1167–1174. IEEE (2012)
3. Anagnostopoulos, M., Kambourakis, G., Kopanos, P., Louloudakis, G., Gritzalis, S.: DNS amplification attack revisited. Comput. Secur. **39**, 475–485 (2013)

4. Atya, A.O.F., Qian, Z., Krishnamurthy, S.V., La Porta, T., McDaniel, P., Marvel, L.: Malicious co-residency on the cloud: attacks and defense. In: IEEE INFOCOM 2017-IEEE Conference on Computer Communications, pp. 1–9. IEEE (2017)
5. Doelitzscher, F., Knahl, M., Reich, C., Clarke, N.: Anomaly detection in IaaS clouds. In: 2013 IEEE 5th International Conference on Cloud Computing Technology and Science, vol. 1, pp. 387–394. IEEE (2013)
6. Ehrenkranz, T., Li, J.: On the state of IP spoofing defense. ACM Trans. Internet Technol. (TOIT) 9(2), 1–29 (2009)
7. Gondim, J.J., de Oliveira Albuquerque, R., Orozco, A.L.S.: Mirror saturation in amplified reflection distributed denial of service: a case of study using SNMP, SSDP, NTP and DNS protocols. Future Gener. Comput. Syst. 108, 68–81 (2020)
8. He, Z., Zhang, T., Lee, R.B.: Machine learning based DDoS attack detection from source side in cloud. In: 2017 IEEE 4th International Conference on Cyber Security and Cloud Computing (CSCloud), pp. 114–120. IEEE (2017)
9. Huistra, D.: Detecting reflection attacks in DNS flows. In: 19th Twente Student Conference on IT (2013)
10. Infosecurity Magazine: DDoS-ers launch attacks from Amazon EC2. https://www.infosecurity-magazine.com/news/ddos-ers-launch-attacks-from-amazon-ec2/
11. Memarian, M.R., Conti, M., Leppänen, V.: EyeCloud: a BotCloud detection system. In: 2015 IEEE Trustcom/BigDataSE/ISPA. vol. 1, pp. 1067–1072. IEEE (2015)
12. Mishra, P., Pilli, E.S., Varadharajan, V., Tupakula, U.: Out-VM monitoring for malicious network packet detection in cloud. In: 2017 ISEA Asia Security and Privacy (ISEASP), pp. 1–10. IEEE (2017)
13. Osanaiye, O.A.: Short paper: IP spoofing detection for preventing DDoS attack in cloud computing. In: 2015 18th International Conference on Intelligence in Next Generation Networks, pp. 139–141. IEEE (2015)
14. Pitropakis, N., Lyvas, C., Lambrinoudakis, C.: The greater the power, the more dangerous the abuse: facing malicious insiders in the cloud (2017)
15. Rudman, L., Irwin, B.: Characterization and analysis of NTP amplification based DDoS attacks. In: 2015 Information Security for South Africa (ISSA), pp. 1–5. IEEE (2015)
16. Singh, G.K., Somani, G.: Cross-VM attacks: attack taxonomy, defense mechanisms, and new directions. In: Conti, M., Somani, G., Poovendran, R. (eds.) Versatile Cybersecurity. AIS, vol. 72, pp. 257–286. Springer, Cham (2018). https://doi.org/10.1007/978-3-319-97643-3_8
17. Soliman, A.K., Salama, C., Mohamed, H.K.: Detecting DNS reflection amplification DDoS attack originating from the cloud. In: 2018 13th International Conference on Computer Engineering and Systems (ICCES), pp. 145–150. IEEE (2018)
18. Yan, Q., Yu, F.R., Gong, Q., Li, J.: Software-defined networking (SDN) and distributed denial of service (DDoS) attacks in cloud computing environments: a survey, some research issues, and challenges. IEEE Commun. Surv. Tutor. 18(1), 602–622 (2015)

Mining Attribute-Based Access Control Policies

Maryam Davari[(✉)] and Mohammad Zulkernine

School of Computing, Queen's University, Kingston, Canada
{maryam.davari,mz}@queensu.ca

Abstract. The flexibility feature of Attribute-Based Access Control (ABAC) makes it a powerful access control model for supporting the authorization demands of complex and dynamic systems. However, the migration from traditional access control models to the ABAC model is challenging. One promising approach to ease the burden of policy migration is policy mining. This paper proposes a bottom-up policy mining approach to automatically extract policies by mining access logs. The approach also employs machine learning techniques to learn ABAC policies. Real and synthetic data sets are employed to evaluate the approach. The experimental results demonstrate that our approach can generate ABAC policy rules efficiently.

Keywords: Attribute-Based Access Control · Policy mining · Constraints · Separation of Duty constraints · Machine learning

1 Introduction

Large businesses need to provide access to users who are distributed across a variety of computing environments and applications. Each application might have a different access control model. Attribute-Based Access Control (ABAC) [10] model has been found to be promising for complex and dynamic systems since they offer a lot of flexibility when it comes to handling authorization requirements. This model grants access depending on users, resources, and environment attributes.

Migrating to the ABAC model from traditional access control is difficult as i) manual policy specification has proven to be tedious, costly, and error-prone [9], ii) policies in collaborative environments cannot be static because they must adapt to different situations and contexts, and iii) the ABAC model has a number of attributes that make policy specification and maintenance difficult. Mining prior access requests and their corresponding decisions to extract policies is one way to construct ABAC policies automatically. It has the potential to lower the cost of policy development. Policy mining identifies rules that define attribute values and conditions that must be satisfied by a user to perform an action on a resource.

Existing policy mining solutions can be classified into top-down and bottom-up approaches. In the top-down approach [21], organizational processes that are

V. R. Badarla et al. (Eds.): ICISS 2022, LNCS 13784, pp. 186–201, 2022.
https://doi.org/10.1007/978-3-031-23690-7_11

functionally independent are identified and associated with required access. In the bottom-up approach [19], existing access in organizations is generalized to generate rules. The limitations of the existing policy mining approaches are as follows. Environmental conditions that can help in the development of dynamic policy rules are ignored. In addition, constraints that express relationships between users and resources are not taken into consideration.

In this paper, we propose a bottom-up-based policy mining approach to mine ABAC rules from access logs, which can help to migrate to this model. The approach can assist security administrators in identifying potential rules from available information (access requests and corresponding decisions). Access requests with similarities are mapped into a cluster. Rules that can satisfy a significant number of records in the data set are chosen from the clusters. Then, the rules are generalized. We employ machine learning techniques to extract ABAC rules automatically from data. Furthermore, the combination of policy mining and machine learning can help extract ABAC rules effectively. The experimental results show that the policy mining approach is more efficient for mining ABAC rules in comparison with the existing work. The extracted rules form the mined ABAC policies. The major contributions of this paper are as follows:

- We propose a clustering-based approach to cluster access requests and rules are extracted from the clusters.
- We optimize the policy mining approach by considering constraints.
- The approach was implemented and evaluated using various ABAC policy rules.

The rest of the paper is organized as follows: Sect. 2 overviews the ABAC model. Section 3 presents the related work. In Sect. 4, we propose our ABAC policy extraction approach. In Sect. 5, we present the experimental evaluation. Finally, Sect. 6 outlines conclusions and future work.

2 Overview of ABAC

We adopt the core components of the ABAC model from the NIST's document [10] and some components are extended or defined for our work as follows:

Definition 1. User attribute. Attributes that describe the characteristics of users. Let U be a finite set of users and Att_u be a finite set of user attributes. The value of attribute $a \in Att_u$ for user $u \in U$ is represented by the function $d_u(a, u)$.

Definition 2. Resource attribute. Attributes that describe the characteristics of resources. Let R be a finite set of resources and Att_r be a finite set of resource attributes. The value of attribute $a \in Att_r$ for resource $r \in R$ is represented by the function $d_r(a, r)$.

Definition 3. Environment attribute. Attributes that represent the current states of system environments (Att_{env}) such as time and location. The environment attributes help in making dynamic access decisions. The value of attribute $a \in Att_{env}$ for environment $env \in Env$ is represented by the function $d_{env}(a, env)$.

Definition 4. Attribute expression. Attribute expression contains a set of attributes, actions, and values (att, act, val). A user attribute expression (e_U) is a function e that for each user attribute $a \in Att_u$, $e_U(a)$ is either special value $\perp$ (that indicates there is no constraint on the value of attribute a) or a set of possible values. Similarly, resource attribute expression (e_R) selects resources.

Definition 5. Access request. An access request is represented as a tuple $<u, r, act>$, where u denotes the user who requested access, r denotes the target resource, and act denotes an action.

Definition 6. Constraint. Constraints in the ABAC model are used to represent relationships between users and resources. One of the key features of this model is that it enables the specification and enforcement of various types of constraints, including Separation of Duty (SOD), User Capability (UC), and Binding Of Duty (BOD) constraints. Some constraints, such as UC, are not related to access control and may reflect various security requirements of organizations [22].

A constraint is formed by a set (or conjunction) of atomic constraints. User u and resource r can satisfy a constraint c (indicated as $<u, r| = c>$), if they satisfy all the atomic constraints in c. A nurse can read medical records of a patient on a ward where she or he works, and the topic of the item is among their specialties. This is an example of two atomic constraints in the health care domain that can be shown by $<u.word = r.word \land topic \in specialties>$. There are various types of constraints in ABAC policy rules.

Separation of Duty (SoD) is one of the important constraints in commercial applications [15]. SoD ensures that no single user can complete all of the steps in a task. The reason is that a single person is more likely to commit fraud than a group of people. Requesting a loan and accepting the loan request, for example, should not be done by a user on a banking application. To obtain SoD, a task is partitioned among a set of users. K-n SoD states that at least k users require to get all n permissions $s <\{t_1, t_2, ..., t_n\}, k>$, where each t_i is a pair of resources and actions (r_i, act_i) and $1 < k \leq n$.

SoD can be static or dynamic. Static SoD (SSoD) enforces constraints independent of the changing environment, while Dynamic SoD (DSoD) imposes constraints based on runtime conditions. DSoD can be defined as $<\{t_1, t_2, ..., t_n\}, k, [st, et]>$, where $[st, et]$ is the time interval. It demonstrates that constraint holds valid from time st to time et. In this work, we focus on the atomic, SSoD, and k-n SSoD constraints.

3   Related Work

ABAC policy mining is studied by some researchers [4,5,7,11–13,18,19,25,25]. Xu and Stoller propose the first algorithms for ABAC policy mining from access logs [25] and access control lists [25]. Their algorithms construct candidate rules by iterating over access control information (e.g., roles and access control logs) and then they generalize each candidate rule. Their algorithms are specific to their policy framework and data model. Medvet et al. [19] propose the first separate and conquer approach for mining ABAC policy. Similar to [25] their approach cannot mine negative rules. In addition, their performance is not much better than [25].

Iyer et al. [11] propose a heuristic ABAC policy mining approach based on PRISM [3]. It inherits the deficiencies of PRISM including a large number of rules and a huge search space for attribute values. It can also mine ABAC policies with the permit and deny decisions. Cotrini et al. [5] present an ABAC rule mining algorithm from sparse logs (i.e., a sparse log only contains a portion of all possible requests) named Rhapsody. The algorithm is based upon subgroup discovery algorithms. They propose a novel metric named reliability that measures how extracted rules are permissive. Moreover, they propose a cross-validation metric for evaluating the mined policy in the case of sparse logs. Their algorithm is not effective for mining logs with many attributes as the number of rules grows exponentially. Rhapsody is based on a machine-learning algorithm named APRIORI-SD to discover subgroups [2].

Cotrini et al. [4] propose a "universal" access control policy mining algorithm that produces policy mining algorithms for a wide range of policy languages. The algorithm gains lower policy quality than the customized algorithm. Gautam et al. [7] present a constrained policy mining algorithm that takes the Access Control Matrix (ACM) as input and builds ABAC authorization rules. In their model, each rule has at most a fixed number of attributes. Mocanu et al. [20] apply a deep learning technique to understand rules from log files. Both permitted and denied access are considered. Karimi et al. [18] propose an ABAC policy learning algorithm from access logs. They use an unsupervised algorithm based on K-modes clustering to simplify the access control policy development process. Following this work, Karimi et al. [17] present an automated policy extraction from access logs containing positive and negative authorizations.

Jabal et al. [12] develop a policy mining approach that uses access requests and their corresponding access control decisions. They use contextual information gained from other resources. Their work deals with several limitations. For example, they are specific to a policy framework and a data model. Their approaches are not able to mine noisy access logs that can contain over-assignments or under-assignments. They are not able to cover authorization rules with negative filters. They lack the capability to mine logs with many attributes. In general, some of the suggested policy mining methods lack interpretability, are confusing, and are complex. Additionally, they do not take SoD constraints into account.

4 ABAC Policy Extraction

In this section, we present a policy mining approach and employ machine learning for policy extraction.

Algorithm 1. Extract Rules

Require: DS^+
1: $Cls_u \leftarrow$ Clustering_DS $(DS^+ - att_u)$
2: **for each** cluster $cl_j \in Cls_u$ **do**
3:   $cl_j.candidate\_rule.att_u \leftarrow \bigcap_{r_i \in cl_j} r_i.att_u$
4: **end for**
5: $Cls_r \leftarrow$ Clustering_DS $(DS^+ - att_r)$
6: **for each** cluster $cl_j \in Cls_r$ **do**
7:   $cl_j.candidate\_rule.att_r \leftarrow \bigcap_{r_i \in cl_j} r_i.att_r$
8: **end for**
9: $candidate\_rules \leftarrow \bigcup_{cl_j \in Cls_u} cl_j.candidate\_rule$
10: $candidate\_rules \leftarrow candidate\_rules \cup (\bigcup_{cl_j \in Cls_r} cl_j.candidate\_rule)$
11: $final\_rules \leftarrow$ Generalize $(candidate\_rules)$
12: **return** $final\_rules$

4.1 Policy Mining

We mine access requests and their corresponding responses to extract rules based on Algorithm 1. The data set is pre-processed and split into two sets (records with "Permit" and "Deny" decisions) (presented in Step 1). Then, we take into account two cases: clustering records in the data sets independent of their user attributes and clustering records in the data sets independent of their resource attributes. In the first case (lines 1–4), the permit data set (DS^+) independent of user attributes is passed to the Algorithm 2 (presented in Step 2). Similarly, in the second case (lines 5–8), the permit data set (DS^+) independent of resource attributes is passed to the clustering algorithm. The clustering algorithm assigns records from the data set to the most appropriate clusters based on similarities. After clustering, the intersections of user attributes of records in each cluster are computed and assigned to the *candidate_rule*. *candidate_rule* is a rule that can support a large number of records. After that, all *candidate_rules* from clusters are merged and generalized (described in Step 4) to find rules with smaller sizes (lines 9–12).

Step 1. Data set pre-processing. The initial step in the policy mining process is data pre-processing. Access request logs may have noisy examples (such as redundancies and inconsistencies). For example, the same record may have two different decisions ("Permit" and "Deny"). To prevent developing inaccurate rules, we detect and delete noisy examples using the approach proposed in [6]. The records are then decomposed into two partitions based on their decisions. Records with the "Permit" decisions belong to DS^+ and records with the "Deny" decisions belong to DS^-. We then go over records of DS^+ to discover rules.

Step 2. Record clustering. We propose a clustering-based approach to mine access logs. There are different clustering algorithms (e.g., K-means [14] and hierarchical clustering [16]) applied to numerical data. There are some more studies on clustering categorical data [8]. These clustering algorithms are associated with some challenges, such as identifying the number of clusters, selecting

Algorithm 2. Clustering Data Set

Require: DS
1: **for each** record $r \in DS$ **do**
2:    **for each** cluster $cl \in Cl_k$ **do**
3:       **if** $(r \ Res \ cl.super\_rule \lor cl.super\_rule \ Res \ r)$ **then**
4:          **if** $r \ Res \ cl.super\_rule$ **then**
5:             $cl.super\_rule \leftarrow r$
6:          **end if**
7:          $support = \mathrm{Sup}(r)$
8:          **if** $support > cl.candidate\_rule.support$ **then**
9:             $cl.candidate\_rule \leftarrow r$
10:          **end if**
11:          *break*
12:       **end if**
13:    **end for**
14:    **if** $\mathrm{No\_cluster}\ (r)$ **then**
15:       $support = \mathrm{Sup}(r)$
16:       **if** $support > minsup$ **then**
17:          $Cl_k.candidate\_rule \leftarrow \mathrm{Create\_cluster}\ (r)$
18:       **end if**
19:    **end if**
20: **end for**
21: **return** Cl_k

---

learning algorithms, initializing clusters, and finding local optima. In this work, we propose Algorithm 2 that does not deal with these challenges. The proposed algorithm does not employ means (or medians) and distances (or dissimilarities) in the clustering process. The approach maps the data set records into clusters and extracts the most appropriate rule from each cluster.

In a data set, it is possible that some records are similar to each other. Our clustering approach creates clusters that are significantly diverse from one another, but the components of each cluster are very similar. Consider rules ρ_1 and ρ_2 where

$$\rho_1 = <\{(role, manager)\}, \{(type, budget)\}, \{approve\}, permit>$$
$$\rho_2 = <\{(role, manager), (dep, dep1)\}, \{(type, budget)\}, \{approve\}, permit>$$

Rule ρ_2 is more restricted than rule ρ_1 since it has additional conditions. Keeping both rules in the rule set is ineffective as it increases the chance of redundancy.

A user attribute p is more restricted than user attribute c ($p \ Res \ c$) if and only if

$$\forall a' \in c.Att_u, \exists \ !\ a \in p.Att_u \mid Att_u(a) = Att_u(a') \land d_u(a') \subseteq d_u(a)$$

We extend this concept to resource and environment attributes. Rule ρ_1 is more restricted than rule ρ_2 ($\rho_1 \ Res \ \rho_2$) if and only if

$(\rho_1.Att_u \; Res \; \rho_2.Att_u) \wedge (\rho_1.Att_r \; Res \; \rho_2.Att_r) \wedge (\rho_1.Att_{env} \; Res \; \rho_2.Att_{env}) \wedge$
$(\rho_1.act \cap \rho_2.act \neq \varnothing) \wedge \rho_1.effect = \rho_2.effect$

In this approach, the most restrictive record in a cluster is referred to as *super_rule*. We go over the records of the data set. A record is assigned to a cluster when *super_rule* of the cluster is more restrictive than the record or the record is more restrictive than the *super_rule*. When a record is more restrictive than *super_rule* (i.e., contains all of *super_rule*'s attributes and attribute values), the *super_rule* is replaced with the record (lines 1–13). When a record cannot be mapped to any cluster, its support value is calculated (by the sup function) based on Step 3. If the support value is greater than *minsup*, a cluster is created and the record is assigned to it (lines 14–19).

Step 3. Support calculation. When a record is assigned to a cluster, support, which is the fraction of the records satisfying the rule [24], is counted. Support is equivalent to statistical significance. The support value can contain the number of records that are exactly covered by the rule or are a superset of the rule. We define the support value for record r as follows:

$$R_{sup}(r) = \{\forall l \in DS \,|\, d_u(r.u_i, a_j) \subseteq d_u(l.u_i, a_j) \wedge d_r(r.r_i, a_j) \subseteq d_r(l.r_i, a_j) \wedge$$
$$l.act \in r.act \wedge l.effect = r.effect\}$$

$$Sup(r) = \frac{|R_{sup}(r)|}{|DS|}$$

where $|DS|$ is the number of records in the data set. When the support value of a rule is not big enough, the rule's consideration is less desirable [1]. The approach mines rules that have a support value greater than a pre-specified value (named *minsup*). If the support value of a rule is higher than *minsup*, the rule holds. Otherwise, it is ignored. The support value of a rule in a cluster is compared to the support value of the cluster candidate rule. If the support value is larger than the support value of *candidate_rule* (i.e., a rule having the highest support value in a cluster), *candidate_rule* is replaced by the rule (lines 8–10).

Step 4. Rule generalization. Following the mapping of all the records to the clusters, the clusters are extracted. Generalization is one way to handle overfitting, which means the approach is good only for the given data. However, generalization must be safe. Replacing the rules with their intersections might not be a safe generalization as it can increase the chance of false positives. The rules in *candidate_rules* may be subsets or supersets of one another. In this work, the subset rules are added as final rules.

Constraints. We optimize the policy mining approach by considering the atomic and static Separation of Duty (SSoD) constraints. All atomic constraints that exist between user u_i and resource r_j are defined as $Constraint(u_i, r_j)$.

To identify the satisfaction of SSoD constraints, we present two functions for authorization rules (ρ) of users and SSoD tuples: $Rule\_Allow\_User(u)$ shows authorization rules that allow user u to perform actions on resources. The function uses a hash table with user ids as the key and a list of relevant rules for the user as the key value. The hash table is updated when a record in the algorithms is analyzed. This can make searching in the data set more efficient. $Rule\_Allow\_Tuple(t)$ presents authorization rules that allow access to tuple t. A SoD can be satisfied if and only if

$$\nexists u \in U, \forall t \in SoD : Rule\_Allow\_Tuple(t) \rightarrow \rho' \wedge Rule\_Allow\_User(u) \rightarrow \rho \wedge$$
$$\rho \cap \rho' \neq \varnothing$$

Consider constraint sod_1 which contains tuples of $sod_1 = \{t_1, t_2, t_3\}$ as an example. At least two users must work together to satisfy this constraint. First, $Rule\_Allow\_Tuple(t)$ identifies the rules that allow access to constraint tuples. $t_1: \{\rho_3, \rho_8\}$, $t_2: \{\rho_1\}$, and $t_3: \{\rho_4, \rho_5\}$. Then, $Rule\_Allow\_User(u)$ discovers rules associated with each user, $u_1: \{\rho_1, \rho_3, \rho_5\}$, $u_2: \{\rho_4\}$, and $u_3: \{\rho_8\}$. Finally, it is determined if all of these constraint tuples are owned by a single user. In this example, if a user owns one of these rule sets $rs_1: \{\rho_3, \rho_1, \rho_4\}$, $rs_2: \{\rho_8, \rho_1, \rho_4\}$, $rs_3: \{\rho_3, \rho_1, \rho_5\}$, $rs_4: \{\rho_8, \rho_1, \rho_5\}$, sod_1 cannot be satisfied. As user $u1$ owns rs_3 (can satisfy all the constraint tuples), sod_1 is dissatisfied. Therefore, enforcement of SSoD constraints in this system might not be controllable.

Running Time of Algorithm. To analyze the time complexity of the algorithm, we consider Algorithm 2. It has two nested for loops, the first loop gets records from the data set and takes $|DS|$. The second loop finds the most appropriate cluster for a record and takes $|CL|$. The running time of the algorithm is $|DS| \times |CL|$ where $|CL|$ depends on $|DS|$. Therefore, the running time is quadratic in terms of the data set size.

In practice, the running time is considerably shorter. Other steps (e.g., attribute value hierarchy and support value computation) in the algorithm take a linear or constant amount of time. The worst-case running time of the Xu et al. [25] algorithm is cubic in terms of the data set size.

4.2   Policy Extraction Using Machine Learning

In the policy mining approach, we do not consider the similarities between access requests for generalization. Assume a record in the data set DS indicates that, when both the user u_i and the resource r_j are in Location A, the user u_i can access the resource r_j. This approach cannot handle similar requests. Consider a new request that asks if user u_i can access the resource r_j when both are in the Location B. Despite the fact that these two requests have similar patterns and different attribute values, the rule is not generalized. We employ machine learning techniques to identify patterns in access requests and responses. The techniques can predict responses to new requests based on their similarities to the previously generated policies. However, the generated rules can be associated with some inaccuracy due to the machine learning techniques. We apply machine learning techniques only to requests that are not addressed by the policy mining approach.

5   Experimental Evaluation

In this section, we evaluate the performance of 1) the policy mining approach, 2) ABAC policies with constraints, and 3) the policy extraction using machine learning techniques. The experiments are conducted on the synthetic and real access logs.

5.1   Performance of Policy Mining Approach

In this section, we evaluate the performance of the policy mining approach and compare it with the approach proposed by Xu et al. [25]. We construct multiple data sets to evaluate the performance of various components of the approach.

Data Sets. Organizations are gradually migrating to the ABAC model while their data sets are not available yet. We adopt access control policies of project management introduced by Xu et al. [25]. Then, we generate a set of random data sets. As Table 1 shows the synthetic data sets have varying numbers of users ($|U|$), resources ($|R|$), user attribute value pairs ($|UAV|$), resource attribute value pairs ($|RAV|$), the maximum length of each rule ($|L|$), and the number of logs. We create data sets with positive and negative records to conduct full analyses.

To assess the effect of parameters on the mining results, we consider three scenarios, i) $|U|$ and $|R|$ vary in the ranges of 100, 1000, and 10000, ii) $|UAV|$ changes in the range of 24, 32, and 40 and $|RAV|$ changes in the range of 15, 19, 23, and iii) $|L|$ varies from 5 to 9 with a step of 2. In each experiment, one parameter varies while the other parameters remain constant. These data sets are inputs to our policy mining approach. The experiments are run five times, and the final results are averaged over all the runs. The number of rules generated by the approach ($|\rho_G|$) and Xu et al.'s approach ($|\rho_{Xu}|$) is shown in the table. The table also includes the running time of the proposed approach (T_G) and Xu et al.'s approach (T_{Xu}).

Table 1. Synthetic access control data sets.

DS	$|U|$	$|R|$	$|UAV|$	$|RAV|$	$|L|$	$|Log|$	$|Log^-|$	$|Log^+|$	$|\rho_G|$	$|\rho_{Xu}|$	$T_G(s)$	$T_{Xu}(s)$
DS_1	100	100	28	17	11	50k	49129	871	14	12	900	1000
DS_2	1000	1000	28	17	11	50k	49037	963	14	13	1000	2000
DS_3	10000	10000	28	17	11	50k	48946	1054	15	16	1050	4000
DS_4	100	100	24	15	11	50k	49159	841	13	12	900	50
DS_5	100	100	32	19	11	50k	49404	596	13	13	910	1000
DS_6	100	100	40	23	11	50k	49720	280	15	11	915	10000
DS_7	100	100	28	17	5	50k	49851	149	11	11	900	60
DS_8	100	100	28	17	7	50k	49534	466	13	12	950	5000
DS_9	100	100	28	17	9	50k	49241	759	12	13	980	4500

The approach is implemented in Java 11. The experiments were conducted on a computer with an Intel Core i7 1.99 GHz processor and 16 GB of RAM.

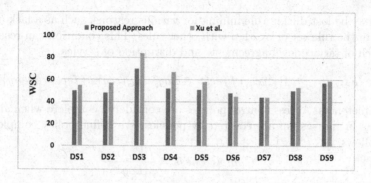

Fig. 1. Comparison of WSC complexity.

Evaluation Metrics. From each cluster, candidate rules with the ability to support more access are chosen from the clusters. In this work, we evaluate the quality of the generated rules with the help of the following metrics.

– The number of generated rules ($|\rho_G|$). The primary goal is to find the minimal set of rules that can satisfy both positive and negative authorizations.
– Weighted Structural Complexity (WSC). We compute Weighted Structural Complexity (WSC) [25] (which was first introduced for RBAC) to generalize rule sizes. They are consistent with the idea that more concise rules are more manageable. The goal is to find rules with minimum WSC weights. The WSC of a rule is defined by $WSC(\rho = <e_u, e_r, env, act, effect>) = w_1WSC(e_u) + w_2WSC(e_r) + w_3WSC(env) + w_4WSC(act)$. We consider all w_i to be 1 in the WSC formula.
– Running time. It is the total time for mining the data set to generate rules.
– Correctness. It refers to ensuring that policies assign the correct decisions to requests. Accuracy and F-measure are computed to calculate the correctness based on True Positive, True Negative, False Positive, and False Negative defied as follows.
Both True Positive (TP) and True Negative (TN) of ρ_G regarding logs indicate that decisions made on mined policies are consistent with the original rule decisions.

$$TP_{\rho_G|Log} = |\{<req, effect> \in Log^+ \mid \rho_G(req).effect = Permit\}|$$
$$TN_{\rho_G|Log} = |\{<req, effect> \in Log^- \mid \rho_G(req).effect = Deny\}|$$

A False Positive (FP) happens when access is inappropriately given based on mined rules while it must be denied based on the original rule. During rule mining, for example, some attribute expressions of a rule are missing. As a result, the rule becomes more relaxed to allow a request that must be denied. It might result in information leakage, privilege escalation, and corruption.

$$FP_{\rho_G|Log} = |\{<req, effect> \in Log^- \mid \rho_G(req).effect = Permit\}|$$

In the False Negative (FN) case, permission should be granted based on original rules but is denied due to mined rules. Some rules from the original rule set may be lost during rule mining for various reasons, such as a lack of samples in the rule set or overlap with other rules. This condition can result in a breach of service level agreements and disruption of service.

$$FN_{\rho_G|Log} = |\{<req, effect> \in Log^+ \mid \rho_G(req).effect = Deny\}|$$

- Completeness. Access control policies are considered complete when all operations in the system are covered by policies. We define policy completeness as follows.

$$Completeness = \frac{TP_{\rho_G|Log}}{|Log^+|}$$

Result and Analysis. We compute the presented metrics for each experiment. Then, the results are compared with the results of Xu et al. [25].

The data sets DS_1 to DS_3 in Table 1 demonstrate that when the numbers of users ($|U|$) and resources ($|R|$) vary while other parameters remain constant, the proposed approach (ρ_G) and Xu et al. (ρ_{Xu}) generate nearly the same number of rules. Moreover, as shown in Fig. 1, the proposed approach outperforms Xu et al. in terms of WSC. In addition, the running time of Xu et al. (T_{Xu}) is longer than the running time of the approach (T_G), as can be observed in the table.

The data sets DS_4 to DS_6 in Table 1 show when the numbers of user attribute values ($<UAV>$) and resource attribute values ($<RAV>$) change, the generated ρ_G and ρ_{Xu} are nearly the same. Nevertheless, the WSC of the proposed approach is smaller than Xu et al. as shown in Fig. 1. Moreover, the running time of Xu et al. (T_{Xu}) rapidly increases, while the proposed approach has a more consistent running time (T_G) for all of the attributes, as shown in the table.

The data sets DS_7 to DS_9 in Table 1 show the impact of varying the length of rules (L). Both approaches generate nearly the same number of rules, similar to the last two scenarios. Also, the WSC of the approach is lower than the WSC of Xu et al. as shown in Fig. 1. Moreover, the running time of the approach (T_G) drops slightly as L increases, while the running time of Xu et al. (T_{Xu}) fluctuates.

The proposed approach performs very well in terms of correctness and completeness. The correctness of the approach is shown via accuracy and F-measure in Figs. 2a and 2b, respectively. The accuracy of all nine data sets is above 80%. Some data sets (DS_7 and DS_8) reach their maximum accuracy. The F-measure is also greater than 60%. As shown in the Fig. 2c, the completeness is greater than 45%.

5.2   Performance of ABAC Policies *with* Constraints

To evaluate the effectiveness of the approach for atomic constraints, we use data sets from Xu et al. The results in Table 2 indicate the effect of having different numbers of atomic constraints from 0 to 4, with a step of 2 for the data set. As the number of constraints increases, the rules grow in complexity. Similar behavior was shown by Xu et al. The WSCs of the proposed approaches are

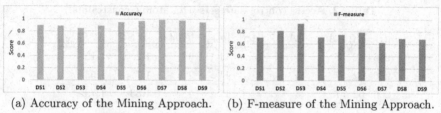

(a) Accuracy of the Mining Approach.   (b) F-measure of the Mining Approach.

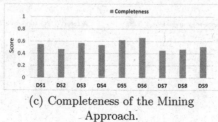

(c) Completeness of the Mining
Approach.

Fig. 2. Evaluation metrics.

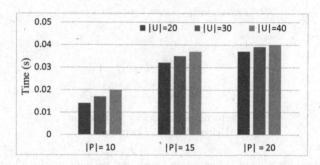

Fig. 3. Average running time for different $|U|$ and $|\rho|$.

divided by the WSC of ρ_{org}. To evaluate the effectiveness of the approach for
enforcing SoD constraints, we employ real data sets from Xu et al. with $|R| =$
34, $|A_u| = 6$, $|A_r| = 5$. Then, we build some synthetic SoD constraints that
can be between 2 and 5 for the data set. Figure 3 indicates the influence of the
number of users ($|U|$) and rules ($|P|$) on the running time. When the number
of users rises while the other parameters remain fixed, the average running time
does not increase significantly. Nonetheless, as the number of rules increases and
the number of users remains constant, the average running time grows clearly.
The reason is that the number of constraints can be greater for a large number
of rules, and the verification time of the larger number of constraints grows.

5.3   Performance of Policy Extraction Using Machine Learning

This section contains a summary of three experiments: the policy mining approach, the policy mining approach combined with machine learning techniques,

Table 2. Access control data sets *with* atomic constraints.

$|U|$	$|R|$	$|Att_u|$	$|Att_r|$	$|Act|$	$|\rho_{org}|$	$|Cons|$	$|WSC|$	$|WSC_{Xu}|$
206	62	7	5	7	11	0	1.2	1.12
206	62	7	5	7	11	2	1.7	1.55
206	62	7	5	7	11	4	1.83	1.79

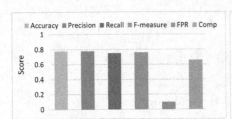

(a) Performance of the Policy Mining Approach.

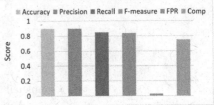

(b) Performance of the Policy Mining Approach and Machine Learning.

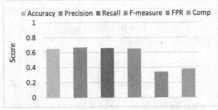

(c) Performance of Policy Extraction Using Machine Learning.

Fig. 4. Performance of policy mining with and without machine learning.

and policy generation using machine learning techniques. A new data set and evaluation metrics are used in these experiments.

Evaluation and Setting. We use a real data set provided by Amazon in the Kaggle competition[1]. The data set contains 12 user attributes, and 1 resource attribute. This data set contains access requests by Amazon's employees over two years. Each record includes a request for a resource and an authorized or not authorized response. The data set contains 12000 users and 7000 resources.

We report accuracy, precision, recall, F-measure, and False Positive Rate (FPR) to evaluate the efficacy of the approach. A false positive happens when access is inappropriately given based on mined rules while it must be denied based on the original rule. We employ five machine learning techniques: Random Forest, Decision Tree, Naive Bayes, Support Vector Machine, and K-Nearest Neighbors. The classifiers might produce different results, and the classifiers

---

[1] https://www.kaggle.com/competitions/amazon-employee-access-challenge/data.

might have inherent classification inaccuracies. As a result, we combine the results of various classifiers using the majority voting technique [23].

Result and Analysis. We conduct three experiments as described below. 1) We apply our policy mining approach (presented in Subsect. 4.1) to the Amazon data set. As Fig. 4a shows, the accuracy, precision, recall, and F-measure of our policy mining approach are close to 80% and the FPR is less than 10%. The completeness of the proposed approach is 65%. 2) The rules produced by the proposed policy mining approach are used to train the machine learning classification models. The machine learning techniques make decisions for access requests that are not addressed by the proposed approach. We then integrate the classifier's findings using majority voting. The accuracy, precision, recall, and F-measure are all greater than 85%, and the FPR is less than 3%. Also, the completeness rate of this approach is close to 80%, which is very promising, as shown in Fig. 4b. 3) The machine learning techniques are applied to the Amazon data set. Figure 4c demonstrates the accuracy, precision, recall, and F-measure of this experiment. All the results are below 65%, and its FPR is 35%. Additionally, this approach has a close to 40% completeness rate, which is low. It can be concluded that combining the proposed policy mining approach with machine learning techniques can be more effective than using only policy mining or machine learning.

6   Conclusion

The ABAC model provides flexibility and benefits for large and dynamic applications. Many organizations using conventional access control models (e.g., DAC, MAC, and RBAC) are eager to move to the ABAC model. However, developing suitable authorization rules, which are essential for the ABAC model, is not simple. In this paper, we propose an efficient solution to ease the burden of migration to the ABAC model by learning ABAC rules from access logs. This approach can simplify the policy specification process and has the capability to assign appropriate rules whenever new resources and users are added to a system. It is a clustering-based approach that supports both positive and negative authorization. It also takes into account atomic and SoD constraints. We experimentally assessed the performance of the proposed approach, and the results show that it is generally faster than the state of the art. As part of the future work, we plan to extend our approach to support more constraints such as binding-of-duty and user-capability.

Acknowledgment. This work was supported in part by the Natural Sciences and Engineering Research Council of Canada (NSERC) and the Canada Research Chairs (CRC) Program.

References

1. Agrawal, R., Imieliński, T., Swami, A.: Mining association rules between sets of items in large databases. In: Proceedings of the ACM SIGMOD International Conference on Management of Data, Washington, DC, USA, pp. 207–216 (1993)
2. Bui, T., Stoller, S.D., Le, H.: Efficient and extensible policy mining for relationship-based access control. In: Proceedings of the 24th ACM Symposium on Access Control Models and Technologies, Toronto, Canada, pp. 161–172 (2019)
3. Cendrowska, J.: PRISM: an algorithm for inducing modular rules. Int. J. Man Mach. Stud. **27**(4), 349–370 (1987)
4. Cotrini, C., Corinzia, L., Weghorn, T., Basin, D.: The next 700 policy miners: a universal method for building policy miners. In Proceedings of the ACM Conference on Computer and Communications Security, London, UK, pp. 95–112 (2019)
5. Cotrini, C., Weghorn, T., Basin, D.: Mining ABAC rules from sparse logs. In: Proceedings of the 3rd European Symposium on Security and Privacy, London, UK, pp. 31–46. IEEE (2018)
6. Davari, M., Zulkernine, M.: Policy modeling and anomaly detection in ABAC policies. In: Luo, B., Mosbah, M., Cuppens, F., Ben Othmane, L., Cuppens, N., Kallel, S. (eds.) CRiSIS 2021. LNCS, vol. 13204, pp. 137–152. Springer, Cham (2022). https://doi.org/10.1007/978-3-031-02067-4_9
7. Gautam, M., Jha, S., Sural, S., Vaidya, J., Atluri, V.,: Poster: constrained policy mining in attribute based access control. In Proceedings of the 22nd ACM on Symposium on Access Control Models and Technologies, Indianapolis, Indiana, USA, pp. 121–123 (2017)
8. Guha, S., Rastogi, R., Shim, K.: ROCK: a robust clustering algorithm for categorical attributes. Inf. Syst. **25**(5), 345–366 (2000)
9. Hachana, S., Cuppens-Boulahia, N., Cuppens, F.: Role mining to assist authorization governance: how far have we gone? Int. J. Secur. Softw. Eng. (IJSSE) **3**(4), 45–64 (2012)
10. Hu, V.C., et al.: Guide to attribute based access control (ABAC) definition and considerations (draft). NIST Special Publication, 800(162), pp. 1–54 (2013)
11. Iyer, P., Masoumzadeh, A.: Mining positive and negative attribute-based access control policy rules. In: Proceedings of the 23rd ACM Symposium on Access Control Models and Technologies (SACMAT), Indianapolis, Indiana, USA, pp. 161–172 (2018)
12. Abu Jabal, A., et al.: Polisma - a framework for learning attribute-based access control policies. In: Chen, L., Li, N., Liang, K., Schneider, S. (eds.) ESORICS 2020. LNCS, vol. 12308, pp. 523–544. Springer, Cham (2020). https://doi.org/10.1007/978-3-030-58951-6_26
13. Jabal, A.A., et al.: Methods and tools for policy analysis. ACM Comput. Surv. (CSUR) **51**(6), 1–35 (2019)
14. Jain, A.K., Dubes, R.C.: Algorithms for Clustering Data. Prentice-Hall, Inc., Upper Saddle River (1988)
15. Jha, S., Sural, S., Atluri, V., Vaidya, J.: Specification and verification of separation of duty constraints in attribute-based access control. IEEE Trans. Inf. Forensics Secur. **13**(4), 897–911 (2017)
16. Johnson, S.C.: Hierarchical clustering schemes. Psychometrika **32**(3), 241–254 (1967)
17. Karimi, L., Aldairi, M., Joshi, J., Abdelhakim, M.: An automatic attribute based access control policy extraction from access logs. IEEE Trans. Depend. Secur. Comput. (TDSC) **19**, 2304–2317 (2021)

18. Karimi, L., Joshi, J.: An unsupervised learning based approach for mining attribute based access control policies. In: Proceedings of the International Conference on Big Data (Big Data), Honolulu, HI, USA, pp. 1427–1436. IEEE (2018)
19. Medvet, E., Bartoli, A., Carminati, B., Ferrari, E.: Evolutionary inference of attribute-based access control policies. In: Gaspar-Cunha, A., Henggeler Antunes, C., Coello, C.C. (eds.) EMO 2015. LNCS, vol. 9018, pp. 351–365. Springer, Cham (2015). https://doi.org/10.1007/978-3-319-15934-8_24
20. Mocanu, D., Turkmen, F., Liotta, A., et al.: Towards ABAC policy mining from logs with deep learning. In: Proceedings of the 18th International Multiconference Information Society (IS), Ljubljana, Slovenia, pp. 124–128 (2015)
21. Narouei, M., Khanpour, H., Takabi, H., Parde, N., Nielsen, R.: Towards a top-down policy engineering framework for attribute-based access control. In: Proceedings of the 22nd ACM on Symposium on Access Control Models and Technologies, Indianapolis, Indiana, USA, pp. 103–114 (2017)
22. Roy, A., Sural, S., Majumdar, A.K., Vaidya, J., Atluri, V.: Enabling workforce optimization in constrained attribute-based access control systems. IEEE Trans. Emerg. Top. Comput. **9**(4), 1901–1913 (2019)
23. Ruta, D., Gabrys, B.: Classifier selection for majority voting. Inf. Fusion **6**(1), 63–81 (2005)
24. Srikant, R., Agrawal, R.: Mining quantitative association rules in large relational tables. In: Proceedings of the ACM SIGMOD International Conference on Management of Data, Montreal, Quebec, Canada, pp. 1–12 (1996)
25. Xu, Z., Stoller, S.D.: Mining attribute-based access control policies. IEEE Trans. Depend. Secur. Comput. **12**(5), 533–545 (2014)

Preventing Privacy-Violating Information Flows in JavaScript Applications Using Dynamic Labelling

Sandip Ghosal[1]([⊠]) [iD] and R. K. Shyamasundar[2]

[1] Department of Information Technology, Uppsala University, Uppsala, Sweden
sandipsmit@gmail.com
[2] Department of Computer Science and Engineering,
Indian Institute of Technology Bombay, Mumbai, India

Abstract. Web browser-based applications deal with humongous user information using applications of web scripts. In particular, JavaScript applications access information through built-in browser APIs that dynamically load remote scripts and execute with the same privilege as that of the applications – usually referred to as mashup model. Unfortunately, this allows malicious JavaScripts to manipulate the given browser functionalities leading to various web attacks violating users' privacy. Moreover, with the rapid growth of e-commerce sectors, malicious scripts pose a significant challenge to digital transactions. In this paper, we propose an approach that prevents various web-based attacks such as code injection, cross-site scripting (XSS). The approach adopts a *Dynamic Labelling* algorithm that generates information flow security policies automatically for local variables in JavaScript based on the given policies for sensitive variables. Unlike existing solutions that are too conservative primarily due to the generic flow policies leading to false-alarms, our solution leads to realizing conditions as to when a script accepts the parameters returned by a dynamic script; thus enabling us to build an automatic platform for preventing information flows to malicious scripts without explicit characterization by programmers or users.

1 Introduction

JavaScript being the most popular scripting language [2], has been an integral part of modern web applications for quite a long time. The popularity continues to grow due to a number of factors such as the flexibility to pull the necessary libraries at run-time from remotely diverse sources, delegate source code over the network to different receivers across the web for execution, and JavaScript APIs that allow sharing the page state with dynamically loaded scripts. Since confidentiality and integrity are major concerns for cross-domain sharing of code and data, modern web browsers enforce the *same-origin policy* (SOP) for isolating content and scripts from different domains. SOP specifies that data of an

---

S. Ghosal—Work done while the author was at Indian Institute of Technology Bombay.

V. R. Badarla et al. (Eds.): ICISS 2022, LNCS 13784, pp. 202–219, 2022.
https://doi.org/10.1007/978-3-031-23690-7_12

origin shall be accessible only by the code from the same origin [8, 45, 49]. However, there are many occasions where browsers can bypass SOP by inspecting properties of cross-origin images, frames, and windows which make the applications vulnerable to attacks such as cross-site scripting (XSS), cross-site request forgery (CSRF), and privacy leaks [3, 4]. Problem is quite pronounced with the folklore "web-mashups", a regular phenomenon these days thanks to "ads" on nearly all websites. Moreover, frequent changes in the script, code reuse and dependencies on unequally trusted third-party libraries [33] pose a significant threat to security and privacy.

Problem Description:
We illustrate the problem through the attack (Cf. [14]) shown in Figs. 1 and 2. For a given website, let a part of the script that does not load external resources be called *context*. On the other hand, the part that dynamically loads resources located remotely is referred to as the *hole*. Consider the script shown in Fig. 1, where the dynamic part loads external resources from B, that eventually re-directs the login parameters to an evil site C instead of the original destination D (Fig. 2). The solution proposed in [14] follows a mechanism called *staged information flow* (SIF) that prevents flows from sensitive variable to hole or

```
 1 /* the context part of the script */
 2 <script type="javascript''>
 3 var initSettings = function(s, i){
 4     baseUrl = s;
 5     version = i;
 6 }

 8 /* set original destination as D */
 9 initSettings(D,1.0);

11 var login = function(){
12     var pwd = PasswordTextBox.value;
13     var uname = UsernameTextBox.value;
14     var params = "u=" + user + "&p=" + pwd;
15     post(baseUrl, params);
16 }
17 </script>
18 <text id="UsernameTextBox">
19 <text id="PasswordTextBox">
20 <button id="ButtonLogin" onclick="login()">

22 /* a hole pulls resources from B */
23 <div id="advertise">
24 <script src="B/ad.js"/>
25 </div>
```

Fig. 1. Script loads an external resources from B

```
1  <script type="javascript''>
2  var z1 = C;
3  var z2 = 1.0;
4  /* destination redirected to C */
5  initSettings(z1, z2);
6  <script/>
```

Fig. 2. Script in B redirects the destination to an evil site C

vice-versa. As per [14], a confidentiality policy is given as $(A, \bullet)$ read as information in A cannot flow to a *hole*. However, it may be observed that blocking information from flowing to a hole beforehand may not be a good idea – makes the system too restrictive. For example, a script might be loaded to calculate the tax amount in different currencies, where the system demands information to flow to a hole but not a nested hole – this cannot be allowed through SIF.

Yang *et al.* [48] argue that information flow control (IFC) subsumes SOP and could provide a stronger notion of confidentiality and integrity. Taking inspiration from [48], in this paper, we propose an IFC-based solution that does not require explicit characterization of a *hole* by the user; however, the security (or insecurity) can be evaluated automatically through a recently proposed compile-time *Dynamic Labelling* (DL) algorithm [21,22]. The algorithm, with respect to a given set of fixed information flow policies for global sensitive objects, dynamically generates security policies for local objects of a program. Failing to generate a security policy for a local object(s) at any program point, the algorithm indicates a potential flow policy violation. We adopt the mechanism of DL algorithm in the context of JavaScript applications to prevent information from flowing to a malicious script or vice-versa.

In summary, the paper makes the following contributions:

- Highlights some of the existing problems for enforcing flow security in JavaScript applications;
- Describes how an extension of IFC-based program certification approach, i.e. *Dynamic Labelling* algorithm, does provide potential solutions to the problems; and
- Propose an algorithm for JavaScript application based on the Dynamic Labelling approach that provides an automatic solution for preventing privacy-violating information flows.

Structure of the Paper: Section 2 provides a brief background about the security label-based information flow control, DL algorithm, and a lattice-based security model, i.e. *Readers-Writers Flow Model*. Section 3 describes the pressing problems for enforcing information flow security in JavaScript applications. Further, we discuss how an extension of DL algorithm could solve these problems. Section 4 describes our proposed approach using DL algorithm that provides an automatic solution for preventing privacy-violating information flows in

JavaScript applications. Section 5 describes the related work, followed by Sect. 6 summarizing the contribution along with the future work.

2   Background

In this section, we briefly introduce concepts of IFC that are necessary to understand the solution this paper presents. We shall start with the notion of security *labels* or *policies* or *classes* (used interchangeably) and the definition of *information flow policy*. Next, we introduce DL algorithm – the backbone of this paper, and a noble security model, i.e. *Readers-Writers Flow Model* (RWFM), required for governing flow transitions and in the event of *declassification* [36,52].

2.1   A Brief Introduction to IFC

Usually, IFC systems govern information propagation by associating a security label with every subject (stakeholder of a system) and object (e.g., variable, file, register) – commonly referred to as *security labeling*. Security labels are used to specify who may read (confidentiality policy) or write data (integrity policy). For example, an object labeled as $\langle readers : \{A, B\}, writers : \{B\}\rangle$ can only be read by A, B and modified by B. In general, the set of security labels are partially ordered over a binary relation $\leqslant$ read *can-flow-to*: for any objects x, y labeled as $\underline{x}, \underline{y}$ respectively, if $\underline{x} \leqslant \underline{y}$ then the policy encoded by $\underline{x}$ is no more restrictive than that of $\underline{y}$. In other words, security policy in $\underline{x}$ is upheld by the policy $\underline{y}$, hence information can flow in the direction $x \rightarrow y$.

Following the semantics of information flow, we can fairly assume two binary class combining operators, *join* ('$\oplus$') and *meet* ('$\otimes$'), that evaluate *least upper bound* (LUB) and *greatest lower bound* (GLB) of two security labels respectively. Next we shall define a universally bounded security lattice w.r.t a partially ordered set $(\mathcal{L}, \leqslant)$, join, and meet operations.

Definition 1 (Information-Flow Lattice [16]). *A given partially ordered set $(\mathcal{L}, \leqslant)$ together with a least upper bound (LUB) operator $\oplus : \mathcal{L} \times \mathcal{L} \rightarrow \mathcal{L}$ and greatest lower bound (GLB) operator $\otimes : \mathcal{L} \times \mathcal{L} \rightarrow \mathcal{L}$, defines a universally bounded lattice $(\mathcal{L}, \leqslant, \oplus, \otimes)$ such that there exist a lower bound $\perp \in \mathcal{L}$ where $\perp \leqslant l$, and upper bound $\top \in \mathcal{L}$ where $l \leqslant \top$ for all $l \in \mathcal{L}$.*

Using the lattice structure, an information flow policy (IFP) is defined as follows: if there is information flow from x to y then the flow is secure iff $\lambda(x) \leqslant \lambda(y)$, where λ is a labeling function that maps subjects and objects of a program to respective security labels from the lattice. Note that a two-point lattice could have only labels *high* and *low*, where information shall only flow in the direction *low* $\rightarrow$ *high*. A program is certified for IFP if there are no violations of the policy during program execution [17].

2.2 Dynamic Labelling (DL) Algorithm [21,22]

The DL algorithm certifies a program for flow security by enforcing IFP at each program point with respect to a given set of fixed security labels of sensitive variables. The algorithm accepts the following input parameters: (i) a program statement S; (ii) a labeling function λ that maps a subject or object to its respective security label in the lattice; and (iii) a clearance label cl – the highest label that the executing subject can achieve. If the statement is flow-secure the algorithm outputs a new labeling function mapping each local variable in S to their respective final label in the lattice. Otherwise, it throws an error indicating a possible IFP violation. The algorithm follows a combination of static and dynamic (or hybrid) binding of security labels with subjects and objects: a set of sensitive variables referred to as global are given fixed or static security labels, whereas the labels of intermediate or local variables, including the program counter (pc), dynamically change as the value changes. We refer to the work [22] for the properties and formal analysis of DL algorithm.

2.3 Readers-Writers Flow Model (RWFM) [32]

We borrow a lattice-based information flow control model, i.e., Readers-Writers Flow Model (RWFM) for labeling subjects and objects and governing information flows in a program. In RWFM, a subject or principal is a string representation of a source of authority such as user, process, also called as *active* agent of a program responsible for information flow. On the other hand, objects are passive agents such as variables, files used for storing information.

A RWFM label l of a subject or object is a three-tuple (s, R, W) ($s, R, W \in$ set of principals P), where s represent the owner of the information and policy, R denote the set of subjects (*readers*) allowed to read the information, and W refer to the set of subjects (*writers*) who have influenced the information so far. The readers and writers set, respectively, specify the confidentiality and integrity policy associated with the information. Information from a source with a RWFM label L_1 can flow to an endpoint having RWFM label L_2 ($L_1 \leqslant L_2$) if it does not violate the confidentiality and integrity policies already imposed by L_1. The definition of *can-flow-to* is given below:

Definition 1 (Can-flow-to relation ($\leqslant$)). *Given any two RWFM labels $L_1 = (s_1, R_1, W_1)$ and $L_2 = (s_2, R_2, W_2)$, the can-flow-to relation is defined as:*

$$\frac{R_1 \supseteq R_2 \quad W_1 \subseteq W_2}{L_1 \leqslant L_2}$$

The join ($\oplus$) and meet ($\otimes$) of any two RWFM labels $L_1 = (s_1, R_1, W_1)$ and $L_2 = (s_2, R_2, W_2)$ are respectively defined as

$$L_1 \oplus L_2 = (-, R_1 \cap R_2, W_1 \cup W_2), \quad L_1 \otimes L_2 = (-, R_1 \cup R_2, W_1 \cap W_2)$$

Then the set of RWFM labels $SC = P \times 2^P \times 2^P$ forms a bounded lattice ($SC, \leqslant$, $\oplus, \otimes, \top, \bot$), where ($SC, \leqslant$) is a partially ordered set and $\top = (-, \emptyset, P)$, and $\bot = (-, P, \emptyset)$ are respectively the maximum and minimum elements.

Definition 2 (Declassification in RWFM). *The declassification of an object o from its current label* (s_2, R_2, W_2) *to* (s_3, R_3, W_3) *as performed by the subject s with label* (s_1, R_1, W_1) *is defined as*

$$\frac{s \in R_2 \quad s_1 = s_2 = s_3 \quad R_1 = R_2 \quad W_1 = W_2 = W_3 \quad R_2 \subseteq R_3}{(W_1 = \{s_1\} \vee (R_3 - R_2 \subseteq W_2))}$$
$$(s_2, R_2, W_2) \textit{ may be declassified to } (s_3, R_3, W_3)$$

This says, the owner of an object can declassify the content to a subject(s) only if the owner is the sole writer of the information or that subject(s) had influenced the information earlier.

3   Security Challenges and Our Approach

In this section, we outline some of the security challenges in JavaScript and illustrate how a natural extension of the DL algorithm can overcome the challenges by enforcing information flow security in JavaScript programs. The following constructs constitute the core of our JavaScript language: assignment, selection, iteration, sequence, eval, and functions. A subset of ECMA-262 [1] standard defines the syntax and semantics of our JavaScript constructs. In addition, we provide a solution to declassification in JavaScript applications that could arise due to decentralized labeling [35] followed by the modern security lattice models.

Before delving into the challenges, we shall briefly revisit the three information flow channels, i.e. *explicit*, *implicit*, and *covert*, responsible for leaking information [42]. An assignment $\ell = h$ is the most prevalent example of information leak through explicit channel where sensitive (or *high*) information in h is directly copied into a public (or *low*) variable ℓ. An implicit channel occurs in a conditional statement such as if..then..else when a branch is selected based on a condition involving sensitive values. Finally, covert channels refer to all other side channels where information leaks may occur depending on the program (non)termination, power consumption, or execution time.

In the presence of any of the above information channels, the program violates the non-interference property [23,46]. Usually, enforcement of the global policy of non-interference ensures information shall flow only in the upward direction in the lattice (*low* → *high*). While there has been impressive progress in both the static [12,24,37] and dynamic [6,50,53] flow security analyses, however, their applications for enforcing non-interference in JavaScript are limited due to the reasons discussed in the following.

3.1   Flow Sensitivity

Since JavaScript is a dynamically typed language, the type of variables and fields changes as per the information flow during execution, making the type system information flow sensitive. However, classical dynamic flow sensitive analyses [20,26,40] might allow the following program to copy sensitive information (0 or 1) in h (labeled *high*) to public variable ℓ (labeled *low*) via temporary variable t without upgrading the security label of ℓ.

$$\ell = 0; \, t = 1; \, \texttt{if} \, (h == 0) \, t = 0; \, \texttt{if} \, (t! = 0) \, \ell = 1;$$

Our Approach: DL algorithm follows a hybrid labeling approach where the labels of global variables h and ℓ are static, but the label of t is dynamic. As it encounters an implicit flow from h to t conditioned on h, eventually updates the label of t to *high*. Therefore, in the following branch, the algorithm can identify a violation of non-interference caused by the implicit flow $t \rightarrow \ell$.

Table 1. DL algorithm for JavaScript assignment statements

Statement	Flow constraints
`baseUrl = s`	$\lambda(s) \oplus \lambda(pc) \leqslant \lambda(baseUrl)$
`var pwd = PasswordTextBox.value`	$\lambda(pwd) = \lambda(PasswordTextBox.value) \oplus \lambda(pc)$

For the example shown in Fig. 1, consider objects $baseUrl$ and pwd are global and local respectively. Then Table 1 shows the flow check and label computation performed by DL algorithm for the assignment statements at lines 4 and 12. Since the variable $baseUrl$ has a fixed security label, the algorithm only checks if the label of s can flow to $baseUrl$, otherwise raises an error indicating an incident of possible flow policy violation. On the other hand, the algorithm dynamically updates the label of local variable pwd to accommodate information flow from the object `PasswordTextBox.value`. Therefore, the algorithm follows static labeling when the target is a global variable; whereas, it uses dynamic labeling by updating labels when the target is a local variable. Thus, DL algorithm is flow sensitive for local variables; in addition, it overcomes issues of over-approximation of security labels often encountered in static analyses that could lead to false alarms for security certification. An approach called *no-sensitive-upgrade* [50] overcomes the shortcomings of dynamic analyses for information leaks through implicit channels. The mechanism only allows assignment to variables that have a security label at least as high as the label of the predicate that governs the assignment. Thus, it avoids upgrading variables of only the branch in execution. While the DL algorithm is in line with *no-sensitive-upgrade* method, note that the latter is *termination-insensitive* [5] – could leak information based on (non)termination of the program.

3.2 Termination Sensitivity

The existing IFC mechanisms enforce an imprecise notion of information flow security when it comes to *termination-sensitive* non-interference [5,47]. Under this class of non-interference, information leak takes place depending on whether the program has terminated or not. Askarov *et al.* [5] argued that such an imperfection of flow analysis is the price to pay for having a security condition that is relatively liberal (e.g., allowing while loops whose termination may depend on the value of a secret) and easy to check. According to the authors, in the presence of output to a public channel, the price is higher than just "one-bit" often claimed informally in the literature, and effectively such programs can leak all of their secrets. In the case of JavaScript, the presence of a termination leak could be fatal; e.g., consider the program shown in Fig. 3, where h is a high-security variable storing sensitive information and $img.url$ is an object which stores the path to an image such that $\lambda(h) \not\leq \lambda(img.url)$. Note that the image is displayed only if the value in h is 1; hence the information is leaked depending on the (non)termination of the loop.

```
1 while (h == 0){ }
2 img.url = 'http://abc.com/img.jpg';
```

Fig. 3. An example of information leak through a termination channel in JavaScript

Handling Termination Sensitivity in Our Approach: DL algorithm is termination-sensitive: it captures information leaks through termination channels (covert channel) that could arise due to (non)termination of the loop statements. DL algorithm tracks the pc label and updates it monotonically as it reads a new variable. This enables the algorithm to capture forward information flow that implicitly leaks information from loop predicate to the following statement. A recurring backward information flow could also arise due to multiple loop iterations, which may update the label of local variables in each iteration and could eventually violate IFP. The DL algorithm continues to iterate the loop until it computes the highest possible label of the local variables in the loop. As it can be shown that the highest labels are achieved within three iterations only, DL algorithm terminates the loop after a maximum of three unrolls [22]. Note that the loop might not terminate during actual execution in run time. In this process, the algorithm enforces IFP in the presence of backward information flow. In the above example, the algorithm captures the insecurity in the following way: reads variable h in the predicate; updates the label of pc to the equivalent of h; terminates the while statement after iterating the loop once as it does not have any local variable in the body; moves forward to the next statement; realizes the insecurity as it fails to satisfy the flow constraint $\lambda(pc) \leq \lambda(img.url)$.

Devriese and Piessens [18] proposed an approach called *Secure Multi-Execution* (SME) that enforces termination-sensitive non-interference by executing multiple instances of a program concurrently, once for each security label in the lattice, applying special rules for I/O operations that prevent the information flow from high to low-security variables. An instance of a program executed with the security label ℓ can only write to outputs with security label ℓ and can read from the inputs with security labels $\ell' \leq \ell$. A default input statement replaces the inputs with higher security labels. SME intercepts executions of inputs and outputs that violate the above I/O rules. An execution under SME at a given security label can only produce output with the same label and cannot see inputs from a higher security label. Therefore, outputs produced under SME could not possibly depend on higher inputs.

Unlike DL algorithm, SME framework is built upon a two-point lattice, where the security labels (*high* or *low*) for each program instance shall be given a priori. An extension to a general n-point lattice would require executing n program instances concurrently, which could be limited by the program design, system architecture, and scheduling strategy. Besides, restrictions on I/O operations could limit the application of SME for concurrent programs that exchange information using shared variables. Although the approach adheres to *no-sensitive-upgrade* and enforces non-interference as it prevents secret input from influencing the public output [6], in practice, the information flow usually occurs in the opposite direction, where high-security inputs always influence low-security outputs [41]. Having said that, we arrive at the notion of declassification, a common phenomenon for developing *multi-level security* (MLS) systems. However, how one would define declassification using SME remains unclear. We discuss declassification in JavaScript applications in the sequel.

3.3   Eval Statement

An `eval` instruction in JavaScript could parse and execute a string argument as code at run-time. Thus, `eval` statement could execute a malicious statement with the same privilege as the caller application. Since the string may not be available to a static analyzer, it poses a significant challenge to static flow analyses.

Eval Statement Treatment in Our Approach: Taking inspiration from the work by Jang *et al.* [28, 29], we could follow a rewriting-based source-to-source transformation to generate an intermediate representation of JavaScript code for `eval` statements. For rewriting, we can fairly assume an approximate string-matching function $\mathcal{A}$ that maps a given input string s to command(s) c matched with the JavaScript syntax. Whereas the function $\mathcal{A}_{Rev}$ performs the reverse for a given program statement(s). Then as shown in Fig. 4, the rewriting function $\mathcal{R}$ could interpose either of the following two treatments to the string argument: (i) replace the `eval` statement with the argument itself, or (ii) a function call within the scope of caller application where the function performs the operations that would have executed by the `eval`.

Next, DL algorithm shall generate security labeling for intermediate variables of transformed JavaScript source code. In case of the latter approach, the algorithm performs flow analyses similar to a function call [22]. Note that the clearance label cl for caller application would then be treated as an upper bound for evaluating the function body. Therefore, the execution of an `eval` statement is flow-safe as long as the function call in the transformed JavaScript code does not invalidate the *can-flow-to* relation with the static labels of sensitive variables in the caller application.

$$S' := \text{function } f : \mathcal{A}(s)\#\#S;$$
$$s' := \mathcal{A}_{Rev}(f());$$
$$S' := S[T(\text{eval}(s)) \mapsto \mathcal{A}(s)]; \qquad S'' := S'[T(\text{eval}(s)) \mapsto \text{eval}(s')];$$
$$\text{output } S'; \qquad\qquad\qquad \text{output } S'';$$

Fig. 4. Steps performed by $\mathcal{R}(S)$ for a JavaScript S when the function T transforms eval through replacement (left); and function call (right). The binary operator '##' produces a sequence of program statements.

3.4   Declassification

Often enforcement of the global policy of non-interference is too restrictive to design real systems. In practice, system design often demands information to flow from *high* to *low* as one can intuitively see in the classic *password example*. For this purpose, the notion of declassification [27,31,36,43,52] has been used extensively under rigid conditions so that confidentiality is not violated to the detriment of the usage. Declassification eventually allows more subjects to be readers of the information. However, the addition of readers needs to be genuinely robust as it may otherwise reduce to pure discretionary access control that has severe consequences in a decentralized model.

Motivated by the earlier development of SME [18], Austin & Flanagan [7] proposed the notion of *faceted value*, a pair of raw values (facets) containing *low* and *high* information respectively. In this work, the authors introduce a mechanism called *facet declassification* where information shifts from one facet to another only if the control path has not been influenced by an untrusted label. Although the work follows the definition of *robust declassification* [51], it does not define the drop in confidentiality, i.e., who could be the potential reader of the declassified data, hence it could boil down to discretionary access control. Bauer *et al.* [9] proposed a run-time monitor for web browsers introducing an information-flow label written as a tuple (S, I, D), where S, I, and D denote the secrecy, integrity, and declassification labels respectively. Information can flow from a sender to a receiver, labeled as $(S_1, I_1, \{\})$ and $(S_2, I_2, \{\})$ respectively, only if $S_1 \subseteq S_2$ and $I_1 \supseteq I_2$. The declassification label is often useful to circumvent the above constraints, which otherwise would have failed due to secrecy and integrity tags. However, the declassification could disclose sensitive data to any arbitrary entity if the label is not given judiciously. Moreover, the approach does not follow the notion of *robust declassification* as the mechanism of declassification is independent of secrecy or integrity labels.

Our Approach to Declassification using RWFM: Consider a password manager extension P that stores the username and password for websites (or server or entity) A, B, and C each time a user performs a new login and enables the browser to auto-fill the same for every subsequent login to that respective website. We apply DL algorithm in tandem with RWFM label specification and governing policies for flow transitions and declassification. Firstly, we shall provide static labels for global variables such as username or password for website

A as $\lambda(A) = (A, \{P, A\}, \{A\})$, read as A is the owner, P and A are readers and only A has written the information so far. Secondly, the initial dynamic label for the password manager extension is given as $\lambda(P) = (S, \{*\}, \{\})$, meaning S is the owner (could be the user or browser) of the password storage, $'*'$ denotes anybody can read the information (public), and an empty writer set represents that nobody has written the information so far. Next, the label of P changes dynamically according to flow transitions. The label changes for P are shown in Table 2 where the column "Transitions" represents the information flow direction, i.e. $A \rightarrow P$ when password manager reads username and password entered for the website A, and $P \xrightarrow{d} A$ when P declassifies information to A. Note that the reader set of P becomes more restrictive as it collects information from A, B, and C. As the label of P obtains the highest possible label in the lattice, information cannot flow from P to the websites A, B, or C for the sake of auto-filling the username and password fields on subsequent visits. Therefore, the label of P needs to be declassified to the respective website. During the next login to website A, RWFM declassification eventually includes A into the reader set as A has influenced the information earlier; in other words, A is present in the writer set of P. Unlike the earlier approaches, RWFM declassification clearly defines the drop in confidentiality (readers) policy and prevents declassifying sensitive data to an entity that has not influenced the data in preceding flow transitions. In addition, the approach also automatically generates dynamic labels for local variables, therefore not requiring explicitly providing labels for each entity.

Table 2. Changes in RWFM labels corresponding to information flows

Transitions	Source label	Destination label	Changed label
$A \rightarrow P$	$\lambda(A) = (A, \{P, A\}, \{A\})$	$\lambda(P) = (S, \{*\}, \{\})$	$\lambda(P) = (S, \{P, A\}, \{A\})$
$B \rightarrow P$	$\lambda(B) = (B, \{P, B\}, \{B\})$	$\lambda(P) = (S, \{P, A\}, \{A\})$	$\lambda(P) = (S, \{P\}, \{A, B\})$
$C \rightarrow P$	$\lambda(C) = (C, \{P, C\}, \{C\})$	$\lambda(P) = (S, \{P\}, \{A, B\})$	$\lambda(P) = (S, \{P\}, \{A, B, C\})$
$P \xrightarrow{d} A$	$\lambda(P) = (S, \{P\}, \{A, B, C\})$	$(S, \{P, A\}, \{A, B, C\})$	

There are two possibilities for the placement of declassification construct: (i) have an assertion that ensures declassification explicitly, or (ii) perform declassification implicitly at the JavaScript function return. In this work, we consider the former option as implicit declassification or automatic placement of the construct could lead to security risk – we leave the discussion for our future work.

4   Solution for Preventing Privacy-Violating Flows

We extend the DL algorithm for identifying privacy-violating information flows in JavaScript programs. DL algorithm generates dynamic labels for local objects of a JavaScript program for a given set of user-defined fixed labels of global objects (variables interact with the outside world). Possibility (or otherwise) of labeling the program objects leads to certification (or otherwise) of the program;

the same could be used in the execution monitor for checking flow security at run-time as discussed for `eval` statement in the previous section.

Let W be a website, S and H denote the static and dynamic part of the script respectively, λ be a given labeling function, and cl is the clearance label. The DL algorithm for identifying privacy-violating information flow is shown in Table 3. Note that the information flow between the static and dynamic part of the script is administered by the binary relation *can-flow-to* of the security lattice.

Table 3. DL Algorithm for JavaScript application

$DL(W, \lambda, cl)$ ::
1. $\lambda_1 = DL(S, \lambda, cl)$
2. **WHILE** there exists H then
3.   load H
4. $\lambda_2 = DL(H, \lambda, cl)$
5.   **IF** there is a flow from $S(param)$ to $H(var)$
6.   Check $\lambda_1(param) \leqslant \lambda_2(var)$
7.   **IF** there is a flow from $H(var)$ to $S(param)$
8.   Check $\lambda_2(var) \leqslant \lambda_1(param)$
9.   **IF** H contains H' then
10.   Go to step 2
11.   **ELSE** Exit

Table 4 demonstrates the application of DL algorithm for the example shown in Fig. 1. Consider variables *baseUrl*, *version*, *PasswordTextBox.value*, and *UsernameTextBox.value* as global objects, whereas *pwd*, *uname*, and *params* are local objects. An initial labeling function λ maps the global objects to the corresponding given static security label and local objects to $\perp$. Next, for the given initial mapping λ, our proposed algorithm performs the following tasks: (i) computes the final labels of local variables in the context part, and thus, obtains a new labeling function λ_1; (ii) loads the hole part of the JavaScript; (iii) obtains a labeling function λ_2 that maps each local variables of the hole to their respective final security labels; and (iv) checks if the required flow constraints hold whenever there are information flows from the hole to the context or vice-versa. Thus, the algorithm allows the context part of the script to accept the parameters of a hole only if the required flow constraints at the line `initSettings`$(z1, z2)$ hold good.

Note that unlike SIF [14], our framework built upon the proposed algorithm allows the information to flow to/from a hole as long as it does not violate the flow constraints. Thus, our approach could lead to the development of a flow-secure web browser by modifying the browser core or implementing an OS-agnostic browser extension that would enable us to specify and enforce security policies and analyze information flows in JavaScript against the given policies.

5   Related Work

In this section, we briefly describe previous IFC-based solutions for preventing privacy-violating leaks in JavaScript applications.

Table 4. A solution to example in Fig. 1 using DL algorithm

	Script	Labeling

Context	`var initSettings = function(s, i){`
	    `baseUrl = s;`
	    `version = i;`
	`}`
	
	`initSettings(D, 1.0); /*initial destination D/*`
	
	`var login = function(){`
	    `var pwd = PasswordTextBox.value;`
	    `var uname = UsernameTextBox.value;`
	    `var params = "u = " + user + "&p = " + pwd;`
	    `post(baseUrl, params);`
	`}`
		Global objects:
		$baseUrl, version,$
		$PasswordTextBox.value,$
		$UsernameTextBox.value$
		
		Local Objects:
		$pwd, uname, params$
		
		$\lambda_1 = DL(\text{Context}, \lambda, cl)$

Hole	`var z1 = C;`
	`var z2 = 1.0;`
	`initSettings(z1, z2); /*destination redirected to C/*`
		Loads the Hole
		$\lambda_2 = DL(\text{Hole}, \lambda, cl)$
		
		Checks:
		$\lambda_2(z1) \leqslant \lambda_1(baseUrl)$
		$\lambda_2(z1) \leqslant \lambda_1(version)$

Most of the earlier approaches to IFC in JavaScript are based on dynamic information flow control (DIFC) [19,25,28,38]. DIFC attaches *high* or *low* security labels with sensitive or insensitive values respectively and propagates the labels during program execution. Vogt *et al.* [38] proposed a tainting-based approach that marks sensitive data, and the sensitivity is propagated when the data is accessed by scripts running in the web browsers. Dhawan and Ganapathy [19] proposed a similar approach where a label is associated with each in-memory JavaScript object. The label determines if an object contains sensitive information. The labels are propagated as objects are modified by the JavaScript engine and passed between browser subsystems. The technique raises an alert when a sensitive object is accessed in unsafe way. Jang *et al.* [28] proposed a dynamic code rewriting-based mechanism that enables injecting taints depending on different privacy-violating flows and eventually propagated and blocked. Hedin *et al.* [25] first implemented DIFC in the form of a JavaScript interpreter called *JSFlow* for fine-grained tracking of information flow in large JavaScript applications. However, the above approaches fail to realize termination leaks due to the program's non-termination.

Some variant of inline reference monitor (IRM) performs dynamic inline taint tracking that does not require browser modification but instruments the code or existing JavaScript engine – the interpreter or just-in-time (JIT) compiler [11, 13]. The mechanisms must translate JavaScript to prevent security risks due to dynamic features. Although some of the approaches incur moderate performance overhead, unlike our approach, the non-interference is termination-insensitive.

S. Just *et al.* [30] first introduced a hybrid mechanism that dynamically tracks explicit information flows while tracking intra-and inter-procedural information flows using static analysis. Following the hybrid information flow analysis, Bedford *et al.* [10] proposed a flow-sensitive inline monitoring that uses an oracle to determine loop termination behaviour [34]. While the former approach does not guarantee termination-sensitive non-interference, the notion of declassification is yet to be defined in the latter.

Devriese and Piessens [18] proposed *Secure Multi-Execution* (SME) that executes multiple instances of a JavaScript program concurrently, once for each security label in the lattice, applying special rules for I/O operations that prevent the information flow from high to low-security variables. However, in practice, the information flow usually occurs in the opposite direction, where high-security inputs always influence low-security outputs [41]. Particularly, in cryptographic operations, files are encrypted, sanitized, declassified, and sent over low- level public network. But the implementation of declassification [36,52] in SME and its subsequent developments [15,39] is majorly overlooked.

Recent development claims that the cases of information leaks due to implicit flows are insignificant in web applications, but tracking implicit flows is expensive and incurs performance overhead [44]. Comparatively, a lightweight taint analysis could be sufficient to track insecurity due to explicit flows. Nonetheless, ignoring implicit flows could have a severe security risk; therefore, our approach stands out in this context that could prevent leaks due to implicit, explicit, and termination channels. Furthermore, following RWFM specification provides a robust notion of declassification. We leave the performance evaluation of our framework and comparison with the existing implementation as our future work.

6   Conclusions and Future Work

There are two research aspects for establishing flow security in JavaScript applications. Firstly, identifying the key security challenges for enforcing flow security in JavaScript language, including declassification. Secondly, defining flow security with respect to information flows in different directions in JavaScript applications, such as from context to context, context to hole, hole to context, and hole to hole. In this paper, we have highlighted the security challenges and provided a detailed description of our solution using an IFC-based program certification algorithm. Further, we have provided a solution to prevent cross-script privacy-violating information flows, in particular, and thus, answered the fundamental question that is *when should a script accept the parameters returned by a dynamic script?*. Further, we have proposed an all-in-one automatic solution using *Dynamic Labelling* algorithm and RWFM label specifications that could identify privacy-violating information flows with respect to a given set of security policies associated with sensitive objects. The solution would help coexist the cooperating scripts and encourage the "web-mashup" model - a common practice in web applications; although it involves privacy risk but relevant from business perspectives.

In future, we plan the development of a flow-secure web browser by modifying the browser core or implementing an OS-agnostic browser extension that would enable us to specify and enforce security policies and analyze information flows in JavaScript against the given policies. In addition, our future work includes extensions to handling exceptions and concurrency. In particular, we would be interested in scaling up our approach to deal with real-world applications and evaluate performance against the existing implementation.

References

1. Ecmascript 2023 language specification. https://tc39.es/ecma262/
2. Most popular technologies. https://insights.stackoverflow.com/survey/2020#most-popular-technologies
3. Cross-domain security woes. the strange zen of javascript (2005). http://jszen.blogspot.com/2005/03/cross-domain-security-woes.html
4. Defining safer json-p (2020). https://json-p.org/
5. Askarov, A., Hunt, S., Sabelfeld, A., Sands, D.: Termination-insensitive noninterference leaks more than just a bit. In: Jajodia, S., Lopez, J. (eds.) ESORICS 2008. LNCS, vol. 5283, pp. 333–348. Springer, Heidelberg (2008). https://doi.org/10.1007/978-3-540-88313-5_22
6. Austin, T.H., Flanagan, C.: Efficient purely-dynamic information flow analysis. In: Proceedings of the ACM SIGPLAN 4th Workshop on PLAS, pp. 113–124 (2009)
7. Austin, T.H., Flanagan, C.: Multiple facets for dynamic information flow. In: Proceedings of the 39th Annual ACM SIGPLAN-SIGACT Symposium on Principles of Programming Languages, pp. 165–178 (2012)
8. Barth, A.: The web origin concept. Technical report (2011)
9. Bauer, L., Cai, S., Jia, L., Passaro, T., Stroucken, M., Tian, Y.: Run-time monitoring and formal analysis of information flows in chromium. In: NDSS (2015)
10. Bedford, A., Chong, S., Desharnais, J., Kozyri, E., Tawbi, N.: A progress-sensitive flow-sensitive inlined information-flow control monitor (extended version). Comput. Secur. **71**, 114–131 (2017)
11. Bichhawat, A., Rajani, V., Garg, D., Hammer, C.: Information Flow Control in WebKit's JavaScript Bytecode. In: Abadi, M., Kremer, S. (eds.) POST 2014. LNCS, vol. 8414, pp. 159–178. Springer, Heidelberg (2014). https://doi.org/10.1007/978-3-642-54792-8_9

12. Broberg, N., van Delft, B., Sands, D.: Paragon for practical programming with information-flow control. In: Shan, C.-C. (ed.) APLAS 2013. LNCS, vol. 8301, pp. 217–232. Springer, Cham (2013). https://doi.org/10.1007/978-3-319-03542-0_16
13. Chudnov, A., Naumann, D.A.: Inlined information flow monitoring for javascript. In: Proceedings of the 22nd ACM SIGSAC Conference on Computer and Communications Security, pp. 629–643 (2015)
14. Chugh, R., Meister, J.A., Jhala, R., Lerner, S.: Staged information flow for javascript. In: Proceedings of the 30th ACM SIGPLAN Conference on Programming Language Design and Implementation, pp. 50–62 (2009)
15. De Groef, W., Devriese, D., Nikiforakis, N., Piessens, F.: Flowfox: a web browser with flexible and precise information flow control. In: Proceedings of the 2012 ACM Conference on Computer and Communications Security, pp. 748–759 (2012)
16. Denning, D.E.: A lattice model of secure information flow. CACM **19**(5), 236–243 (1976)
17. Denning, D.E., Denning, P.J.: Certification of programs for secure information flow. Commun. ACM **20**(7), 504–513 (1977)
18. Devriese, D., Piessens, F.: Noninterference through secure multi-execution. In: 2010 IEEE Symposium on Security and Privacy, pp. 109–124. IEEE (2010)
19. Dhawan, M., Ganapathy, V.: Analyzing information flow in javascript-based browser extensions. In: 2009 Annual Computer Security Applications Conference, pp. 382–391. IEEE (2009)
20. Fenton, J.S.: Memoryless subsystems. Comput. J. **17**(2), 143–147 (1974)
21. Ghosal, S., Shyamasundar, R.K., Kumar, N.V.N.: Static security certification of programs via dynamic labelling. In: Proceedings of the 15th International Joint Conference on e-Business and Telecommunications, ICETE 2018 - Volume 2: SECRYPT, 26–28 July 2018, pp. 400–411 Porto, Portugal (2018)
22. Ghosal, S., Shyamasundar, R., Kumar, N.N.: Compile-time security certification of imperative programming languages. In: Obaidat, M.S. (ed.) ICETE 2018. CCIS, vol. 1118, pp. 159–182. Springer, Cham (2019). https://doi.org/10.1007/978-3-030-34866-3_8
23. Goguen, J.A., Meseguer, J.: Security policies and security models. In: 1982 IEEE Symposium on Security and Privacy, pp. 11–11. IEEE (1982)
24. Graf, J., Hecker, M., Mohr, M.: Using joana for information flow control in java programs - a practical guide. In: Proceedings of the 6th Working Conference on Programming Languages (ATPS 2013). LNI, vol. 215, pp. 123–138. Springer, Berlin (2013)
25. Hedin, D., Birgisson, A., Bello, L., Sabelfeld, A.: Jsflow: tracking information flow in javascript and its apis. In: Proceedings of the 29th Annual ACM Symposium on Applied Computing, pp. 1663–1671 (2014)
26. Hedin, D., Sabelfeld, A.: Information-flow security for a core of javascript. In: Computer Security Foundations Symposium (CSF), 2012 IEEE 25th, pp. 3–18. IEEE (2012)
27. Hicks, B., Ahmadizadeh, K., McDaniel, P.: From languages to systems: Understanding practical application development in security-typed languages. In: 2006 22nd Annual Computer Security Applications Conference (ACSAC 2006), pp. 153–164. IEEE (2006)
28. Jang, D., Jhala, R., Lerner, S., Shacham, H.: An empirical study of privacy-violating information flows in javascript web applications. In: Proceedings of the 17th ACM Conference on Computer and Communications Security, pp. 270–283 (2010)

29. Jang, D., Jhala, R., Lerner, S., Shacham, H.: Rewriting-based dynamic information flow for javascript. In: 17th ACM Conference on Computer and Communications Security (2010)

30. Just, S., Cleary, A., Shirley, B., Hammer, C.: Information flow analysis for javascript. In: Proceedings of the 1st ACM SIGPLAN International Workshop on Programming Language and Systems Technologies for Internet Clients, pp. 9–18 (2011)

31. King, D., Jha, S., Jaeger, T., Jha, S., Seshia, S.A.: On automatic placement of declassifiers for information-flow security. Technical report, Technical Report NASTR-0083-2007, Network and Security Research Center (2007)

32. Kumar, N.V.N., Shyamasundar, R.: A complete generative label model for lattice-based access control models. In: Cimatti, A., Sirjani, M. (eds.) SEFM 2017. LNCS, vol. 10469, pp. 35–53. Springer, Cham (2017). https://doi.org/10.1007/978-3-319-66197-1_3

33. Mitropoulos, D., Louridas, P., Salis, V., Spinellis, D.: Time present and time past: analyzing the evolution of javascript code in the wild. In: 2019 IEEE/ACM 16th International Conference on Mining Software Repositories (MSR), pp. 126–137. IEEE (2019)

34. Moore, S., Askarov, A., Chong, S.: Precise enforcement of progress-sensitive security. In: Proceedings of the 2012 ACM Conference on Computer and Communications Security, pp. 881–893. ACM (2012)

35. Myers, A.C., Liskov, B.: A Decentralized Model for Information Flow Control, vol. 31. ACM (1997)

36. Myers, A.C., Liskov, B.: Protecting privacy using the decentralized label model. ACM Trans. Software Eng. Methodol. 9(4), 410–442 (2000)

37. Myers, A.C., Zheng, L., Zdancewic, S., Chong, S., Nystrom, N.: Jif: java information flow (2001). http://www.cs.cornell.edu/jif

38. Nentwich, F., Jovanovic, N., Kirda, E., Kruegel, C., Vigna, G.: Cross-site scripting prevention with dynamic data tainting and static analysis. In: Proceeding of the Network and Distributed System Security Symposium (NDSS 2007). Citeseer (2007)

39. Ngo, M., Bielova, N., Flanagan, C., Rezk, T., Russo, A., Schmitz, T.: A better facet of dynamic information flow control. In: Companion Proceedings of the The Web Conference 2018, pp. 731–739 (2018)

40. Russo, A., Sabelfeld, A.: Dynamic vs. static flow-sensitive security analysis. In: 2010 23rd IEEE Computer Security Foundations Symposium, pp. 186–199. IEEE (2010)

41. Ryan, P., McLean, J., Millen, J., Gligor, V.: Non-interference: who needs it? In: CSFW, p. 0237. IEEE (2001)

42. Sabelfeld, A., Myers, A.C.: Language-based information-flow security. IEEE J. Selected Areas Commun. 21(1), 5–19 (2003)

43. Sabelfeld, A., Myers, A.C.: A Model for delimited information release. In: Futatsugi, K., Mizoguchi, F., Yonezaki, N. (eds.) ISSS 2003. LNCS, vol. 3233, pp. 174–191. Springer, Heidelberg (2004). https://doi.org/10.1007/978-3-540-37621-7_9

44. Staicu, C.A., Schoepe, D., Balliu, M., Pradel, M., Sabelfeld, A.: An empirical study of information flows in real-world javascript. In: Proceedings of the 14th ACM SIGSAC Workshop on Programming Languages and Analysis for Security, pp. 45–59 (2019)

45. Van Kesteren, A., et al.: Cross-origin resource sharing. W3C Working Draft WD-cors-20100727, latest version available at< (2010). http://www.w3.org/TR/cors (2010)

46. Volpano, D., Irvine, C., Smith, G.: A sound type system for secure flow analysis. J. Comput. Secur. **4**(2–3), 167–187 (1996)
47. Volpano, D., Smith, G.: Eliminating covert flows with minimum typings. In: Proceedings 10th Computer Security Foundations Workshop, pp. 156–168. IEEE (1997)
48. Yang, E., Stefan, D., Mitchell, J., Mazières, D., Marchenko, P., Karp, B.: Toward principled browser security. In: 14th Workshop on Hot Topics in Operating Systems (HotOS XIV) (2013)
49. Zalewski, M.: Browser security handbook. Google Code (2010)
50. Zdancewic, S.A., Myers, A.: Programming Languages for Information Security. Cornell University (2002)
51. Zdancewic, S.: A type system for robust declassification. Electron. Notes Theoretical Comput. Sci. **83**, 263–277 (2003)
52. Zdancewic, S., Myers, A.C.: Robust declassification. CSFW. **1**, 15–23 (2001)
53. Zheng, L., Myers, A.C.: Dynamic security labels and static information flow control. Int. J. Inform. Secur. **6**(2–3), 67–84 (2007)

On the Impact of Model Tolerance in Power Grid Anomaly Detection Systems

Srinidhi Madabhushi[✉] and Rinku Dewri

University of Denver, Denver, CO 80208, USA
`nidhi.madabhushi@du.edu`, `rdewri@cs.du.edu`

Abstract. Rapid development in deep learning-based detection systems for numerous industrial applications has opened opportunities to apply them in power grids. A consumer's power consumption can be monitored to recognize any anomalous behavior in their household. When building such detection systems, evaluating their robustness to adversarial samples is critical. It has been shown that when we provide adversarial samples to deep learning models, they falsely classify instances, even when the perturbation or noise added to the original data is very small. On the other hand, these models should be able to detect attack instances correctly and raise few to no false alarms. While this expectation can be difficult to attain, we are allowed to choose a threshold that decides the extent to which the detection and false alarm rates are compromised. To this end, we explore the threshold selection problem for state-of-the-art deep learning-based detection models such that it can recognize attack instances. We show that selecting a threshold is challenging, and even if an appropriate threshold is chosen, the tolerance of a model to adversarial samples can still leave avenues for an attack to be successful.

Keywords: Anomaly detection · Deep learning · Model sensitivity · Power consumption · Threshold selection

1 Introduction

Industrial control systems support critical national infrastructure that are essential for managing various industries like electricity generation and distribution, water treatment and supply, oil and gas production and many more. Disruption of such infrastructure at any time can lead to serious effects on the society and can impact the safety and economy of a nation. A large scale attack on a power grid allows adversaries to take control and operate other industrial control systems as well. Moreover, the attack surface for a power grid has increased over the past decade with the advent of IoT devices. As these devices are designed with security as an afterthought, they become easy targets for attackers. By controlling IoT devices of consumers, an attacker can regulate the power demand that can lead to grid failures. Therefore, using anomaly detection and monitoring

V. R. Badarla et al. (Eds.): ICISS 2022, LNCS 13784, pp. 220–234, 2022.
https://doi.org/10.1007/978-3-031-23690-7_13

systems to detect anomalous power consumption can help in identifying such cases in advance, facilitating grid operators to take necessary action. Machine learning and deep learning methods are proposed for many anomaly detection applications, and neural networks are well known for their ability to learn patterns, making them applicable for time series data. However, it is possible for adversaries to modify the input data to deceive the model. Adversarial attacks on such models were first shown in image applications where perturbed images of animals and traffic signs were mis-classified, when small perturbations are introduced in the images [6,16]. Previous work also showed that by perturbing the time series data in small amounts, a deep neural network can still be deceived for time series classification applications [5,14].

In this paper, we study how susceptible deep learning-based anomaly detection models are to adversarial samples that manipulate the power demand through compromised consumer devices. First, we provide a simple yet easily generalizable method to create adversarial samples that is parameterized by the frequency and strength of the attack (Sect. 3). This allows us to compare any generic anomaly detection system against another in a black box setting. Second, we provide a comparative assessment of the detection efficiency of three state-of-the-art deep learning models for power consumption anomaly detection under different levels of attack aggressiveness. Choosing a right cut-off threshold is critical for such systems because they differentiate anomalous values from the normal ones. Hence, third, we demonstrate through a detailed exercise that it can be challenging to choose a threshold that can detect the various attack scenarios, and provide a low false alarm rate at the same time (Sect. 4). We show that a model may perform well for certain levels of attack aggressiveness, but is unable to provide coverage across all scenarios. Lastly, we delve deeper into the types of undetected attacks in each model, providing insights on the characteristics of the models and the trade-off between the model's noise tolerance levels and the attacker's wattage requirement (Sect. 5). Unfortunately, there always appears to be sufficient room for an attacker to bypass detection by adjusting their manipulation frequency and strength. We conclude the paper in Sect. 6 with references to future work.

2 Background and Related Work

In this section, we discuss demand manipulation attacks (MAD) and their effects on the power grid. We explain the role of anomaly detection algorithms for detecting MAD attacks. We further discuss existing literature for anomaly detection in the power consumption domain, and adversarial attacks demonstrated on deep learning models.

2.1 Demand Manipulation Attacks

Demand manipulation attacks, also known as MAD attacks, occur when an adversary manipulates the demand of the power grid from the utility side using consumer devices. These devices are assumed to be in a residential setting and are manipulated either directly by the attacker or by the consumer. Such attacks can be performed by controlling a botnet of IoT devices that can manipulate the power demand much faster than the power plants can react [4]. When an attacker has access to various high wattage IoT devices, they can synchronously switch them on and off which leads to the disruption of the power grid [17]. The attacker can also influence the behavior of the consumers by sending false messages to fake maintenance shutdown alerts, suggesting the consumers to use appliances during peak consumption periods [15]. Such attacks have adverse effects on the power grid such as (i) frequency instability that can lead to a sudden generation tripping, or disrupting a grid re-start, (ii) line failures and cascading failures, and (iii) an increase in operating costs leading to the Independent System Operators (ISOs) having to purchase additional power in the form of reserve generators [17].

2.2   Anomaly Detection Mechanism

The power consumption data of a household that is collected from a smart meter provides an opportunity to detect sudden changes in the consumption as a result of a demand manipulation attack. Anomaly detection mechanisms are designed for detecting attacks and alerting the consumer and the power grid operator. This allows the power grid personnel to take necessary action to avoid potential damage to the power grid equipment. An anomaly detection mechanism consists of a prediction method followed by a scoring technique which provides a score specifying how anomalous the instance is. A thresholding mechanism is then used to provide a cut-off beyond which the instance will be flagged as an anomaly.

2.3   Related Work

A review for several anomaly detection systems proposed for power consumption data was conducted by Himeur et al. focusing on artificial intelligence-based (AI) models [8]. They categorized models based on different aspects like the type of algorithm and application. While this work covers different AI models, we focus on deep learning and neural network-based models. As power consumption data is a time series, long short term memory (LSTM) neural networks are predominantly used for time series prediction applications. Wang et al. proposed an LSTM-based detection model where the predictions are used to calculate anomaly scores for each time unit and two thresholds are used to mark anomalies in the data [19]. Clustering-based approaches like K-means can also be applied instead of scores to identify anomalous instances [2].

Neural networks are often combined with other techniques to capture events that can be detected by both models. While taking advantage of LSTM's ability to remember previous observations, it can be combined with traditional time series methods like ARIMA to model the non-linear components of the data [9]. Autoregression models (AR) can also be combined with feed forward neural networks (NN) to form a hybrid model called NNAR [3]. Kim et al. combined two neural networks, CNN and LSTM, for predicting power consumption data [10]. Other examples of two neural networks used in conjunction include combining autoencoders with Online Sequential Extreme Learning Machine (OS-ELM) and LSTM [18,20].

Adversarial attacks on deep neural network models were demonstrated by Goodfellow et al. in a computer vision application [7]. Different adversarial attack generation methods on neural networks have been proposed including fast gradient sign method (FGSM) [7] and basic iterative method (BIM) [12] among many others. These methods are designed for a threat model where the adversary has full knowledge of their target model (white-box). However, due to the transferability of adversarial samples across models, these methods are effective for gray-box (knowledge limited to model structure) and black-box (can only query the model) threat models [16]. In the literature, different adversarial sample generation models have been compared by applying them to neural networks used for time series classification tasks, including power consumption applications [5]. This was also demonstrated for multivariate time series regression models specifically for CNNs, LSTMs and GRUs (Gated Recurrent Unit) [14].

In this work, we do not assume a target model and generate adversarial samples by incrementally increasing the power injection and proportion of perturbation. We then pass the generated adversarial samples to three detection models to assess their performance. While adversarial attacks have been demonstrated on detection systems used in power grids as well as other industrial control systems [13,21], we focus on exploring whether a detection system when tuned to detect such adversarial samples, succeeds or not.

3 Methodology

Anomaly detection systems that are semi-supervised are trained on normal data and when provided with new data, the model identifies anomalies based on how different the data is from what it learned. However, there may be cases where the data is anomalous, but the model is unable to detect it. The same applies to when the data is normal but the model identifies it as abnormal, because it is slightly different from what it has seen. In order to explore the research question of how well a model can avoid giving false classifications, we develop a methodology where different attack data are generated and tested on state-of-the-art models to evaluate their performance. The minute-level consumption values from the previous hour (60 min) represented by $d_{t-60}, d_{t-59}, ..., d_{t-2}, d_{t-1}$ are used to predict the power consumption at time t represented by d'_t. An anomaly score s_t is then calculated using the actual and predicted consumption values (d_t and d'_t). The threshold th is used to decide whether the consumption value at time t is an anomaly, by checking if the score s_t is greater than th.

3.1 Power Consumption Data

The data used in this paper is the individual household electric power consumption dataset obtained from the UCI Machine Learning Repository[1]. It consists

---

[1] https://archive.ics.uci.edu/ml/datasets/individual+household+electric+power+consumption.

of readings for nine attributes collected for every minute over a period of almost four years. As we focus only on power consumption, we use three attributes which consists of the date, time and global active power in kilowatt collected during the years 2007, 2008 and 2009. There are 25,979 missing values in the data that are handled using linear interpolation which is particularly useful for time series. The training and validation data consists of power consumption values for the years 2007 and 2008, whereas the testing data consists of values for the year 2009. For predicting the power consumption at time t, the consumption values at times $t - 1$, $t - 2$, $t - 3$,..., $t - 60$ are passed as the input to the model. The training input for each neural network is a dataframe consisting of 60 columns that represent the previous 60 consumption values for each time unit and 920,100 rows representing the inputs for timestamps for 21 months, starting from 2007-01-01 00:00:00 to 2008-09-30 23:59:00 with minute level sampling. The validation data consists of consumption values for three months starting from 2008-10-01 00:00:00 to 2008-12-31 23:59:00. All the consumption values for the year 2009 are used as test data.

3.2   Model Training

We select three prediction models from the literature, each representing a different type of neural network—multi layer perceptron (MLP) [3], long short term memory (LSTM) [2] and convolutional neural network LSTM (CNN-LSTM) [10]. We follow semi-supervised training in which the training data is considered to be normal and does not contain any anomalies. For each model, we use the same number of layers that the authors from the literature use. We tune the hyperparameters of the neural network by starting off with the values that the literature uses and going higher and lower than the suggested value in powers of two. We perform this search for the number of nodes, dropout, batch size and number of epochs. The search is controlled by the mean squared error and provides the model that has the least error on the validation data. The number of nodes per layer and other parameters for the final models are shown in Table 1. The layers are listed in the order of their placement in the architecture. There are two convolution layers for the CNN-LSTM model for which the parameters for each layer are given in the format *(number of filters, kernel size)*. The number of input features for each model is 60 and the output is a single value, the prediction. Mean squared error is used as the loss function, Adam [11] as the optimizer and TensorFlow [1] on the back-end.

3.3   Anomaly Score

An anomaly score gives the extent to which the data point should be considered as an anomaly. We use the score s_t adopted by Wang et al. [19], given as

$$s_t = \frac{|predicted_t - observed_t|}{avg_{i \in T}(|predicted_i - observed_i|)}, \tag{1}$$

where $predicted_t$ is the prediction for consumption at time t, $observed_t$ is the observed consumption at time t and all previous times $\{1, 2, 3, ..., t-2, t-1\} \in T$.

Table 1. Model architecture for MLP, LSTM and CNN-LSTM

Parameter	MLP	LSTM	CNN-LSTM
Convolution layer	n/a	n/a	(64, 2), (64, 2)
LSTM layer	n/a	32, 32, 64	128
Dense layer	100	n/a	32, 64
Dropout	n/a	0.07, 0.03	n/a
Number of epochs	30	5	30
Batch size	2048	2048	4096

Table 2. Thresholds calculated for each model using the validation data with varying percentiles

Percentile	MLP	LSTM	CNN-LSTM
60.0	0.39	0.63	0.41
70.0	0.54	0.74	0.58
80.0	0.92	1.03	0.92
90.0	2.14	2.11	2.37
95.0	4.52	4.08	4.75
98.0	8.74	7.4	8.04
99.0	11.94	10.21	11.16
99.5	15.68	13.21	14.06
99.9	21.8	18.93	19.78
99.999	39.4	34.88	36.08

3.4 Thresholding Mechanism

A threshold is a value that is applied to an anomaly score above which a point is flagged as an anomaly. We use a percentile-based approach to calculate ten different thresholds that vary by the percentile values. This lets us explore the threshold that fits best with the data. The percentile values used are 60, 70, 80, 90, 95, 98, 99, 99.5, 99.9 and 99.999 which starts from the strictest threshold and is loosened till the 99.999^{th} percentile. The threshold values calculated for each model are shown in Table 2. The percentiles are calculated using anomaly scores for the validation data.

3.5 Attack Profiles

An attack profile represents a dataset that consists of attack instances and is created by adding perturbations to the original dataset. We generate 2,000 attack profiles using a perturbation model that randomly chooses the time instances that are injected with extra wattage in the test data. The number of attack instances in the data depends on the proportion of perturbation ranging from

0.05 to 1.0 in steps of 0.05, giving a total of 20 proportions to choose from. The perturbation that is added ranges from 1 kW to 100 kW in steps of 1 kW, giving 100 different perturbation values. We choose to limit at 100 kW as the injection is performed for a single household and it is unlikely to get a wattage as high as 100 kW. We extend the perturbations till 100 kW to study the model performance for increasing wattage. The following steps are used to generate the attack profiles.

1. For a proportion p, randomly choose the list of indices I (or timestamps) in the dataframe that will be treated as attack instances from the entire test dataset D.

$$I = random(n = length(D), r = length(D) \times p) \qquad (2)$$

where n is the total number of indices in the dataset D, r is the number of attack instances to select from D and $random$ chooses r values from 0 to n.

2. Add the perturbation ϵ to the chosen attack instances to create the attack profile D'.

$$D' = D[I] + \epsilon \qquad (3)$$

3. Repeat steps 1 and 2 for each proportion $p \in$ 0.05, 0.1, 0.15,..., 0.95, 1.0 and $\epsilon \in$ 1, 2, 3,..., 99, 100.

4   Threshold Selection

Prediction-based anomaly detection systems require a threshold to be selected such that it is able to detect majority of the attack instances and give least number of false alarms at the same time. In this section, we explore different thresholds in order to choose a value that is able to perform well in both cases. The metrics for the threshold selection used are detection rate (DR) and false alarm rate (FAR). Detection rate measures the proportion of true anomalous instances that are correctly identified. False alarm rate measures the proportion of normal instances that are incorrectly classified as anomalies.

To make it easier for visual analysis, we categorize the combination of the amount of perturbation (injected power wattage) and the frequency of the attacks (percentage of attack instances) into nine attack configurations that represent the strength of the attack as shown in Fig. 1. As both values get higher, it represents a more aggressive attack. We also overlay this grid on the plots to get a general overview of the performance of the metrics.

4.1   The Threshold Dilemma

The threshold dilemma represents the inability to choose a threshold based on the detection and false alarm rates in order to achieve the best performance for adversarial samples. It involves going back and forth with the threshold selection because there is a downside with one metric when a threshold is chosen using the

high perturbation less frequent	high perturbation moderately frequent	high perturbation more frequent
moderate perturbation less frequent	moderate perturbation moderately frequent	moderate perturbation more frequent
low perturbation less frequent	low perturbation moderately frequent	low perturbation more frequent

Fig. 1. Types of attacks varying by amount of perturbation and frequency of attacks

other metric. A chosen threshold must be able to detect most of the anomalies while keeping the false alarms low. This means it should have a high detection rate i.e. having a value closer to 1.0 and a low false alarm rate i.e. having a value closer to 0. The detection and false alarm rates are plotted for each threshold and each plot shows the performance across different attacks. Figure 2 shows the metrics when using four different thresholds that are calculated using the 60th, 70th, 80th and 90th percentile values (going from bottom to top). Though we calculate results for all the ten thresholds as described in Sect. 3.4, we choose to display only these four thresholds due to space constraints. The results for the other thresholds are predictable based on the patterns observed in the displayed plots. The x-axis represents the attack frequency that tells what proportion of attack instances are perturbed, whereas the y-axis represents the amount of perturbation or the power wattage that is injected to the chosen attack instances. As the models are trained using attack-free instances, it can be observed in the plots that the detection rates are invalid for all models where the percentage of attack instances or amount of perturbation is zero (i.e. no attack).

In general, the false alarm rates are the best for the highest threshold and the detection rates are the best for the least threshold. For all the models, we start off by choosing a threshold using a single metric and change the selection based on the performance of the other metric. We repeat this and go through all the thresholds which eventually causes a dilemma of what threshold is the best. We demonstrate this process in detail for the MLP model and generalize it for the LSTM and CNN-LSTM models.

We begin by choosing a threshold for the MLP model based on the performance results shown in Fig. 2 . When selecting a threshold, it is preferred to have the least false alarm rate because it would be flustering to have false alarms raised too often. For this reason, we start by choosing the highest threshold of 2.14 calculated using the 90th percentile. Note that the false alarm rate is the least for a 99.999^{th} percentile threshold, but we are only considering the displayed four thresholds for easy reference to the readers. When looking at the results for the 90th percentile threshold, the model has low false alarm rates for majority of the attack configurations. But it is unable to maintain it as the attack frequency increases, thus failing in the right strip of the plot particularly when 80 to 100 percent of data is injected with any amount of wattage. If we are willing to accept the high false alarm rates for the higher proportions, the choice of threshold may seem fit. However, the detection rate for the same threshold

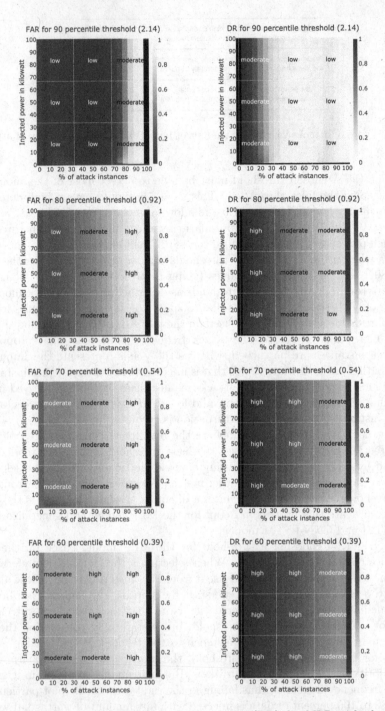

Fig. 2. False alarm rate (FAR) and detection rate (DR) for MLP with thresholds ranging from 60th to 90th percentile

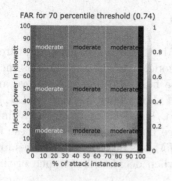
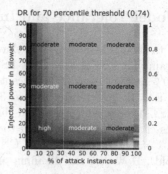

Fig. 3. False alarm rate and detection rate for LSTM for a selected threshold

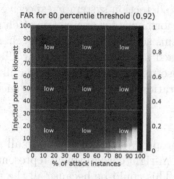
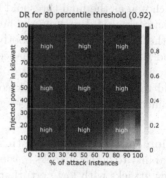

Fig. 4. False alarm rate and detection rate for CNN-LSTM for a selected threshold

of 90th percentile (top-right of Fig. 2) is poor even when 25% or more data is perturbed. Six out of nine attack configurations are almost never detected. In an attempt to improve the detection rate to the highest value possible, we will intuitively choose the least threshold of 60th percentile (bottom-right of Fig. 2), because it is able to detect majority of attacks across all attack zones compared to the others. However, when looking at the false alarm rates for the same threshold (bottom-left of Fig. 2), the proportion of false alarms are between moderate and high for all attack configurations starting from the least to the highest possible perturbation and attack frequency. To improve the false alarm rates, we can increase the threshold to the highest unexplored threshold which is at 80th percentile. There is an improvement in the false alarm rates throughout for this threshold compared to the 60th percentile. While this seems to have given us a better threshold, the detection rates again are observed to be between moderate and low for attack frequencies greater than 50%. The only available threshold is at 70th percentile, which provides an improvement for the detection rates. However, the false alarm rates have worsened in this case compared to the previous 80th percentile threshold. This leads to a dilemma as to which threshold must be chosen to balance both metrics. Even if a threshold is chosen, the compromise that occurs with either of the metrics leads to the conundrum again.

5   Model Tolerance and Impact

Similar to the MLP model, the behavior of both metrics to changing thresholds is the same for LSTM and CNN-LSTM models. As the threshold is increased from 60th percentile to 90th percentile, the false alarm rates improve and the detection rates deteriorate. Figures 3 and 4 shows both metrics for LSTM and CNN-LSTM models for a selected threshold. The decision to choose a threshold becomes challenging while trying to balance both the metrics for these models as well. Compared to all models, CNN-LSTM has high detection rates for most thresholds. However, the dilemma arises when deciding how much of the false alarm rates we are willing to compromise.

Through the above exercise, we observe that there exists a dilemma of what is to be chosen as the final threshold for the detection system irrespective of the neural network used. Pursuing the best performance for one metric often results in the other metric performing poorly. In this section, we discuss the characteristics and the prediction performance of each model to analyze their effects on the detection and false alarm rates. We also explore whether the inability of a threshold to detect certain attack configurations, can still lead to a successful and significant attack on the power grid.

Detection Model Characteristics. A property that is common to all models is the inability to detect attacks in the bottom-right corner, which represents high frequency attacks with low perturbations. This could be because all the models start adapting to the small injections in the consumption that is performed to majority of the instances. The more the model starts seeing these small changes, the more it accepts it to be normal. However, the detection system is able to correctly identify sudden increase or decrease in the power consumption.

When we look at model-specific characteristics, the MLP model has linearly varying detection rates and false alarm rates based on the proportion of perturbation. As observed in Fig. 2, if we choose 10% of instances to be perturbed, irrespective of the power injected, the MLP model has high detection rates throughout. On the other hand, the LSTM model follows an exponential shape for high detection rates as observed in Fig. 3. It is able to detect all of small proportions and small power injections. For example, a perturbation value of 6 kW is consistently detected for any proportion. The CNN-LSTM model starts to fail detection in the bottom right corner as seen in Fig. 4, and slowly propagates towards the left in an exponential shape. The detection rate at 100% perturbation proportion is different from the rest of the proportions for all thresholds in all models. This can be observed in Figs. 2, 3 and 4 that there is a different behavior for only the 100% perturbation with progressively changing detection rates going from low to high for different perturbations.

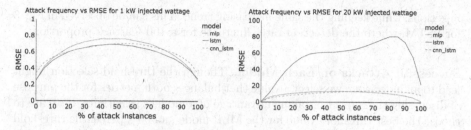

Fig. 5. Root mean squared error for different models when different proportions of attack instances are injected with 1 kW (left) and 20 kW (right)

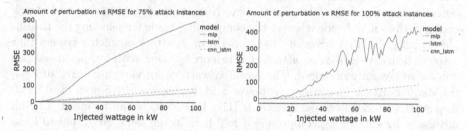

Fig. 6. Root mean squared error for different models when different values of power are injected for 75% (left) and 100% (right) of attack proportions

Model Prediction Performance. The root mean squared error for the trained MLP, LSTM and CNN-LSTM models on validation data are 0.099, 0.114 and 0.145 respectively. In terms of predicting the power consumption values, MLP performs the best having the least error, followed by LSTM which has similar performance as MLP and lastly, CNN-LSTM. Figure 5 shows how the root mean squared error (RMSE) changes for each model as the percentage of attack instances increases. We can see that when the attack instances are perturbed with 1 kW increase in power, the RMSE values follow an inverted parabolic curve. This suggests that the prediction errors are lower when the proportion of attack instances are either very low or very high. This can be observed in the results from the previous section where the detection rates start becoming poor when there is a large proportion of attack instances. As the injected wattage is increased, MLP and CNN-LSTM models maintain the same shape, but the LSTM model starts to deviate from it. This can be observed in the plot for the 20 kW case, where the errors for LSTM model increase quickly, thus being sensitive to higher perturbation values. When we keep the percentage of attack instances constant and plot the RMSE values for increasing amount of injected wattage, the LSTM model again has a different behavior compared to the MLP and CNN-LSTM models. As seen in Fig. 6, when the proportion of attack instances is 75%, the RMSE has increasing trend for all models. However, LSTM model increases very quickly for increasing wattage values. Whereas, for a 100% proportion case, the RMSE values for LSTM increase and decrease for different values of power injections, while keeping the same increasing trend. This can be observed in Fig. 3 for LSTM, where the detection rates fluctuate for a 100% attack proportion.

Successful Attacks on Each Model. Though the threshold selection might lead to an indecision, we select a value that balances both metrics for the purpose of discussing the impact of taking advantage of a model's sensitivity. If we are to choose the best threshold value for the MLP model, an 80th percentile threshold with a value of 0.92 is able to give correct results, at least until 70% proportion of perturbed data. For the LSTM and CNN-LSTM models, the 70th percentile and the 80th percentile thresholds respectively, have a good balance between the detection rates and the false alarm rates. Now, we look into undetected attack configurations and decide whether the compromise made for selecting the threshold is negligible. If an adversary has to perform an attack on such a system that involves neural networks, an attack that is more frequent with low perturbations will be successfully obscured. The required wattage for carrying out a successful MadIoT attack to disrupt the power grid as proposed by Soltan et al. is 30 megawatt with 300 bots per megawatt [17]. This wattage can be injected by an adversary by controlling compromised IoT bots in the same geographical location. The number of bots required for the attack is even lower with high wattage devices. If an adversary has access to 3,000 bots, the wattage per bot requirement would be 10kW for a successful attack. Similarly, with access to 6,000 and 100,000 bots, it would require 5 kW/bot and 0.3 kW/bot respectively.

When we look at the metrics for the chosen threshold of the MLP model which is 80th percentile in Fig. 2, the right vertical strip of the plot with proportions greater than 70% are not detected. Let us assume that the attacker has access to 3,000 bots each contributing 10 kW of additional wattage. Given that for a single household, the detection is low for the MLP model, irrespective of the power injection for an 80% perturbation, the attack will be successful with access to 10 kW devices in 3,000 households. With access to 20 kW or more per device and perturbing more than 30% of the consumption, the attacker can attain low detection rates with below 50% of the attack being detected in an LSTM model with the chosen threshold at 70th percentile. As observed in the LSTM plot for 70th percentile threshold in Fig. 3, the detection rates are the least with lower injected wattage per device and more than 50% of the data perturbed. With this configuration, the attacker requires access to 6,000 devices with each device contributing a lower wattage of 5 kW. If we go with the chosen 80th percentile for the CNN-LSTM model, the attacker can again perform a successful attack by choosing devices under 30 kW and injecting it in more than 70% of the data as seen in Fig. 4. The attack is possible with less than 3,000 devices contributing more than 10 kW each. If we choose a higher threshold of 70th percentile to combat this behavior, there is still a possibility for the adversary to use between 1 kW to 5 kW devices requiring 6,000 to 9,000 devices to carry out a successful attack.

In summary, the MLP model is easily vulnerable because of its exposure to a variety of small and large power injection attacks when 70% or more of instances are perturbed. LSTM model cannot detect higher power injection with moderate to high frequency attacks, and low power injection with high frequency attacks, with the latter being more feasible. Though an attacker can have a tough time staying undetected for majority of the attack configurations in a CNN-LSTM model, there is still a slight possibility for this to take place for lower power injections with high attack frequencies. Tightening or increasing the threshold for any of these models to improve the detection rates leads to the threshold dilemma as the false alarm rates will be significantly high. Therefore, going past this dilemma and choosing an appropriate threshold will still lead to successful attacks on the power grid as the attacker can work within the noise tolerance levels of a model to stay undetected.

6   Conclusion and Future Work

In this work, we train three state-of-the-art neural network models that are integrated into anomaly detection systems for power consumption data. We generate adversarial samples with increasing power wattage and attack frequency for the selected detection systems. We then demonstrate the threshold dilemma showing the inability to choose a single threshold that will be able to detect all power grid attacks. We discuss the model characteristics and the impact of the undetected attacks on the power grid. Using some of these insights, a possible future direction would be to investigate why neural network-based models fail when detecting attacks that have low power injection but high proportion of attack instances. As this is a common case observed in all models, it could be possible to offset that behavior by introducing a new parameter or model into the detection system to capture such instances. Though the metrics calculated for these cases have different behaviors visually, the errors for all models follow the same pattern except for LSTM. As LSTMs are commonly used for time series predictions, it would be interesting to look into why the model has increasing errors with high perturbation and proportion of attack instances.

References

1. Abadi, M., et al.: TensorFlow: large-scale machine learning on heterogeneous systems (2015). https://www.tensorflow.org/. (software available from tensorflow.org)
2. Chahla, C., Snoussi, H., Merghem, L., Esseghir, M.: A deep learning approach for anomaly detection and prediction in power consumption data. Energy Efficiency **13**(8), 1633–1651 (2020). https://doi.org/10.1007/s12053-020-09884-2
3. Chou, J.S., Telaga, A.S.: Real-time detection of anomalous power consumption. Renew. Sustain. Energy Rev. **33**, 400–411 (2014)
4. Dabrowski, A., Ullrich, J., Weippl, E.R.: Grid shock: coordinated load-changing attacks on power grids: the non-smart power grid is vulnerable to cyber attacks as well. In: 33rd Annual Computer Security Applications Conference, pp. 303–314 (2017)
5. Fawaz, H.I., Forestier, G., Weber, J., Idoumghar, L., Muller, P.A.: Adversarial attacks on deep neural networks for time series classification. In: 2019 International Joint Conference on Neural Networks, pp. 1–8. IEEE (2019)

6. Gnanasambandam, A., Sherman, A.M., Chan, S.H.: Optical adversarial attack. In: IEEE/CVF International Conference on Computer Vision, pp. 92–101 (2021)
7. Goodfellow, I.J., Shlens, J., Szegedy, C.: Explaining and harnessing adversarial examples. arXiv preprint arXiv:1412.6572 (2014)
8. Himeur, Y., Ghanem, K., Alsalemi, A., Bensaali, F., Amira, A.: Artificial intelligence based anomaly detection of energy consumption in buildings: a review, current trends and new perspectives. Appl. Energy **287**, 116601 (2021)
9. Hollingsworth, K., et al.: Energy anomaly detection with forecasting and deep learning. In: 2018 IEEE International Conference on Big Data, pp. 4921–4925. IEEE (2018)
10. Kim, T.Y., Cho, S.B.: Predicting the household power consumption using CNN-LSTM hybrid networks. In: Yin, H., Camacho, D., Novais, P., Tallón-Ballesteros, A.J. (eds.) IDEAL 2018. LNCS, vol. 11314, pp. 481–490. Springer, Cham (2018). https://doi.org/10.1007/978-3-030-03493-1_50
11. Kingma, D.P., Ba, J.: Adam: a method for stochastic optimization. arXiv preprint arXiv:1412.6980 (2014),
12. Kurakin, A., Goodfellow, I.J., Bengio, S.: Adversarial examples in the physical world. In: Artificial Intelligence Safety and Security, pp. 99–112. Chapman and Hall/CRC (2018)
13. Li, J., Yang, Y., Sun, J.S.: Exploiting vulnerabilities of deep learning-based energy theft detection in AMI through adversarial attacks. arXiv preprint arXiv:2010.09212 (2020)
14. Mode, G.R., Hoque, K.A.: Adversarial examples in deep learning for multivariate time series regression. In: 2020 IEEE Applied Imagery Pattern Recognition Workshop, pp. 1–10. IEEE (2020)
15. Raman, G., Peng, J.C.H., Rahwan, T.: Manipulating residents' behavior to attack the urban power distribution system. IEEE Trans. Indust. Inform. **15**(10), 5575–5587 (2019)
16. Ren, K., Zheng, T., Qin, Z., Liu, X.: Adversarial attacks and defenses in deep learning. Engineering **6**(3), 346–360 (2020)
17. Soltan, S., Mittal, P., Poor, H.V.: BlackIoT: IoT botnet of high wattage devices can disrupt the power grid. In: 27th USENIX Security Symposium, pp. 15–32 (2018)
18. Tsukada, M., Kondo, M., Matsutani, H.: A neural network-based on-device learning anomaly detector for edge devices. IEEE Trans. Comput. **69**(7), 1027–1044 (2020)
19. Wang, X., Zhao, T., Liu, H., He, R.: Power consumption predicting and anomaly detection based on long short-term memory neural network. In: 2019 IEEE 4th International Conference on Cloud Computing and Big Data Analysis, pp. 487–491. IEEE (2019)
20. Weng, Y., Zhang, N., Xia, C.: Multi-agent-based unsupervised detection of energy consumption anomalies on smart campus. IEEE Access **7**, 2169–2178 (2018)
21. Zizzo, G., Hankin, C., Maffeis, S., Jones, K.: Adversarial attacks on time-series intrusion detection for industrial control systems. In: 2020 IEEE 19th International Conference on Trust, Security and Privacy in Computing and Communications, pp. 899–910. IEEE (2020)

WiP: Control Plane Saturation Attack Mitigation in Software Defined Networks

Neminath Hubballi[✉] and Kanishk Patel

Department of Computer Science and Engineering,
Indian Institute of Technology Indore, Indore, India
{neminath,cse180001025}@iiti.ac.in

Abstract. Recent works have shown that the interaction between control and data plane in the Software Defined Networks can be chocked by an adversary with saturation attack. This attack is generated by sending large number of new flows to a switch exploiting the switch-controller communication. A switch sends a packet-in message to the controller if a new flow is seen. A flux of new flows results in a large number of packet-in messages at the controller. In this paper, we present `SaturationGuard` which mitigates this attack by adopting an early attack detection method. An anomaly detection method deployed at the controller observes the patterns of packet-in messages and identifies the attack. In particular, we capture normal interaction between switch and controller using the arrival rate of packet-in messages with a probability distribution. To mitigate the attack, we propose to throttle the bandwidth of the affected switch port in proportion to the arrival rate of new flows. We implement a proof of concept solution with Mininet and an external controller and show that `SaturationGuard` is effective in handling the saturation attacks with early stage detection.

Keywords: Saturation attack · Anomaly detection · Mitigation ·
Bandwidth throttling · Software defined networking

1 Introduction

Software Defined Networking (SDN) simplifies the task of network management by separating the control and data planes in the network. It concentrates the control plane operation into a software entity which has a global visibility of the network. This central entity called the controller makes decisions of what action should be taken on packet(s) at the data plane. The action to be taken is indicated by installing a set flow rules in the relevant switches. Centralized decision making brings several advantages including programmibility, resource optimization and also innovative application development. OpenFlow [1] is the standard interface between the control plane and data plane. SDN has also been used to design new security solutions for the traditional security issues. However, it also brings several new security issues [12] including new DoS attacks.

© The Author(s), under exclusive license to Springer Nature Switzerland AG 2022
V. R. Badarla et al. (Eds.): ICISS 2022, LNCS 13784, pp. 235–246, 2022.
https://doi.org/10.1007/978-3-031-23690-7_14

Denial of Service and Distributed Denial of Service attacks have been studied very extensively. Peng et al. [10] argue that several design decisions of TCP/IP network protocols have led to such attacks. More recently these attacks have taken the form of targeting the application layer protocols [15] and also software defined networks [14]. There are methods to detect and possibly mitigate the effects of traditional DoS and DDoS attacks. However the DoS attack on SDN is unique and the conventional methods to handle the DoS attacks will not be effective. In the traditional DoS attack a specific server, application is targeted. However a single attack can be launched against control plane in SDN affecting the entire network.

Saturation Attack: This attack is a consequence of scalability issues of Open-Flow. Typically a SDN switch has a set of flow rules installed by the controller and if a new flow is seen for which there is no flow rule, the switch sends a packet-in message to the controller asking for a new flow rule to handle this packet. To mount the attack, an adversary generate a flux of new flows potentially with spoofed addresses which hogs the bandwidth between the switch and controller. This can also overwhelm the controller and switches also become saturated as they have limited buffering ability. A flow is defined with five attributes namely source and destination IP addresses, source and destination port numbers and layer four protocol. By changing one or more attributes in these fields an adversary can generate a flux of flows and generate the attack. As there are many attributes available for manipulation, the attack can be very easily generated with a program which can craft custom packets and send it.

In this paper we describe a method to detect and subsequently mitigate the control plane DoS attacks. Our proposed model has two sub-modules. The first one detects the attacks against control plane using anomaly detection technique and second one takes remedial action to mitigate the attack. In particular we make the following contributions in this paper.

(i) We describe an anomaly detection system to detect attacks against controller by modeling the packet-in messages as a probability distribution.

(ii) We propose a method to mitigate the attack or minimize the effect of attack by throttling the bandwidth of the affected port proportinal to the intensity of the attack.

(iii) Perform simulation experiments with Mininet to validate the proposed method.

2   Literature Review

In this section, we present the related works on saturation attack detection and mitigation. The existing works majorly fall into following three categories.

(i) Proxy-Based Mitigation: These works propose to add state information to the switches and convert them to proxies. AVANT-GUARD [14] described a data-plane solution to handle saturation attacks resulting from TCP SYN flood attacks. It proposes to use Connection Migration where the SDN switch acts as a proxy and handles the TCP 3-way handshake without maintaining state information. Only the flows completing 3-way handshake will be notified to the controller. It proposes to delay the notification till a valid data packet arrives on that TCP connection. Unfortunately this introduces another vulnerability called buffer saturation and also has significant limitations as shown by Ambrosin et al. [6]. Alternatively the authors of [6] suggest to proxy the TCP connection probabilistically on per IP basis which they adopted in their design of LineSwitch to show that it required much less resources.

(ii) Anomaly Based Detection: These methods monitor the state of controller and take necessary action which are either in the form of blocking the source of attack or diverting the packets arriving to other switches or buffer them in the switch. Li et al. [9] propose an anomaly based detection system using the arrival patterns of incoming packet-in messages. They argue that the control plane traffic is self-similar and if an anomaly is detected the model installs a flow rule to redirect the packet-in messages to a cache. OFF-Guard [16] uses a threshold to detect saturation attack by counting the number of packet-in messages. FloodGuard [17] proposes to install proactive-rules to mitigate the attack by observing the controller status. FlowRanger [18] detects anomalies in the incoming packet-in messages and uses job scheduling technique to penalize attack sources. FloodDefender [13] installs a flow rule at the affected switch to detour attack flows to the victim's neighbor switches. Some works also use machine learning [8] algorithms for detecting anomalies originating from a saturation attack.

(iii) Source Validation: These methods rely on the fact that spoofed source IP addresses are used for launching the saturation attack. Hence, they initiate the validation of source addresses. Zhang et al [19] use this method and deploy verification on switches connecting to end hosts. FSDM [7] also invokes a verification method to validate the source IP address when the attack is detected.

From the above discussion, it is clear that proxy based methods require switch to be intelligent and track TCP state information. This requires additional resources at the switch. In addition successive packets may not flow in the same path, they may not be available at the same switch which makes these proxy schemes ineffective. Further source verification also requires maintaining similar state at the switch which can become bottleneck. Both proxy schemes and source verification techniques requires modification to switch functionality and add complexity. Taking motivation from this, we propose an anomaly based attack detection and mitigation technique in this paper.

3   Proposed Approach

In this section we describe our proposed method `SaturationGuard` for mitigating the control plane saturation attack. Precursor to the mitigation is the detection of attack. We propose a method to detect the attack and subsequently describe a way to handle the attack. We consider a reference architecture shown in Fig. 1

to present our detection and mitigation methods. This has three SDN switches (can be any number), a controller, an attacker and a web server. Dotted lines in the graph indicate a logical connection between the switch and the controller and other lines indicate a direct connection. As mentioned earlier, every time a new flow (new combination of packet attributes) is detected the switch sends a packet-in message to the controller. In `SaturationGuard`, the attack detection module runs on the controller and for mitigation it communicates an action to be taken to one or more switches. In the following two sub-sections the detection and mitigation techniques are elaborated.

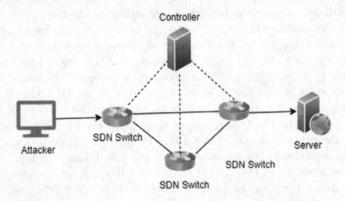

Fig. 1. Control plane saturation attack mitigation setup

3.1 Saturation Attack Detection

In order to detect the attack, we model the communication between the switch and controller as seen in a normal condition. There are two ways to model this communication, first is where individual switches communication with controller is modelled and the second is modelling the aggregated communication of all switches. First one can not scale to large networks. Later one has the advantage of being simpler and one model suffices for the entire network. It serves our purpose as it does not matter whether the packet-in messages are coming from a single switch or many switches. In `SaturationGuard`, we represent the arrival of packet-in messages as a probability distribution. The idea is to capture the probability or the likelihood of packet-in message ranges and identify the deviations. In particular, we model it as a Poisson probability distribution [11]. The choice of using this distribution is motivated by the fact that this distribution captures the average number of such messages in an interval and represent the normal behavior. We want to identify the abnormal behavior or deviations particularly large number of packet-in messages using this distribution.

Poisson probability distribution is a discrete probability distribution which uses mean number of events λ obtained from $\mathcal{N}$ observation intervals. In our case this is the number of packet-in messages as observed by the controller. The probability distribution function of Poisson distribution is given by Eq. 1.

$$P(X = n) = \frac{e^\lambda \times \lambda^n}{n!} \tag{1}$$

In this equation, X is a discrete random variable, n is a non negative integer value. $P(X = n)$ represent the probability of random variable X taking the value n. An important feature of this discrete distribution is that, the maximum probability value is around the mean λ. The probability value of random variable decrease on either side of mean. Figure 2 is a sample distribution generated with a λ value of 4.5. By taking the mean number of packet-in messages as seen in the controller, we generate a distribution and to detect the attack, we identify an event which has a low probability value with increased number of packet-in messages. The value of n at this probability will become the threshold for detecting the attack. If the number of packet-in messages are larger than this threshold number, saturation attack is detected. In order to set this threshold value, we use chebyshev's one sided inequality which is given by Eq. 2.

$$P(X \geq \lambda + C) \leq \frac{\sigma^2}{\sigma^2 + C^2} \tag{2}$$

In Eq. 2, σ is the standard deviation and C is a positive constant. We set this value of $\lambda + C$ as a multiple of λ i.e. $\gamma \times \lambda$ such that a major portion of the probability distribution is covered under normal case and rare events falling in the tail of distribution are detected as saturation attack.

Fig. 2. Poisson probability distribution

3.2 Attack Mitigation

Once the attack is detected (by the method in the previous stage) the next step is to minimize the effect of the attack. There are many options one can think of. If the attack is generated using a single source (one source IP address) by modifying the other attributes like destination IP address, layer 4 port numbers, etc. mitigation is very easy which is to just block that source. However if the attack is generated with spoofed address (which is likely the case), then blocking is not the solution. We propose to handle this by looking at the port number of switch from which the packet-in messages have originated and reduce the bandwidth of the particular port on that switch proportionately using traffic policing techniques. This we estimate by calculating a probability value which indicates by what factor the bandwidth needs to be reduced. The probability value is calculated as in Eq. 3.

$$prob = 1 - e^{\frac{threshold-observed}{threshold}} \qquad (3)$$

In this equation threshold is the value used to detect the saturation attack as calculated in the previous phase. SaturationGuard requires the bandwidth reduction to be proportional to the probability value calculated in Eq. 3. The choice of Eq. 3 is motivated by a similar use-case in handling network congestion with Random Early Detection [5] where the packets arriving at a router are dropped based on the queue length which indicate what fraction of the input queue is full. As the probability value ranges between 0.0 to 1.0 and there are infinitely many values in between. For easier handling, we divide the range for probability values into $\mathcal{K}$ blocks as shown in Fig. 3. Depending on which block the probability value $prob$ falls, the bandwidth of the port from which these packets are originating is throttled. This is done by defining different transmission rate corresponding to every block and setting the switch to operate at that rate. In the diagram low probability values indicate less aggressive transmission and probability value close to 1 indicate aggressive transmission. Thus if the value is above 0.8 which falls in the last block $T5$, transmission on that port is completely blocked for a fixed duration.

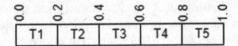

Fig. 3. Probability ranges

4   Experiments and Evaluation

In this section we describe the experimental setup and evaluations done with our proposed method SaturationGuard.

Experimental Setup: We used two systems running Ubuntu 20.0 having 8 GB RAM with Intel i5 processor. In one of the machine we setup Mininet [2] emulator and in the other machine we setup pox controller. The controller was able to install flow rules in the Mininet switch. We designed a network topology with ten systems and emulated it in Mininet. The topology is shown in Fig. 4. It has a SDN switch and all the hosts connect to this host in a star topology. In the diagram clients are denoted as C_i's and Servers are marked as S_i's. Out of five servers in two we ran web servers, other two were accessed with iperf tool and the remaining one is pinged by clients. In this setup all the servers also act as clients connecting to other servers. In our experiments, we limit the bandwidth between the switch and controller to 2 Mbps using Netem tool [3] installed on the controller.

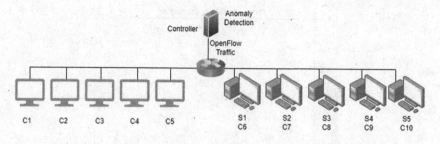

Fig. 4. Experimental setup

Algorithm 1. Generating Normal Traffic

Input: η - Total Number of Servers
Input: t_1 and t_2: Minimum and Maximum Time Delay

1: **while** not interrupted **do**
2:    $K_1 \leftarrow$ RandomNumber($1,\eta$)
3:    ConnectToServer(K_1)
4:    AccessService(K_1)
5:    $K_2 \leftarrow$ RandomNumber(t_1,t_2)
6:    Sleep(K_2)

Simulating the Normal Traffic: In order to mimic the normal operation in the network, we generated traffic by setting up interaction between different clients and servers. Algorithm 1 shows the connection and service accesses established. Every client randomly chose a server to connect to and establishes a connection request for some service and subsequently sleep for a random amount of time. These interactions between the systems generate some number of flows. The controller installs rules in the switch for those flows. We used a timer of 10 s for rule expiry after which the rule will be flushed from the switch. We collected the packet-in messages and calculated the average number of such messages in a window period of 5 s. Using this mean number (λ), we generated the probability distribution as shown in Fig. 5. As the mean number of packet-in messages were around 30, the distribution graph has the highest probability at this value.

Generating the Saturation Attack: Saturation attack requires generating packets which belong to different flows such that each one of them results in a packet-in message to the controller. This can be generated by changing the source and destination addresses, source and destination port numbers. We used a tool named hping3 [4] to generate the attack. This tool has the ability to send different packet types and using different protocol types. It can also send the packets by randomizing the source and destination addresses.

SaturationGraurd Implementation: We implemented the two parts (detection and mitigation) with python scripts running on the controller. The detection part will read the packet-in messages and periodically compare the intensity

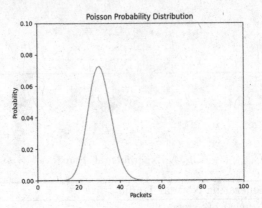

Fig. 5. Probability distribution of packet-in messages

with baseline observation and mitigation part will send appropriate flow rules to switch(es) through controller.

Impact of Attack on Controller CPU Utilization: We generated the attack by sending packets with random addresses (source and destination) from client C1 (Fig. 4) with different intensity by scheduling the time delay between successive packets in hping3. These packets generated packet-in messages to the controller. We measured the CPU utilization on the controller when the attack was on. Figure 6a shows the variation of CPU utilization with attack intensity. The X axis in the graph shows the number of packets per second and Y axis is the percentage of CPU utilization. We can notice that, as the attack intensity increases the CPU utilization also increases almost linearly and saturates at about 500 packets per second rate nearly with 100% utilization. This observation is consistent with other works [17].

Impact of the Attack on RTT: In order to assess the impact of the attack on the communication of other hosts connected to the switch, we measured Round Trip Time (RTT) variation with attacks of different intensity. In particular two client machines (C2 and C3) and one client (C4) and server machine (S1) connected to the switch. This we measure with and without SaturationGuard. For the attack detection we use a probability threshold which is 20 times the mean (λ). Figure 6b shows this variation of RTT values. We can notice that till the saturation point is reached the RTT values are very low and more or less constant and when the saturation occurs (which is about 500 PPS) the RTT values increase significantly in the absence of SaturationGuard. The low RTT values even when the attack is on is due to the fact that, a small amount of bandwidth available at the switch is good enough to establish a communication. When the saturation attack is peaked, the switch is no longer able to handle the new flows that's when the RTT increases significantly. However, when the proposed mitigation method is used, the RTT values are still maintained around the same range as in the previous case. This is becuase SaturationGuard throttled the bandwidth (using traffic policing techniques) of the corresponding input port early on which enabled the flows corresponding to RTT measurement handled successfully.

Availability of Bandwidth: SaturationGuard throttles the bandwidth of the affected switch based on the intensity of the attack. In order to assess the impact of this when the saturation attack is on, we conducted a study by measuring the available bandwidth between the switch and the controller. We measure this bandwidth by successively generating the attack with different intensities as in the previous case. Figure 6c shows the variation of available bandwidth between switch and controller. We can notice that for lower intensity attacks the available bandwidth difference is small, however as the attack intensity increases, SaturationGuard preserves the available bandwidth between switch and the controller and the difference is significant. This is due to the fact that SaturationGuard throttles the bandwidth proportionate to the attack intensity. For higher intensity attacks, the rate of throttling is also higher which preserves bandwidth between the switch and the controller.

Impact of Detection Threshold on Attack Detection Time: It is worth noting that probability threshold used for detecting the attack determines when the attack is detected. If the threshold is too small, then the attack is detected quickly and bandwidth is throttled quickly. On the other hand if the threshold is high then the attack is detected very late and by that time the attack might have caused significant damage. We study the sensitivity of threshold on the latency in the attack detection. For this we fixed the attack PPS at 500 and measured the delay in the detection of attack i.e. first throttling of bandwidth by varying the threshold used for detecting the attack between 10 times of λ to 80 times of the λ. Figure 6d shows the variation of delay in detecting the attack. We can notice that as the probability threshold increases the delay also proportionately increases.

Impact of Blocking the Switch Port: When the attack intensity is very high then the probability of throttling will be close to 1. This in our case is mapped to blocking the port(s) of impacted switch(es). Once a port is blocked, it is blocked for a duration of 30 s. Subsequently even if the source is continuing with the attack those packets will not impact the controller. Infinitely blocking a port is not a feasible solution either. In order to validate how a continuous high intensity attack is handled by SaturationGuard, we performed an experiment by flooding the switch with randomly generated flows. As the rate is quite high, it triggered blocking of the port. Figure 6e shows (few initial seconds) the on-off periods during which there were some packet-in messages generated or not to the controller. We can see that when the attack is detected for the next 30 s there is no communication (indicated with blank) generated and once the port is unblocked the communication is restored for a very short duration of 2 s. This is the time lag for detecting the attack at the threshold which is 20 times the mean as seen in Fig. 6d.

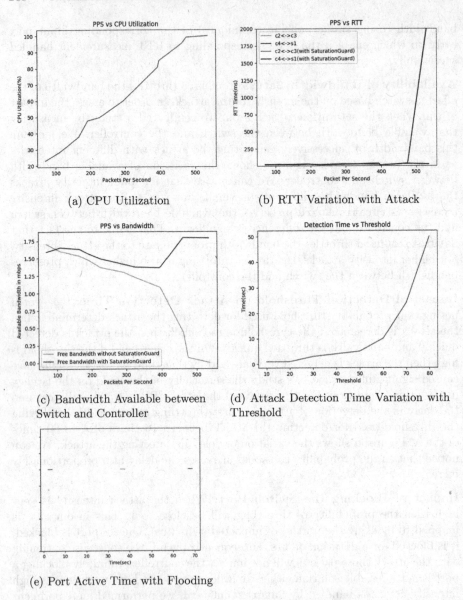

(a) CPU Utilization

(b) RTT Variation with Attack

(c) Bandwidth Available between Switch and Controller

(d) Attack Detection Time Variation with Threshold

(e) Port Active Time with Flooding

Fig. 6. Behavioral changes with saturation attack

Collateral Damage of SaturationGaurd: The proposed detection and mitigation solution SaturationGaurd can be easily used with switches deployed at the edge of the network where the hosts directly connect to the switch. In this deployment scenario there is no collateral damage of blocking the port of the switch. However, when the packet-in messages are observed from a switch located in the backbone of the network then blocking a port can cause collateral damage impacting other communications passing through that port. We argue that, this is a rare case and happens when the intensity is very high. Otherwise bandwidth throttling in the worst will reduce the available bandwidth to other communications as well. In addition, if the solution is used with every switch it is the edge switch which is likely to report all the packet-in messages rather than a switch in the backbone. In order for a switch in the backbone to generate these many packet-in messages, an adversary has to intelligently craft an attack such that switches at the edge do not generate packet-in messages, which we believe is not easy to achieve.

5 Conclusion

Saturation attack chokes the communication between a SDN controller and switch by sending large number of new flows. This can cause Denial of Service to other legitimate traffic and services as these connections are affected. In this paper, we described the working of SaturationGuard which can mitigate the effect of such attacks by throttling the rate of transmission at the affected switches. An anomaly detection system running at the controller observes the rate of arrival of packet-in messages and detects the attack. By identifying the infected ports of switch, it throttles the bandwidth available at the switch in proportion to the attack intensity. We implemented and evaluated a working prototype of SaturationGuard with Mininet and an external controller.

References

1. https://www.section.io/engineering-education/openflow-sdn/. Accessed 22 July 2022
2. http://mininet.org/. Accessed 29 July 2022
3. https://www.linux.org/docs/man8/tc-netem.html. Accessed 29 July 2022
4. https://www.kali.org/tools/hping3/. Accessed 28 July 2022
5. David, D., et al.: Recommendations on Queue Management and Congestion Avoidance in the Internet. RFC 2309, RFC Editor (1998). https://datatracker.ietf.org/doc/html/rfc2309
6. Ambrosin, M., Conti, M., De Gaspari, F., Poovendran, R.: Lineswitch: tackling control plane saturation attacks in software-defined networking. IEEE/ACM Trans. Network. 25(2), 1206–1219 (2017)
7. Huang, X., Xue, K., Xing, Y., Hu, D., Li, R., Sun, Q.: FSDM: fast recovery saturation attack detection and mitigation framework in SDN. In: MASS 2020: IEEE 17th International Conference on Mobile Ad Hoc and Sensor Systems, pp. 329–337 (2020)
8. Khamaiseh, S., Serra, E., Li, Z., Xu, D.: Detecting saturation attacks in SDN via machine learning. In: ICCCS 2019: 4th International Conference on Computing, Communications and Security, pp. 1–8 (2019)
9. Li, Z., Xing, W., Khamaiseh, S., Xu, D.: Detecting saturation attacks based on self-similarity of openflow traffic. IEEE Trans. Network Serv. Manage. 17(1), 607–621 (2020)

10. Peng, T., Leckie, C., Ramamohanarao, K.: Survey of network-based defense mechanisms countering the dos and ddos problems. ACM Comput. Surv. **39**(1), 1–42 (2007)
11. Ross, S.M.: A First Course in Probability. 5th edn. (1998)
12. Scott-Hayward, S., O'Callaghan, G., Sezer, S.: SDN security: a survey. In: SDN4FNS 2013: IEEE SDN for Future Networks and Services, pp. 1–7 (2013)
13. Shang, G., Zhe, P., Bin, X., Aiqun, H., Kui, R.: Flooddefender: protecting data and control plane resources under SDN-aimed dos attacks. In: INFOCOM 2017: IEEE Conference on Computer Communications, pp. 1–9 (2017)
14. Shin, S., Yegneswaran, V., Porras, P., Gu, G.: Avant-guard: scalable and vigilant switch flow management in software-defined networks. In: CCS 2013: Proceedings of the 2013 ACM SIGSAC Conference on Computer & Communications Security, pp. 413–424 (2013)
15. Tripathi, N., Hubballi, N.: Application layer denial-of-service attacks and defense mechanisms: a survey. ACM Comput. Surv. **54**(4) (2021)
16. Wang, H., Xu, L., Gu, G.: Of-guard: a dos attack prevention extension in software-defined networks. In: USENIX 2014, pp. 1–2 (2014)
17. Wang, H., Xu, L., Gu, G.: Floodguard: a dos attack prevention extension in software-defined networks. In: DSN 2015: 45th Annual IEEE/IFIP International Conference on Dependable Systems and Networks, pp. 239–250 (2015)
18. Wei, L., Fung, C.: Flowranger: a request prioritizing algorithm for controller dos attacks in software defined networks. In: ICC 2015: IEEE International Conference on Communications, pp. 5254–5259 (2015)
19. Zhang, M., Bi, J., Bai, J., Li, G.: FloodShield: Securing the SDN infrastructure against denial-of-service attacks. In: TrustCom 2018: 17th IEEE International Conference On Trust, Security And Privacy In Computing And Communications, pp. 687–698 (2018)

WiP: EventTracker-Event Driven Evidence Collection for Digital Forensics

Aniket Sangwan, Sarthak Jain, and Neminath Hubballi[✉]

Department of Computer Science and Engineering,
Indian Institute of Technology Indore, Indore, India
{cse180001005,cse180001047,neminath}@iiti.ac.in

Abstract. Digital forensics involves credible evidence collection from digital assets and analysis to conclusively attribute events to users and sources. Traditional forensic methods only focus on preserving the evidence and audit trail generated. Further they have the standard practices for evidence collection by invoking these methods manually. In this paper, we present EventTracker which has the features of traditional methods to monitor and track file system and user activity, and can also dynamically invoke evidence collection based on events of interest. EventTracker allows the user to specify the kind of evidence required for an event type giving more flexibility to the user. It also allows users to define custom event types and monitor the system and evidence be logged safely. We implement a proof of concept code of EventTracker integrating several open source facilities and also furnish details of experiments with a handful of custom event types. We also perform a measurement study with file monitoring and quantify the frequency and number of changes typical system operations do to the underlying file system and conclude that the number of changes is often high which warrants automated techniques for investigation.

Keywords: Digital forensics · Event tracking · Evidence collection · Activity monitoring

1 Introduction

Digital forensics is a branch of science that uses evidence collected from digital assets like computers, networks, server logs and CCTV cameras to assist in crime investigation. Many of these devices and network elements keep information that is useful to this end. Existing literature in digital forensics mainly concentrate on identifying the sources of information and how to preserve, analyze and present it. Several tools like FTK [1] and EnCase [2] rely on methods designed to process structured information rather than unstructured information. Often evidence collected through one source is incomplete and noisy, making it difficult to establish an act of crime using such conventional tools. Typically forensic investigators do manual screening of the data which is a tedious task.

© The Author(s), under exclusive license to Springer Nature Switzerland AG 2022
V. R. Badarla et al. (Eds.): ICISS 2022, LNCS 13784, pp. 247–259, 2022.
https://doi.org/10.1007/978-3-031-23690-7_15

Recently some efforts have been made to automate this action using correlation techniques. However these methods do not completely leverage the rich source of information that systems, applications and other digital assets offer.

There are two important issues that require a careful balancing act in a digital forensic evidence source. If the logs or information about the events is kept to a minimal, then we may not have enough information to correlate and establish an event and, on the other hand, if a very detailed event trail is maintained, we may have everything that has happened and is required for analysis. However, logging everything can become overwhelming and requires a large amount of storage, processing (even if it is automated) and time for the analysis. In this paper, we consider the problem of collecting evidence based on the type and severity of a suspected activity. The idea is to collect the evidence dynamically as soon as something suspicious is detected. This involves collecting the necessary information by identifying the type of event. In particular we make the following contributions in this paper.

(i) We propose `EventTracker` which is a tool designed to gather evidence from monitored computer systems.

(ii) `EventTracker` identifies/recognizes a set of predefined cyber security events and decides the kind of evidence required to be captured based on the event. We do a proof of concept evaluation with few sample event types.

(iii) Change detection is an essential operation of `EventTracker`. We perform a measurement study using automated software update operations to quantify the extent of changes these operations bring to the system.

2   Literature Review

In this section we review the existing literature in the area of event detection and evidence collection. Broadly there are three categories of work.

(i) Traditional Forensic Tools: There are several tools [1,2] developed for collecting evidence from computing devices. Such evidence is typically collected from memory, disk, network, etc. Collected evidence is in the form of memory image which has the in-memory contents, running processes, registry files and temporary files on the system. These tools are used after occurence of some cyber event and evidence is collected from suspected devices by manually invoking such tools.

(ii) Host based Intrusion Detection Systems: These are responsible for detecting attacks or intrusions against a monitored system. There are both open source and commercial HIDS tools available. OSSEC [3], Tripwire [4] and Auditbeat [5] are some of the popular open source tools. All of these provide the ability to monitor and detect changes to files of interest, identify suspicious logins and other important events in digital forensic investigation. Over the years these tools have matured and now have very easy to use graphical interfaces and dashboards. Some of these tools also allow remote monitoring using client-server architecture providing the ability for a system administrator to view activities of a large number of systems in the network. However these tools only log the basic evidence for an event and do not have facility for collecting any additional evidence based on the event type. We have listed out a detailed comparison of these tools with our proposed tool in the Table 5. The reviewed tools are either expensive or lack different functionalities, which serves as the motivation for the development of EventTracker.

(iii) Log Analysis and Correlation: Logs are an important source of information for postmortem analysis. Several infosec tools (e.g. HIDS, NIDS, DNS, DHCP, firewall, etc.) generate such logs. However logs generated by individual sources may not reveal the complete picture. Thus a body of work describe collection, analysis and correlation of logs from different sources [18]. Different methods of correlation like complementary evidence based correlation [14,19,22], attack graphs [15,21], casual relationship [20], machine learning [12,13] and multi-step correlation techniques [16,17] are used for this purpose.

3 Proposed Approach

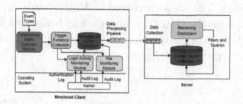

Fig. 1. EventTracker evidence collection setup

In this section, we describe the working of EventTracker for evidence collection from monitored systems. It works by having a database of events listed along with the evidence needed to be collected from the client/monitored machine as shown in Table 1. For every event, there is one or more sources/types of evidence collected from the target machine. The overall architecture of EventTracker is shown in Fig. 1. It has two components - one running at the client and the other running at the server. In the following two subsections we elaborate the working of both components.

Table 1. Events and corresponding evidence collected

Event	File operation	Login	Memory	Disk	Process	Network settings
E_1		✓		✓		
E_2	✓		✓		✓	
E_3		✓	✓	✓		✓

I. Components of Monitored Client: These are responsible for collecting evidence from the client by observing activities happening in the system. The evidence is collected by monitoring activities related to files, user logins, detecting attacks, and also by identifying suspicious events. The choice of monitoring these is due to the fact that occurrence of cyber attacks and other events results into changes to these. Thus monitoring these components will help in attributing certain events to users, sources, etc. The client side implementation mainly has three components out of which two are doing the basic level monitoring just like any other forensic tool namely file operations and user logins and third one has the list of user defined events. These three components are elaborated below.

(i) **File Monitoring**: Unauthorized users can access, modify or delete the files on a system. The file monitoring module in our evidence collection setup is tasked to monitor changes to the important files and directories. This module uses kernel audit feature offered by the Operating System. It serves the purpose of tracking all the modifications so that unwanted changes can be detected. It detects filesystem events namely creation, deletion, modification and move operation for important files and directories and maintains an integrity check for each of the monitored file. This is done by maintaining the hash values of these files. Once any filesystem event is detected, the evidence around the event is collected and stored. The steps involved in this module are shown in Fig. 2a. There are three steps involved in this module which are as follows:

a) A list of files and directories to be monitored is provided to the file monitoring module which sets up event triggers on them.

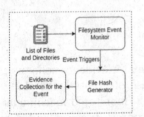

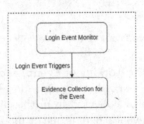

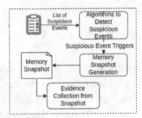

(a) File Monitoring Module

(b) Login Monitoring Module

(c) Suspicious Event Detection Module

Fig. 2. Modules in EventTracker

b) Once a trigger is generated for a filesystem event, file hash is generated for the file that triggered the event to maintain an integrity check.

c) Evidence for the filesystem event is collected and stored in the local database along with the calculated hash value.

(ii) **Login Activity Monitoring**: Unauthorized users after gaining access to the systems can do many things including installing new software, making changes to the files, directories, etc. Thus, in order to keep track of logged in users, their location, login time, along with other necessary information, EventTracker keeps track of all these activities and collects necessary evidence.

The login activity monitoring module detects both successful logins and failed login attempts and stores evidence around those attempts. This enables us to identify the source of events/attacks and also, identify the users who made unwanted changes in the monitored files and directories. The steps involved in the evidence collection related to this module are shown in Fig. 2b and it has two steps as follows:

a) Setup triggers for login attempts made to the system.

b) Once a trigger is generated for a login attempt, evidence around the login attempt is collected and stored in the local database.

(iii) Suspicious Event Detection: This component is in-charge of detecting cyber attacks and events of interest. The idea here is to store evidence when something suspicious is noticed in the system. Attacks and events can be detected by developing a software similar to an intrusion detection system. This can be done by monitoring network traffic or identifying changes to the files located at specific places or in general any activity which the user considers as unusual. The set of activities which are considered as suspicious is defined in a file or a database as shown in Table 1. These events might indicate a cyber-attack or presence of an adversary on the monitored host system. Once a suspicious event is detected, it triggers specific evidence collection for the event. For e.g. a login from unusual location may not trigger disk image generation but the authentication logs and file activities might be tracked. On the other hand, if a malware is detected on the system we may require all types of evidence collection including memory snapshot, disk image, network settings, etc. The collected evidence can be temporarily stored in a local database (till it is exported to the server). The steps involved in this module are shown in Fig. 2c and are as follows:

a) Setup event detection module to look for suspicious activities. This can be a custom detection method and can also consult the logs generated by the file monitoring and login monitoring modules.

b) Once an event is detected, the information related to the event is stored in the local database.

c) Memory, disk and other forensic evidence is collected for the event and stored separately in the local database with a timestamp attached to it.

(iv) Exporting Evidence: The ultimate goal is to export the evidence collected from a monitored host to a remote server. Thus a data processing module exports this evidence to the server using client-server communication setup. This module takes details from the local database instance which is maintained on every client being monitored. The local database can serve as temporary safe storage of evidence in case of communication issues with the server. It is worth noting that different evidence types collected require different kind of storage and this module maintains separate collection in the database to facilitate this storage. The newly generated evidence is pushed to the server storage after every write operation performed on the database and can be subsequently removed from the local storage.

II. Components on the Evidence Collector: The server or evidence collector/logger has three important components namely data receiver, database logger and a dashboard as detailed below.

(i) `Data Collection Module`: This is a companion of data dispatcher available at the other end (monitored client). It establishes a network connection with the dispatcher and receives the evidence exported by the client and stores it in the database.

(ii) `Central Database`: The server database collects and stores data coming from all the clients being monitored by maintaining separate indices for each category of logs.

(iii) `Dashboard`: The server has a front end dashboard which retrieves the logged events from the database and presents them on an interactive panel. Users can choose to view logs or evidence collected from a particular system, type of logs, etc. It allows the user to apply different filters and queries on the stored logs to facilitate investigation of specific scenarios.

4   Implementation and Evaluation

In this section, we elaborate the system setup along with the software utilities, technologies and frameworks used in the development of the proposed `EventTracker` tool.

4.1   System Setup

We setup a client and server/monitoring machine using two virtual machine instances of Ubuntu 20.04, with each of them containing 32 GB RAM and a 12-core processor. The client machine has all the modules mentioned above implemented as python programs, while the other one acted as the server running the database and a dashboard application as mentioned above. The client primarily has file monitoring, user login monitoring and suspicious event detection modules as shown in Fig. 1.

Client Side Implementation:

(i) `File Event Monitoring`: In order to track the filesystem events, `EventTracker` uses Watchdog [6]. This is a Python library which monitors and generates alerts on filesystem events. The required evidence is collected by monitoring the alerts raised by it.

(ii) `Linux Auditing System`: The Linux Auditing System [7] facilitates incident investigation by establishing an audit trail that collects specific type of system activity. We used it to collect evidence of both monitored files and login activity.

(iii) `Client Side Database`: EventTracker uses MongoDB, [8] a free and open-source NoSQL database, to store the event details and evidence locally (till the evidence is exported to the server).

(iv) `LiME`: LiME [9] is a Loadable Kernel Module (LKM) that allows Linux and Linux-based devices to acquire volatile memory. `EventTracker` uses this module to generate memory snapshot of the monitored client. This is invoked when a suspicious event is detected and memory forensic data is required for it.

(v) `Volatility`: It is a framework [10] written in Python for extracting digital artifacts from volatile memory (RAM) samples. In our implementation, we used this utility to collect evidences such as bash history and running processes from the memory snapshot generated with LiME.

(vi) `Logstash`: Logstash [11] is a data processing pipeline that can process data from a variety of sources and transform it into different formats as required by a variety of use-cases. We used logstash to transform each MongoDB collection in the database to JSON, find the estimated location of the IP addresses using its geoip filter and push them to corresponding Elasticsearch indices on the server. It observes changes to the database and triggers the data processing pipeline once they are detected.

Server-Side Implementation: The server side implementation of `EventTracker` uses an utility called Elastic Stack in place of a conventional database. This is intended to assist users in extracting data from any source and in any format. It assists in the real-time search, processing, and visualisation of evidence. We used the following components from elastic stack:

(i) `Elasticsearch`: Elasticsearch [11] is a search and analytic engine that can handle a large amount of data in different formats like textual, numerical, geospatial, structured and unstructured data using multiple distributed nodes at a very high speed. We used elasticsearch to store, filter and query logs and evidence on the server.

(ii) `Kibana`: Kibana [11] is a free and open source user interface for visualising Elasticsearch data and managing the Elastic Stack. We used kibana as the frontend dashboard to display, filter and visualize the data uploaded to Elasticsearch. It consists of views present on multiple dashboards displaying all the essential logs.

Data Collection: We created watchdog observers for each file/directory to be monitored in the client (monitored machine), along with the */var/log/auth.log* which contains the authentication logs. In addition, we setup audit rules to collect evidence around modifications to the specified files and directories. The evidence collected is parsed and required information is extracted and inserted into the local MongoDB database. The suspicious event detection module detects the events by monitoring the required source of information (network traffic, file operations, user logins, new installations, etc.). Upon detection of an event, it triggers evidence collection specific to the event detected. Table 2 shows the different types of evidence that can be collected by invoking the memory snapshot module.

4.2 Evaluation

In this subsection, we describe the evaluation done with `EventTracker`. We performed evaluation with a few selected events as suspicious events to trigger the forensic evidence collection. We discuss the events and the evidence gathered by the tool below.

Table 2. Evidence collected from the memory snapshot

Data collected	Description
Bash History	The bash history shows the history of commands ran by a user using shell along with their timestamp.
Kernel Logs	These logs are generated by the kernel whenever changes are made to it.
Process Information	This keeps track of information about the running processes such as pid, command line, environment variables and sockets used.
Kernel Modules	Kernel modules are object files that contain code to extend the running kernel. These modules run with privileges similar to kernel.
Network Interfaces	This keeps track of the network interfaces that were connected/added to the machine.
Mount Information	This keeps track of all the memory devices mounted on the system.
ARP Cache	This keeps track of ARP cache stored on the machine which helps in identifying suspicious machines connecting to or access the monitored machine

timeStamp	operation	fileDir	fileName	fileHash	executable
Apr 9, 2022 @ 22:56:54.221	CREATE	/home/ubuntu/testDir	b.txt	e3b0c44298fc1c149afbf4c8996fb92427ae41e4649b934ca495991b7852b855	/usr/bin/touch
Apr 9, 2022 @ 22:57:31.218	MODIFIED	/home/ubuntu/testDir	b.txt	5891b5b522d5df080d0ff0b110fbd9d21bb4fc7163af34d08286a2e846f5be03	/usr/bin/echo
Apr 9, 2022 @ 23:03:13.093	RENAMED to /home/ubuntu/testDir/a.txt	/home/ubuntu/testDir	b.txt	(empty)	/usr/bin/mv
Apr 9, 2022 @ 23:03:17.625	DELETE	/home/ubuntu/testDir	a.txt	(empty)	/usr/bin/rm

Fig. 3. Sample logs generated for file monitoring

(i) **File Events:** The goal here is to track events related to various files and directories. In particular the events like creation, deletion, modification and access to different files of interest are monitored and necessary evidence is collected for the same. For this we created a watchdog observer for a directory /home/ubuntu/testDir. Subsequently we performed few file operations inside this directory. Figure 3 shows sample logs generated from these operations displayed on the EventTracker's dashboard. We can notice that, each row has details of filename, the operation performed, the timestamp of the event, the new hash signature (if applicable). These logs are initially stored in the client database and subsequently exported to remote server. The sample entries in Fig. 3 pertain to the following sequence of events:

a) File /home/ubuntu/testDir/b.txt was created using the command *touch*.
b) File /home/ubuntu/testDir/b.txt was modified by piping the output of the command *echo* to the file.
c) File /home/ubuntu/testDir/b.txt was renamed to file /home/ubuntu/testDir/a.txt using the command *mv*.
d) File /home/ubuntu/testDir/a.txt was deleted using the command *rm*.

(ii) `Login Monitoring`: To test `EventTracker`'s ability to detect logins, we performed three login operations from two different locations. We made two failed login attempts by providing wrong username and wrong password in the initial attempts and we provided the correct credentials in the final attempt. Table 3 shows the logs/evidence generated from these login activities along with its details. We can see that it has details of remote IP address, username, whether the login was successful or failed, timestamp of login, when the user logged out and a description of this event.

(iii) `Suspicious Event Detection`: As mentioned previously, an important contribution of our tool is the evidence collection when certain suspicious events occur. In order to test the implementation of the same, we considered the following four events as sample cases for detection and subsequent evidence collection from the monitored host.

Table 3. Sample evidence collected from login monitoring module

IP Address	Username	Success	Login time	Logout time	Description
10.241.11.242	citc	false	2022-04-09T17:57:23Z	2022-04-09T17:59:24Z	SSH login attempt using wrong password
172.16.2.91	(invalid user)	false	2022-03-22T13:29:55Z	2022-03-22T13:29:55Z	SSH login attempt using wrong username
10.241.11.242	citc	true	2022-04-09T17:57:27Z	2022-04-09T17:59:23Z	Successful login attempt

1. *Bruteforce Login Attack*: This attack consists of an adversary trying to access a machine by bruteforcing the usernames and their passwords on that machine. This attack can be detected by looking at the number of login attempts within a fixed time-frame either from a single IP address or multiple IP addresses (distributed bruteforce attack). For every login attempt, the suspicious event detection module checks if a bruteforce attempt is detected. If login attempts are unsuccessful, we store the event description which contains the event type and IP address used in the attack. If the adversary successfully logs in after a bruteforce attempt, it is an indication of a serious event hence the memory forensic evidence is collected in detection. We performed this attack by using a python script to bruteforce passwords for SSH login of a user on the client machine. We specified the bruteforce threshold to be equal to 30 and made 30 failed login attempts over a period of an hour from multiple locations. This generated the bruteforce event logs. We followed this up with a successful login attempt, which triggered the memory forensic data collection.

2. *Successful Login from Unknown IP Address*: This event detects successful login to an user account from an unknown IP address. The login history for a chosen user is monitored using the local database running on the client side, which is not accessible to any non-root user. If a successful login attempt is made from an IP address which has previously not been used to login for a user, it is considered as a suspicious event. Every occurrence of this event triggers the memory forensic data collection. Initially, we used two different

IP addresses to login for a week. This served as the profile of login history After this period, we generated a successful login from a different IP address (with a different ISP) and it was detected by EventTracker after searching for the IP address prefix in the login history of the user.

3. *Changes in High-Risk Directories*: This event detects changes made in directories maintained by either the kernel or the organization because the user ideally shouldn't have access to them. Once any of the monitored files and directories are modified, we add the details of file name and file path (directory) fields in the logs. Once the event is detected, the required forensic data from memory is collected using appropriate components. We considered */boot* to be a high-risk directory since it contains the compiled kernel image and boot configuration files. This event was successfully detected by EventTracker when we created a new file inside */boot* directory and evidence was collected for the event.

4. *File Changes with Specific Commands*: This is an event which detects changes made to the list of monitored files by execution of specific commands.

We look at the executable field in the file monitoring module's logs generated upon any operation and if it is present in the monitored commands list, an event of interest is detected and memory forensics data is collected. We used a system configuration file */etc/resolv.conf* to verify this event. We added the following three commands - *touch*, *echo* and *rm*, to the suspicious commands list. We updated its modification time using *touch* command, appended content to the end of it using *echo* command and then used the *rm* command to remove it. This generated three different logs for this event and triggered the memory forensic data collection.

4.3 Measurement Study

As mentioned previously, EventTracker is able to monitor file changes, user logins and also suspicious events and collect necessary evidence. It is common nowadays for the software to do automated updates and installations. These actions will also result into changes in the filesystem. We used the tool to track changes made to the filesystem over a longer time period to understand the frequency of changes and also the number of times changes are made. For this study we used a fresh installation of Ubuntu 20.04 without any extra packages and software installed on the machine. We monitored this system for 14 d by allowing it to perform auto updates. We collected the data EventTracker generated over a period of 14 d by marking the following directories */bin, /boot, /etc, /lib, /lib32, /lib64, /libx32, /opt, /sbin* on the client machine for tracking. The summary of this monitoring activity is shown in Table 4.

During this 14 d time period the Linux system's update manager fetched system updates seven times and it generated 4213 log entries related to this activity. In total 1059 files were modified which were located in 77 different directories (sub directories of above list). We noticed that all these changes were done by five different executables. Figure 4 shows the number of files changed in

Table 4. Summary of monitoring linux system

Number of Updates	7
Number of Log Entries	4213
Number of unique files modified	1059
Number of unique directories changed	77
Number of unique executables responsible for modifications	5

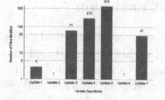

Fig. 4. Files modified in every update

every update operation. We can notice that the changes vary with few updates being small and others modifying large number of files. As there is a likelihood of very large number of changes being done frequently, hence warrants some kind of automation.

4.4 Comparison with Existing Tools

We compare the features of `EventTracker` with other similar host based IDS. Table 5 summarises this comparison between our proposed tool, OSSEC [3], Tripwire [4] and Auditbeat [5]. We can notice that `EventTracker` has all the basic features that other tools have, but it also has the advantage of having the ability to define the new events of interest and integrate with `EventTracker`. We are currently working to add API support for integration with SIEM tools.

Table 5. Comparison with existing tools

Features	EventTracker	OSSEC [3]	Tripwire [4]	Auditbeat [5]
Filesystem Monitoring	Yes	Yes	Yes	Yes
File Integrity Monitoring	Yes	Yes	Yes	Yes
Login Monitoring	Yes	No	No	Yes (on Linux)
Detection of Predefined Suspicious Events	Yes	Yes	Yes	No
Forensic Data Collection	Yes	No	Yes	Yes
Interactive Dashboard	Yes	No	Yes	Yes
Tamperproof Storage of Data	Yes	Yes	Yes	Yes
Support for Multiple Clients	Yes	Yes	Yes	No
Database Used	MongoDB and Elasticsearch	Mysql or Postgresql	Sql based	Elasticsearch
Add Custom Events and Evidence Collection	Yes	No	No	No
API's to Export Logs to SIEM Tools	No	No	Yes	No

5 Conclusion

In this paper we described EventTracker which is a tool developed to define and track events of interest and also collect necessary evidence for forensic investigation. We implemented a proof of concept code integrating the other open source utilities available and evaluated its ability to detect events and also log the details. We also performed a measurement study tracking changes made by the update managers to the underlying filesystem to conclude that changes are often large.

Acknowledgement. This work is financially supported by funding through SPARC project via grant number "SPARC/2018-2019/P448".

References

1. accessdata.com. Accessed 18 July 2022
2. security.opentext.com/encase-forensic . Accessed 20 July 2022
3. www.ossec.net. Accessed 12 July 2022
4. www.tripwire.com. Accessed 12 July 2022
5. www.elastic.co/beats/auditbeat. Accessed 12 July 2022
6. github.com/gorakhargosh/watchdog. Accessed 12 July 2022
7. access.redhat.com/documentation/en-us/red_hat_enterprise_linux/8/html/security_hardening/auditing-the-system_security-hardening. Accessed 12 July 2022
8. www.mongodb.com. Accessed 12 July 2022
9. github.com/504ensicsLabs/LiME. Accessed 12 July 2022
10. www.volatilityfoundation.org. Accessed 12 July 2022
11. www.elastic.co/elastic-stack. Accessed 12 July 2022
12. Chen, L., et al.: Detecting advanced attacks based on linux logs. In: BigDataSecurity'20: Proceedings of the IEEE 6th International Conference on Big Data Security on Cloud, pp. 60–64 (2020)
13. Cheng, Q., Wu, C., Zhou, S.: Discovering attack scenarios via intrusion alert correlation using graph convolutional networks. IEEE Commun. Lett. **25**(5), 1564–1567 (2021)
14. Debar, H., Wespi, A.: Aggregation and correlation of intrusion-detection alerts. In: Lee, W., Mé, L., Wespi, A. (eds.) RAID 2001. LNCS, vol. 2212, pp. 85–103. Springer, Heidelberg (2001). https://doi.org/10.1007/3-540-45474-8_6
15. Feng, Y., et al.: Attack graph generation and visualization for industrial control network. In: CCC 2020: Proceedings of the 39th Chinese Control Conference, pp. 7655–7660 (2020)
16. Haas, S., Fischer, M.: Gac: graph-based alert correlation for the detection of distributed multi-step attacks. In: SAC 2018: Proceedings of the 33rd Annual ACM Symposium on Applied Computing, pp. 979–988 (2018)
17. Haas, S., Fischer, M.: On the alert correlation process for the detection of multi-step attacks and a graph-based realization. SIGAPP Appl. Comput. Rev. **19**(1), 5–19 (2019)
18. Hubballi, N., Suryanarayanan, V.: False alarm minimization techniques in signature-based intrusion detection systems: A survey. Comput. Commun. **49**, 1–17 (2014)

19. Porras, P.A., Fong, M.W., Valdes, A.: A mission-impact-based approach to INFOSEC alarm correlation. In: Wespi, A., Vigna, G., Deri, L. (eds.) RAID 2002. LNCS, vol. 2516, pp. 95–114. Springer, Heidelberg (2002). https://doi.org/10.1007/3-540-36084-0_6
20. Qin, X., Lee, W.: Attack plan recognition and prediction using causal networks. In: 20th Annual Computer Security Applications Conference, pp. 370–379 (2004)
21. Roschke, S., Cheng, F., Meinel, C.: A new alert correlation algorithm based on attack graph. In: CISIS 2011: Proceedings of the 4th International Conference on Computational Intelligence in Security for Information Systems, pp. 58–67 (2011)
22. T, C., Nadjm-Tehrani, S., Burschka, S., Burbeck, K.: Alarm reduction and correlation in defence of IP networks. In: 13th IEEE International Workshops on Enabling Technologies: Infrastructure for Collaborative Enterprises, pp. 229–234 (2004)

WiP: Characterizing the Impact of Multiplexed DoS Attacks on HTTP and Detection

Shaurya Sood, Pritesh Palod, and Neminath Hubballi[(⊠)]

Department of Computer Science and Engineering,
Indian Institute of Technology Indore, Indore, India
{phd1801201007,cse180001038,neminath}@iiti.ac.in

Abstract. Application layer Denial of Service attacks can severely impact the services and at worst render them useless. As many of these come in the form of flooding attacks, traditional detection methods work with thresholds. These are easy to evade using multiplexed attacks where multiple type of attacks are launched in parallel. In this paper, we study the impact of multiplexed attacks using carefully chosen behavioral parameters. Subsequently, we use the observations to propose detection methods. By experimenting with three types of attacks and their combinations against HTTP, we show that using the behavioral parameters, these attacks can be detected.

Keywords: Denial of service · Multiplexed attacks · Application layer attacks · Performance impact · Detection method

1 Introduction

Denial of Service (DoS) attacks are increasingly becoming powerful and impacting the applications. Recent DoS attacks exploit the application layer behavior [17]. Objective of these attacks is to exhaust the system resources. These application layer attacks can be generated with minimal efforts. Traditional intrusion detection techniques which detect these attacks are of two types as anomaly based and signature based. These detection techniques use thresholds on the occurrence of certain type of packets/requests. Threshold based detection methods are very easy to evade [2] as any requests falling below the thresholds will not be detected. Further an attacker can render these methods ineffective by launching multiplexed attacks. Hence a different approach for detection is to rely on a rugged detection mechanism based on multiple features to detect these attacks. Taking motivation from this, we study the characteristics of such attacks on the system and applications using few behavioral parameters.

We consider multiplexed DoS attacks on HTTP by evaluating three attacks namely SYN Flood, HTTP GET Flood and Slowloris. We study these attacks individually and in all combinations. Flood attacks on one hand are volumetric

V. R. Badarla et al. (Eds.): ICISS 2022, LNCS 13784, pp. 260–271, 2022.
https://doi.org/10.1007/978-3-031-23690-7_16

attacks and application layer attacks like Slowloris on other hand leave a trail of incomplete requests. We identify some behavioral parameters and subsequently use these parameters to detect multiplexed attacks.

Background In our study following three attacks are considered.

(i) `SYN Flood Attack`: This is a TCP based attack generated with half open connections. Here the attacker does not complete the three-way handshake. Only the initial SYN packet is sent to the server and SYN-ACK sent by the server is subsequently not acknowledged. These half open connections are retained by the server for a certain time period by creating state information in the form of Transmission Control Block. A flux of half open connections consume the available memory at the server rendering it unusable.

(ii) `HTTP Flood Attack`: It is a volumetric attack on HTTP. A coordinated botnet can generate multiple requests to the target web server creating large volume. The server gets overwhelmed with these flood requests and may not be able to service the legitimate requests. There are two types of flood requests HTTP GET Flood and HTTP POST Flood. The GET flood targets the server requesting images, files and other resources from server whereas POST flood is targeted on web forms. In either case the server's capacity gets saturated.

(iii) `Slowloris Attack`: In this attack an adversary sends incomplete HTTP requests and keeps them alive by repeatedly sending parts of requests. The server waits to service the request until the complete request is received. However, the attacker never completes the request, instead mounts several such open connections to exhaust the available connection pool at the server rendering it useless to service the legitimate requests.

Related Literature. The attacks considered are known for sometime and several previous works have attempted to propose methods for detecting and mitigating these.

(i) `SYN Flood Detection and Mitigation`: Several detection and mitigation techniques can be found for SYN flood attack [4]. The main detection works include sequential change point detection [18], using machine learning algorithms [6]. RFC 4987 [7] suggests several mitigation techniques for SYN flood attack. Some recent works [8] use features of SDN to mitigate the flooding attacks.

(ii) `HTTP Flood Detection`: There are commercial offering [1] for mitigating the effects of HTTP flood attacks. Using CAPTCHA [10] is another popular method for mitigating this attack.

(iii) `Slowloris Detection and Mitigation`: There are some modules available for mitigating these attacks namely 'Core' [5], 'Antiloris' [11], 'Limitipconn' [12] and 'mod_reqtimeout' [13] which either limit the number of requests per client or delay sending the HTTP request till it completely arrives. Recently Sood et al. [14] proposed a detection method using behavioral parameters.

There are also some research efforts to understand the effect of attacks either individually or in combination. Jiang et al. [9] study the effect of attacks in terms of CPU and memory utilization. Zebari et al. [19] study the CPU load and response time of two web servers. Beckett and Sezer [3], and Tripathi and Hubballi [16] show that HTTP/2 has more threat vectors compared to HTTP/1.1 and hence susceptible to DoS attacks.

2 Impact Study

In order to study the impact of attacks we setup a testbed with a web server and the changes are captured with a set of carefully chosen behavioral parameters. These two are elaborated below.

Testbed Setup: We study the impact of different attacks on a web server. For this study, we created a testbed with three systems installing two VMs in each. These machines were connected in star topology as shown in Fig. 1. In one of the VM we installed Apache web server, one VM is used for generating HTTP traffic with Jmeter instance. Another VM is used to measure the response time from the server. Three attacker terminals (depicted in red) generated different attacks using tools *Hping3*, *Hulk* and one implementation of *Slowloris*. We wrote a script in python for measuring server parameters for discrete time windows which in our case was set to 15 s. This code invokes *Scapy* and *psutil* library for these measurements.

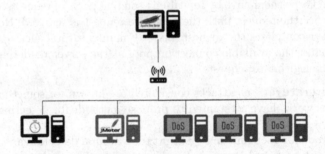

Fig. 1. Network topology

We carefully select seven parameters for this impact study. These parameter are listed below.

Parameters Considered:
(i) Number of Incomplete Requests: These are HTTP incomplete requests sent by the client.
(ii) Number of Log 200 Messages: The server logs HTTP response code 200 when the request made by the client is serviced successfully.
(iii) Number of Log 400 Messages: HTTP response code 400 indicate an error and server will not process it or failed to process it.
(iv) Response Time: The round trip time for a HTTP request as measured from a client is Response Time. It depends on external factors like network congestion and server load.

(v) **Number of HTTP Responses**: Count of HTTP response messages sent by the server.

(vi) **Number of Server Responses**: Count of total number of packets sent by the server.

(vii) **Server CPU Utilization**: This parameter measure the CPU utilization on the server.

Observations: In order to understand the impacts of attacks on these parameters, we used the testbed shown in Fig. 1 and measured all the parameters on the server for seven minutes duration. In the measurement period, we launched different attacks for three minutes duration in the middle (starting and last two minutes are benign and in between three minutes attack). Figures 2, 3, 4, 5, 6, 7, and Fig. 8 show the behavioral response of the server with different attacks. In these figures red colored lines represent the duration of attack and blue colored lines represent benign windows. The behaviour of server is summarized in Table 1. This table reports the observed behaviour for each parameter along with the severity of the effect either positively or negatively. An upward arrow indicates increase in the value or quantity and their number indicates magnitude. Similarly downward arrow indicates the corresponding parameter has a decreased value. A marking of NA indicates the corresponding parameter is not affected by the attack. For example considering the first row of Table 1 following can be interpreted. In case of SYN flood attack number of incomplete requests are not affected, number of log 200 messages significantly decrease, log 400 messages are not affected, the server response time increases significantly (a value of 100 s is considered as timeout and 999 s is considered as no response), number of HTTP response messages decrease considerably, the total number of bytes sent by the server increase to a great extent and the CPU utilization of the server increases significantly. Similar interpretation goes for other attack combinations as well.

3   Detecting Attacks

Considering the behavioral changes observed during different attacks, we propose methods for detecting these attacks. We consider three machine learning algorithms with these behavioral parameters for attack detection including the multiplexed attacks. The algorithms used and a very brief overview follows[1].

(i) **Decision Tree Classifier**: It is a supervised machine learning algorithm which constructs a tree to represent a set of rules. These rules are in the form of if-then-else format. Each child indicate a decision. These decisions are based on information gain calculated with training samples. Every leaf node represent a class label or decision.

(ii) **Random Forest Classifier**: It is an ensemble supervised machine learning algorithm which creates multiple decision trees. It picks random tuples as seed through a process called bootstrapping. A subset of features are selected

---

[1] More details can be found in [15].

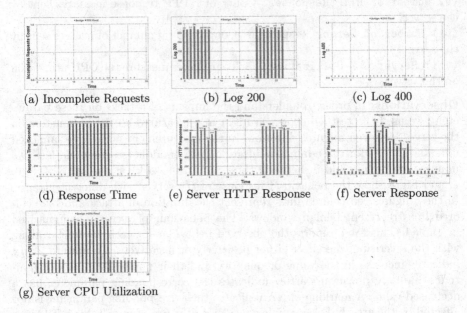

(a) Incomplete Requests   (b) Log 200   (c) Log 400

(d) Response Time   (e) Server HTTP Response   (f) Server Response

(g) Server CPU Utilization

Fig. 2. SYN flood attack

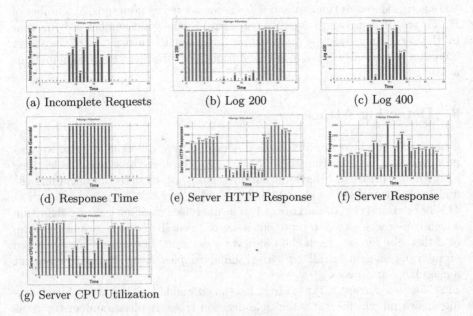

(a) Incomplete Requests   (b) Log 200   (c) Log 400

(d) Response Time   (e) Server HTTP Response   (f) Server Response

(g) Server CPU Utilization

Fig. 3. Slowloris attack

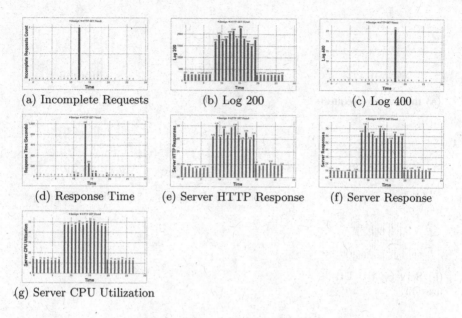

(a) Incomplete Requests   (b) Log 200   (c) Log 400

(d) Response Time   (e) Server HTTP Response   (f) Server Response

(g) Server CPU Utilization

Fig. 4. HTTP GET flood attack

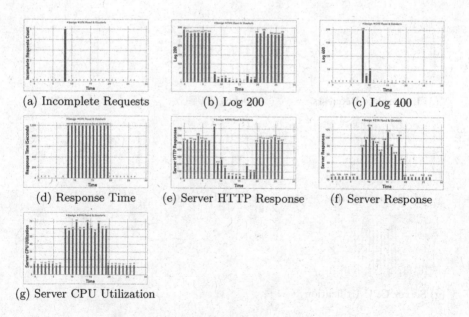

(a) Incomplete Requests   (b) Log 200   (c) Log 400

(d) Response Time   (e) Server HTTP Response   (f) Server Response

(g) Server CPU Utilization

Fig. 5. SYN flood and slowloris attack

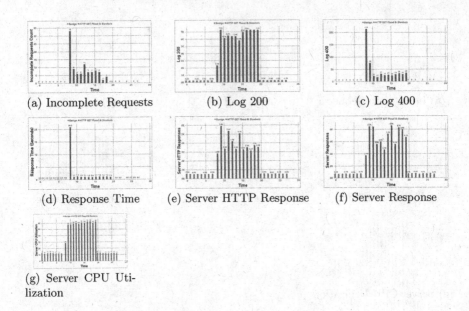

(a) Incomplete Requests   (b) Log 200   (c) Log 400

(d) Response Time   (e) Server HTTP Response   (f) Server Response

(g) Server CPU Utilization

Fig. 6. HTTP GET flood and slowloris attack

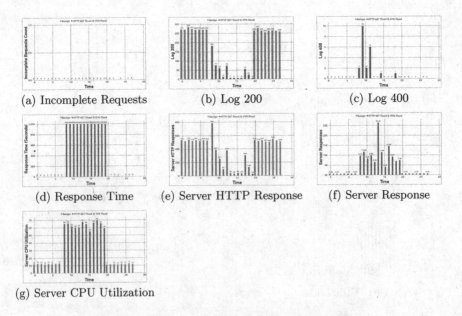

(a) Incomplete Requests   (b) Log 200   (c) Log 400

(d) Response Time   (e) Server HTTP Response   (f) Server Response

(g) Server CPU Utilization

Fig. 7. HTTP GET flood and SYN flood attack

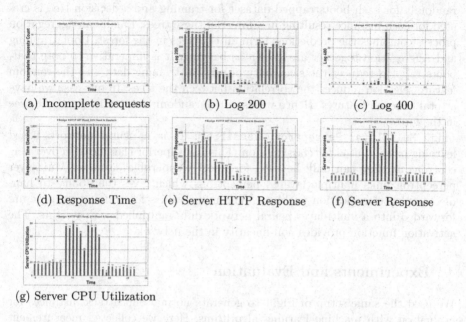

(a) Incomplete Requests   (b) Log 200   (c) Log 400

(d) Response Time   (e) Server HTTP Response   (f) Server Response

(g) Server CPU Utilization

Fig. 8. HTTP GET flood, SYN flood and slowloris attack

Table 1. Summary of behavioural changes under different attacks

Attack Type	Incomplete Requests	Log 200	Log 400	Response Time	Server HTTP Response	Server Response	Server CPU Utilization
SYN Flood	NA	⇓⇓⇓	NA	⇑⇑⇑	⇓⇓⇓	⇑⇑	⇑⇑⇑
Slowloris	⇑⇑	⇓⇓⇓	⇑⇑⇑	⇑⇑⇑	⇓⇓	⇑	⇓⇓
HTTP GET Flood	NA	⇑⇑	NA	⇑	⇑⇑	⇑⇑	⇑⇑
SYN Flood & Slowloris	⇑	⇓⇓	⇑	⇑⇑⇑	⇓⇓	⇑⇑	⇑⇑⇑
HTTP GET Flood & Slowloris	⇑⇑	⇑⇑⇑⇑	⇑⇑	⇑⇑⇑	⇑⇑	⇑⇑⇑	⇑⇑
HTTP GET Flood & SYN Flood	NA	⇓⇓	⇑⇑	⇑⇑	⇓⇓	⇑⇑	⇑⇑⇑
HTTP GET Flood, SYN Flood & Slowloris	⇑	⇓⇓	⇑⇑	⇑⇑⇑	⇓⇓	⇑⇑	⇑⇑

randomly for each bootstrapped dataset for training and a decision tree is created for each instance resulting in a forest of these trees. Finally an aggregation process combines the predictions form all the trees in the forest. Bootstrapping and Aggregation together are known as bagging. It is imperative to note that, bootstrapping reduces the sensitivity of original training data and the random feature selection reduces the correlation between the trees. In our case we have a total of seven features. Hence we use three random features for each sub-tree in the forest.

(iii) Multilayer Perceptron Classifier: It is a neural network based learning method used for classification. This has superior classification over perceptrons as they can only be used for linearly separable datasets. Multilayer perceptron links multiple layered perceptrons which gives the ability to handle complex classification problems. The input values for training purpose are forwarded into a multi-layer neural network duly multiplied with weights. The activation function provides non-linearity in the network.

4   Experiments and Evaluation

We used the same setup of Fig. 1 to generate normal and attack instances for evaluation with machine learning algorithms. Here we collected measurement data for one hour duration for every attack type. In this one hour, thirty minutes of benign traffic generated only with Jmeter and remaining thirty minutes of attack traffic generated with specific attack type (or combination) along with the background traffic generated with Jmeter. With 15 s measurement intervals this resulted into 120 benign measurements and 120 measurements with attack. We used the dataset so generated to evaluate the detection performance of machine learning algorithms individually with 10 fold cross validation. Table 2 shows the confusion matrices of all 21 experiments (seven attack types and three algorithms). It is easy to see that the detection performance is very high with more than 97% accurate classification. The number of false positives are also limited and are within acceptable range.

Combined Attack Detection Performance: In the previous experiment, we used the dataset generated from the individual cases i.e. one hour data is used for training and testing. Here we perform a combined detection with two scenarios (i) all attack instances irrespective of their type is labeled as attack (ii) all benign and seven attack instances are combined with their individual labels. First is a case of binary classification and later is a multi-class classification instance. We used the dataset generated previously by combining all measurement instances for this experiment too with appropriate labeling. Table 3 shows the results of the first experiment. We can notice that all the three algorithms performed well with very few misclassifictions. Table 4 shows the performance of detection in the second case with multilayer perceptron (We omit reporting performance with other algorithms due to space constraints). Here the classification performance is degraded with misinterpretations i.e. one class labeled as the other particularly for the flooding attack combinations and when all the three attacks are

Table 2. Attack Detection Performance

Attack Type	Decision Tree			Random Forest			Multi Perception		
SYN Flood		Normal	Attack		Normal	Attack		Normal	Attack
	Normal	120	0	Normal	120	0	Normal	118	2
	Attack	0	120	Attack	0	120	Attack	1	119
Slowloris		Normal	Attack		Normal	Attack		Normal	Attack
	Normal	119	1	Normal	120	0	Normal	118	2
	Attack	3	117	Attack	2	118	Attack	1	119
HTTP Get Flood		Normal	Attack		Normal	Attack		Normal	Attack
	Normal	119	1	Normal	120	0	Normal	120	0
	Attack	1	119	Attack	1	119	Attack	0	120
SYN Flood + Slowloris		Normal	Attack		Normal	Attack		Normal	Attack
	Normal	118	2	Normal	119	1	Normal	118	2
	Attack	1	119	Attack	0	120	Attack	0	120
HTTP GetFlood + Slowloris		Normal	Attack		Normal	Attack		Normal	Attack
	Normal	118	2	Normal	120	0	Normal	120	0
	Attack	4	116	Attack	0	120	Attack	1	119
HTTP Get Flood + SYN Flood		Normal	Attack		Normal	Attack		Normal	Attack
	Normal	119	1	Normal	118	2	Normal	120	0
	Attack	1	119	Attack	0	120	Attack	0	120
SYN Flood+ HTTP GetFlood + Slowloris		Normal	Attack		Normal	Attack		Normal	Attack
	Normal	119	1	Normal	119	1	Normal	119	1
	Attack	1	119	Attack	0	120	Attack	1	119

Table 3. Detection Performance with Two Classes

Attack Windows	Benign Windows	Decision Tree			Random Forest			Multilayer Perceptron		
840	840		Normal	Attack		Normal	Attack		Normal	Attack
		Normal	833	7	Normal	835	5	Normal	831	9
		Attack	9	831	Attack	1	839	Attack	7	833

Table 4. Detection Performance with Multiple Classes

Attack Type	Benign	SYN Flood	Slowloris	HTTP GET Flood	SYN Flood & Slowloris	HTTP GET Flood & Slowloris	HTTP GET Flood & SYN Flood	HTTP GET Flood, SYN Flood & Slowloris
Benign	838	0	0	0	0	0	0	2
SYN Flood	1	107	0	0	0	0	7	5
Slowloris	2	0	118	0	0	0	0	0
HTTP GET Flood	1	0	0	119	0	0	0	0
SYN Flood & Slowloris	0	1	0	0	70	0	26	23
HTTP GET Flood & Slowloris	1	0	4	1	0	114	0	0
HTTP GET Flood & SYN Flood	0	18	0	1	42	0	40	19
HTTP GET Flood, SYN Flood & Slowloris	0	8	0	1	28	0	15	68

used together. A careful analysis reveals that flooding attacks generate slightly similar behavioral changes. However, it is worth noting that the mis-labeling is happening to another attack type where at least one of the constituent attack is part of. This way at least one attack type is identified by the detection methods. We believe that this helps a system administrator to further examine the case.

5   Conclusion

Multiplexed DoS attacks pose challenges for threshold based detection techniques and can be easily evaded. However, their combined effect can adversely affect the service. In this paper, we reported attack characterization using some behavioral parameters by launching three attacks against HTTP. Although these attacks can be detected using a combination of behavioral features, more than two types of attacks together pose challenge for identifying exact combination. However detecting them as attacks can still be performed.

Acknowledgement. This work is financially supported by funding through SPARC project via grant number "SPARC/2018-2019/P448".

References

1. https://www.cloudflare.com/en-in/learning/ddos/http-flood-ddos-attack/. Accessed 03 April 2022
2. Aqil, A., et al.: Detection of stealthy TCP-based dos attacks. In: MILCOM 2015–2015 IEEE Military Communications Conference, pp. 348–353 (2015)
3. Beckett, D., Sezer, S.: Http/2 cannon: Experimental analysis on http/1 and http/2 request flood DDOS attacks. In: EST 2017: Seventh International Conference on Emerging Security Technologies, pp. 108–113 (2017)
4. Carl, G., Kesidis, G., Brooks, R., Rai, S.: Denial-of-service attack-detection techniques. IEEE Internet Comput. **10**(1), 82–89 (2006)
5. Core: (2019). https://httpd.apache.org/docs/2.4/mod/core.html. Accessed 28 April 2022
6. Daneshgadeh, S., Baykal, N., Ertekin, S.: DDoS attack modeling and detection using smo. In: ICMLA 2017: 16th IEEE International Conference on Machine Learning and Applications, pp. 432–436 (2017)
7. Eddy, W.: TCP SYN Flooding Attacks and Common Mitigations. RFC 4987, RFC Editor (2007). https://datatracker.ietf.org/doc/html/rfc4987
8. Fichera, S., Galluccio, L., Grancagnolo, S.C., Morabito, G., Palazzo, S.: Operetta: an openflow-based remedy to mitigate TCP synflood attacks against web servers. Comput. Networks **92**, 89–100 (2015)
9. Jiang, M., Wang, C., Luo, X., Miu, M., Chen, T.: Characterizing the impacts of application layer DDoS attacks. In: ICWS 2017: IEEE International Conference on Web Services, pp. 500–507 (2017)
10. Kandula, S., Katabi, D., Jacob, M., Berger, A.: Botz-4-sale: surviving organized DDoS attacks that mimic flash crowds. In: NSDI 2005: Proceedings of the 2nd Conference on Symposium on Networked Systems Design & Implementation - Volume 2, pp. 287–300. USENIX Association (2005)
11. mod_antiloris: (2013). https://sourceforge.net/projects/mod-antiloris/. Accessed 28 April 2022
12. mod_limitipconn: (2002). http://dominia.org/djao/limitipconn.html. Accessed 28 April 2022

13. mod_reqtimeout: (2019). https://httpd.apache.org/docs/trunk/mod/mod_reqtime out.html. Accessed 28 July 2022
14. Sood, S., Saikia, M., Hubballi, N.: WiP: slow rate HTTP attack detection with behavioral parameters. In: Tripathy, S., Shyamasundar, R.K., Ranjan, R. (eds.) ICISS 2021. LNCS, vol. 13146, pp. 26–37. Springer, Cham (2021). https:// doi.org/10.1007/978-3-030-92571-0_2
15. Tan, P.N., Steinbach, M., Karpatne, A., Kumar, V.: Introduction to Data Mining, 2nd edn. Pearson (2018)
16. Tripathi, N., Hubballi, N.: Slow rate denial of service attacks against http/2 and detection. Comput. Secur. **72**(C), 255–272 (2018)
17. Tripathi, N., Hubballi, N.: Application layer denial-of-service attacks and defense mechanisms: a survey. ACM Comput. Surv. **54**(4) (2021)
18. Wang, H., Zhang, D., Shin, K.G.: Detecting syn flooding attacks. In: Proceedings of the Twenty-First Annual Joint Conference of the IEEE Computer and Communications Societies, vol. 3, pp. 1530–1539 (2002)
19. Zebari, R.R., Zeebaree, S.R.M., Jacksi, K.: Impact analysis of http and syn flood DDoS attacks on apache 2 and IIS 10.0 web servers. In: ICOASE 2018: International Conference on Advanced Science and Engineering, pp. 156–161 (2018)

Author Index

Printed in the United States
by Baker & Taylor Publisher Services

Printed in the United States
by Baker & Taylor Publisher Services